W9-AGO-247

enVision math 2.0

Volume 2 Topics 9-15

Authors

Randall I. Charles
Professor Emeritus
Department of Mathematics
San Jose State University
San Jose, California

Jennifer Bay-Williams
Professor of Mathematics Education
College of Education and Human Development
University of Louisville
Louisville, Kentucky

Robert Q. Berry, III
Associate Professor of Mathematics Education
Department of Curriculum, Instruction and Special Education
University of Virginia
Charlottesville, Virginia

Janet H. Caldwell
Professor of Mathematics
Rowan University
Glassboro, New Jersey

Zachary Champagne
Assistant in Research
Florida Center for Research in Science, Technology, Engineering, and Mathematics (FCR-STEM)
Jacksonville, Florida

Juanita Copley
Professor Emerita, College of Education
University of Houston
Houston, Texas

Warren Crown
Professor Emeritus of Mathematics Education
Graduate School of Education
Rutgers University
New Brunswick, New Jersey

Francis (Skip) Fennell
L. Stanley Bowlsbey Professor of Education and Graduate and Professional Studies
McDaniel College
Westminster, Maryland

Karen Karp
Professor of Mathematics Education
Department of Early Childhood and Elementary Education
University of Louisville
Louisville, Kentucky

Stuart J. Murphy
Visual Learning Specialist
Boston, Massachusetts

Jane F. Schielack
Professor of Mathematics
Associate Dean for Assessment and Pre K-12 Education, College of Science
Texas A&M University
College Station, Texas

Jennifer M. Suh
Associate Professor for Mathematics Education
George Mason University
Fairfax, Virginia

Jonathan A. Wray
Mathematics Instructional Facilitator
Howard County Public Schools
Ellicott City, Maryland

SAVVAS
LEARNING COMPANY

Mathematicians

Roger Howe
Professor of Mathematics
Yale University
New Haven, Connecticut

Gary Lippman
Professor of Mathematics and
Computer Science
California State University, East Bay
Hayward, California

ELL Consultants

Janice R. Corona
Independent Education Consultant
Dallas, Texas

Jim Cummins
Professor
The University of Toronto
Toronto, Canada

Copyright © 2019 by Savvas Learning Company LLC. All Rights Reserved. Printed in the United States of America.

This publication is protected by copyright, and permission should be obtained from the publisher prior to any prohibited reproduction, storage in a retrieval system, or transmission in any form or by any means, electronic, mechanical, photocopying, recording, or otherwise. For information regarding permissions, request forms, and the appropriate contacts within the Savvas Learning Company Rights Management group, please send your query to the address below.

Savvas Learning Company LLC, 15 East Midland Avenue, Paramus, NJ 07652

Savvas™ and **Savvas Learning Company™** are the exclusive trademarks of Savvas Learning Company LLC in the U.S. and other countries.

Savvas Learning Company publishes through its famous imprints **Prentice Hall®** and **Scott Foresman®** which are exclusive registered trademarks owned by Savvas Learning Company LLC in the U.S. and/or other countries.

enVisionMATH® and **Savvas Realize™** are exclusive trademarks of Savvas Learning Company LLC in the U.S. and/or other countries.

Unless otherwise indicated herein, any third party trademarks that may appear in this work are the property of their respective owners, and any references to third party trademarks, logos, or other trade dress are for demonstrative or descriptive purposes only. Such references are not intended to imply any sponsorship, endorsement, authorization, or promotion of Savvas Learning Company products by the owners of such marks, or any relationship between the owner and Savvas Learning Company LLC or its authors, licensees, or distributors.

SAVVAS
LEARNING COMPANY

ISBN-13: 978-0-328-96832-9
ISBN-10: 0-328-96832-3
7 2021

Digital Resources

Go to SavvasRealize.com

MP
Math Practices Animations to play anytime

Solve
Solve & Share problems plus math tools

Learn
Visual Learning Animation Plus with animation, interaction, and math tools

Glossary
Animated Glossary in English and Spanish

Tools
Math Tools to help you understand

Assessment
Quick Check for each lesson

Help
Another Look Homework Video for extra help

Games
Math Games to help you learn

eText
Student Edition online

ACTIVe-book
Student Edition online for showing your work

SAVVAS realize™ Everything you need for math anytime, anywhere

Hi, we're here to help you.
Have a great year!
I'm Jada.
I'm Emily.
I'm Carlos.
I'm Marta.
I'm Alex.
I'm Daniel.
I'm Jackson.

Contents

Digital Resources at SavvasRealize.com

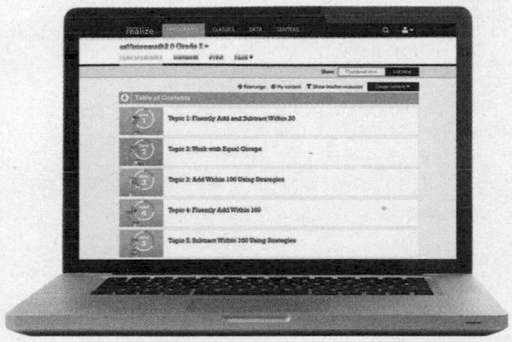

TOPICS

1 Fluently Add and Subtract Within 20

2 Work with Equal Groups

3 Add Within 100 Using Strategies

4 Fluently Add Within 100

5 Subtract Within 100 Using Strategies

6 Fluently Subtract Within 100

7 More Solving Problems Involving Addition and Subtraction

8 Work with Time and Money

9 Numbers to 1,000

10 Add Within 1,000 Using Models and Strategies

11 Subtract Within 1,000 Using Models and Strategies

12 Measuring Length

13 More Addition, Subtraction, and Length

14 Graphs and Data

15 Shapes and Their Attributes

TOPIC 9
Numbers to 1,000

Math and Science Project 503
Review What You Know 504
Vocabulary Cards 505

VA 5 **Ordinal Numbers*** VA23

9-1 **Understand Hundreds** 511

9-2 **Models and 3-Digit Numbers** 517

9-3 **Name Place Values** 523

9-4 **Read and Write 3-Digit Numbers** 529

9-5 **Different Ways to Name the Same Number** 535

9-6 **Place-Value Patterns with Numbers** 541

9-7 **Skip Count by 5s, 10s, and 100s to 1,000** 547

9-8 **Compare Numbers Using Place Value** 553

9-9 **Compare Numbers on the Number Line** 559

9-10 **PROBLEM SOLVING: Look For and Use Structure** 565

Fluency Practice Activity 571
Vocabulary Review 572
Reteaching 573
Topic Assessment 577
Topic Performance Assessment 581

*Lesson exclusively for Virginia at the end of this volume

Copyright © Savvas Learning Company LLC. All Rights Reserved.

TOPIC 10
Add Within 1,000 Using Models and Strategies

Math and Science Project 583
Review What You Know 584

10-1 **Add 10 and 100** 585

10-2 **Add on an Open Number Line** 591

10-3 **Add Using Mental Math** 597

10-4 **Add Using Partial Sums** 603

10-5 **Use Models to Add** 609

10-6 **Explain Addition Strategies** 615

10-7 **PROBLEM SOLVING: Repeated Reasoning** 621

Fluency Practice Activity 627
Vocabulary Review 628
Reteaching 629
Topic Assessment 631
Topic Performance Assessment 633

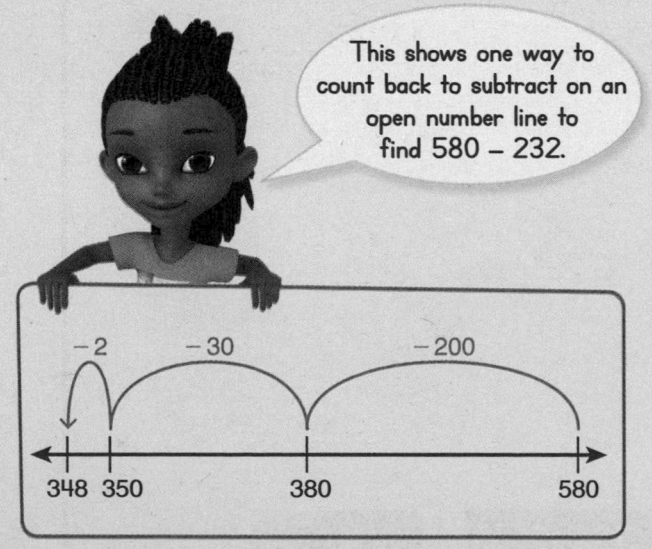

TOPIC 11
Subtract Within 1,000 Using Models and Strategies

Math and Science Project 635
Review What You Know 636

11-1 **Subtract 10 and 100** 637

11-2 **Count Back to Subtract on an Open Number Line** 643

11-3 **Add Up to Subtract on an Open Number Line** 649

11-4 **Subtract Using Mental Math** 655

11-5 **Use Models to Subtract** 661

11-6 **Explain Subtraction Strategies** 667

11-7 **PROBLEM SOLVING: Make Sense and Persevere** 673

Fluency Practice Activity 679
Vocabulary Review 680
Reteaching 681
Topic Assessment 683
Topic Performance Assessment 685

Copyright © Savvas Learning Company LLC. All Rights Reserved.

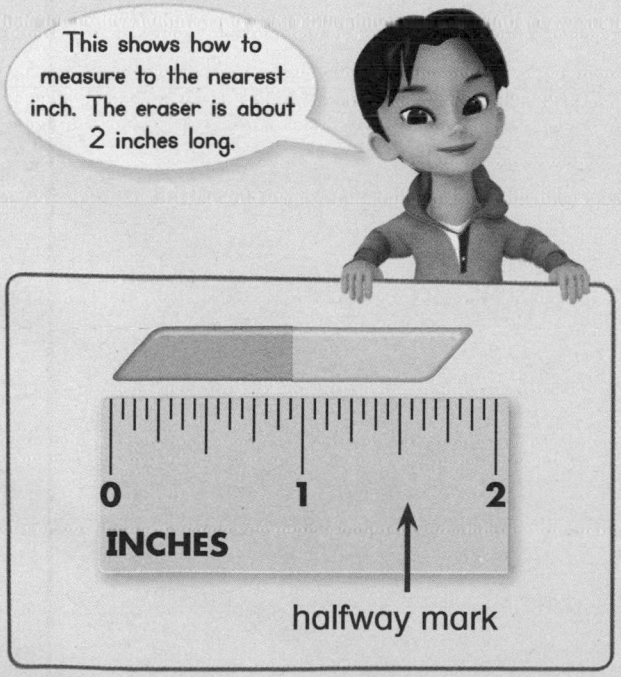

TOPIC 12
Measuring Length

Math and Science Project 687
Review What You Know 688
Vocabulary Cards 689

12-1 **Estimating Length** 693
12-2 **Measure with Inches** 699
12-3 **Inches, Feet, and Yards** 705
12-4 **Measure Length Using Different Customary Units** 711
12-5 **Measure with Centimeters** 717
12-6 **Centimeters and Meters** 723
12-7 **Measure Length Using Different Metric Units** 729
12-8 **Compare Lengths** 735
12-9 **PROBLEM SOLVING: Precision** 741
VA 6 **Estimate and Measure Weight*** VA27
VA 7 **Temperature*** VA31

Fluency Practice Activity 747
Vocabulary Review 748
Reteaching 749
Topic Assessment 753
Topic Performance Assessment 757

*Lesson exclusively for Virginia at the end of this volume

Amelia walks 17 blocks before dinner.
She walks 8 blocks after dinner.

How many more blocks does she walk before dinner than after dinner?

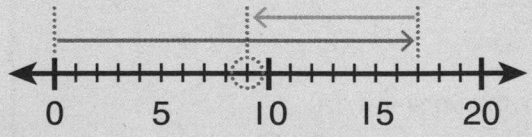

TOPIC 13
More Addition, Subtraction, and Length

Math and Science Project 759
Review What You Know 760

13-1 **Add and Subtract with Measurements** 761

13-2 **Find Unknown Measurements** 767

13-3 **Continue to Find Unknown Measurements** 773

13-4 **Add and Subtract on a Number Line** 779

13-5 **PROBLEM SOLVING: Use Appropriate Tools** 785

Fluency Practice Activity 791
Vocabulary Review 792
Reteaching 793
Topic Assessment 795
Topic Performance Assessment 797

Copyright © Savvas Learning Company LLC. All Rights Reserved.

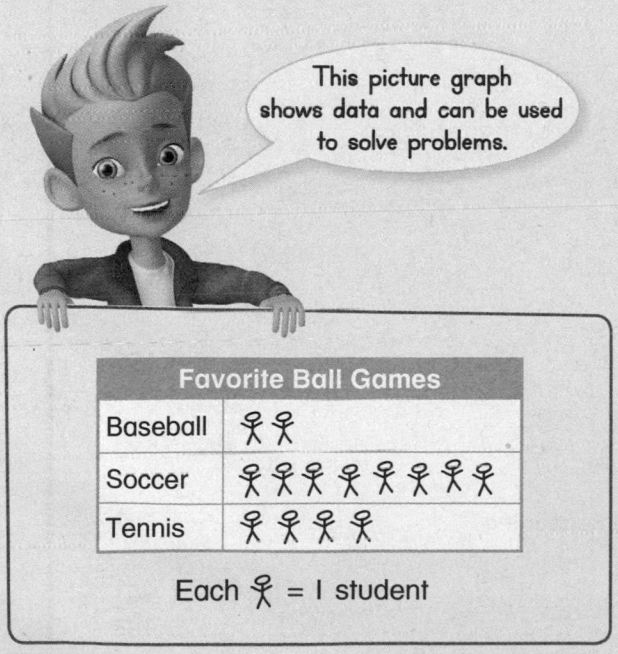

TOPIC 14
Graphs and Data

Math and Science Project 799
Review What You Know 800
Vocabulary Cards 801

14-1 **Line Plots** 803
14-2 **More Line Plots** 809
14-3 **Bar Graphs** 815
14-4 **Picture Graphs** 821
14-5 **Draw Conclusions from Graphs** 827
14-6 **PROBLEM SOLVING: Reasoning** 833
VA 8 **Predict Outcomes*** VA37

Fluency Practice Activity 839
Vocabulary Review 840
Reteaching 841
Topic Assessment 845
Topic Performance Assessment 849

*Lesson exclusively for Virginia at the end of this volume

SavvasRealize.com

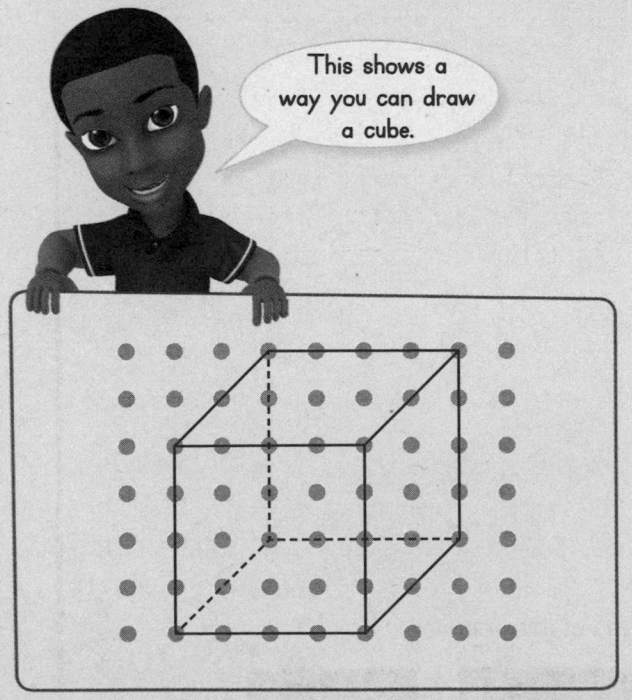

TOPIC 15
Shapes and Their Attributes

Math and Science Project 851
Review What You Know 852
Vocabulary Cards 853

15-1 **2-Dimensional Shapes** 859
15-2 **Polygons and Angles** 865
15-3 **Draw 2-Dimensional Shapes** 871
15-4 **Cubes** 877
VA 9 **Compare 2-Dimensional with 3-Dimensional Shapes*** VA43
15-5 **Divide Rectangles into Equal Squares** 883
VA 10 **Symmetry*** VA47
15-6 **Partition Shapes** 889
15-7 **Equal Shares, Different Shapes** 895
VA 11 **Fraction Names*** VA51
VA 12 **Fractions of a Set*** VA55
VA 13 **Equal Shares, Length*** VA59
VA 14 **Compare Unit Fractions*** VA63
15-8 **PROBLEM SOLVING: Repeated Reasoning** 901

Fluency Practice Activity 907
Vocabulary Review 908

*Lesson exclusively for Virginia at the end of this volume

Copyright © Savvas Learning Company LLC. All Rights Reserved.

STEP UP to Grade 3

STEP UP Opener 919

1 **Multiplication as Repeated Addition** 921

2 **Arrays and Multiplication** 925

3 **Division as Sharing** 929

4 **Division as Repeated Subtraction** 933

5 **Add with Partial Sums** 937

6 **Models for Adding 3-Digit Numbers** 941

7 **Subtract with Partial Differences** 945

8 **Models for Subtracting 3-Digit Numbers** 949

9 **Divide Regions into Equal Parts** 953

10 **Fractions and Regions** 957

Glossary G1

Problem Solving Handbook

Problem Solving Handbook

Math Practices

1. Make sense of problems and persevere in solving them.
2. Reason abstractly and quantitatively.
3. Construct viable arguments and critique the reasoning of others.
4. Model with mathematics.
5. Use appropriate tools strategically.
6. Attend to precision.
7. Look for and make use of structure.
8. Look for and express regularity in repeated reasoning.

Copyright © Savvas Learning Company LLC. All Rights Reserved.

1 Make sense of problems and persevere in solving them.

MP

Good math thinkers know what the problem is about. They have a plan to solve it. They keep trying if they get stuck.

My plan is to use counters as trucks. I can act out the problem.

A store has some toy trucks.
Mike buys 2 of the trucks.
Now the store has 3 trucks.
How many trucks did the store have at the start?

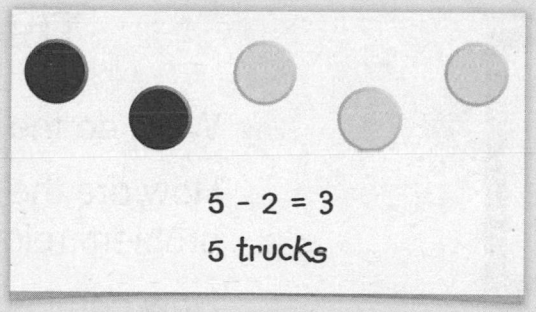

Thinking Habits

What do I need to find?

What do I know?

What's my plan for solving the problem?

What else can I try if I get stuck?

How can I check that my solution makes sense?

2 Reason abstractly and quantitatively.

MP

I completed a part-part-whole model. It shows how things in the problem are related.

Good math thinkers know how to think about words and numbers to solve problems.

Tony has 10 apples. 6 are red. The rest are green. How many apples are green?

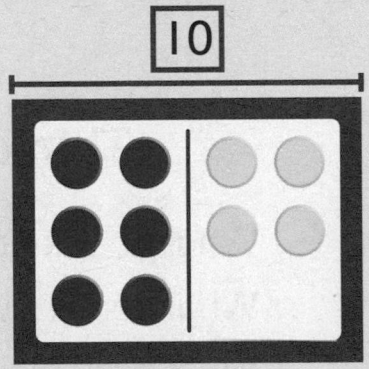

10 - 6 = 4

4 apples are green.

Thinking Habits

What do the numbers stand for?

How are the numbers in the problem related?

How can I show a word problem using pictures or numbers?

How can I use a word problem to show what an equation means?

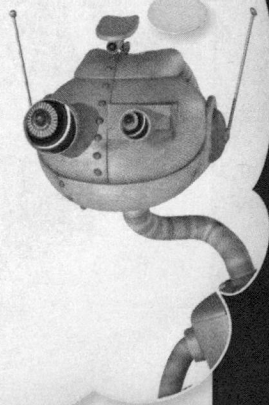

Copyright © Savvas Learning Company LLC. All Rights Reserved.

3 Construct viable arguments and critique the reasoning of others.

MP

I can use place-value blocks to check Paula's thinking. My explanation is clear and complete.

Good math thinkers use math to explain why they are right. They talk about math that others do, too.

Paula added 34 + 5.
She says she had to regroup the ones.
Is she correct? Show how you know.

34 has 4 ones.
4 ones and 5 ones are 9 ones.
Paula is incorrect.
You do not need to regroup ones.

Tens	Ones

34 + 5 = 39

Thinking Habits

How can I use math to explain my work?

Am I using numbers and symbols correctly?

Is my explanation clear?

What questions can I ask to understand other people's thinking?

Are there mistakes in other people's thinking?

Can I improve other people's thinking?

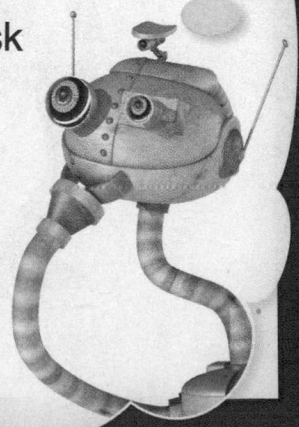

4 Model with mathematics.

MP

Good math thinkers use math they know to show and solve problems.

I can use ten-frames and counters to show the problem.

14 dogs are playing at a park.
9 dogs go home.
How many dogs are still at the park?

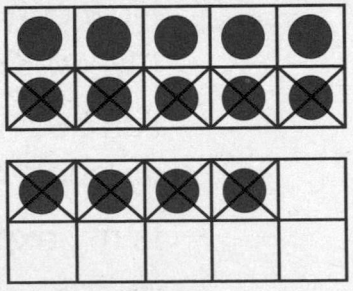

14 - 9 = 5

5 dogs

Thinking Habits

How can I use the math I know to help solve this problem?

Can I use a drawing, diagram, table, graph, or objects to show the problem?

Can I write an equation to show the problem?

Copyright © Savvas Learning Company LLC. All Rights Reserved.

5 Use appropriate tools strategically.

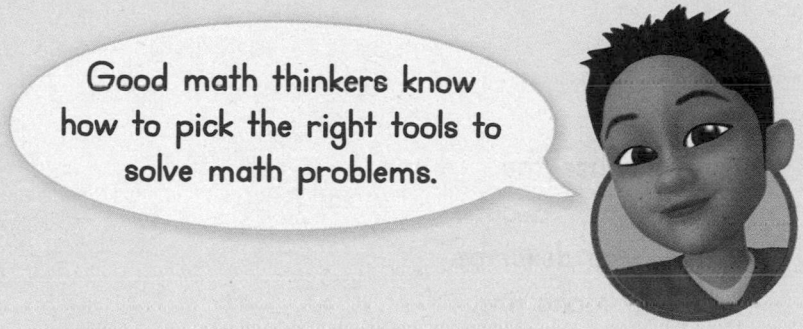

Kai and Maddie each pick 6 apples.
Then Maddie picks 1 more apple.
How many apples do they pick in all?

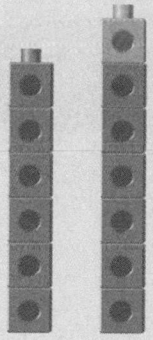

6 + 7 = 13

13 apples

Thinking Habits

Which tools can I use?

Is there a different tool I could use?

Am I using the tool correctly?

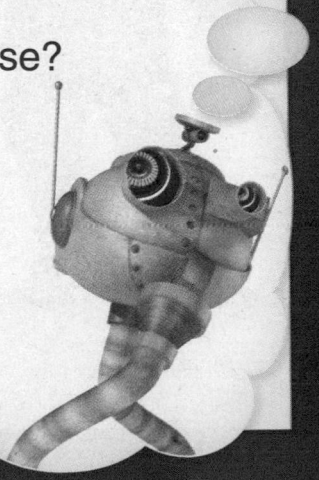

6 Attend to precision.

MP

Good math thinkers are careful about what they write and say, so their ideas about math are clear.

I can use the definition of a cube to help me describe what it looks like.

Circle each cube below.

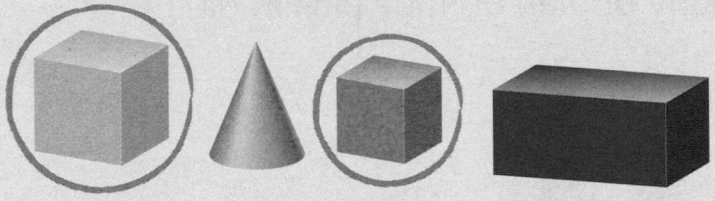

Describe what a cube looks like.

A cube has 6 flat surfaces.

Each flat surface is the same size.

A cube has 12 edges.

Thinking Habits

Am I using numbers, units, and symbols correctly?

Am I using the correct definitions?

Is my answer clear?

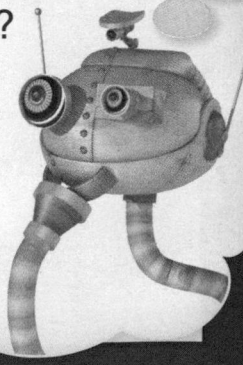

Copyright © Savvas Learning Company LLC. All Rights Reserved.

7 Look for and make use of structure.

It is hard to add three numbers at once. I can add any two numbers first. I added 6 + 4 first to make the problem easier.

Good math thinkers look for patterns in math to help solve problems.

Jeff saw 6 brown frogs, 3 green frogs, and 4 spotted frogs.
How many frogs did Jeff see in all?

Show your work and explain your answer.

6 + 3 + 4 = 13

10

I made 10 then added 3 to make the problem easier.

Thinking Habits

Is there a pattern?

How can I describe the pattern?

Can I break the problem into simpler parts?

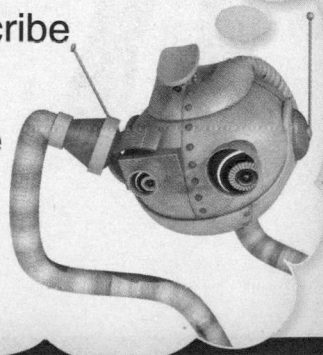

8 Look for and express regularity in repeated reasoning.

MP

Good math thinkers look for things that repeat in a problem. They use what they learn from one problem to help them solve other problems.

I can compare the tens first. If the tens are the same, I can compare the ones.

Compare each pair of numbers. Write <, >, or =. Tell how you will compare each pair of numbers.

57 < 75 49 < 52

36 > 34 61 = 61

Thinking Habits

Does something repeat in the problem?

How can the solution help me solve another problem?

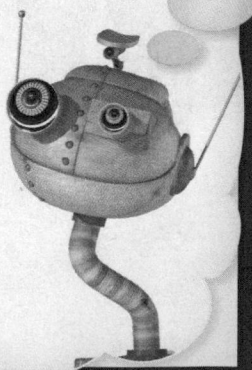

Copyright © Savvas Learning Company LLC. All Rights Reserved.

Problem Solving Handbook

Problem Solving Guide

Make Sense of the Problem

Reason

- What do I need to find?
- What given information can I use?
- How are the quantities related?

Think About Similar Problems

- Have I solved problems like this before?

Persevere in Solving the Problem

Model with Math

- How can I use the math I know?
- How can I show the problem?
- Is there a pattern I can use?

Use Appropriate Tools

- What math tools could I use?
- How can I use those tools?

Check the Answer

Make Sense of the Answer

- Is my answer reasonable?

Check for Precision

- Did I check my work?
- Is my answer clear?
- Is my explanation clear?

Some Ways to Show Problems

- Draw a Picture
- Draw a Number Line
- Write an Equation

Some Math Tools

- Objects
- Rulers
- Technology
- Paper and Pencil

Problem Solving Recording Sheet

Name Mary

Teaching Tool 1

Problem Solving Recording Sheet

Problem:
John bikes for 17 miles on Monday.
He bikes for 15 miles on Tuesday.
How many miles does John bike in all?

MAKE SENSE OF THE PROBLEM

Need to Find

I need to find how many miles John bikes in all.

Given

John bikes 17 miles on Monday and 15 miles on Tuesday.

PERSEVERE IN SOLVING THE PROBLEM

Some Ways to Represent Problems
- ☑ Draw a Picture
- ☐ Draw a Number Line
- ☑ Write an Equation

Some Math Tools
- ☐ Objects
- ☐ Rulers
- ☐ Technology
- ☑ Paper and Pencil

Solution and Answer

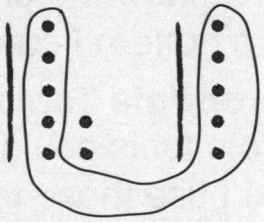

17 + 15 = 32

I made a 10.
John bikes 32 miles in all.

CHECK THE ANSWER

I checked my drawing of blocks.
They matched the problem and show 32 in all.

TT1

Copyright © Savvas Learning Company LLC. All Rights Reserved.

TOPIC 9

Numbers to 1,000

Essential Question: How can you count, read, and show numbers to 1,000?

Digital Resources

Solve Learn Glossary

Tools Assessment Help Games

Math and Science Project: Breaking Apart and Putting Together

Find Out Collect sets of building blocks. Take turns and work together. Use the blocks to build a model. Then take that model apart and use the same blocks to build a different model.

Journal: Make a Book Show your models in a book. In your book, also:

- Tell how many pieces you used to build your models.
- Show how to use place-value blocks to model different names for the same number.

Name _____

Review What You Know

Vocabulary

1. Circle the coin with the **least value**. Put a square around the coin with the **greatest value**.

2. Circle the number that has 5 **ones** and 4 **tens**.

54

45

40

5

3. Tom is having breakfast. The minute hand on the clock shows **half past** 7 **o'clock**. Circle the time on the clock.

7:15 a.m.

7:30 a.m.

7:15 p.m.

7:30 p.m.

Counting Money

4. Circle coins that total 83¢.

Breaking Apart Numbers

5. Break apart each number into tens and ones.

23 = _____ + _____

47 = _____ + _____

96 = _____ + _____

Math Story

6. Howie has $13. A backpack costs $30. How much more money does Howie need to buy the backpack?

$_____

Copyright © Savvas Learning Company LLC. All Rights Reserved.

My Word Cards

Study the words on the front of the card.
Complete the activity on the back.

A-Z Glossary

hundred

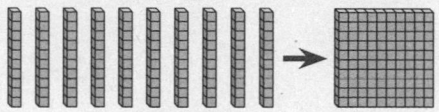

thousand

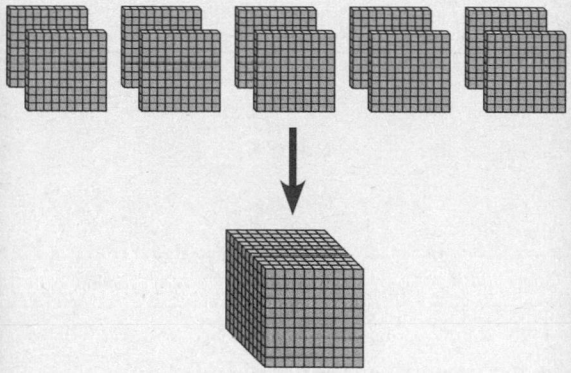

digits

43

2 digits

815

3 digits

place-value chart

Hundreds	Tens	Ones
3	4	8

expanded form

$400 + 60 + 5$

standard form

465

My Word Cards

Use what you know to complete the sentences.
Extend learning by writing your own sentence using each word.

Numbers are made up of 1 or more

_____.

10 hundreds make 1

_____.

10 tens make 1

_____.

_____

is a way to write a number using only its digits.

_____

is a way to write a number showing the place value of each digit.

A _____

_____

matches each digit of a number with its place.

Copyright © Savvas Learning Company LLC. All Rights Reserved.

My Word Cards

Study the words on the front of the card.
Complete the activity on the back.

A-Z Glossary

word form

four hundred sixty-five

compare

$> \; < \; =$

greater than (>)

$325 > 299$

less than (<)

$411 < 438$

equals (=)

$75 = 75$

increase

$224 \rightarrow 324 \rightarrow 424$

increase by 100

My Word Cards

Use what you know to complete the sentences.
Extend learning by writing your own sentence using each word.

325 is _____

_____ 299.

When you _____

numbers, you find out if a number is greater than, less than, or equal to another number.

_____

is a way to write a number using only words.

Numbers that

_____

become greater in value.

75 _____ 75.

411 is _____

_____ 438.

Copyright © Savvas Learning Company LLC. All Rights Reserved.

My Word Cards

Study the words on the front of the card.
Complete the activity on the back.

A-Z Glossary

decrease

424 → 324 → 224

decrease by 100

My Word Cards

Use what you know to complete the sentences.
Extend learning by writing your own sentence using each word.

Numbers that

_____

become lesser in value.

Copyright © Savvas Learning Company LLC. All Rights Reserved.

Name _____

Solve

Lesson 9-1
Understand Hundreds

I can ...
understand place value and count by hundreds to 1,000.

SOL 2.1a

Solve & Share

What is another way to show 100? Draw a picture and explain.

Way 1

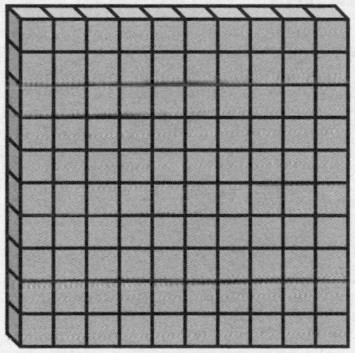

Way 2

10 ones make 1 ten.

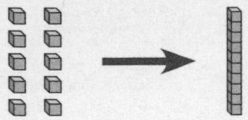

10 tens make 1 hundred.

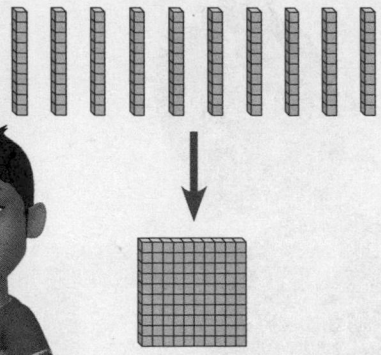

10 hundreds make 1 **thousand**.

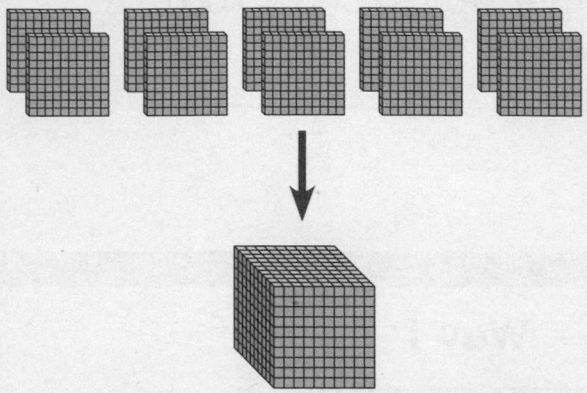

What is the number?

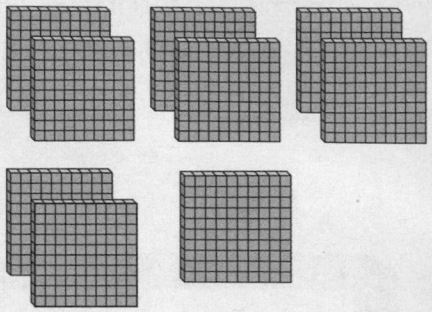

900 equals 9 hundreds, 0 tens, and 0 ones.

Do You Understand?

Show Me! 10 ones make 1 ten. 10 tens make 1 hundred. 10 hundreds make 1 thousand. Do you see a pattern? Explain.

Guided Practice

Complete each sentence. Use models if needed.

1. 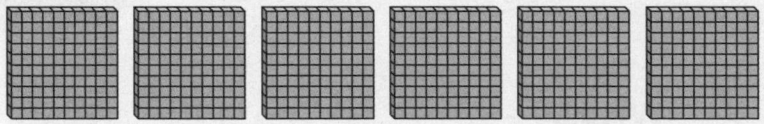

600 equals 6 hundreds, 0 tens, and 0 ones.

2. 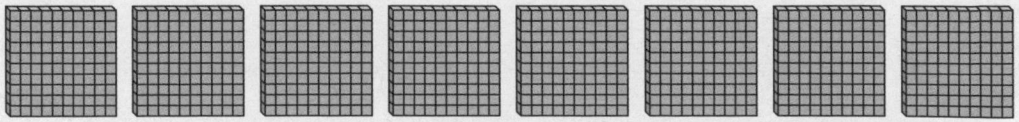

_____ equals _____ hundreds, _____ tens, and _____ ones.

Copyright © Savvas Learning Company LLC. All Rights Reserved.

Name _____

Tools Assessment

Independent Practice

Complete each sentence. Use models if needed.

3. 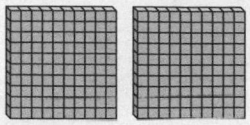

_____ equals _____ hundreds, _____ tens, and _____ ones.

4. 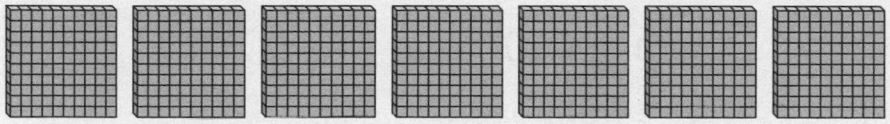

_____ equals _____ hundreds, _____ tens, and _____ ones.

5. 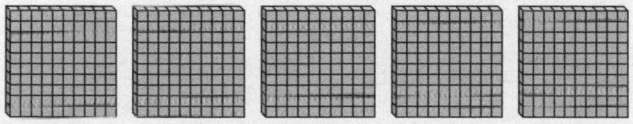

_____ equals _____ hundreds, _____ tens, and _____ ones.

6. 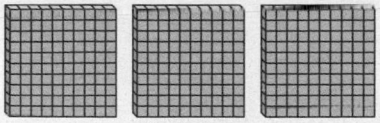

_____ equals _____ hundreds, _____ tens, and _____ ones.

7. **Number Sense** Complete the pattern.

100	200	300		500		700	800	900	

Problem Solving Solve each problem. Use models if needed.

8. **Use Tools** Lucy picked a number. She says her number has 8 hundreds, 0 tens, and 0 ones.

   What is Lucy's number?

   _____

9. **Vocabulary** Complete the sentences using the words below.

   hundred **tens** **ones**

   There are 100 _____ in one hundred.

   There are 10 _____ in one _____.

Higher Order Thinking Farrah and Cory are playing beanbag toss. Circle the two other numbers they each must get to score 1,000 points.

10. Farrah has 300 points.

    200 500 600 300

11. Cory has 500 points.

    100 200 400 700

12. **Assessment** Each box has 100 pencils. Count by hundreds to find the total. Which number tells how many pencils are in the boxes?

Ⓐ 170 Ⓒ 800

Ⓑ 700 Ⓓ 900

Copyright © Savvas Learning Company LLC. All Rights Reserved.

Name _____

Help Tools Games

Homework & Practice 9-1
Understand Hundreds

Another Look! You can show hundreds with models.

Circle the models to show 500.

500 equals __5__ hundreds, 0 tens, and 0 ones.

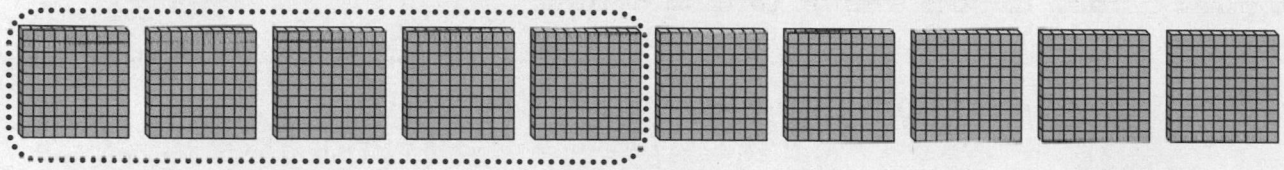

Remember that 10 ones = 1 ten, 10 tens = 1 hundred

and 10 hundreds = 1 thousand.

HOME ACTIVITY Ask your child to count by hundreds to solve the following problem. *Each box of paper clips has one hundred paper clips. Joe has 6 boxes of paper clips. How many paper clips does Joe have in all?*

Circle the models to show each number. Write the number of hundreds.

1. 200 How many hundreds? _____

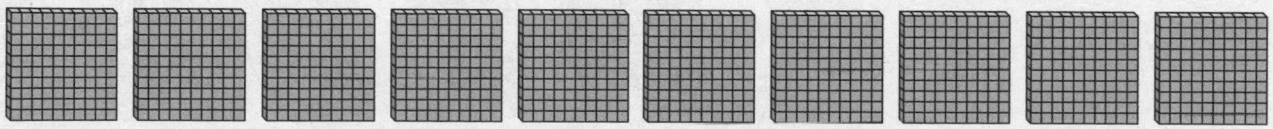

2. 700 How many hundreds? _____

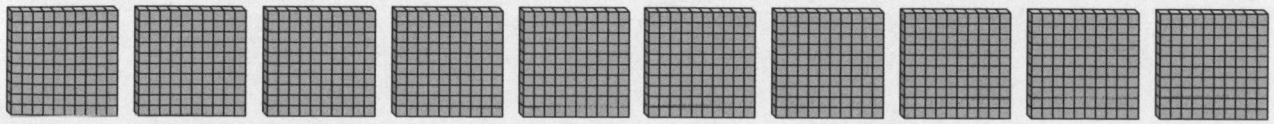

Model Circle the models to show each number. Write the number of hundreds.

3. 900 How many hundreds? _____

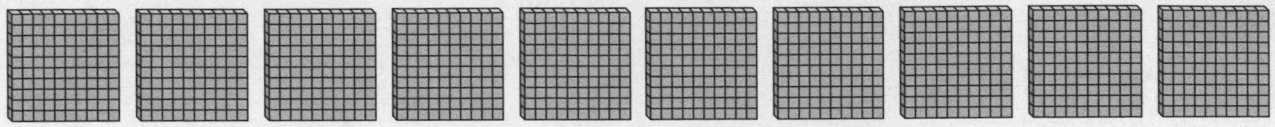

4. 1,000 How many hundreds? _____

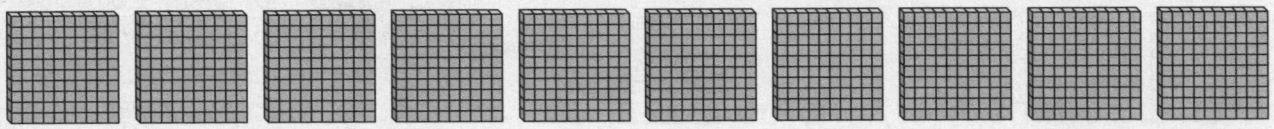

Solve each problem below.

5. Use tens blocks to build 100. Think about how many tens make 100. Draw a picture of your model.

6. **Higher Order Thinking** Patrick picked two numbers. The first number has 7 hundreds, 0 tens, and 0 ones. The second number has 2 fewer hundreds than the first number. Which two numbers did Patrick pick?

Patrick's numbers are _____

and _____.

7. **Assessment** Each bag has 100 pretzels. Count by hundreds to find the total. Which is the total number of pretzels in the bags?

Ⓐ 150 Ⓑ 400 Ⓒ 500 Ⓓ 550

Copyright © Savvas Learning Company LLC. All Rights Reserved.

Name _____

Solve

Lesson 9-2
Models and 3-Digit Numbers

I can ...
use place-value blocks and drawings to model and write 3-digit numbers.

SOL 2.1a

Solve & Share

How can you use place-value blocks to show 125? Explain.

Draw your blocks to show what you did.

Digital Resources at SavvasRealize.com

Learn Glossary

What number do the models show?

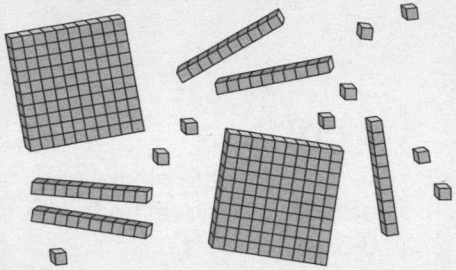

Remember, 10 ones make 1 ten.
10 tens make 1 hundred.

First, count the hundreds.

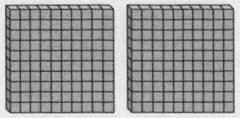

Use a **place-value chart** to show the value of each **digit**.

Hundreds	Tens	Ones
2		

Then count the tens.

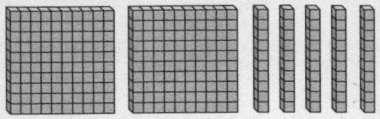

Hundreds	Tens	Ones
2	5	

Then count the ones.

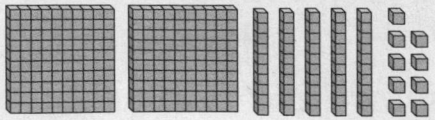

Hundreds	Tens	Ones
2	5	9

Do You Understand?

Show Me! How many hundreds are in 395? How many tens? How many ones?

Guided Practice

Write the numbers shown.
Use models and your workmat if needed.

1.

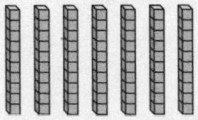

Hundreds	Tens	Ones
	7	0

70

2.

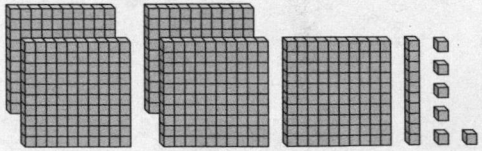

Hundreds	Tens	Ones

_____

Copyright © Savvas Learning Company LLC. All Rights Reserved.

Name _____

Tools Assessment

Independent Practice

Write the numbers shown. Use models and your workmat if needed.

3.

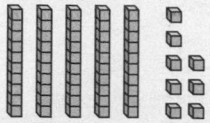

Hundreds	Tens	Ones

_____

4.

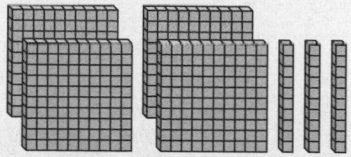

Hundreds	Tens	Ones

_____

5.

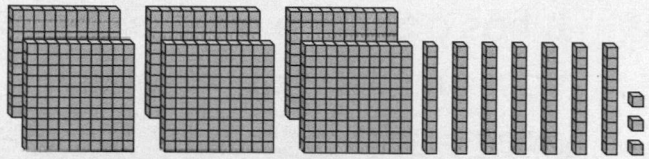

Hundreds	Tens	Ones

_____

6.

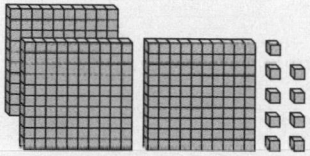

Hundreds	Tens	Ones

_____

7.

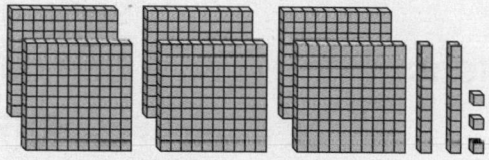

Hundreds	Tens	Ones

_____

8.

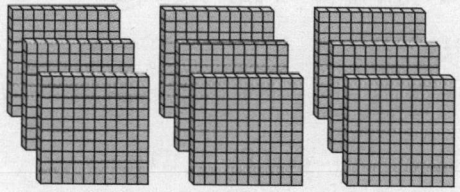

Hundreds	Tens	Ones

_____

9. **Higher Order Thinking** Find the number. It has 5 hundreds. The digit in the tens place is between 5 and 7. The number of ones is 2 less than 4. _____

Problem Solving Solve the problems below.

10. **Make Sense** Complete the chart. A number has an 8 in the hundreds place. It does not have any tens. It has a 3 in the ones place. Check that your answer makes sense.

Hundreds	Tens	Ones

What is the number? _____

11. Draw models to show the 1 hundred, 4 tens, and 3 ones. Then write the number in the chart.

Hundreds	Tens	Ones

12. **Higher Order Thinking** Choose a three-digit number. Draw models to show the hundreds, tens, and ones for your number. Write the number below.

_____

13. **Assessment** Katie used these models to show a number. Which number would be shown if Katie used 1 more hundreds flat?

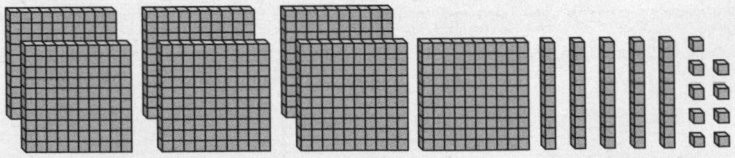

Ⓐ 758

Ⓑ 768

Ⓒ 858

Ⓓ 859

Copyright © Savvas Learning Company LLC. All Rights Reserved.

Name _____

Help Tools Games

Homework & Practice 9-2
Models and 3-Digit Numbers

HOME ACTIVITY Give your child 50 paper clips or other small, countable objects. Ask your child how many ones make 5 tens.

Another Look! Use models and your workmat to sort and count.

First, put the hundreds flats on your mat. Next, put the tens rods on your mat. Last, put the ones cubes on your mat.

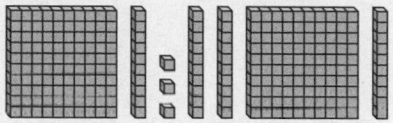

Write the number of hundreds, tens, and ones.

Hundreds	Tens	Ones
2	4	3

Write the numbers.
Use models and your workmat if needed.

1.

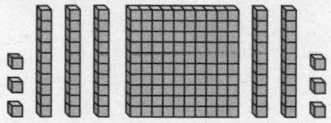

Hundreds	Tens	Ones

2.

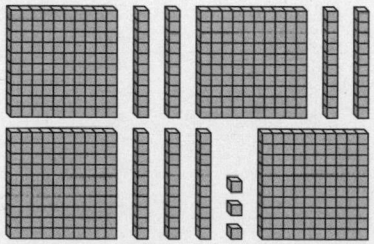

Hundreds	Tens	Ones

Solve each problem. Use models and your workmat if needed.

3. **Model** Write the number based on the model shown.

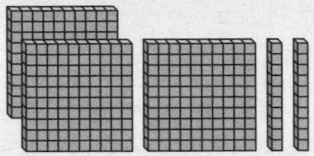

Hundreds	Tens	Ones

4. **Number Sense** Use the clues to solve the number puzzle.

I have a 5 in my ones place.
The digit in my tens place is 3 plus the digit in my ones place. The digit in my hundreds place is 2 less than the digit in my ones place. What number am I?

_____

5. **Higher Order Thinking** Look back at Item 4. Write your own place-value number puzzle. Give it to a friend to solve.

_____

_____

_____

_____

_____

6. **Assessment** Which number is shown?

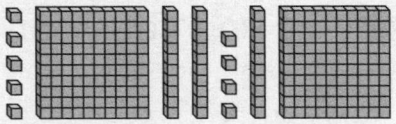

Ⓐ 239

Ⓑ 329

Ⓒ 293

Ⓓ 339

Copyright © Savvas Learning Company LLC. All Rights Reserved.

Name _____

Solve

Lesson 9-3

Name Place Values

I can ...

tell the value of a digit by where it is placed in a number.

SOL 2.1a

Solve & Share

Jake says the 3 in 738 has a value of 3. He shows this with 3 ones blocks. Do you agree with Jake? Explain. Use the chart to help.

Hundreds	Tens	Ones

_____

_____

_____

_____

What number do the place-value blocks show?

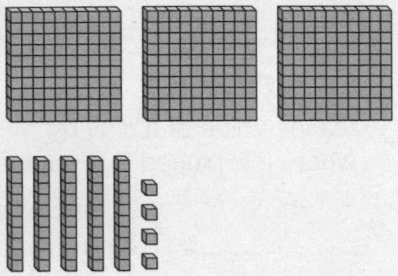

Remember, you can use a place-value chart to show the value of each digit.

Hundreds	Tens	Ones
3	5	4

354

The 3 has a value of 3 hundreds or 300.

The 5 has a value of 5 tens or 50.

The 4 has a value of 4 ones or 4.

Do You Understand?

Show Me! How can you find the value of a digit using a place-value chart?

Guided Practice

Complete the place-value chart. Then write the value of each digit.

1.

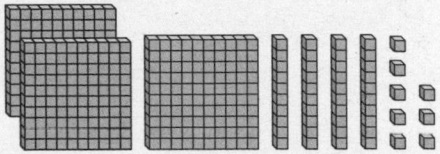

Hundreds	Tens	Ones
3	4	8

The 3 has a value of 3 hundreds or 300.

The 4 has a value of 4 tens or 40.

The 8 has a value of 8 ones or 8.

Copyright © Savvas Learning Company LLC. All Rights Reserved.

Name _____

Tools Assessment

Independent Practice

Circle the correct values for the underlined digit in each number.

2.	17<u>3</u>	3	30	3 hundreds	3 ones	3 tens
3.	<u>4</u>39	4 tens	4 hundreds	4	40	400
4.	6<u>6</u>1	6 hundreds	60	6 tens	600	6 ones
5.	<u>5</u>18	500	5 tens	5 hundreds	5	50
6.	74<u>2</u>	20	200	2	2 tens	2 ones

7. Use the number to answer each question.

902

What is the value of the 9?

_____

What is the value of the 0?

_____

What is the value of the 2?

_____

8. **Higher Order Thinking** Write the number that has the following values.

- The tens digit has a value of 70.
- The ones digit has a value of 5 ones.
- The hundreds digit has a value of 8 hundreds.

_____

Problem Solving

Use place value to solve each problem.

9. Complete the chart to find the number.

The number has 9 hundreds.
It has 5 tens
It has 8 ones.

Hundreds	Tens	Ones

What is the number? _____

10. **Model** Courtney drew a picture of place-value blocks to show the number 793. Draw the blocks to show what Courtney's picture may have looked liked.

11. **Higher Order Thinking** A class needs to build the number 123 with place-value blocks but does **NOT** have any hundreds blocks. How can they build 123 using other place-value blocks?

_____

_____

_____

_____

12. **Assessment** What is the value of the 6 in the number 862?

Ⓐ 6
Ⓑ 10
Ⓒ 60
Ⓓ 600

Copyright © Savvas Learning Company LLC. All Rights Reserved.

Name _____

Help Tools Games

Homework & Practice 9-3

Name Place Values

Another Look! You can find the value of each digit of a number by its place.

Hundreds	Tens	Ones
2	4	3

The value of the 2 is 2 hundreds or 200.

The value of the 4 is 4 tens or 40.

The value of the 3 is 3 ones or 3.

HOME ACTIVITY Choose two three-digit numbers. Ask your child to name the values of each digit in each number.

Use the number in the place-value chart. Write the value of each digit.

1.

Hundreds	Tens	Ones
8	2	1

The value of the 8 is _____ hundreds or _____.

The value of the 2 is _____ tens or _____.

The value of the 1 is _____ one or _____.

2.

Hundreds	Tens	Ones
5	7	9

The value of the 5 is _____ hundreds or _____.

The value of the 7 is _____ tens or _____.

The value of the 9 is _____ ones or _____.

Use place value to solve each problem.

3. Complete the chart to find the number.

The number has 0 ones.
It has 7 hundreds.
It has 8 tens.

Hundreds	Tens	Ones

What is the number? _____.

4. **Explain** Stacy says the 4 in 643 has a value of 4 tens or 40. Do you agree with Stacy's reasoning? Explain. Use pictures, words, or numbers in your answer.

5. **Higher Order Thinking** Kayla wrote a three-digit number. The value of the digit in the hundreds place is 6 hundreds. The digit in the tens place is 3 less than the digit in the hundreds place. The sum of all three digits is 12. What is Kayla's number?

Kayla's number is _____.

6. **Assessment** What is the value of the 7 in the number 763?

Ⓐ 7

Ⓑ 70

Ⓒ 100

Ⓓ 700

Copyright © Savvas Learning Company LLC. All Rights Reserved.

Name _____

Solve

Lesson 9-4

Read and Write 3-Digit Numbers

I can ...

read and write 3-digit numbers in expanded form, standard form, and word form.

SOL 2.1a

Solve & Share

What is another way to write the number 231? Explain.

Way 1

231

Way 2

What number is shown by the models?

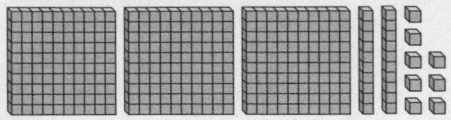

You can write the number in different ways.

Way 1
Write the number in **expanded form**.

$300 + 20 + 8$

Way 2
Write the number in **standard form**.

328

Write the hundreds first, then the tens, then the ones.

Way 3
Write the number in **word form**.

three hundred twenty-eight

All three ways show the same number!

$328 = 300 + 20 + 8$

Do You Understand?

Show Me! How many hundreds, tens, and ones does the number six hundred forty have?

Guided Practice

Use the models to solve each problem.

1. Write the number in expanded form. Then write it in standard form.

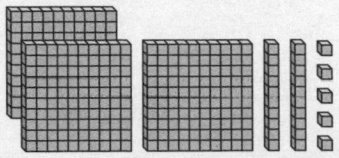

300 + 20 + 5

325

2. Write the number in expanded form. Then write it in word form.

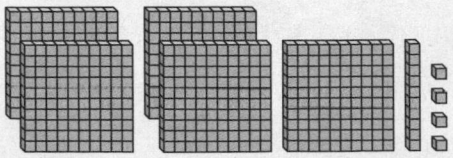

____ + ____ + ____

____

____

Copyright © Savvas Learning Company LLC. All Rights Reserved.

Name _____

Tools Assessment

Independent Practice

Write the number in word form and standard form.

3. 300 + 80 + 2

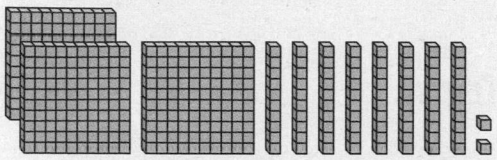

_____

_____

4. 200 + 6

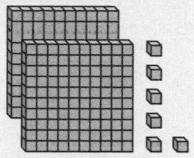

_____

_____

5. 600 + 90 + 5

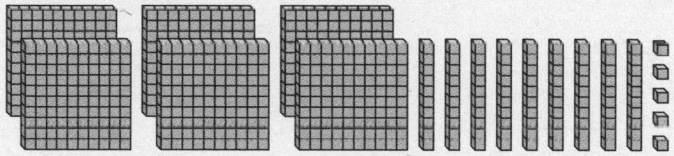

_____

_____

6. 500 + 30 + 3

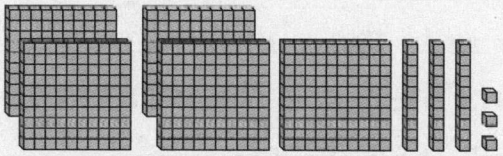

_____

_____

7. Write eight hundred seventy-four in expanded form and standard form.

_____

_____

8. Write 478 in expanded form and word form.

_____

_____

9. **Higher Order Thinking** Write the number in two different ways. It has 5 hundreds. The tens digit is 1 less than the hundreds digit. The ones digit is 2 more than the hundreds digit.

Standard form: _____ Expanded form: _____

Problem Solving

Use place-value models to help you solve the problems below.

10. **Vocabulary** There are 493 pages in a book.

Write the number 493 in **expanded form**.

_____ + _____ + _____

Write the number 493 in **word form**.

_____

11. **Higher Order Thinking** Draw hundreds, tens, and ones to show a three-digit number. Then write the number in expanded form. Then use the word form of the number in a sentence.

12. **Assessment** The model shows a three-digit number. Which is the standard form of the number?

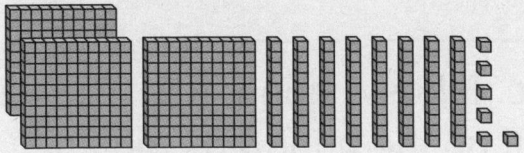

Ⓐ 300 + 80 + 6 Ⓑ 386 Ⓒ 300 + 90 + 7 Ⓓ 397

Copyright © Savvas Learning Company LLC. All Rights Reserved.

Name _____

Help Tools Games

Homework & Practice 9-4

Read and Write 3-Digit Numbers

Another Look! You can write and show numbers in different ways.

Expanded form uses plus signs to show hundreds, tens, and ones.

200 + 60 + 4

You can draw models to show the expanded form.

The **word form** is two hundred sixty-four.

The **standard form** is 264.

HOME ACTIVITY Say a three-digit number, such as eight hundred fifty-one. Write it down in word form. Ask your child to write the number in both standard form and expanded form.

Solve each problem.

1. Draw models to show the expanded form. Write the number in standard form.

400 + 30 + 8

four hundred thirty-eight

_____

2. Write the number in expanded form and standard form.

three hundred fifty-four

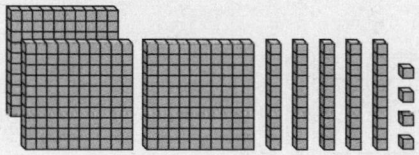

_____ + _____ + _____

_____

3. **Vocabulary** Write the number in **standard form**.
Then write it in **word form**.

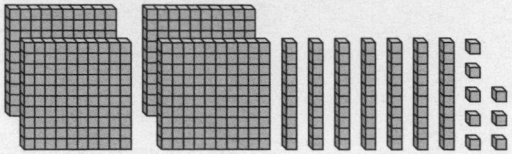

400 + 70 + 8

_____

_____

4. **Assessment** 329 cars and 293 trucks are parked in a parking lot.

Which is the expanded form of the number of cars parked?

Ⓐ 200 + 90 + 3

Ⓑ 300 + 20 + 9

Ⓒ 300 + 90 + 2

Ⓓ 600 + 20 + 2

Higher Order Thinking Use the clues to complete the number puzzle.

Across

5. 500 + 20 + 3

7. 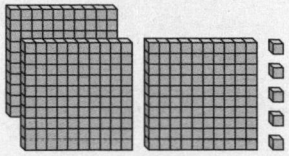

9. 400 + 20 + 9

10. 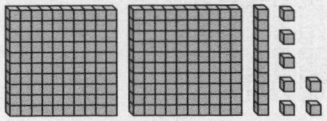

13. Two hundred sixty-nine

Down

6. 300 + 40 + 7

7. Three hundred ninety-seven

8. 500 + 60 + 9

11. 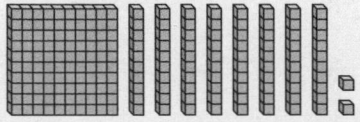

12. Four hundred thirty-eight

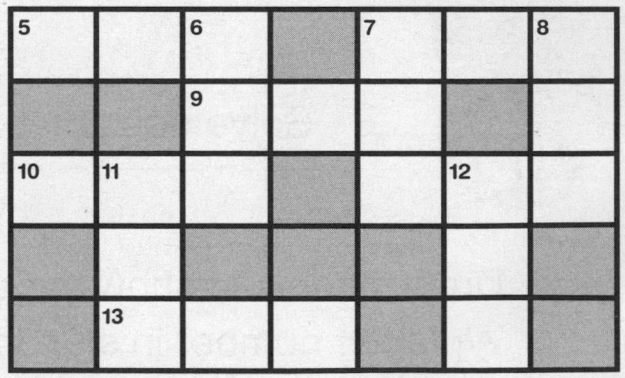

Copyright © Savvas Learning Company LLC. All Rights Reserved.

Name _____

Solve

Lesson 9-5

Different Ways to Name the Same Number

I can ...
make and name a number in different ways to show the same value.

SOL 2.1a

Solve & Share

Use place-value blocks. Show two ways to make 213. Then draw each way. Tell how your ways are alike and different.

Make your models here.

Draw your models here.

Way 1

Way 2

Do You Understand?

Show Me! How can you show that 5 hundreds and 4 tens has the same value as 4 hundreds and 14 tens?

Guided Practice

Use place-value blocks to count the hundreds, tens, and ones. Show two other ways to make the number.

1.

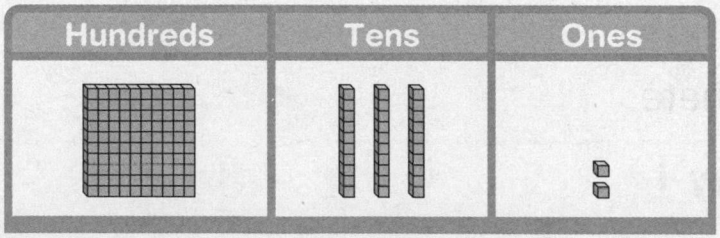

132 = 100 + 30 + 2

132 = _____

132 = _____

Copyright © Savvas Learning Company LLC. All Rights Reserved.

Name _____

Tools Assessment

Independent Practice

Use place-value blocks to count the hundreds, tens, and ones. Then show two other ways to make the number.

2.

Hundreds	Tens	Ones

418 = _____

418 = _____

418 = _____

3.

Hundreds	Tens	Ones

163 = _____

163 = _____

163 = _____

4.

Hundreds	Tens	Ones

225 = _____

225 = _____

225 = _____

Algebra Write the missing number.

5. 698 = 500 + _____ + 8

6. 939 = 900 + 20 + _____

Problem Solving Solve the problems below.

7. Carl made this model to show a number.

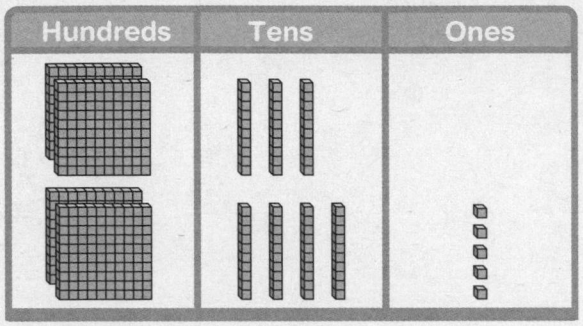

What number is shown? _____

Draw models to show another way Carl could make this number.

8. **Explain** Neha wants to make the same number in different ways. She says 300 + 130 + 9 equals the same number as 500 + 30 + 9. Do you agree with Neha? Explain.

_____

_____

_____

9. **Higher Order Thinking** Make 572 as hundreds, tens, and ones. Write as many ways as you can.

_____

_____

_____

_____

10. **Assessment** Which is a way to show 687? Choose all that apply.

- ☐ 600 + 70 + 17
- ☐ 600 + 80 + 7
- ☐ 600 + 180 + 7
- ☐ 500 + 180 + 7

Copyright © Savvas Learning Company LLC. All Rights Reserved.

Name _____

Help Tools Games

Homework & Practice 9-5

Different Ways to Name the Same Number

Another Look! You can show a number in different ways.

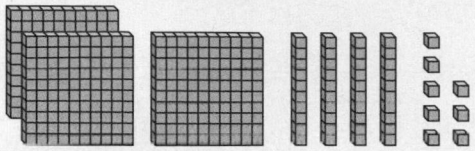

Remember that 10 tens makes 1 hundred. So, 1 hundred and 4 tens is the same as 14 tens.

3 hundreds, 4 tens, and 8 ones

348 = 300 + 40 + 8 is the same as

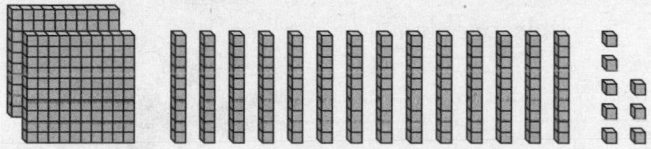

2 hundreds, 14 tens, and 8 ones

348 = 200 + 140 + 8

HOME ACTIVITY Write the expanded form of a number and ask your child to tell you another way to show the number. For example, write 200 + 10 + 6 or 900 + 40 + 3.

Show two different ways to name the number. You can use place-value blocks to help.

1. 734 = _____ hundreds, _____ tens, and _____ ones.

   734 = _____ + _____ + _____

   734 = _____ hundreds, _____ tens, and _____ ones.

   734 = _____ + _____ + _____

2. **Be Precise** What number does the model show?

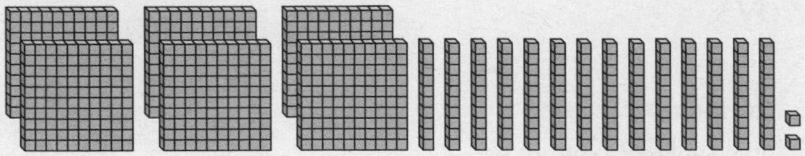

_____

3. **Number Sense** Write a three-digit number. Then write it in two different ways.

My Number _____

Way 1 _____

Way 2 _____

4. **Math and Science** Matt built a house with 164 blocks. The main part of his house has 100 blocks. The roof has 50 blocks. The chimney has 14 blocks. Write another way to use the same number of blocks for a new house.

5. **Higher Order Thinking** Write 936 two different ways using the charts.

Hundreds	Tens	Ones

Hundreds	Tens	Ones

6. **Assessment** Which is a way to show 764? Choose all that apply.

- ☐ 600 + 150 + 4
- ☐ 600 + 150 + 14
- ☐ 700 + 50 + 14
- ☐ 700 + 60 + 4

Copyright © Savvas Learning Company LLC. All Rights Reserved.

Name _____

Solve

Lesson 9-6

Place-Value Patterns with Numbers

I can ...

use place-value patterns to mentally count by 1s and 10s from a given number.

SOL 2.16, 2.1b, 2.2a

Solve & Share

Write the missing numbers in the chart.
Be ready to explain how you found the missing numbers.

51	52	53	54	55	56	57	58	59	60
61	62	63	64	65	66	67	68	69	70
71	72	73	74	75	76	77	78	79	80
	82	83		85				89	
91			94		96	97	98		100
101	102	103	104	105	106	107	108	109	110
111	112	113	114	115	116	117	118	119	120
	122	123		125				129	
131			134				138		

Digital Resources at SavvasRealize.com

You can use place-value patterns and mental math to count by 1s and 10s to 100.

31	32	33	34	35	36	37
41	42	43	44	45	46	47
51	52	53	54	55	56	57

The ones digits go up by 1 from left to right.
The tens digits go up by 1 from top to bottom.

You can also use place-value patterns and mental math to count by 1s and 10s to 1,000.

531	532	533	534	535	536	537
541	542	543	544	545	546	547
551	552	553	554	555	556	557

The ones digits go up by 1 from left to right.
The tens digits go up by 1 from top to bottom.

Do You Understand?

Show Me! Use mental math and place-value patterns to write each missing number.

536, 537, _____, 539, 540

531, 541, _____, 561, 571

☆ Guided Practice ☆

Use place-value patterns and mental math to find the missing numbers.

1.

784	785	786	787	788	789	790
794	795	796	797	798	799	800
804	805	806	807	808	809	810

2.

412		414		416		418
422			425		427	
432	433		435	436	437	

Copyright © Savvas Learning Company LLC. All Rights Reserved.

Name _____

Tools Assessment

Independent Practice

Use place-value patterns and mental math to find the missing numbers.

3.

884			887		889
	895			898	
904	905		907	908	

4.

	146	147			150
155				159	
	166	167		169	170

5. 456, 457, 458, _____, _____,
461, 462, _____, _____, _____

6. 620, 630, 640, _____, 660, _____,
680, 690, _____, 710, _____

7. 232, 242, _____, 262, _____,
_____, 292, 302, _____, _____

8. 175, 176, _____, _____, 179,
_____, 181, _____, 183, _____

Number Sense Describe each number pattern.

9. 130 → 230 → 330 → 430 → 530

_____

_____

10. 320 → 330 → 340 → 350 → 360

_____

_____

Problem Solving Solve each problem.

11. **Look for Patterns** Sally sees a pattern in these numbers. Describe the pattern.

500, 501, 502, 503, 504, 505

_____

_____

_____

12. **Look for Patterns** Yoshi sees a pattern in these numbers. Describe the pattern.

341, 351, 361, 371, 381, 391

_____

_____

_____

13. **Higher Order Thinking** Write your own three-digit numbers. Describe the number pattern for your numbers.

_____, _____, _____, _____, _____

_____

_____

_____

14. **Assessment** Use the numbers on the cards. Write the missing numbers in the number chart.

222	214	224	231

210	211	212	213		215
220	221		223		225
230		232	233	234	235

Copyright © Savvas Learning Company LLC. All Rights Reserved.

Name _____

Help Tools Games

Homework & Practice 9-6

Place-Value Patterns with Numbers

Another Look! The digits in numbers can help you find patterns.

975	976	977	978	979	980
985	986	987	988	989	990
995	996	997	998	999	1,000

Pick a row in the chart. Read the numbers across the row.

The ones digits go up by ____.

Pick a column in the chart and read the numbers from top to bottom.

The tens digits go up by ____.

HOME ACTIVITY Write a three-digit number such as 120. Ask your child to write four more numbers after it, counting by 1s. Then ask your child to start at the number and write four more numbers below it, counting by 10s.

Use place-value patterns and mental math to find the missing numbers.

1.

633		635		637	
	644			647	648
653			656	657	

2.

	285	286			289
294	295		297		299
304			307		

Solve each problem.

3. **Explain** Manuel thinks the tens digit goes up by 1 in these numbers. Do you agree? Explain.

460, 470, 480, 490, 500, 510

_____

_____

_____

4. **Explain** Maribel thinks the tens digit goes up by 1 in these numbers. Do you agree? Explain.

864, 865, 866, 867, 868, 869

_____

_____

_____

5. **Higher Order Thinking** Write 5 three-digit numbers. From left to right, the ones digit in your numbers should go up by 1.

_____, _____, _____, _____, _____

Write 5 three-digit numbers. From left to right, the tens digit in your numbers should go up by 1.

_____, _____, _____, _____, _____

6. **Assessment** Use the numbers on the cards. Write the missing numbers in the number chart.

557 539 545 547

535	536	537	538		540
	546		548	549	550
555	556		558	559	560

Copyright © Savvas Learning Company LLC. All Rights Reserved.

Name _____

Solve

Lesson 9-7

Skip Count by 5s, 10s, and 100s to 1,000

I can ...

skip count by 5s, 10s, and 100s using a number line.

SOL 2.2a, 2.1b, 2.16

Solve & Share

Use the number line to skip count by 5s, starting at 0. Write the two missing numbers. Describe any patterns you see.

_____

_____

_____

This number line shows skip counting by 5s.

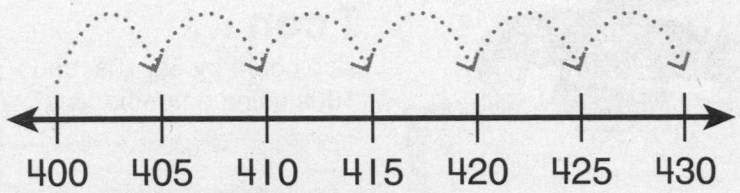

This number line shows skip counting by 100s.

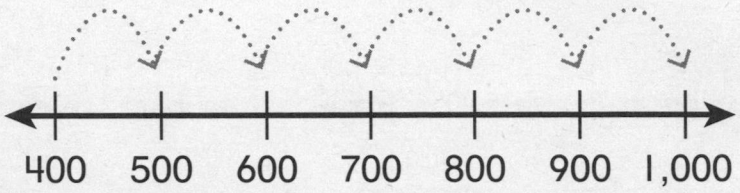

Do You Understand?

Show Me! How could you use the number line in the first box above to skip count by 10s starting at 400?

Guided Practice

Skip count on the number line. Write the missing numbers.

1.

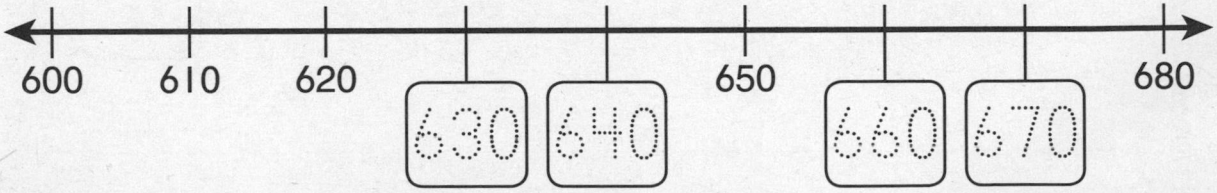

2.

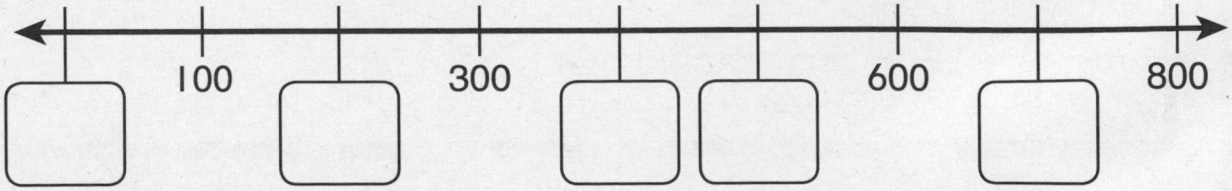

Copyright © Savvas Learning Company LLC. All Rights Reserved.

Name _____

Tools Assessment

Independent Practice

Skip count on the number line.
Write the missing numbers.

3.

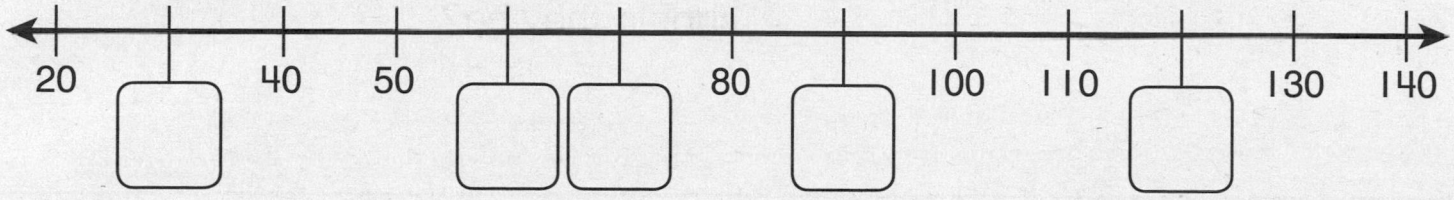

4.

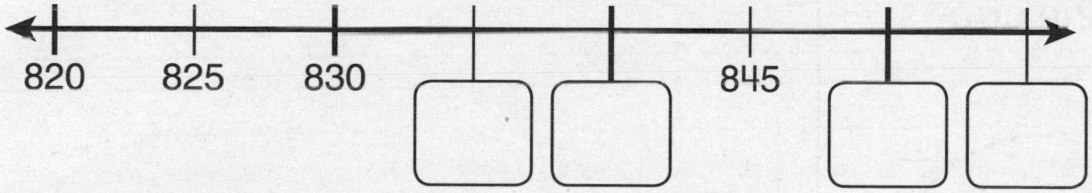

Look at the skip counting pattern. Write the missing numbers.

5. 100, 200, 300, 400, _____, _____

6. 930, 940, _____, 960, 970, _____

7. 480, 490, 500, _____, _____, 530

8. 745, 750, _____, _____, 765, _____

9. **Algebra** Write the missing numbers.

300 + _____ = 400

85 + _____ = 90

990 + _____ = 1,000

Problem Solving Solve the problems below.

10. **Reasoning** Greg is skip counting. He writes 430, 435, 440 on paper. Greg wants to write 3 more numbers after 440. What should they be?

_____, _____, _____

11. **Reasoning** Zoe is skip counting. She writes 300, 400, 500 on paper. Zoe wants to write 3 more numbers after 500. What should they be?

_____, _____, _____

12. **Higher Order Thinking** What number is used to skip count on this number line? How do you know? What numbers did the arrows land on at the jumps?

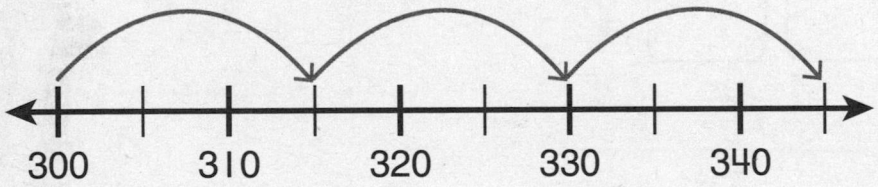

13. **Assessment** Roy played 4 video games. He scored 110, 115, 120, and 125 points.

Skip counting by what number from 110 to 125 is shown on the number line?

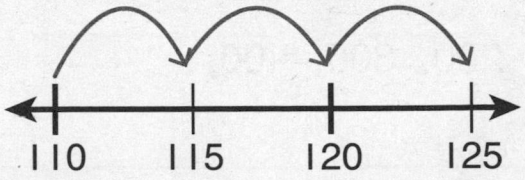

Ⓐ 2 Ⓑ 5 Ⓒ 10 Ⓓ 100

Copyright © Savvas Learning Company LLC. All Rights Reserved.

Name _____

Help Tools Games

Homework & Practice 9-7

Skip Count by 5s, 10s, and 100s to 1,000

Another Look! Skip count on the number line. Write the missing numbers.

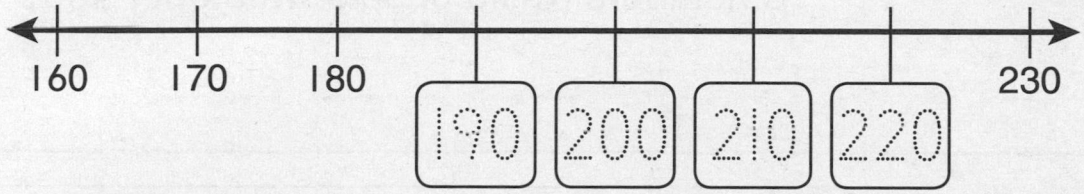

Find the difference between two given numbers that are next to each other. That tells you which number you are skip counting by.

HOME ACTIVITY Draw a number line with numbers that go up by 5s. Have your child tell you what number he or she can skip count by. Repeat this activity with numbers that go up by 10s.

Skip count on the number line. Write the missing numbers.

1.

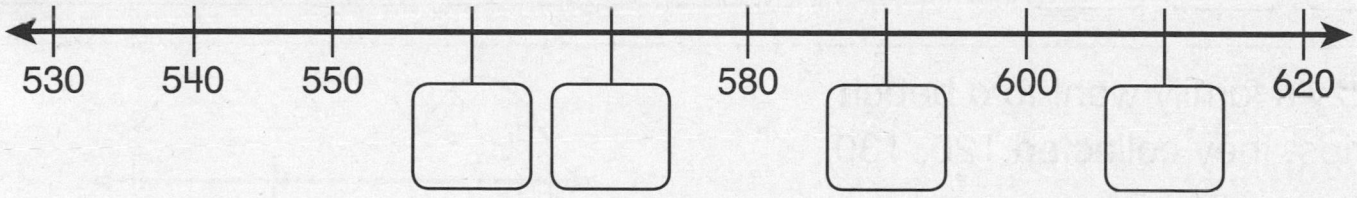

2.

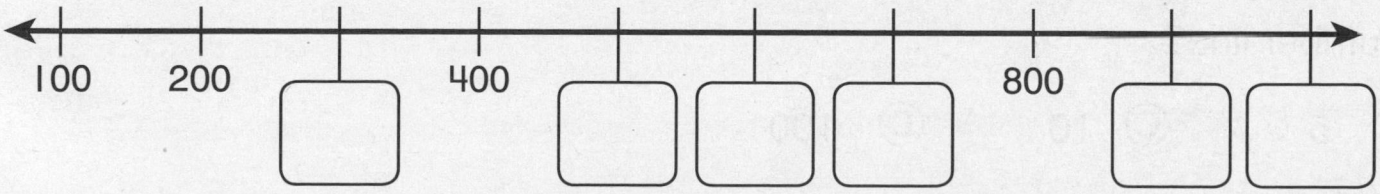

Solve the problems below.

3. **Look for Patterns** Bill wants to skip count by 10s from 710. He writes 710, 720, 730 on paper. What are the next 5 numbers Bill should write after 730?

_____, _____, _____, _____, _____

4. **Look for Patterns** Krista wants to skip count by 100s from 200. She writes 200, 300, 400 on paper. What are the next 5 numbers Krista should write after 400?

_____, _____, _____, _____, _____

5. **Higher Order Thinking** Linda wants to show skip counting by 5s from a number to get to 1,000. Write the numbers she should put on her number line below. How do you know?

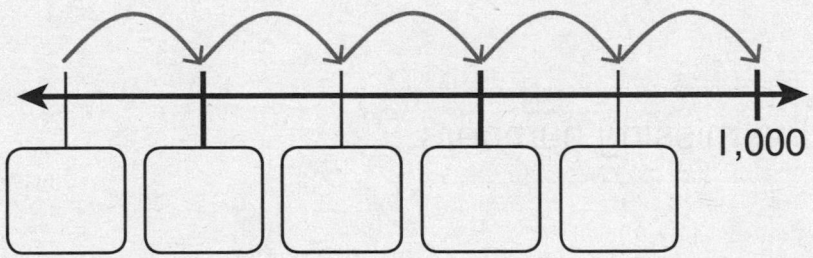

6. **Assessment** Izzy's family went to a beach 4 times. On their trips, they collected 120, 130, 140, and 150 shells.

Skip counting by what number from 120 to 150 is shown on the number line?

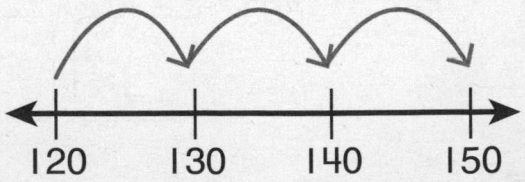

Ⓐ 2 Ⓑ 5 Ⓒ 10 Ⓓ 100

Copyright © Savvas Learning Company LLC. All Rights Reserved.

Name _____

Solve

Lesson 9-8

Compare Numbers Using Place Value

I can ...
compare numbers using place value.

SOL 2.1c

Solve & Share

Joy and Zach flipped three number cards. Then they each made a number. Joy made 501 and Zach made 510.

Who made the greater number? How do you know? Use place-value blocks to help you solve.

Hundreds	Tens	Ones

_____ is greater than _____.

Digital Resources at SavvasRealize.com

Compare 325 and 225.

Hundreds	Tens	Ones
3	2	5
2	2	5

Compare the hundreds first.

300 is **greater than** 200.

So, 325 > 225.

Compare 736 and 756.

Hundreds	Tens	Ones
7	3	6
7	5	6

If the hundreds are equal, compare the tens.

30 is **less than** 50.

So, 736 < 756.

Compare 897 and 897.

Hundreds	Tens	Ones
8	9	7
8	9	7

The hundreds, the tens, and the ones are **equal**.

897 is equal to 897.

So, 897 = 897.

Do You Understand?

Show Me! How would you compare 995 and 890?

Guided Practice

Compare. Write greater than, less than, or equal to. Then write >, <, or =.

1. 264 is greater than 178.

264 > 178

Hundreds	Tens	Ones
2	6	4
1	7	8

2. 816 is _____ 819.

816 ◯ 819

Hundreds	Tens	Ones

Copyright © Savvas Learning Company LLC. All Rights Reserved.

Name _____

Tools Assessment

Independent Practice

Compare. Write greater than, less than, or equal to. Then write >, <, or =.

3.
572 is _____ 577.

572 ◯ 577

4.
256 is _____ 243.

256 ◯ 243

5.
837 is _____ 837.

837 ◯ 837

6.
486 is _____ 468.

486 ◯ 468

7.
208 is _____ 208.

208 ◯ 208

8.
936 is _____ 836.

936 ◯ 836

9.
821 is _____ 821.

821 ◯ 821

10.
347 is _____ 437.

347 ◯ 437

11.
286 is _____ 189.

286 ◯ 189

12. Higher Order Thinking Find one number that will make all three comparisons true.

_____ < 111 _____ > 109 _____ = 110

Problem Solving

Compare. Write >, <, or =. Then answer the question.

13. Reasoning Ming sells 319 tickets. Josie sells 315 tickets. Who sells more tickets?

319 ◯ 315

_____ sells more tickets.

14. Reasoning Jared earned 189 pennies doing chores. Tara earned 200 pennies doing chores. Who earned more pennies?

189 ◯ 200

_____ earned more pennies.

15. Higher Order Thinking Compare the numbers 298 and 289. Write the comparison two ways. Then explain your thinking.

_____ ◯ _____

_____ ◯ _____

_____

_____

_____

_____

_____

16. Assessment Solve the riddle to find the number of coins in the second chest. Then compare the numbers.

The two numbers have the same digits.
The hundreds digits are the same.
The tens and ones digits are in different orders.

Ⓐ 556 < 665

Ⓑ 556 > 565

Ⓒ 556 = 565

Ⓓ 556 < 565

Copyright © Savvas Learning Company LLC. All Rights Reserved.

Name _____

Help Tools Games

Homework & Practice 9-8

Compare Numbers Using Place Value

Another Look! To compare two numbers, first compare the digits with the greatest place value.

If the hundreds are equal, compare the tens.
If the tens are equal, compare the ones.

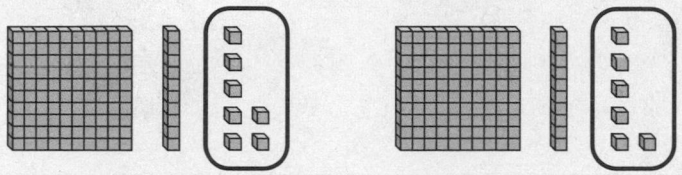

117 116

7 is greater than 6.

So 117 > 116.

Hundreds	Tens	Ones
1	1	7
1	1	6

Use models to help!

> means greater than.
< means less than.
= means equals.

HOME ACTIVITY Ask your child if 540 is greater than or less than 524. Then have your child explain his or her answer.

Compare. Write >, <, or =. Use place-value blocks to help if needed.

1. 341 ◯ 432
2. 990 ◯ 290
3. 621 ◯ 639
4. 890 ◯ 880
5. 546 ◯ 546
6. 999 ◯ 995

Make Sense Use the numbers in the triangles as digits. Write a number that will make each comparison true.

7. 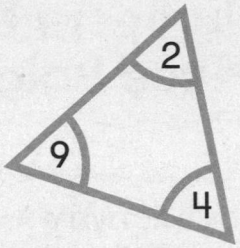

_____ < 942

8. 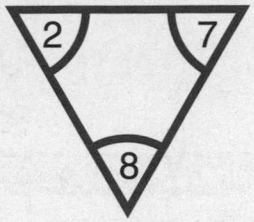

872 > _____

9. Nyla compared 790 and 709. Her work is shown at the right.

Is Nyla's comparison correct? If not, correct her mistake.

_____

_____

_____

Nyla's work
790 < 709
I compared the ones.
0 is less than 9.
So, 790 < 709.

10. **Higher Order Thinking** A number is less than 200 and greater than 100. The ones digit is 5 less than 10. The tens digit is 2 more than the ones digit. What is the number?

_____

11. **Assessment** This week, 161 fans watched a soccer game. Last week, 116 fans watched a soccer game. Which correctly compares the number of soccer fans in these two weeks?

Ⓐ 116 = 116

Ⓑ 161 < 116

Ⓒ 116 > 161

Ⓓ 116 < 161

Copyright © Savvas Learning Company LLC. All Rights Reserved.

Name _____

Solve

Lesson 9-9

Compare Numbers on the Number Line

I can ...

compare and write a three-digit number that is greater than or less than another three-digit number.

SOL 2.1c

Solve & Share

This number line shows only one number. Name a number that is greater than 256. Then, name a number that is less than 256. Show your numbers on the number line and explain why you are correct.

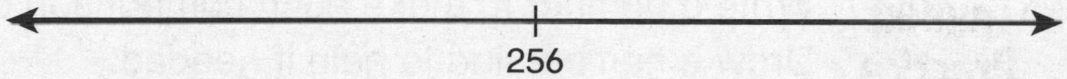

_____ is greater than 256.

_____ is less than 256.

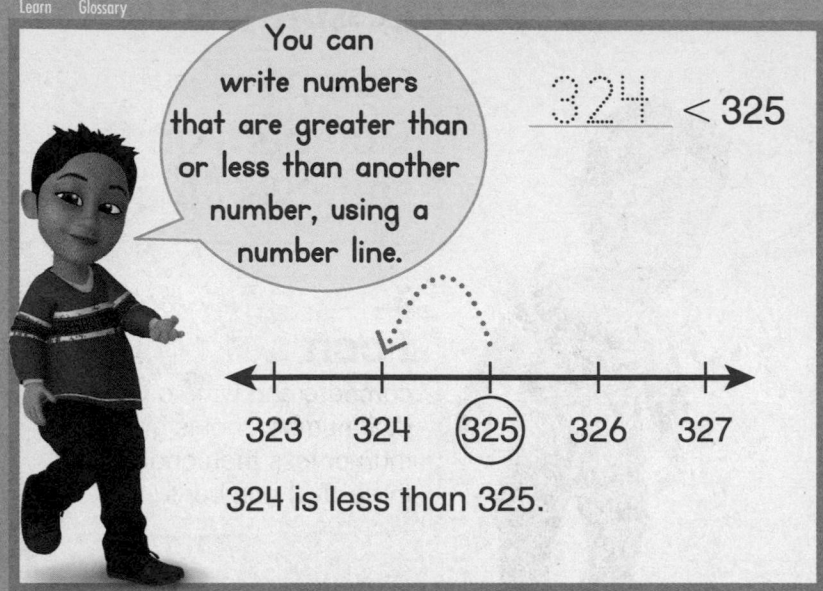

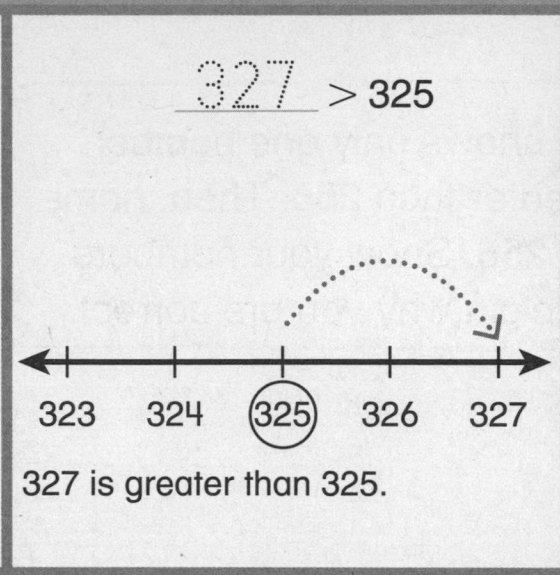

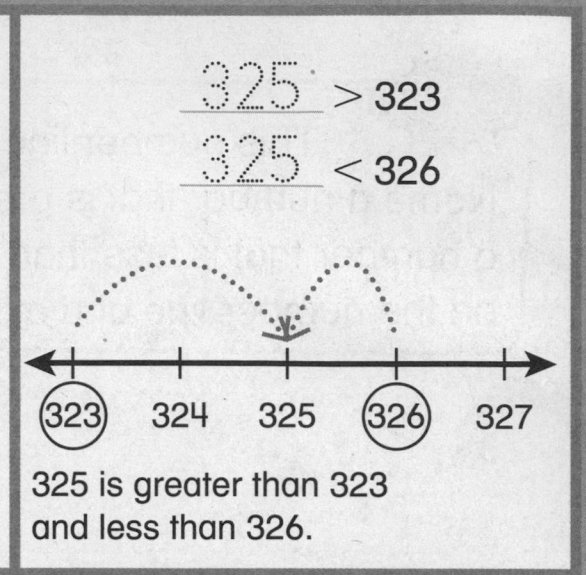

Do You Understand?

Show Me! Can you write a number that is less than 325, and that is not shown on the number line above? Explain.

Guided Practice

Write a number to make each comparison correct. Draw a number line to help if needed.

1. 461 < 467
2. _____ < 470
3. 132 < _____
4. 263 < _____
5. 675 > _____
6. 684 = _____

Copyright © Savvas Learning Company LLC. All Rights Reserved.

Name _____

Tools Assessment

Independent Practice

Write a number to make each comparison correct. Draw a number line to help if needed.

7. 421 > _____

8. _____ < 884

9. 959 < _____

10. _____ < 619

11. 103 = _____

12. 566 > _____

13. 394 < _____

14. _____ < 417

15. _____ > 789

Write <, >, or = to make each comparison correct.

16. 107 ◯ 106

17. 630 ◯ 629

18. 832 ◯ 832

19. **Higher Order Thinking** Write a number to make each comparison correct. Place the numbers on the number lines.

_____ < 780 < _____

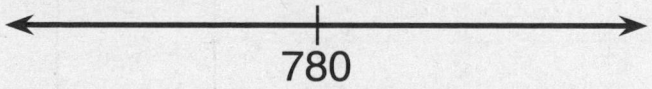

_____ > 457 > _____

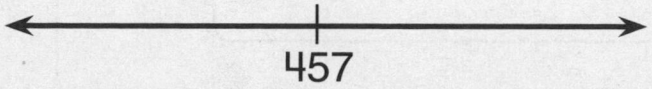

Problem Solving Solve the problems below.

20. **Reasoning** Kim is thinking of a number.
It is greater than 447.
It is less than 635.
What could the number be?

_____

21. **Reasoning** Don is thinking of a number.
It is less than 982.
It is greater than 950.
What could the number be?

_____

22. **Higher Order Thinking** Monty picked a number card. The number is greater than 282. It is less than 284. What is the number? _____

Explain how you know.

23. **Assessment** What number is neither greater than nor less than the number shown? Explain how you know.

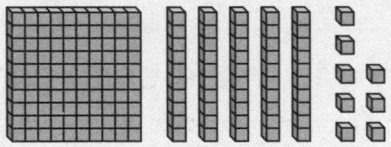

Copyright © Savvas Learning Company LLC. All Rights Reserved.

Name _____

Help Tools Games

Homework & Practice 9-9

Compare Numbers on the Number Line

Another Look! Think about the order of numbers.

159 160 161 162 163 164 165 166 167 168

Numbers go on forever in both directions on a number line. So, 170 is also greater than 167.

Write a number to make each comparison correct.

160 is **less than** 163. 168 is **greater than** 167.

161 is **greater than** 160 and **less than** 162.

HOME ACTIVITY Have your child choose a three-digit number. Then ask your child to name a number that is greater than that number and a number that is less than that number.

Write a number to make each comparison correct. Use the number line to help you.

303 304 305 306 307 308 309 310 311 312 313 314 315 316

1. _____ is **less than** 304.

2. _____ is **greater than** 307.

3. _____ is **greater than** 314 and **less than** 316.

Generalize Write three different numbers to make each comparison correct. Draw a number line to help if needed.

4. 805 > _____ > 795
   805 > _____ > 795
   805 > _____ > 795

5. 457 < _____ < 462
   457 < _____ < 462
   457 < _____ < 462

6. 200 > _____ > 190
   200 > _____ > 190
   200 > _____ > 190

7. **Higher Order Thinking** Match each soccer player with a team number. Write the number in the box.

Team Numbers			
192	319	198	420

My number is greater than 197 and less than 199.

_____
Carlos

My number is less than Carlos's number.

_____
Jada

My number is less than 421 and greater than 419.

_____
Marta

My number is greater than Carlos's number and less than Marta's number.

_____
Jackson

8. **Assessment** Which comparisons are correct? Choose all that apply.

- ☐ 294 < 293
- ☐ 296 > 295
- ☐ 295 < 298
- ☐ 297 = 297

9. **Assessment** Write two numbers that are less than 909 and greater than 868. Explain how you know.

Copyright © Savvas Learning Company LLC. All Rights Reserved.

Name _____

Solve & Share

Sort the numbers 500, 800, 600, 400, and 700 from least to greatest.
Describe any number patterns that you see.
Are there any other numbers that fit the pattern?

Number patterns

Problem Solving

Lesson 9-10
Look for and Use Structure

I can ...
look for patterns to help me solve problems.

SOL 2.16, 2.1c, 2.1b

Thinking Habits

Are there things in common that help me?

Is there a pattern? How does it help?

Digital Resources at SavvasRealize.com

The red team is sorting their jersey numbers from least to greatest. What is the next jersey number?

First sort the numbers. Then look for a number pattern.

How can I use patterns to help me solve the problem?

The tens and ones digits do not change. The hundreds increase by one hundred each time.

The pattern rule is increase by 100. The next red jersey number is 624.

The pattern will decrease if the team sorts the numbers from greatest to least.

Do You Understand?

Show Me! How can you use the pattern to find the next three red jersey numbers?

☆ Guided Practice

Look for a pattern to solve each problem.

1. The yellow team is sorting their uniforms.

Sort the first four jersey numbers from least to greatest.

_____, _____, _____, _____

2. Look for a pattern in the sorted jersey numbers. What is the pattern rule?

_____

3. What is the next greatest yellow jersey number? _____

Copyright © Savvas Learning Company LLC. All Rights Reserved.

Name _____

Tools Assessment

Independent Practice

Break the problem into simpler parts to solve. Use a hundreds chart, a number line, or place value chart if you need to.

4. The blue team wants to sort their jersey numbers from greatest to least. After they sort the numbers, what number would come next?

List the jersey numbers from greatest to least.

_____, _____, _____, _____

Compare two numbers at a time to help you put the numbers in order.

Look for a pattern in the sorted jersey numbers. What is the pattern rule?

_____

What jersey number is next in the pattern?

_____

5. A librarian sorted these books.
Find the missing book number. _____

Describe one pattern you notice.

_____

_____

_____

Problem Solving

Performance Assessment

Mail Delivery

Sam delivered mail to four houses numbered 115, 120, 110, and 105. He started at the house with the least number and continued to the house with the greatest number.

If the number pattern continues, what are the next three house numbers?

6. **Reasoning** Sort the numbers of the first four houses from least to greatest. Then write the sorted numbers on the houses in the top row above.

_____

7. **Look for Patterns** What is the pattern rule for the four house numbers you sorted?

_____

_____

What are the next three house numbers?

_____

Write the numbers of the houses in the bottom row of houses above.

8. **Explain** Why do you sort the numbers before looking for a pattern? Explain.

_____

_____

Copyright © Savvas Learning Company LLC. All Rights Reserved.

Name _____

Help Tools Games

Homework & Practice 9-10

Look for and Use Structure

Another Look! Sam needs to paint his taxi number on his taxi. His number is the next greatest number in the pattern. What is Sam's taxi number?

First sort the numbers from least to greatest.

400, 405, 410, 415

Then look for a pattern and name the pattern rule.

The hundreds digit stays the same. The numbers increase by 5 each time.

The pattern rule is increase by 5! Sam's taxi number is 420.

HOME ACTIVITY Write the numbers 285, 265, 255, 275, and 245 on small pieces of paper. Ask your child to sort the numbers from least to greatest. Then ask your child to tell you the pattern rule and to find the next number in the pattern.

Look for a number pattern to solve.

1. James wants to sort the numbers on his teddy bears from greatest to least. After he sorts the numbers, what number would come next?

First sort the numbers from greatest to least.

_____, _____, _____, _____

Then look for a pattern and name the pattern rule.

_____

What number is next in the pattern? _____

Performance Assessment

Bicycle Race

Jack and Sara join the purple team for the bike race. Their bike numbers will be the next two greater numbers in the pattern.

Help them find their bike numbers.

2. **Reasoning** List the bike numbers from least to greatest.

_____, _____, _____, _____, _____

3. **Look for Patterns** Look for a pattern and name the pattern rule. What are Jack's and Sara's bike numbers?

_____

_____

_____

_____

4. **Look for Patterns** Suppose new bike numbers are given in decreasing order. Then what numbers would Jack and Sara be given? Explain.

_____

_____

_____

Copyright © Savvas Learning Company LLC. All Rights Reserved.

Name _____

TOPIC 9 **Fluency Practice Activity**

Follow the Path

Color a path from **Start** to **Finish**. Follow the sums and differences that are even numbers. You can only move up, down, right, or left.

I can ...
add and subtract within 100.

Start

66 − 28	15 + 12	64 − 27	57 + 36	99 − 66	53 − 14	23 + 46	75 − 22	52 + 13
15 + 35	59 − 28	57 + 22	87 − 74	56 − 12	78 − 52	61 + 15	42 − 29	29 + 16
53 + 43	44 + 39	90 − 18	47 − 23	61 + 39	61 − 36	24 + 38	15 + 58	73 − 52
85 − 39	56 + 17	43 − 11	25 + 26	81 − 28	61 + 14	53 − 37	33 + 38	45 − 18
33 + 57	78 − 52	56 + 12	87 − 32	16 + 45	93 − 24	63 + 15	26 + 44	27 − 19

Finish

A-Z Glossary

Understand Vocabulary

Write *standard form*, *expanded form*, or *word form*.

1. 400 + 30 + 7 _____
2. four hundred thirty-seven _____
3. 437 _____

Label each picture. Use terms from the Word List.

4. 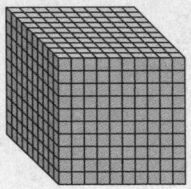 _____
5. 

_____
6. 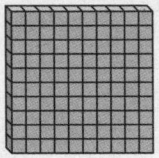 _____

Compare. Complete each sentence.

7. 901 is _____ 910.
8. 429 _____ 400 + 20 + 9.

Word List

- compare
- decrease
- digits
- equals (=)
- expanded form
- greater than (>)
- hundred
- increase
- less than (<)
- ones
- place-value chart
- standard form
- tens
- thousand
- word form

Use Vocabulary in Writing

9. What is the next number in the pattern?
   911, 921, 931, 941, _____

   Explain how you solved the problem.
   Use terms from the Word List.

_____
_____
_____
_____
_____

Copyright © Savvas Learning Company LLC. All Rights Reserved.

Name _____

TOPIC 9

Reteaching

Set A

10 tens make 1 hundred.
You can count by hundreds.

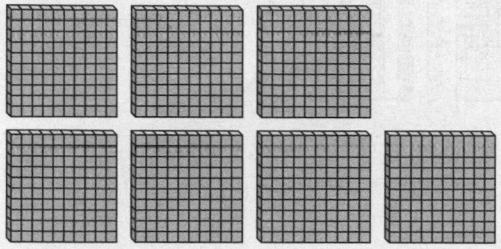

700 equals 7 hundreds,
0 tens, and 0 ones.

Complete the sentence.
Use models if needed.

1. 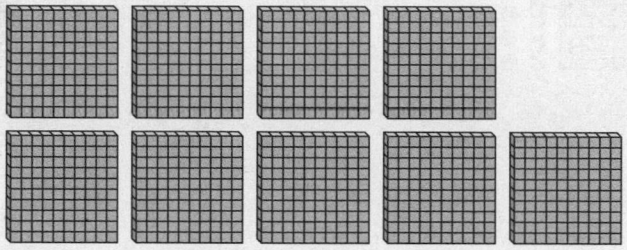

_____ equals _____ hundreds,
_____ tens, and _____ ones.

Set B

You can use place value to help you write numbers.

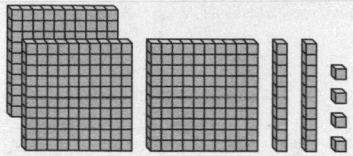

Hundreds	Tens	Ones
3	2	4

324

There are 3 hundreds, 2 tens, and 4 ones in 324.

Write the numbers. Use models and your workmat if needed.

2. 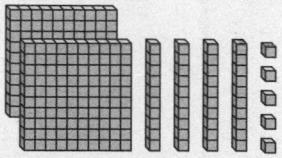

Hundreds	Tens	Ones

_____

3. 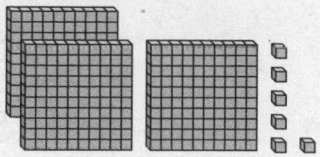

Hundreds	Tens	Ones

_____

Set C

You can write a number using the standard form, expanded form, and word form.

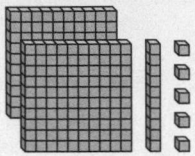

215

200 + 10 + 5

two hundred fifteen

Write the number in standard form, expanded form, and word form.

4.

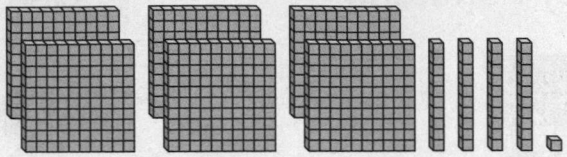

_____

_____ + _____ + _____

_____

Set D

You can show different ways to make numbers.

Hundreds	Tens	Ones
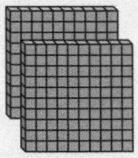	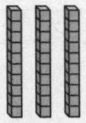	

238 = 200 + 30 + 8

238 = 200 + 20 + 18

238 = 230 + 8

Look at the models in the chart.
Show three different ways to make the number.

5.

Hundreds	Tens	Ones
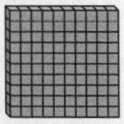	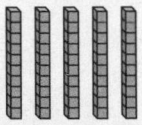	

153 = _____ + _____ + _____

153 = _____ + _____ + _____

153 = _____ + _____

Copyright © Savvas Learning Company LLC. All Rights Reserved.

Name _____

Set E

Reteaching Continued

You can look for patterns with numbers on a hundreds chart.

342	343	344	345	346	347
352	353	354	355	356	357
362	363	364	365	366	367

From left to right, the ones digit goes up by 1.

From top to bottom, the tens digit goes up by 1.

Use place-value patterns to find the missing numbers.

6.

574		576	577	578	
584		586		588	589
	595	596	597		

7.

	222		224	225	
	232		234	235	236
241	242		244		246

Set F

You can skip count by 5s, 10s, and 100s on a number line.

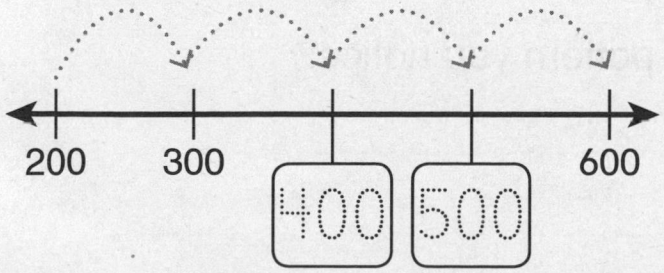

Skip count on the number line. Write the missing numbers.

8.

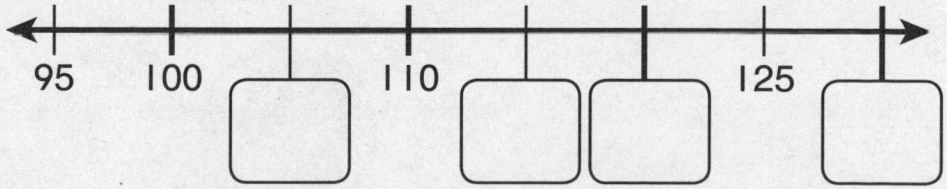

Set G

You can use place value to compare numbers.

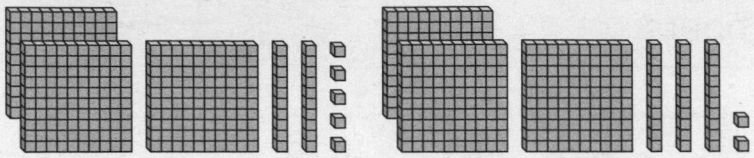

325 332

The hundreds are equal, so compare the tens. 20 is less than 30.

So, 325 < 332.

Compare each pair of numbers. Write >, <, or =.

9. 785 ◯ 793
10. 199 ◯ 198
11. 452 ◯ 452
12. 805 ◯ 810
13. 902 ◯ 897
14. 451 ◯ 516
15. 636 ◯ 629
16. 754 ◯ 754

Set H

Thinking Habits

Look for and Use Structure

Are there things in common that help me?

Is there a pattern? How does it help?

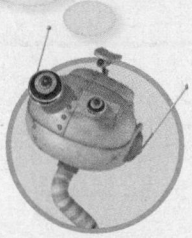

Look for a pattern to solve the problem.

17. These tags are in a drawer.

Describe a pattern you notice.

_____

_____

What is the missing number? _____

Copyright © Savvas Learning Company LLC. All Rights Reserved.

Name _____

TOPIC 9 Assessment

1. Each box has 100 crayons.
Count by hundreds to find the total.
Which number tells how many crayons are in all of the boxes?

Ⓐ 600

Ⓑ 700

Ⓒ 800

Ⓓ 900

2. Danny made this model.
Write the number in three different forms.

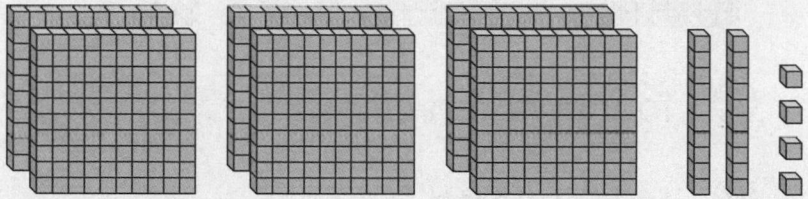

Standard form _____

Expanded form _____

Word form _____

_____

3. Write the number the model shows.
Use the chart.

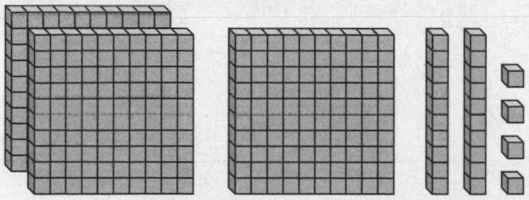

Hundreds	Tens	Ones

4. Which is the value of the 8 in the number 789?

Ⓐ 8

Ⓑ 10

Ⓒ 80

Ⓓ 800

5. Which is the word form of the number shown by the blocks?

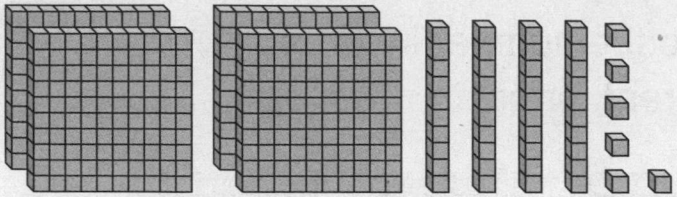

Ⓐ four hundred fifty-six

Ⓑ four hundred forty-six

Ⓒ 400 + 40 + 6

Ⓓ 446

6. Which is the standard form of the number shown by the blocks?

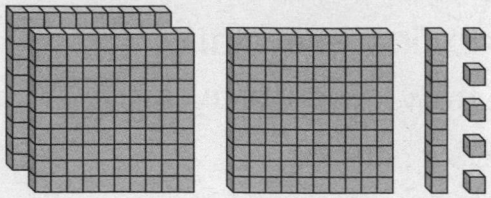

Ⓐ 315

Ⓑ three hundred fifteen

Ⓒ 300 + 10 + 5

Ⓓ 351

7. Draw a line from each number form to its example.

expanded form	standard form	word form
one hundred twenty-one	100 + 20 + 1	121

8. Kate made this model. What number does it show? Write the number and complete the sentence.

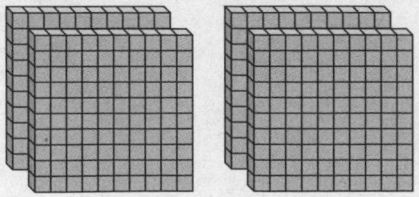

_____ equals _____ hundreds, _____ tens, and _____ ones.

Copyright © Savvas Learning Company LLC. All Rights Reserved.

Name _____

TOPIC 9 Assessment Continued

9. Lee and Maria collect pennies.
Lee has 248 pennies.
Maria has 253 pennies.
Who has more pennies?

_____

Write >, <, or = to compare the number of pennies.

248 ◯ 253

10. Jeff is thinking of a number.
The number has 2 hundreds.
It has more ones than tens.
It has 7 tens.

Which could be the number?
Choose all that apply.

☐ 276 ☐ 279
☐ 278 ☐ 289

11. Compare. Write >, < or =.

429 ◯ 294 849 ◯ 984

12. Write a number that makes the comparison correct.

327 < ____ 716 > ____

13. There are 367 girls and 326 boys at a school. Which is the expanded form for the number of boys?

Ⓐ 200 + 30 + 6 Ⓑ 300 + 20 + 6 Ⓒ 300 + 60 + 2 Ⓓ 300 + 60 + 7

14. Which is a way to show 576? Choose all that apply.

☐ 500 + 60 + 16 ☐ 500 + 70 + 6 ☐ 500 + 6 ☐ 400 + 170 + 6

15. Use the numbers on the cards. Write the missing numbers in the number chart.

333	340	321	331

320		322	323	324
330		332		334
	341	342	343	344

16. Candy counts 405, 410, 415, 420, 425, 430. By what number does Candy skip count?

Ⓐ 2

Ⓑ 5

Ⓒ 10

Ⓓ 100

17. Skip count on the number line. Write the missing numbers.

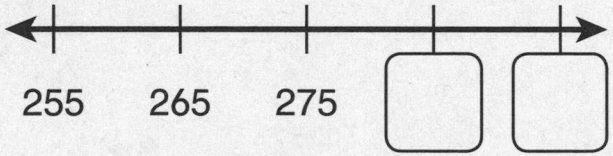

18. Is the statement true? Choose Yes or No.

576 < 675	○ Yes	○ No
435 > 354	○ Yes	○ No
698 < 896	○ Yes	○ No
899 < 799	○ Yes	○ No

Copyright © Savvas Learning Company LLC. All Rights Reserved.

Name _____

TOPIC 9 Performance Assessment

Reading Record

These students love to read!

These books show the number of pages each student has read so far this year.

1. Write the number of pages Tim read in expanded form.

_____ + _____ + _____

Write the number in word form.

_____

2. Complete the place-value chart to show the number of pages Ruth read.

Hundreds	Tens	Ones

Show two other ways to write the number.

_____ + _____ + _____

_____ + _____ + _____

3. Show two ways to compare the number of pages that Luisa read with the number of pages that Ruth read. Use > and <.

_____ ○ _____

_____ ○ _____

4. This number line shows the total number of minutes Diane read each week for 3 weeks.

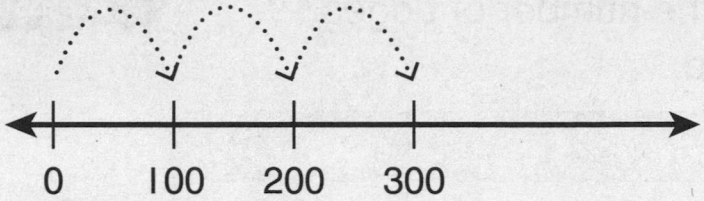

How many minutes did she read after the first week? _____ minutes

After the second week? _____ minutes

After the third week? _____ minutes

How many minutes did she read each week? Explain how you know.

5. Diane reads the same number of minutes each week. How many minutes does she read after 4 weeks? After 5 weeks? Skip count on the number line above to find the answers.

After 4 weeks: _____ minutes

After 5 weeks: _____ minutes

6. The table shows how many pages Jim read in three different months. If he follows the pattern, how many pages will Jim read in April and May?

Number of Pages Read	
January	210
February	220
March	230
April	?
May	?

Part A

What pattern do you see in the table?

Part B

How many pages will Jim read in April and May?

Copyright © Savvas Learning Company LLC. All Rights Reserved.

TOPIC 10 Add Within 1,000 Using Models and Strategies

Essential Question: What are strategies for adding numbers to 1,000?

Digital Resources

Solve Learn Glossary

Tools Assessment Help Games

Math and Science Project: Building Up to 1,000

Find Out Use spaghetti sticks and mini marshmallows. The total for both cannot be more than 1,000. First, decide how many of each to use. Then share. Build the tallest buildings you can.

Journal: Make a Book Describe your building in a book. In your book, also:

- Tell how many spaghetti sticks and mini marshmallows you used.
- Tell how you would make a better building if you did it again.

Name _____

Review What You Know

Vocabulary

1. Circle all of the **hundreds digits** in the numbers below.

502

58

1,000

2. Write the **expanded form** of the number.

846

_____

3. Write the **word form** of the number.

265

_____

_____

Open Number Lines

4. Use the open number line to find the sum.

54 + 13 = _____

Mental Math

5. Use mental math to find each sum.

40 + 37 = _____

6 + 77 + 4 = _____

Partial Sums

6. Use partial sums to add.

$$\begin{array}{r} 46 \\ +\,53 \\ \hline \end{array} \qquad \begin{array}{r} 29 \\ +\,61 \\ \hline \end{array}$$

Copyright © Savvas Learning Company LLC. All Rights Reserved.

Name _____

Solve

Lesson 10-1
Add 10 and 100

I can ...
add 10 or 100 mentally using what I know about place value.

SOL 2.1b

Solve & Share

Forest Park has 565 trees.
Lake Park has 10 trees. Sunset Park has 100 trees.

How many trees do Forest Park and Lake Park have in all?

How many trees do Forest Park and Sunset Park have in all?

Use mental math. Be ready to explain how.

$565 + 10 =$ _____

$565 + 100 =$ _____

Digital Resources at SavvasRealize.com

You can use mental math to add 10 or 100 to three-digit numbers.

Find 243 + 10.
Find 243 + 100.

How can I add 10 or 100 mentally?

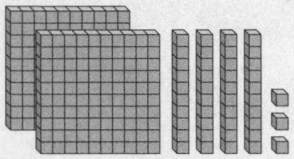

243

Adding 10 makes the tens digit go up by 1.

I know 4 + 1 = 5.
So, 243 + 10 = 253.

Adding 100 makes the hundreds digit go up by 1.

I know 2 + 1 = 3.
So, 243 + 100 = 343.

Sometimes adding 10 changes the tens and hundreds digits.
Find 290 + 10.

I know 290 = 29 tens.
29 tens + 1 ten = 30 tens or 300.
So, 290 + 10 = 300.

Do You Understand?

Show Me! Use mental math to find 567 + 10 and 567 + 100. Explain your reasoning.

☆ Guided Practice ☆

Add using mental math. Use models if needed.

1. 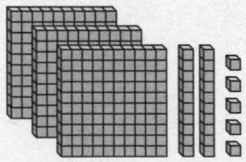

plus 10
plus 100

325 + 10 = 335
325 + 100 = 425

2. 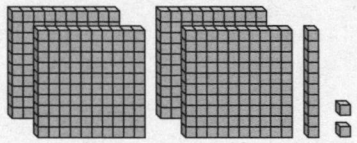

plus 10
plus 100

____ + ____ = ____
____ + ____ = ____

3. 900 + 10 = ____
900 + 100 = ____

4. 790 + 10 = ____
790 + 100 = ____

Copyright © Savvas Learning Company LLC. All Rights Reserved.

Name _____

Tools Assessment

Independent Practice

Add using mental math. Use models if needed.

5.

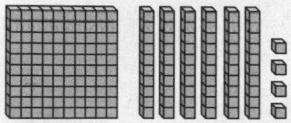

plus 10
plus 100

_____ + _____ = _____

_____ + _____ = _____

6.

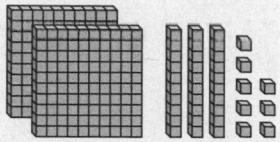

plus 10
plus 100

_____ + _____ = _____

_____ + _____ = _____

7.

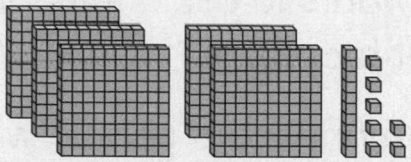

plus 10
plus 100

_____ + _____ = _____

_____ + _____ = _____

8. 391 + 10 = _____

9. 693 + 100 = _____

10. 803 + 100 = _____

11. 460 + 10 = _____

12. 185 + 10 = _____

13. 723 + 100 = _____

Algebra Find the missing numbers. Use mental math to solve.

14. 572 + ☐ = 672

15. 285 + ☐ = 385

16. 709 = 699 + ☐

17. 322 + ☐ = 422

18. 615 + ☐ = 625

19. ☐ + 590 = 600

Problem Solving Solve each problem.

20. **Math and Science** The Science Club asked 178 people about recycling. The club wants to ask a total of 188 people about recycling.

How many more people will the Science Club need to ask?

_____ more people

21. **Generalize** Bob plays a game. He scores 473 points. Bob plays again and scores 100 points. How many points did Bob score in both games?

_____ points

22. **Higher Order Thinking** Think of a 3-digit number. Write a story about adding 100 to your number. Then write an equation to show your solution.

_____ + _____ = _____

23. **Assessment** Sharon counts 328 marbles. David counts 100 more marbles than Sharon.
How many marbles does David count?

Ⓐ 656
Ⓑ 528
Ⓒ 428
Ⓓ 228

Copyright © Savvas Learning Company LLC. All Rights Reserved.

Name _____

Help Tools Games

Homework & Practice 10-1
Add 10 and 100

HOME ACTIVITY Choose a number between 200 and 300. Ask your child to add 10 to the number and tell you the sum. Repeat with adding 100 to the number.

Another Look! Use mental math to add 10 or 100 to three-digit numbers.
Find 315 + 10 and 315 + 100.

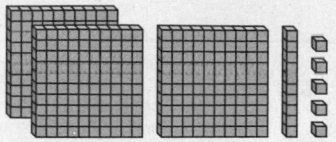

plus 10
plus 100

The tens digit goes up by 1 when you add 10.

315 + 10 = 3[2]5

The hundreds digit goes up by 1 when you add 100.

315 + 100 = [4]15

Add using mental math. Use models if needed.

1.

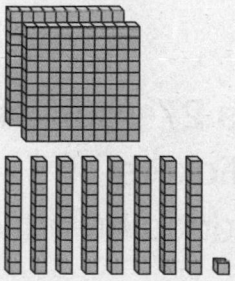

plus 10
plus 100

_____ + 10 = _____

_____ + 100 = _____

2.

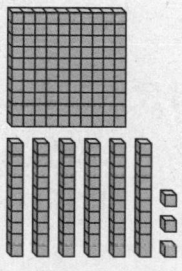

plus 10
plus 100

_____ + 10 = _____

_____ + 100 = _____

3.

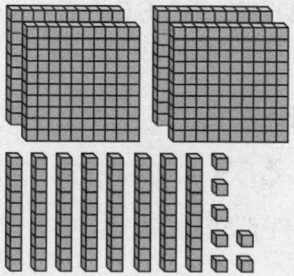

plus 10
plus 100

_____ + 10 = _____

_____ + 100 = _____

Look for Patterns Use mental math. Write the missing digit.

4. 100 + ☐00 = 200

5. 223 + ☐00 = 323

6. 10 + 351 = 3☐1

Vocabulary Use mental math. Write the missing digit. Then complete the sentence with **addend** or **sum**.

7. 6☐3 + 10 = 683

683 is the _____.

8. ☐35 + 100 = 535

The _____ is 535.

9. 802 + 10 = 81☐

802 is an _____.

Higher Order Thinking Write the missing digits.

10. 22☐ + 100 + 105 = 4☐8

11. ☐12 + 205 + 10 = 32☐

Use mental math to solve.

12. **Assessment** Tanner has 679 stamps. She has 669 stamps in her album. How many stamps are **NOT** in her album?

Ⓐ 10
Ⓑ 20
Ⓒ 100
Ⓓ 689

13. **Assessment** Darrin has 274 basketball stickers and 100 football stickers. How many sports stickers does he have?

Ⓐ 174
Ⓑ 184
Ⓒ 284
Ⓓ 374

Copyright © Savvas Learning Company LLC. All Rights Reserved.

Name _____

Solve

Lesson 10-2

Add on an Open Number Line

I can ...

use an open number line to add 3-digit numbers.

SOL 2.6b, 2.6c

Solve & Share

Use the open number line to find 598 + 123. Explain your work.

_____ + _____ = _____

Learn Glossary

Find 481 + 122. Use an open number line.

One Way

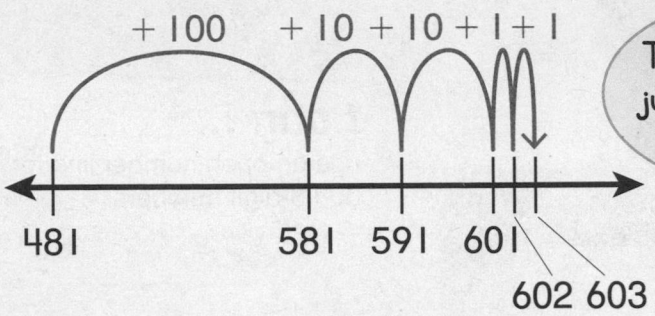

481 + 122 = 603

This way shows jumps by 100s, 10s, and 1s.

Another Way

This way shows how you can make bigger jumps.

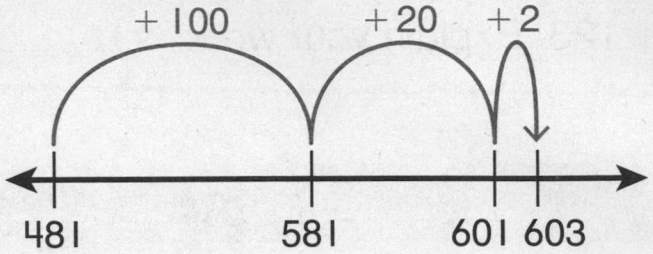

Both ways are correct.

Do You Understand?

Show Me! Explain how you can use an open number line to find 599 + 205.

Guided Practice

Use an open number line to find each sum.

1. 375 + 118 = _____

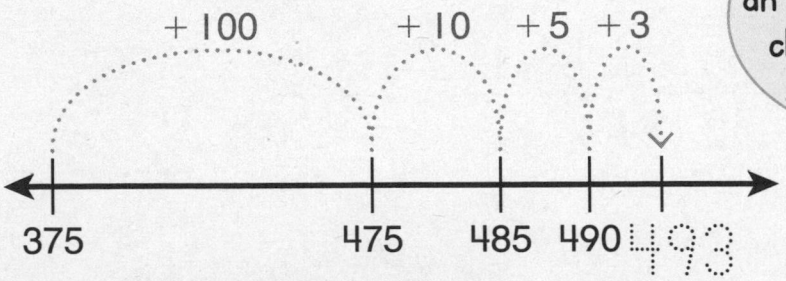

Breaking apart an addend does not change the value being added.

2. 670 + 232 = _____

Copyright © Savvas Learning Company LLC. All Rights Reserved.

Name _____

Tools Assessment

Independent Practice

Use an open number line to find each sum.

3. 278 + 152 = _____

4. 637 + 242 = _____

5. 197 + 523 = _____

6. 202 + 598 = _____

7. **Higher Order Thinking** Lisa finds 550 + 298 using the open number line below. Is her work correct? Explain.

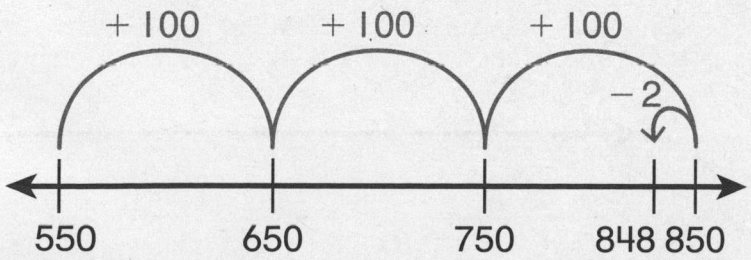

Problem Solving Use an open number line to find each sum.

8. **Reason** Jose has 181 cards. He collects 132 more. How many cards does he have now?

_____ cards

9. **Vocabulary** Complete the sentence using two of these terms.

add **tens** **open number line** **rule**

An _____

can be used to

_____.

10. **Higher Order Thinking** Use open number lines to find 446 + 215 in two different ways.

446 + 215 = _____

11. **Assessment** Mary uses an open number line to find 286 + 137. All of the jumps she draws are greater than 1. Draw what Mary could have done. Write the sum.

286 + 137 = _____

Copyright © Savvas Learning Company LLC. All Rights Reserved.

Name _____

Help Tools Games

Homework & Practice 10-2

Add on an Open Number Line

HOME ACTIVITY Ask your child to show how he or she would find 153 + 162 using an open number line.

Another Look! Find 284 + 231.

Way 1:

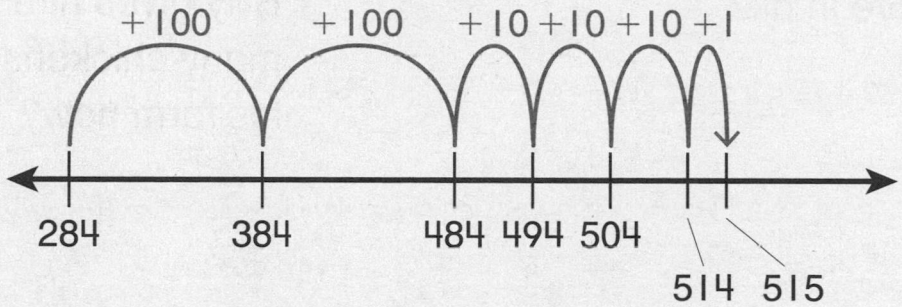

Way 2:

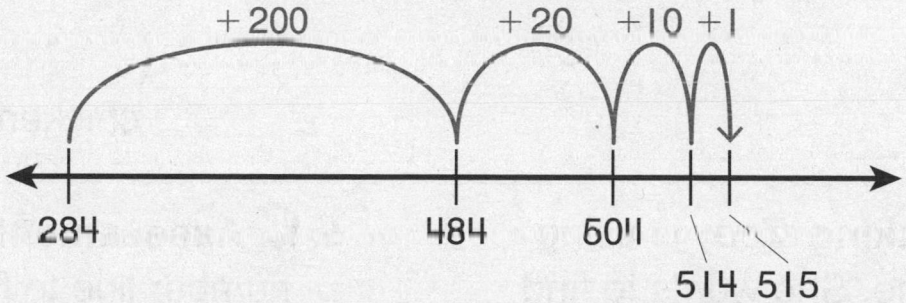

Use an open number line to find each sum.

1. 483 + 172 = _____

2. 288 + 324 = _____

Solve each problem. Use the number line to show your work.

3. **Reasoning** Jeb has 264 blocks in a box. Mia gives Jeb 341 more blocks. How many blocks does Jeb have in all?

_____ blocks

4. Josh has 509 chickens on his farm. Bob gives Josh 111 chickens, and Billy gives him 21 chickens. How many chickens does Josh have on his farm now?

_____ chickens

5. **Higher Order Thinking** Zoey is using an open number line. She wants to find 232 + 578. Which addend should she place on the number line to start? Explain.

_____

_____

_____

6. **Assessment** John uses an open number line to find 570 + 241. One of his jumps is + 40. Draw what John could have done. Write the sum.

570 + 241 = _____

Copyright © Savvas Learning Company LLC. All Rights Reserved.

Name _____

Solve

Lesson 10-3
Add Using Mental Math

I can ...
add 3-digit numbers using mental math strategies.

SOL 2.6b, 2.6c

Solve & Share

On Monday, 248 people visit the museum.
On Tuesday, 325 people visit the museum.
How many people visit the museum on Monday and Tuesday?
Solve any way you choose. Be prepared to explain your thinking.

_____ people

Digital Resources at SavvasRealize.com

Learn Glossary

Use any strategy to find 365 + 196.

I'll make numbers that are easy to work with in my head.

I'll break apart the addends by place value.

One way to add is to add the hundreds, the tens, and the ones.

300	60	5
+ 100	+ 90	+ 6
400	150	11

I can add these sums in any order.

400 + 150 + 11 = **561**

Another way to add is to use easier numbers.

196 is 200 − 4. So, I can add 200, then take away 4.

365	565
+ 200	− 4
565	**561**

So, 365 + 196 = 561.

We both used mental math! Both ways get the same answer!

Do You Understand?

Show Me! How could you use easier numbers to find 303 + 418?

Guided Practice

Use any strategy to add. Show your work.

1. 223 + 106 = 329

2. 149 + 362 = _____

3. 171 + 202 = _____

4. 421 + 397 = _____

Copyright © Savvas Learning Company LLC. All Rights Reserved.

Name _____

Tools Assessment

Independent Practice

Use any strategy to add. Show your work.

5. 151 + 324 = _____

6. 250 + 298 = _____

7. 258 + 109 = _____

8. 187 + 246 = _____

9. 236 + 318 = _____

10. 432 + 365 = _____

11. **Number Sense** Jamal says that the sum of 183 + 198 is less than 300. Is Jamal's answer reasonable? Why or why not?

_____

_____

_____

Problem Solving

Use any strategy to solve each problem. Show your work.

12. **Reasoning** 156 children in a school are girls. 148 children in that school are boys. How many children go to that school?

_____ children

13. **Higher Order Thinking** Write an addition problem about stickers. Use 3-digit numbers. Then solve the problem.

_____

_____

_____

_____

14. **Assessment** Maggie collects stickers. She gives 129 stickers to her friend. Now she has 268 stickers left.

How many stickers does Maggie have before she gives some away?

Ⓐ 292

Ⓑ 294

Ⓒ 389

Ⓓ 397

Copyright © Savvas Learning Company LLC. All Rights Reserved.

Name _____

Help Tools Games

Homework & Practice 10-3

Add Using Mental Math

Another Look! Use any strategy to find 358 + 213.

One Way You can add the hundreds, the tens, and the ones.

Add hundreds.	Add tens.	Add ones.
300	50	8
+ 200	+ 10	+ 3
500	60	11

Add the partial sums.

500 + 60 + 11 = 571

So, 358 + 213 = 571 .

Or you can use easier numbers to find 358 + 213.

Another Way

358 is 360 − 2.

360 + 213 = 573

Take away 2.

573 − 2 = 571

HOME ACTIVITY Ask your child to show you how to add 305 + 497. Have your child explain how he or she does the addition.

Use any strategy to solve each problem. Show your work.

1. 248 + 455 = _____

2. 209 + 376 = _____

3. 597 + 122 = _____

Algebra Write each missing number.

4. 285 + 507 = _____

5. _____ = 378 + 142

6. 802 = _____ + 431

Be Precise Find the total number of buttons for each. Use the chart. Add any way you choose.

Button	Number
animal	378
sport	142
fruit	296
holiday	455

7. Mrs. Jones buys all of the animal and fruit buttons.

_____ + _____ = _____

_____ buttons

8. Mr. Frost buys all of the sport and holiday buttons.

_____ + _____ = _____

_____ buttons

9. **Higher Order Thinking** A theater wants to add 140 seats. Then the theater will have a total of 375 seats. How many seats does the theater have now?

_____ seats

10. **Assessment** Rob has 225 marbles. Jake has 69 more marbles than Rob. How many marbles do they have in all?

294 Ⓐ 509 Ⓑ 519 Ⓒ 529 Ⓓ

Copyright © Savvas Learning Company LLC. All Rights Reserved.

Name _____

Solve

Lesson 10-4
Add Using Partial Sums

I can ...
add 3-digit numbers using partial sums.

SOL 2.6b, 2.6c

Solve & Share

Use place-value blocks to find 243 + 354.
Tell which place value you added first and why.
Then draw a picture to show your work.

Hundreds	Tens	Ones

243 + 354 = _____

Digital Resources at SavvasRealize.com

Find 518 + 327.

Use place value. First, add the hundreds.

Then add the tens. Then add the ones.

	Hundreds	Tens	Ones
	5	1	8
+	3	2	7
Hundreds:	8	0	0
Tens:		3	0
Ones:		1	5
Sum =	8	4	5

Add the partial sums to find the sum.

Here is how you can write out the addition.

$$\begin{array}{r} 518 \\ +\,327 \\ \hline 800 \\ 30 \\ 15 \\ \hline 845 \end{array}$$

So, 518 + 327 = 845.

Do You Understand?

Show Me! Explain why you can use partial sums to find 281 + 276. Find the sum.

Guided Practice

Add. Use partial sums. Show your work. Use place-value blocks if needed.

1. 425 + 148 = 573

	Hundreds	Tens	Ones
	4	2	5
+	1	4	8
Hundreds:	5	0	0
Tens:		6	0
Ones:		1	3
Sum=	5	7	3

2. 394 + 276 = _____

$$\begin{array}{r} 394 \\ +\,276 \\ \hline \end{array}$$

Keep place values in line when you write each partial sum.

Copyright © Savvas Learning Company LLC. All Rights Reserved.

Name _____

Tools Assessment

Independent Practice

Add. Use partial sums. Show your work.

3. $\begin{array}{r} 347 \\ +\,242 \\ \hline \end{array}$

4. $\begin{array}{r} 193 \\ +\,243 \\ \hline \end{array}$

5. $\begin{array}{r} 281 \\ +\,406 \\ \hline \end{array}$

6. $\begin{array}{r} 367 \\ +\,423 \\ \hline \end{array}$

7. $\begin{array}{r} 508 \\ +\,347 \\ \hline \end{array}$

8. **Higher Order Thinking** Mark found the sum of 127 and 345. Explain his mistake. What is the correct sum?

_____

_____

_____

Mark's Work

$\begin{array}{r} 127 \\ +\ 345 \\ \hline 400 \end{array}$

Hundreds: 400

Tens: 6

Ones: $\begin{array}{r} +\ 12 \\ \hline 418 \end{array}$

9. **Number Sense** Find the sum of 137 + 324. Then write the sum two different ways.

Way 1 _____

Way 2 _____

Problem Solving Solve each problem.

10. **Look for Patterns** 349 people are on a boat. 255 people are on another boat. How many people are on both boats?

_____ people

11. 163 students are in first grade. 217 students are in second grade. How many students are in both grades?

_____ students

12. **Higher Order Thinking** Choose a number between 100 and 400. Add 384 to your number. What is the sum? Show your work.

Explain the steps you took to find the sum.

_____

_____

_____

13. **Assessment** Which is the same amount as 238 + 164? Choose all that apply.

☐ 200 + 190 + 12 ☐ 300 + 90 + 12 ☐ 402 ☐ 400 + 10 + 2

Copyright © Savvas Learning Company LLC. All Rights Reserved.

Name _____

Help Tools Games

Homework & Practice 10-4

Add Using Partial Sums

Another Look! You can use place value to add 2 three-digit numbers.

164 + 253 = ?

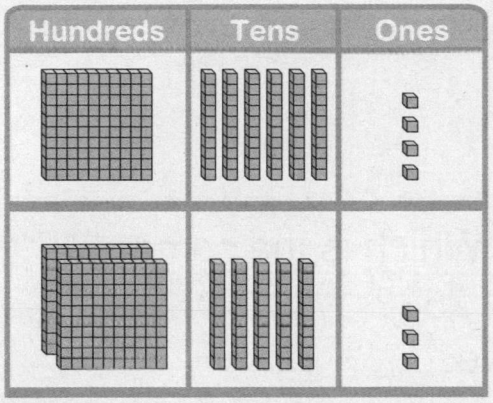

1. Add the hundreds.
2. Add the tens.
3. Add the ones.
4. Add the partial sums.

	Hundreds	Tens	Ones
	1	6	4
+	2	5	3
	3	0	0
	1	1	0
			7
	4	1	7

So, 164 + 253 = 417.

HOME ACTIVITY Write 581 + 294 on a sheet of paper. Ask your child to use partial sums to find the sum.

Add. Use partial sums. Show your work. Use place-value blocks if needed.

1. 218 + 136

	Hundreds	Tens	Ones
	2	1	8
+	1	3	6
Hundreds:	3	0	0
Tens:		4	0
Ones:		1	4
Sum =			

2. 365 + 248

	Hundreds	Tens	Ones
	3	6	5
+	2	4	8
Hundreds:			
Tens:			
Ones:			
Sum =			

Generalize Add. Use partial sums. Show your work.

3. $\begin{array}{r} 714 \\ +135 \\ \hline \end{array}$

4. $\begin{array}{r} 168 \\ +423 \\ \hline \end{array}$

5. $\begin{array}{r} 266 \\ +592 \\ \hline \end{array}$

6. $\begin{array}{r} 474 \\ +238 \\ \hline \end{array}$

7. $\begin{array}{r} 567 \\ +137 \\ \hline \end{array}$

8. **Higher Order Thinking** Fill in the missing numbers to make the addition problem true.

	Hundreds	Tens	Ones
	2	☐	8
+	☐	7	☐
Hundreds:	☐	0	0
Tens:		☐	0
Ones:		☐	☐
Sum =	8	9	0

9. **Assessment** Which is the same amount as 462 + 253? Choose Yes or No.

600 + 11 + 5 ○ Yes ○ No

600 + 110 + 5 ○ Yes ○ No

600 + 100 + 15 ○ Yes ○ No

715 ○ Yes ○ No

Copyright © Savvas Learning Company LLC. All Rights Reserved.

Name _____

Solve

Lesson 10-5
Use Models to Add

I can ...
use models to add 3-digit numbers.

SOL 2.6b, 2.6c

Solve & Share

Oak School has 256 students. Pine School has 371 students. How many students do the schools have in all?
Use place-value blocks to help. Draw your blocks below and solve.

Hundreds	Tens	Ones

	Hundreds	Tens	Ones
+			

Digital Resources at SavvasRealize.com

You can draw a model and use regrouping to add three-digit numbers. Find 173 + 244. First add the ones.

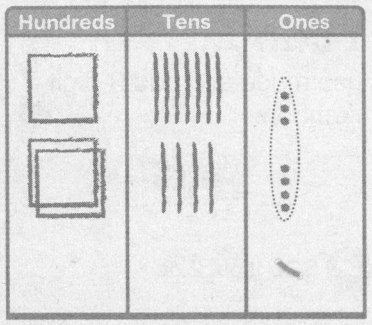

	Hundreds	Tens	Ones
	1	7	3
+	2	4	4
			7

Then add the tens.

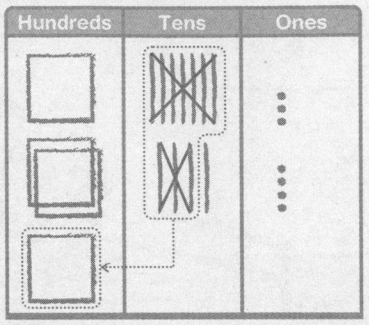

	Hundreds	Tens	Ones
	1	7	3
+	2	4	4
		1	7

Regroup 10 tens to make 1 hundred!

Then add the hundreds.

	Hundreds	Tens	Ones
	1		
	1	7	3
+	2	4	4
	4	1	7

So, 173 + 244 = 417.

Do You Understand?

Show Me! Explain why regrouping works in the problem above.

Guided Practice

Add. Draw place-value blocks to show your work. Regroup if needed.

1.

	Hundreds	Tens	Ones
	2	3	6
+	2	5	2
	4	8	8

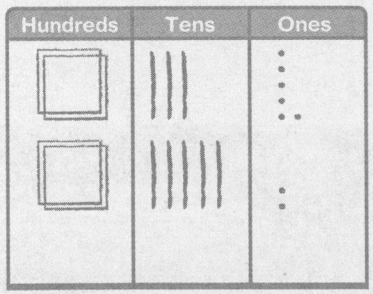

2.

	Hundreds	Tens	Ones
	3	2	8
+	1	2	4

Hundreds	Tens	Ones

3.

	Hundreds	Tens	Ones
	1	6	5
+	4	7	3

Hundreds	Tens	Ones

Copyright © Savvas Learning Company LLC. All Rights Reserved.

Name _____

Tools Assessment

Independent Practice

Add. Draw place-value blocks to show your work. Regroup if needed.

4.

	Hundreds	Tens	Ones
	☐	☐	
	3	7	2
+	2	8	1

Hundreds	Tens	Ones

5.

	Hundreds	Tens	Ones
	☐	☐	
	3	4	9
+	1	8	2

Hundreds	Tens	Ones

6.

	Hundreds	Tens	Ones
	☐	☐	
	2	7	3
+	2	5	9

Hundreds	Tens	Ones

7. Higher Order Thinking Ben said that the sum of 157 and 197 is 254. Nikki said that Ben made a mistake. Who is correct? Explain.

_____

_____

_____

Problem Solving

Solve each problem below.
You can use models to help.

8. **Model** On Friday, 354 people went to the fair. On Saturday, 551 people went to the fair.

   How many people went to the fair in all?

	Hundreds	Tens	Ones
+			

_____ people

9. **Higher Order Thinking** Write an addition problem that shows regrouping both the ones and the tens. Use 3-digit numbers between 100 and 400 as addends. Find the sum.

	Hundreds	Tens	Ones
+			

10. **Assessment** Use the numbers on the cards. Write the missing digits in each sum.

6	1	4	7

```
  169        448
+ 475      + 323
  □□4        7□□
```


Copyright © Savvas Learning Company LLC. All Rights Reserved.

Name _____

Help Tools Games

Homework & Practice 10-5
Use Models to Add

Another Look! You can follow these steps to add three-digit numbers.

Step 1: Add the ones. Regroup if needed.
Step 2: Add the tens. Regroup if needed.
Step 3: Add the hundreds.

HOME ACTIVITY Have your child draw place-value blocks to model the addition of 158 + 146.

	Hundreds	Tens	Ones
135			
248			

135 + 248 = 383

Add. Regroup if needed. Draw models to help.

1. 341 + 127 = _____

Hundreds	Tens	Ones

2. 524 + 249 = _____

Hundreds	Tens	Ones

Digital Resources at SavvasRealize.com

Add. Look for the pattern.

Look for Patterns Write and solve the next addition problem that follows each pattern.

3.

	Hundreds	Tens	Ones
		☐	
	2	0	9
+	1	2	3

	Hundreds	Tens	Ones
		☐	
	3	0	9
+	2	2	3

	Hundreds	Tens	Ones
		☐	
	4	0	9
+	3	2	3

	Hundreds	Tens	Ones
		☐	
+			

4.

	Hundreds	Tens	Ones
		☐	
	3	1	5
+	4	2	7

	Hundreds	Tens	Ones
		☐	
	4	1	5
+	3	2	7

	Hundreds	Tens	Ones
		☐	
	5	1	5
+	2	2	7

	Hundreds	Tens	Ones
		☐	
+			

5. **Higher Order Thinking** Write and solve an addition story for 482 + 336.

_____

_____

_____

_____

_____

6. **Assessment** Use the numbers on the cards. Write the missing digits in each sum.

1	8	6	4

```
  235        652
+ 182      + 216
  ☐☐7        8☐☐
```


Copyright © Savvas Learning Company LLC. All Rights Reserved.

Name _____

Solve

Lesson 10-6

Explain Addition Strategies

I can ...

use different addition strategies and explain why they work.

SOL 2.6b, 2.6c

Solve & Share

Find 375 + 235. Explain your strategy.

Learn Glossary

Lauren, Nate, and Josh use different ways to find 257 + 126.

Lauren uses an open number line. She starts at 257 and mentally adds up the hundreds, the tens, and the ones.

Lauren's Number Line

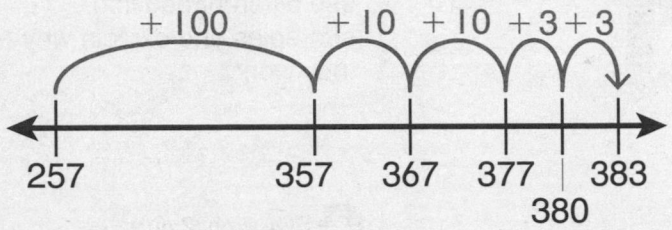

Nate draws place-value blocks. He regroups 10 ones as 1 ten.

Nate's Place-Value Blocks

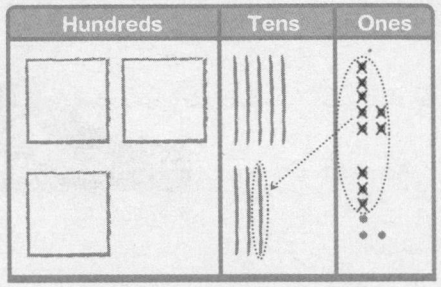

257 + 126 = 383

Josh uses place value to write the addends in a column. He regroups 10 ones as 1 ten.

Josh's Addition

$$\begin{array}{r} {\scriptstyle 1} \\ 257 \\ +\ 126 \\ \hline 383 \end{array}$$

Do You Understand?

Show Me! Choose a strategy shown above. Explain how it works.

Guided Practice

Choose any strategy to solve the problem. Show your work. Then explain your work.

1. 624 + 248 = 872

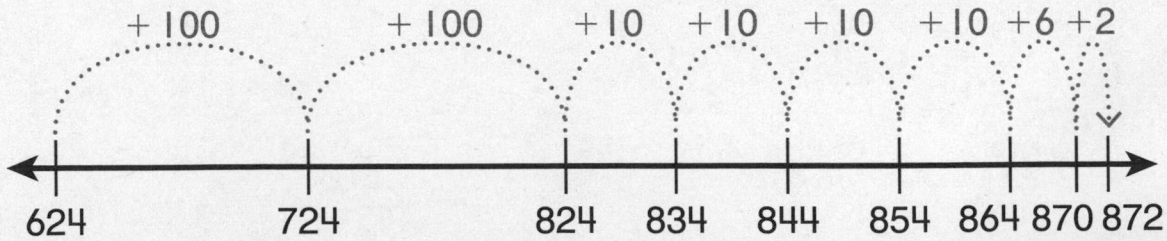

Start at 624. Add 2 hundreds. Then add 4 tens. Count on 6 to get to 870, then add 2 more to reach 872. The jumps add up to 248.

Copyright © Savvas Learning Company LLC. All Rights Reserved.

Name _____

Tools Assessment

Independent Practice

Choose any strategy to solve each addition problem. Show your work. Then explain.

2. 212 + 487 = _____

3. 874 + 109 = _____

4. 419 + 532 = _____

5. 650 + 270 = _____

Problem Solving

Solve each problem any way you choose. Show your work.

6. **Reasoning** Lee School needs 407 folders for its students. Jefferson School needs 321 folders for its students. How many folders do both schools need?

_____ folders

7. **Reasoning** There are 229 people at the football game. 108 more people arrive at the game. How many people are at the football game now?

_____ people

8. **Higher Order Thinking** Tommy found 125 + 598. Since 598 is close to 600, he added 125 + 600 = 725. Then he subtracted 2 to get 723.

Why did Tommy subtract 2? Explain.

9. **Assessment** There are 192 ants on an ant farm. 397 more ants join the ant farm. How many ants are on the ant farm now?

Use the number line to solve. Explain.

Copyright © Savvas Learning Company LLC. All Rights Reserved.

Name _____

Help Tools Games

Homework & Practice 10-6

Explain Addition Strategies

HOME ACTIVITY Ask your child to explain how to solve 429 + 378.

Another Look! Find 219 + 468.

One Way

You can use mental math and an open number line to keep track of your thinking.
You can add numbers in any order.
You can start with 468 and add 219.

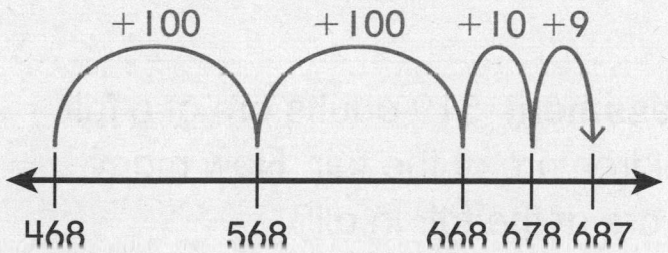

Another Way

You can also use paper and pencil to find the sum. Regroup if you need to.

$$\begin{array}{r} {}^{1} \\ 219 \\ +\,468 \\ \hline 687 \end{array}$$

Choose any strategy to solve the addition problem. Show your work. Then explain your work.

1. 192 + 587 = _____

2. 269 + 658 = _____

Reasoning Choose any strategy to solve the addition problem. Show your work. Then explain your work.

3. 635 + 284 = _____

4. 701 + 103 = _____

5. **Higher Order Thinking** Explain TWO different ways to find 562 + 399.

One Way

Another Way

6. **Assessment** 519 adults are at a fair. 369 children are at the fair. How many people are at the fair in all?

Use the number line to solve. Explain.

Copyright © Savvas Learning Company LLC. All Rights Reserved.

Name _____

Solve

Problem Solving

Lesson 10-7
Repeated Reasoning

I can ...
think about and check my work as I solve a problem.

SOL 2.6b, 2.6c

Solve & Share

Solve the problems in Group 1.
Then, solve the problems in Group 2.

Tell how the problems in Group 1 are alike.
Tell how the problems in Group 2 are alike.

Group 1	Group 2
$\begin{array}{r} 23 \\ +14 \\ \hline \end{array}$ $\quad$ $\begin{array}{r} 525 \\ +261 \\ \hline \end{array}$	$\begin{array}{r} 28 \\ +27 \\ \hline \end{array}$ $\quad$ $\begin{array}{r} 337 \\ +124 \\ \hline \end{array}$

Thinking Habits

What can I use from one problem to help with another problem?

Are there things that repeat?

Digital Resources at SavvasRealize.com

When you use this way to add, you need to use repeated reasoning.

$$\begin{array}{r} 235 \\ +\ 489 \\ \hline \end{array}$$

How can I use repeated reasoning?

I can use what I know, look for things that repeat, and check my work as I add each place.

Add each place from right to left.

Decide if you need to regroup to make a ten or a hundred.

$$\begin{array}{r} {\scriptstyle 1\,1} \\ 235 \\ +\ 489 \\ \hline 724 \end{array}$$

Do You Understand?

Show Me! What is 5 + 9? How is it shown in the problem 235 + 489?

	Hundreds	Tens	Ones
	☐	☐	
	2	3	5
+	4	8	9

Guided Practice

Use repeated reasoning to solve each problem. Circle any problem where you regrouped to make a ten or a hundred.

1. $\begin{array}{r} {\scriptstyle 1} \\ 157 \\ +\ 229 \\ \hline 386 \end{array}$

2. $\begin{array}{r} 214 \\ +\ 331 \\ \hline \end{array}$

3. $\begin{array}{r} 544 \\ +\ 265 \\ \hline \end{array}$

4. $\begin{array}{r} 651 \\ +\ 232 \\ \hline \end{array}$

5. $\begin{array}{r} 455 \\ +\ 223 \\ \hline \end{array}$

6. $\begin{array}{r} 738 \\ +\ 162 \\ \hline \end{array}$

Copyright © Savvas Learning Company LLC. All Rights Reserved.

Name _____

Tools Assessment

Independent Practice

Solve each problem.

7. Write a problem where you need to regroup to make a ten or a hundred. Each addend must be three digits. Solve your problem. Then explain why you needed to regroup.

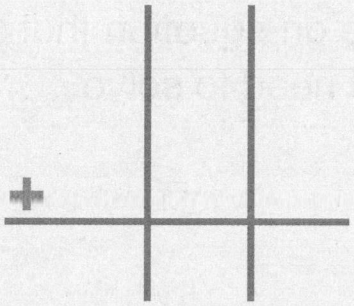

8. Write a problem where you do not need to regroup to make a ten or a hundred. Each addend must be three digits. Solve your problem. Then explain why you don't need to regroup.

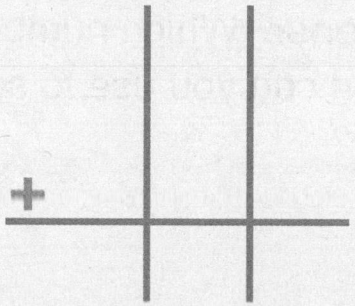

Problem Solving

Performance Assessment

Tickets Sold

The table shows how many tickets were sold at a theater.

How many tickets were sold on Thursday and Saturday?

TICKETS

25145843

Tickets Sold	
Thursday	198
Friday	245
Saturday	367

25145843

9. **Make Sense** Which numbers and operation can you use to solve the problem?

_____

_____

_____

10. **Model** Write an equation that shows the problem you need to solve.

_____ ◯ _____ = _____

11. **Generalize** Use what you know about adding 3-digit numbers to solve the problem. Explain what you did.

_____

_____

_____

_____

Copyright © Savvas Learning Company LLC. All Rights Reserved.

Name _____

Help Tools Games

Homework & Practice 10-7
Repeated Reasoning

HOME ACTIVITY Ask your child to solve 204 + 738 and 504 + 187. For each problem, ask your child to explain how he or she solved the problem.

Another Look!

When you add problems like this, you use repeated reasoning.

You need to check each place as you add. Sometimes, you don't need to regroup.

$$\begin{array}{r} 421 \\ +\ 258 \\ \hline 679 \end{array}$$

Sometimes, you do need to regroup to make a ten or a hundred.

$$\begin{array}{r} {}^{1} \\ 264 \\ +\ 226 \\ \hline 490 \end{array}$$

Use repeated reasoning to solve each problem. Circle any problem where you regrouped to make a ten or a hundred.

1.
$$\begin{array}{r} 242 \\ +\ 139 \\ \hline \end{array}$$

2.
$$\begin{array}{r} 432 \\ +\ 257 \\ \hline \end{array}$$

3.
$$\begin{array}{r} 192 \\ +\ 406 \\ \hline \end{array}$$

4.
$$\begin{array}{r} 371 \\ +\ 240 \\ \hline \end{array}$$

Performance Assessment

Field Trip Costs

Don's class rents a bus for $168. They want to take the bus to the theater. What is the total cost of the bus rental and theater tickets?

Place	Ticket Cost
Science Museum	$158
Horse Farm	$225
Theater	$137

5. **Make Sense** What do you know? What are you asked to find?

6. **Model** Write an equation that shows the problem you need to solve.

_____ ◯ _____ = _____

7. **Generalize** Use what you know about adding 3-digit numbers to solve the problem. Explain what you did.

Copyright © Savvas Learning Company LLC. All Rights Reserved.

Name _____

TOPIC 10 **Fluency Practice Activity**

I can ...
subtract within 100.

Point & Tally

Find a partner. Get paper and a pencil. Each partner chooses a different color: light blue or dark blue.

Partner 1 and Partner 2 each point to a black number at the same time. Both partners subtract Partner 2's number from Partner 1's number.

If the answer is on your color, you get a tally mark. Work until one partner gets seven tally marks.

Partner 1

59
78
92
82
64

53	19	43	62	37	30
48	65	81	32	51	76
14	71	58	66	48	25
44	37	55	47	33	67

Partner 2

45
27
16
11
34

Tally Marks for Partner 1

Tally Marks for Partner 2

TOPIC 10 Vocabulary Review

A-Z Glossary

Word List
- addend
- break apart
- digits
- hundreds
- mental math
- open number line
- partial sum
- sum

Understand Vocabulary

Choose a term from the Word List to complete each sentence.

1. When adding 193 + 564, the sum of 90 + 60 is called a _____.
2. In 709 + 187, 709 is an _____.
3. You can use an _____ to count on.

4. In 841, there are _____ hundreds.

5. Give the value of each digit in 610.

_____

6. Use mental math to find 198 + 362.

_____

Use Vocabulary in Writing

7. Use words to tell how to find 249 + 201. Use terms from the Word List.

_____
_____
_____
_____
_____

Copyright © Savvas Learning Company LLC. All Rights Reserved.

Name _____

TOPIC 10

Reteaching

Set A

You can use mental math to add 10 or 100 to a number.

$362 + 10 = ?$

The tens digit goes up by 1.

$362 + 10 = 372$

$362 + 100 = ?$

The hundreds digit goes up by 1.

$362 + 100 = 462$

Add using mental math.

1. $600 + 10 =$ _____

   $600 + 100 =$ _____

2. $543 + 10 =$ _____

   $543 + 100 =$ _____

3. $799 + 10 =$ _____

   $799 + 100 =$ _____

Set B

You can use an open number line to add. Find $327 + 126$.

First, place 327 on the line.

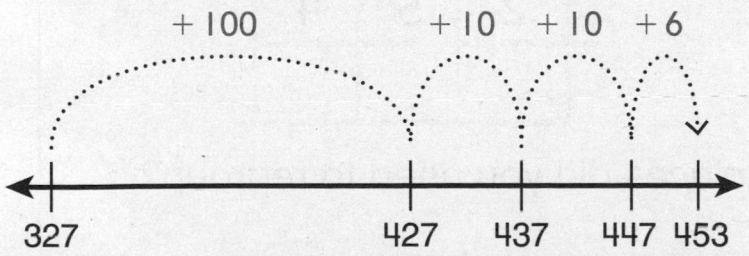

Count on by 100s, 10s, and 6 more on the line.

So, $327 + 126 =$ 453.

Use an open number line to find each sum.

4. $594 + 132 =$ _____

5. $157 + 245 =$ _____

Set C

You can draw place-value blocks to show addition. Find 163 + 144.

	Hundreds	Tens	Ones
	1	6	3
+	1	4	4
	3	0	7

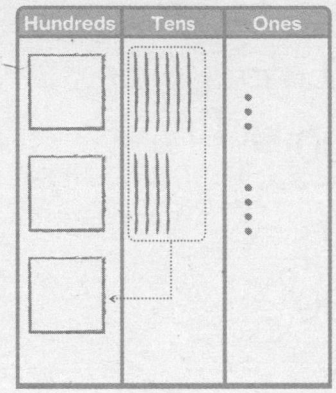

Add. Regroup and draw models if needed.

6.

	Hundreds	Tens	Ones
	4	0	8
+	3	2	6

7.

	Hundreds	Tens	Ones
	2	2	5
+	3	6	1

Set D

Thinking Habits

Repeated Reasoning

What can I use from one problem to help with another problem?

Are there things that repeat?

Solve the problem. Use repeated reasoning.

8. Find the sum.

	Hundreds	Tens	Ones
	5	6	8
+	2	5	4

Which places did you need to regroup?

_____

How does regrouping work?

_____

_____

Copyright © Savvas Learning Company LLC. All Rights Reserved.

Name _____

TOPIC 10 Assessment

1. Emily has 100 sun stickers. She has 382 star stickers and 10 moon stickers. How many sun and star stickers does Emily have?

Ⓐ 492 Ⓒ 393

Ⓑ 482 Ⓓ 392

2. Tyrone collects baseball cards. He gives 138 cards to his friend. Now he has 428 cards. How many baseball cards did Tyrone have before he gave some away?

Ⓐ 290 Ⓒ 556

Ⓑ 550 Ⓓ 566

3. Use the open number line to solve the problem. Write the missing numbers in the boxes.

421 + 250 = ?

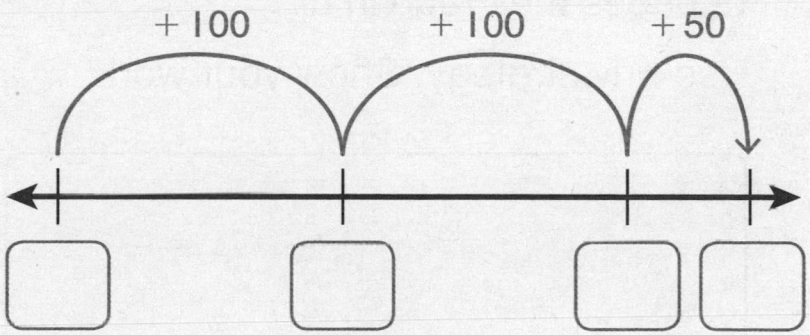

421 + 250 = _____

4. Which is the same amount as 528 + 167? Choose all that apply.

☐ 500 + 80 + 15 ☐ 500 + 180 + 15 ☐ 600 + 90 + 5 ☐ 600 + 80 + 15

5. Is the sum equal to 488? Choose Yes or No.

478 + 10 = ? ○ Yes ○ No

388 + 100 = ? ○ Yes ○ No

248 + 240 = ? ○ Yes ○ No

188 + 300 = ? ○ Yes ○ No

6. Rich has 335 pennies.
Beth has 58 more pennies than Rich.
How many pennies do they have in all?

Ⓐ 277

Ⓑ 393

Ⓒ 628

Ⓓ 728

7. Use the numbers on the cards.
Write the missing digits.

2	3	6	7

$$\begin{array}{r} 472 \\ +256 \\ \hline \square\square 8 \end{array} \qquad \begin{array}{r} 434 \\ +259 \\ \hline \square 9 \square \end{array}$$

8. Molly reads 184 pages. Pat reads 294 pages. What is the total number of pages they read in all?

Use any strategy. Show your work.

_____ pages

9. On Saturday, 449 people visit the zoo.
On Sunday, 423 people visit the zoo.
How many people visit the zoo in all?

Use the open number line to solve.
Explain your work.

Copyright © Savvas Learning Company LLC. All Rights Reserved.

Name _____

TOPIC 10 Performance Assessment

Recycling Race

Westbrook School is having a recycling contest. The table shows the number of cans each grade collected in February.

Cans Collected in February	
First grade	264
Second grade	302
Third grade	392
Fourth grade	425

1. How many cans did the first-grade students and the second-grade students collect in all?
   Use the open number line to solve.

_____ cans

2. Bruce used partial sums to find how many cans the third-grade students and fourth-grade students collected in all.

	392
	+ 425
Hundreds:	700
Tens:	11
Ones:	+ 7
	718

Do you agree with his answer?
Circle **yes** or **no**.

Explain your answer.

_____

_____

_____

_____

_____

_____

3. Which two grades collected a total of 689 cans? Choose any strategy to solve the problem. Show your work. Explain which strategy you used.

The _____ grade and the _____ grade collected a total of 689 cans.

4. The second-grade students collected 432 cans in March. They collected 198 cans in April. Tom and Bill each add to find how many cans the class collected in all. One of them checks his work and finds the correct sum.

Tom's Way	Bill's Way
11 432 + 198 630	432 + 198 520

Who added correctly? Explain.

Who answered incorrectly? What did he do wrong?

Copyright © Savvas Learning Company LLC. All Rights Reserved.

TOPIC 11 Subtract Within 1,000 Using Models and Strategies

Essential Question: What are strategies for subtracting numbers to 1,000?

Digital Resources

Solve · Learn · Glossary · Tools · Assessment · Help · Games

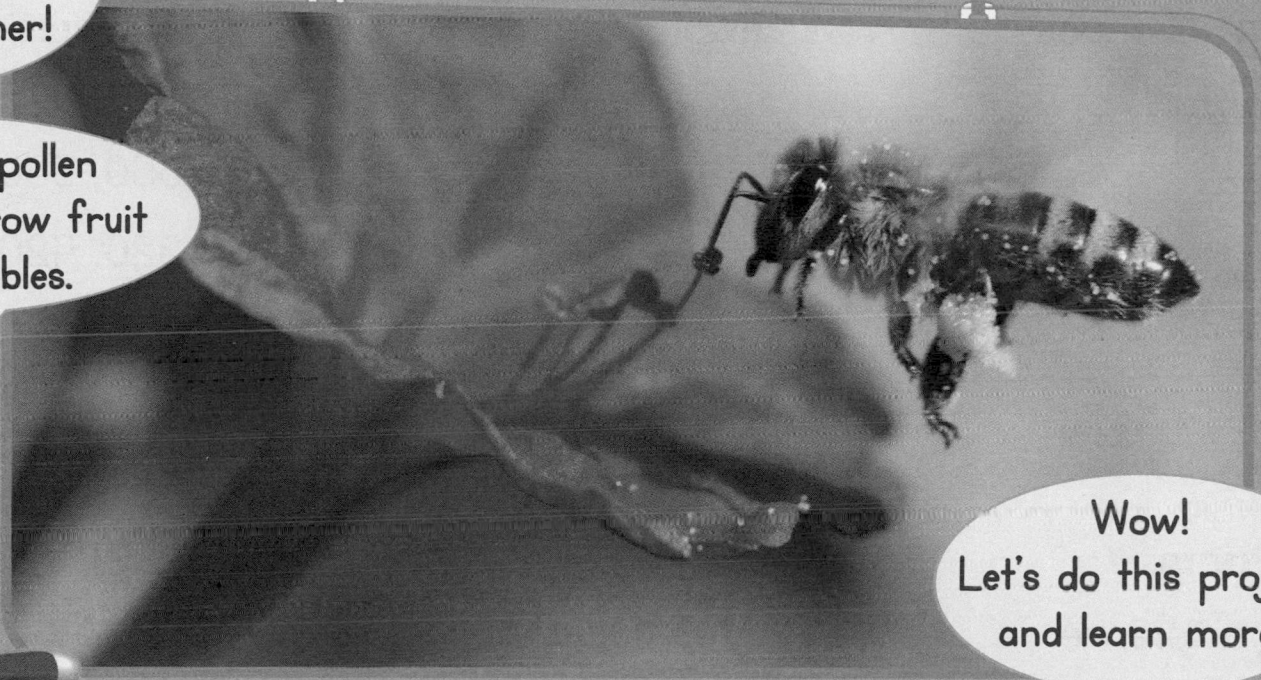

Math and Science Project: Making Models

Find Out Use a paintbrush as a model of a bee's leg. Dip the brush in a bowl of sugar. Then dip the brush in a bowl of pepper. Take turns. What happens to the sugar? What happens to the pepper?

Journal: Make a Book Show what you learn in a book. In your book, also:

- Tell how bees help move pollen between plants.
- Show how to use a model to help subtract three-digit numbers.

Name _____

Review What You Know

Vocabulary

1. Circle each number that is **less than** 607.

598

608

706

2. Circle each number that is **greater than** 299.

352

300

298

3. Circle the group of numbers that **decrease** by 100 from left to right.

650, 550, 450, 350

320, 420, 520, 620

570, 560, 550, 540

Subtraction Facts

4. Write each difference.

$$\begin{array}{r} 14 \\ -\ 7 \\ \hline \end{array} \qquad \begin{array}{r} 11 \\ -\ 4 \\ \hline \end{array} \qquad \begin{array}{r} 16 \\ -\ 9 \\ \hline \end{array}$$

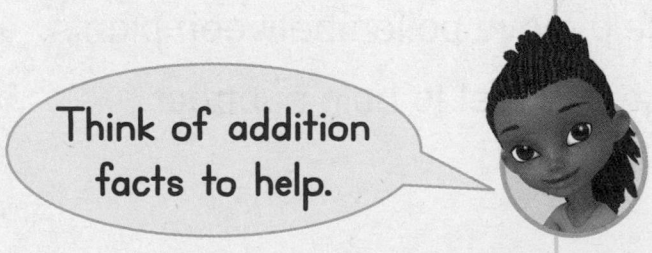

Regrouping

5. Use regrouping to find the difference. Be ready to explain your work.

$$\begin{array}{r} 54 \\ -\ 29 \\ \hline \end{array}$$

Math Story

6. Ben has 64 comic books. He gives 36 comic books to friends. How many comic books does Ben have left?

_____ comic books

Copyright © Savvas Learning Company LLC. All Rights Reserved.

Name _____

Solve

Lesson 11-1
Subtract 10 and 100

I can ...
subtract 10 or 100 mentally using what I know about place value.

SOL 2.1b

Solve & Share

There are 456 ears of corn growing in a field.
How many ears will be left if 10 ears are harvested?
How many ears will be left if 100 ears are harvested?

How can you use mental math to find your answers?

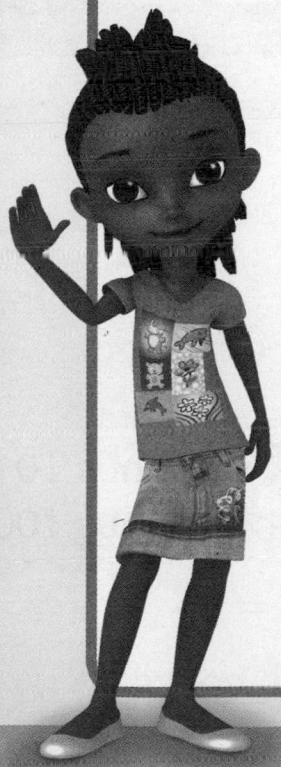

456 − 10 = _____

456 − 100 = _____

Digital Resources at SavvasRealize.com

Learn Glossary

You can use mental math to subtract 10 or 100 from three-digit numbers.

Find 328 − 10.
Find 328 − 100.

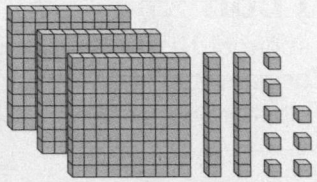

328

Place value can help me subtract mentally.

Subtracting 10 makes the tens digit go down by 1.

I know
2 − 1 = 1.
So, 328 − 10 = 318.

Subtracting 100 makes the hundreds digit go down by 1.

I know
3 − 1 = 2.
So, 328 − 100 = 228.

Sometimes subtracting 10 changes the tens and hundreds digits.
Find 500 − 10.

I know
500 = 50 tens.
50 tens − 1 ten = 49 tens or 490.
So, 500 − 10 = 490.

Do You Understand?

Show Me! Use mental math to find 457 − 10 and 457 − 100. Explain your reasoning.

Guided Practice

Subtract using mental math. Use models if needed.

1.

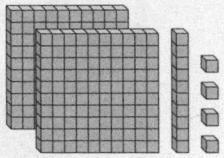

minus 10
minus 100

214 − 10 = 204

214 − 100 = 114

2.

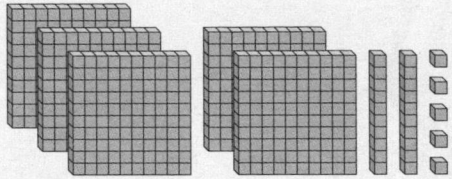

minus 10
minus 100

____ − ____ = ____

____ − ____ = ____

3. 738 − 10 = ____

738 − 100 = ____

4. 100 − 10 = ____

100 − 100 = ____

Copyright © Savvas Learning Company LLC. All Rights Reserved.

Name _____

Tools Assessment

Independent Practice

Subtract using mental math. Use models if needed.

5. 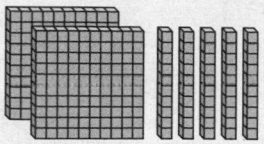

minus 10
minus 100

_____ − _____ = _____

_____ − _____ = _____

6. 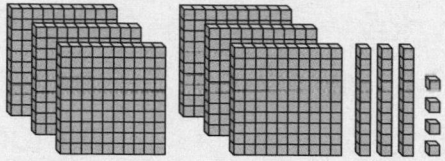

minus 10
minus 100

_____ − _____ = _____

_____ − _____ = _____

7. 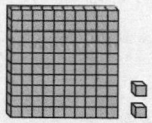

minus 10
minus 100

_____ − _____ = _____

_____ − _____ = _____

8. 719 − 10 = _____

9. 400 − 100 = _____

10. 308 − 10 = _____

11. 520 − 100 = _____

12. 975 − 10 = _____

13. 143 − 100 = _____

Algebra Find the missing numbers. Use mental math to solve.

14. 362 − ☐ = 352

15. 801 − ☐ = 701

16. 449 = 549 − ☐

17. 657 − ☐ = 647

18. 215 − ☐ = 205

19. 700 − ☐ = 690

Problem Solving Solve each problem.

20. **Math and Science** Marni is studying facts about bees. She finds that one type of bee can pollinate 955 plants each day. A different type of bee pollinates 100 fewer plants. How many plants does it pollinate?

_____ − _____ = _____

_____ plants

21. **Model** There was a marathon in Dundee. 10 of the runners did **NOT** finish the marathon. How many runners finished the marathon? Model by writing an equation.

_____ − _____ = _____

_____ runners

22. **Higher Order Thinking** Think of a 3-digit number. Write a story about subtracting 100 from your number. Then complete the equation to show your subtraction.

_____

_____

_____

_____

_____ − _____ = _____

23. **Assessment** Which is equal to 100 less than 463? Choose all that apply.

- ☐ 363
- ☐ 300 + 60 + 3
- ☐ 563
- ☐ 500 + 60 + 3

Copyright © Savvas Learning Company LLC. All Rights Reserved.

Name _____

Help Tools Games

Homework & Practice 11-1

Subtract 10 and 100

Another Look! Use mental math to subtract 10 or 100 from 3-digit numbers.

Find 278 − 10 and 278 − 100.

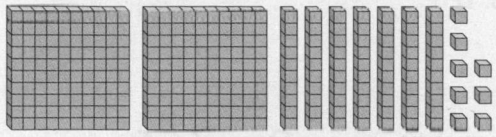

minus 10

minus 100

The tens digit goes down by 1 when you subtract 278 − 10.

278 − 10 = 2 6 8

The hundreds digit goes down by 1 when you subtract 278 − 100.

278 − 100 = 1 78

HOME ACTIVITY Choose a number between 300 and 400. Ask your child to subtract 10 from the number and tell you the difference. Repeat with subtracting 100 from the same number.

Subtract using mental math. Use models if needed.

1.

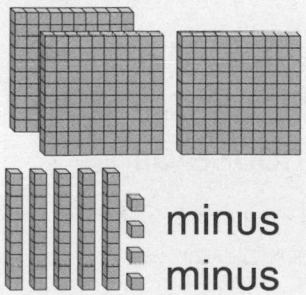

minus 10

minus 100

_____ − 10 = _____

_____ − 100 = _____

2.

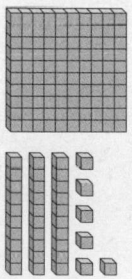

minus 10

minus 100

_____ − 10 = _____

_____ − 100 = _____

3.

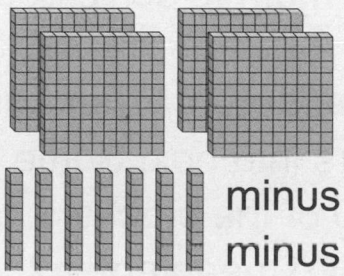

minus 10

minus 100

_____ − 10 = _____

_____ − 100 = _____

Look for Patterns Use mental math. Write the missing digit.

4. $\square 69 - 100 = 469$

5. $\square 00 - 10 = 790$

6. $402 - 10 = 3\square 2$

Vocabulary Use mental math. Write the missing digit. Then complete the sentence with **greater than** or **less than**.

7. $271 - 100 = 1\square 1$

171 is 100 _____ 271.

8. $475 - 100 = \square 75$

475 is 100 _____ 375.

9. $612 - \square 0 = 602$

602 is ten _____ 612.

10. **Higher Order Thinking** Adam is subtracting 708 − 10 mentally. He thinks the tens digit and the hundreds digit will change. He gets 698 for his answer. Is Adam's thinking correct? Explain.

_____

_____

_____

Use mental math to solve each story problem.

11. **Assessment** There are 287 animal crackers in a box. Some second graders eat 100 of the crackers. How many crackers have **NOT** been eaten?

Ⓐ 387 Ⓒ 187

Ⓑ 277 Ⓓ 87

12. **Assessment** Which is equal to 10 less than 145? Choose all that apply.

☐ 135 ☐ 155

☐ 100 + 30 + 5 ☐ 100 + 50 + 5

Copyright © Savvas Learning Company LLC. All Rights Reserved.

Name _____

Solve

Lesson 11-2

Count Back to Subtract on an Open Number Line

I can ...

use an open number line to count back to subtract 3-digit numbers.

SOL 2.6b, 2.6c

Solve & Share

Marcus had 306 stickers. He gave 211 stickers to Juan. How many stickers does Marcus have left?

Use the open number line to solve.

_____ − _____ = _____

Learn Glossary

Find 580 – 232. Use an open number line.

One Way

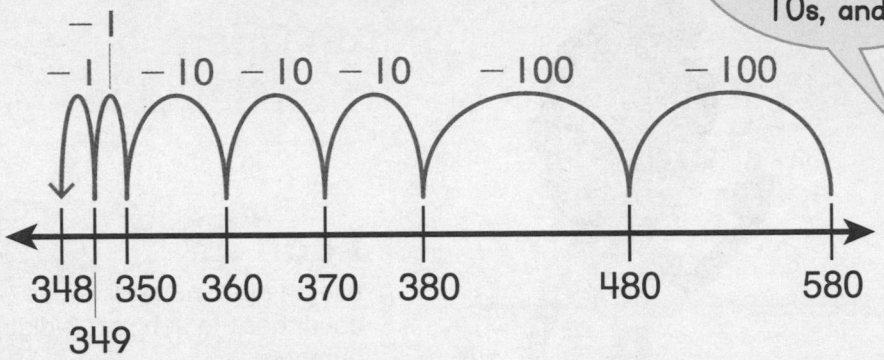

580 – 232 = 348

This way shows counting back by jumps of 100s, 10s, and 1s.

Another Way

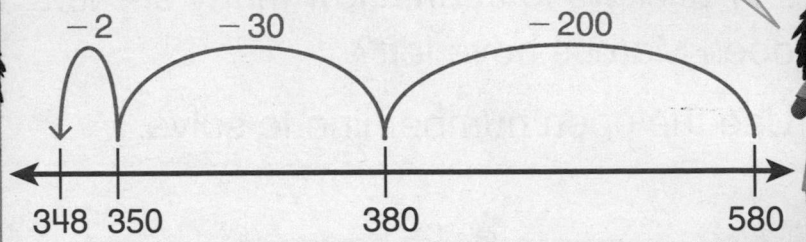

This way shows how you can count back by bigger jumps. Both ways are correct.

Do You Understand?

Show Me! How can an open number line help you keep track as you count back?

Guided Practice

Use an open number line to subtract.

1. 425 – 115 = _____

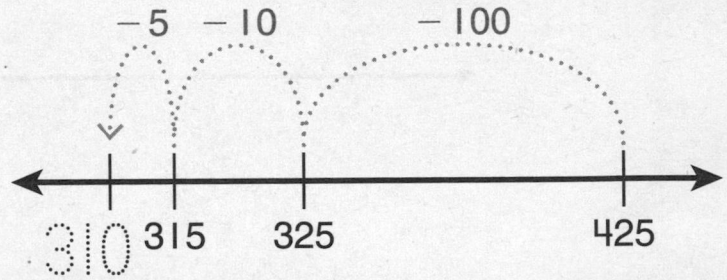

2. 693 – 218 = _____

Copyright © Savvas Learning Company LLC. All Rights Reserved.

Name _____

Tools Assessment

Independent Practice

Use an open number line to find each difference.

3. 451 − 132 = _____

4. 735 − 242 = _____

5. 873 − 225 = _____

6. 492 − 314 = _____

7. **Higher Order Thinking** Show two different ways to find 680 − 237. Use the open number lines.

680 − 237 = _____

Problem Solving

Solve each problem using an open number line.

8. **Model** There are 541 raffle tickets to sell. The second grade class sells 212 raffle tickets. How many raffle tickets are left to sell?

_____ raffle tickets

9. **Model** Fran has 712 stamps. Bill has 137 fewer stamps than Fran. How many stamps does Bill have?

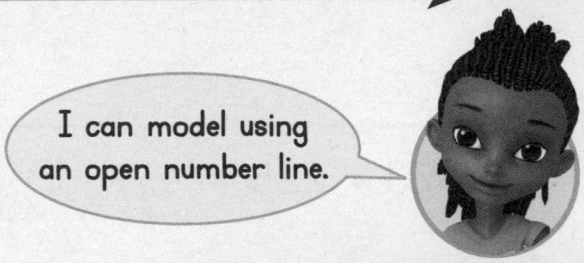

_____ stamps

10. **Higher Order Thinking** Count back on the number line to find 962 – 233. Write how many hundreds, tens, and ones you counted back. Then write the equation.

I counted back _____ hundreds, _____ tens, and _____ ones.

_____ ◯ _____ = _____

11. **Assessment** The open number line below shows a subtraction problem. Complete the equation. Write the numbers that are used to subtract and the difference.

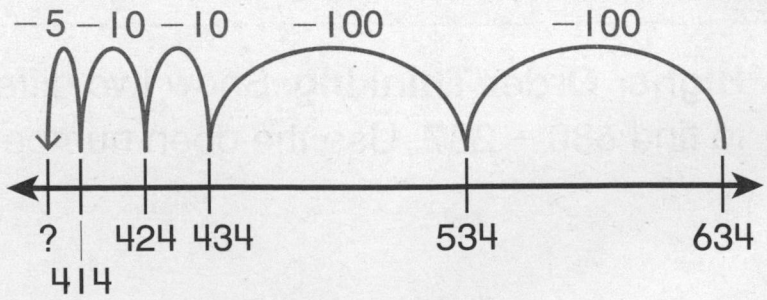

_____ – _____ = _____

Copyright © Savvas Learning Company LLC. All Rights Reserved.

Name _____

Help Tools Games

Homework & Practice 11-2

Count Back to Subtract on an Open Number Line

Another Look! Find 917 − 322.

Here is one way.

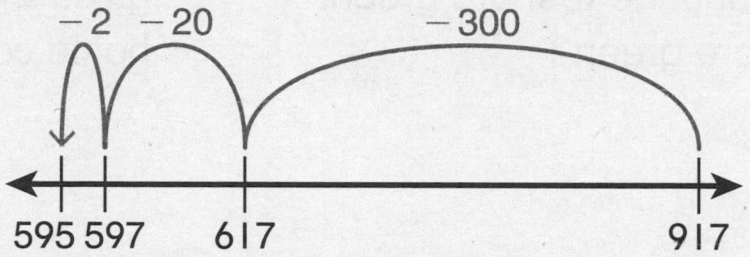

So, 917 − 322 = 595

HOME ACTIVITY Tell your child to find 445 − 152 using an open number line.

Use an open number line to find each difference.

1. 925 − 230 = _____

2. 384 − 126 = _____

Solve each problem using an open number line.

3. **Model** 464 grapes are in a basket. 126 of the grapes are red and the rest are green. How many grapes are green?

_____ green grapes

4. **Model** Gabby has 592 bottle caps. She gives 215 bottle caps to Leroy. How many bottle caps does Gabby have left?

_____ bottle caps

5. **Higher Order Thinking** Write a math story for 348 − 144. Draw an open number line to solve the problem.

_____

_____

_____

_____

348 − 144 = _____

6. **Assessment** The open number line below shows a subtraction problem. Complete the equation. Write the numbers that are used to subtract and the difference.

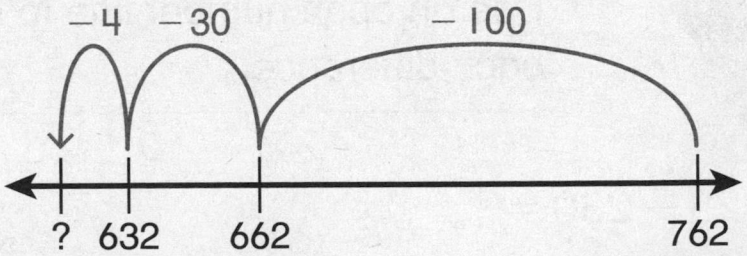

_____ − _____ = _____

Copyright © Savvas Learning Company LLC. All Rights Reserved.

Name _____

Solve

Lesson 11-3

Add Up to Subtract on an Open Number Line

I can ...

use an open number line to add up to subtract 3-digit numbers.

SOL 2.6b, 2.6c

Solve & Share

There are 224 girls and some boys in a parade. There are 471 children in the parade. How many boys are in the parade?

Use the open number line to solve the problem. Show your work.

_____ − _____ = _____

Find 482 – 247.
Add up to find the difference.

Add up from 247, the number you are subtracting. Stop at 482.

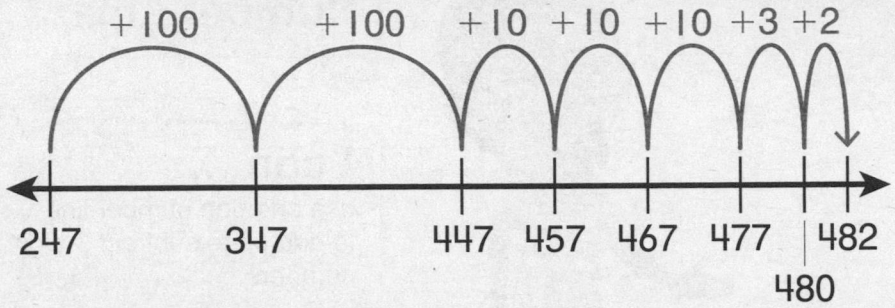

100 + 100 + 10 + 10 + 10 + 3 + 2 = 235

How much did you add up from 247 to get to 482? That's the difference!

So, 482 – 247 = 235.

You can check your work by adding.

247 + 235 = 482.
So, 235 is correct.

Do You Understand?

Show Me! What is another way you could add up to find 482 – 247?

Guided Practice

Add up to subtract. Check your work.

1. 573 – 459 = _____ _____ + _____ = _____

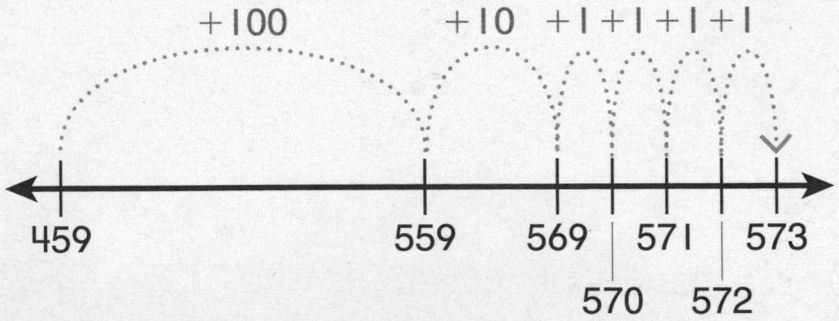

2. 672 – 547 = _____ _____ + _____ = _____

Copyright © Savvas Learning Company LLC. All Rights Reserved.

Name _____

Tools Assessment

Independent Practice

Add up on the open number line to find each difference. Then add to check your work.

3. 530 − 318 = _____

_____ + _____ = _____

4. 735 − 429 = _____

_____ + _____ = _____

5. 802 − 688 = _____

_____ + _____ = _____

6. **Vocabulary** Complete the sentences using each word below once.

ones **add** **number**

You can add up to subtract on an open number line.

Start at the _____ you are subtracting.

_____ up hundreds, tens, and _____.

Stop at the number you subtract from.

Problem Solving Solve each problem. Check your work.

7. **Reasoning** Yun has 780 blocks. Marsha has 545 fewer blocks than Yun. How many blocks does Marsha have?

_____ − _____ = _____ blocks

_____ + _____ = _____

8. **Higher Order Thinking** Vic wants to find 463 − 258 on an open number line. Should he count back or add up? Explain.

_____

_____

_____

_____

_____

_____

9. **Assessment** Write a math story for 653 − 529. Add up on the open number line to solve. Add to check your work.

_____

_____

_____

_____

_____

_____

_____ − _____ = _____

_____ + _____ = _____

Copyright © Savvas Learning Company LLC. All Rights Reserved.

Name _____

Help Tools Games

Homework & Practice 11-3

Add Up to Subtract on an Open Number Line

Another Look! Find 664 – 450.

Here is one way.

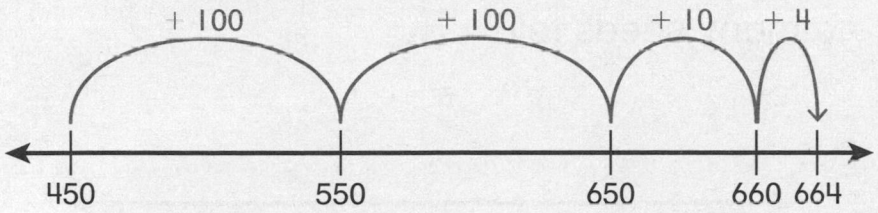

I can add up to subtract!
So, 664 – 450 = 214.

Check: 214 + 450 = 664

Add hundreds, tens, and ones. 100 + 100 + 10 + 4 = 214

HOME ACTIVITY Have your child add up to subtract 873 – 659 on an open number line. Then have your child check the answer using addition.

Add up on the open number line to find each difference. Then add to check your work.

1. 994 – 770 = _____

_____ + _____ = _____

2. 831 – 716 = _____

_____ + _____ = _____

Solve each problem. Check your work.

3. **Reasoning** April has 365 stickers. She gives 238 stickers to Gwen. How many stickers does April have left?

_____ stickers

4. **Math and Science** A group of birds had 362 seeds. Some seeds fell to the ground. Now the birds have 237 seeds. How many seeds fell?

_____ seeds

5. **Higher Order Thinking** Ricky added up on the number line and found 535 − 315 = 210. Is his work correct? Explain.

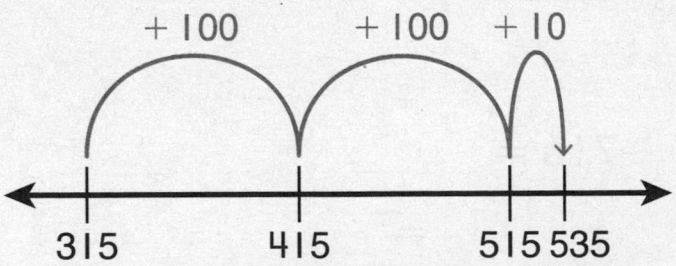

6. **Assessment** Show one way to add up on the open number line to find 560 − 340. Write the difference. Then explain your work.

560 − 340 = _____

Copyright © Savvas Learning Company LLC. All Rights Reserved.

Name _____

Solve

Lesson 11-4
Subtract Using Mental Math

I can ...
use mental math to subtract.

SOL 2.6b, 2.6c

Solve & Share

Ami and Jorge enter their pumpkins in the Giant Pumpkin Contest. Ami's pumpkin weighs 335 pounds. Jorge's pumpkin weighs 302 pounds. How many more pounds does Ami's pumpkin weigh?

Show how you can use mental math to solve.

_____ – _____ = _____

_____ more pounds

Digital Resources at SavvasRealize.com

Use any strategy to find 372 − 123.

I'll count back to find the answer.

I'll try to think of numbers that are easier to work with to help me.

One way to subtract is to count back.

Start at 372. Count back 1 hundred, then 2 tens, then 3 ones.

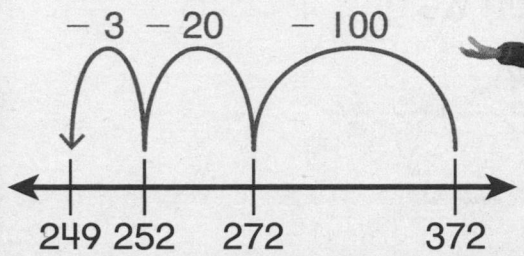

Another way to subtract is to use easier numbers.

$$\begin{array}{r} 372 \\ -\ 122 \\ \hline 250 \end{array} \qquad \begin{array}{r} 250 \\ -\ \ \ 1 \\ \hline 249 \end{array}$$

123 = 122 + 1
So, I can take away 122. Then take away 1 more.

Both ways get the same answer!

So, 372 − 123 = 249.

Do You Understand?

Show Me! How could you count back to find 430 − 241? What is the difference?

Guided Practice

Use any strategy to subtract. Show your work.

1. 485 − 136 = 349

2. 457 − 261 = _____

3. 342 − 134 = _____

4. 321 − 115 = _____

Copyright © Savvas Learning Company LLC. All Rights Reserved.

Name _____

Tools Assessment

Independent Practice

Use any strategy to subtract. Show your work.

5. 598 − 319 = _____

6. 794 − 452 = _____

7. 871 − 355 = _____

8. 649 − 525 = _____

9. 463 − 244 = _____

10. 304 − 198 = _____

11. **Number Sense** Leo says that the difference of 526 − 217 is greater than 200. Is what Leo says reasonable? Why or why not?

_____

_____

_____

_____

Problem Solving

Use any strategy to solve each problem. Show your work.

12. Tia collected cans to raise money for school. She collected 569 cans on Monday. Tia collected some more cans on Tuesday. Now she has 789 cans. How many cans did Tia collect on Tuesday?

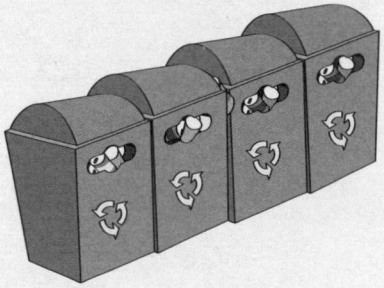

_____ cans

13. **Reasoning** Felipe has 453 stamps in his collection. Emily has 762 stamps in her collection. How many more stamps does Emily have?

_____ more stamps

14. **Higher Order Thinking** Write a subtraction problem about recycling. Use 3-digit numbers. Use pictures, numbers, or words to solve the problem.

15. **Assessment** On Saturday, 28 fewer boys than girls played in soccer matches. If 214 girls played, how many boys played?

Ⓐ 186

Ⓑ 166

Ⓒ 156

Ⓓ 136

Copyright © Savvas Learning Company LLC. All Rights Reserved.

Name _____

Help Tools Games

Homework & Practice 11-4

Subtract Using Mental Math

HOME ACTIVITY Ask your child to show you how to subtract 431 − 216. Have your child explain every step of the subtraction.

Another Look! Find 361 − 142.

One Way

Start at 361 and count back 142.

Remember, 142 is
1 hundred, 4 tens, and 2 ones.

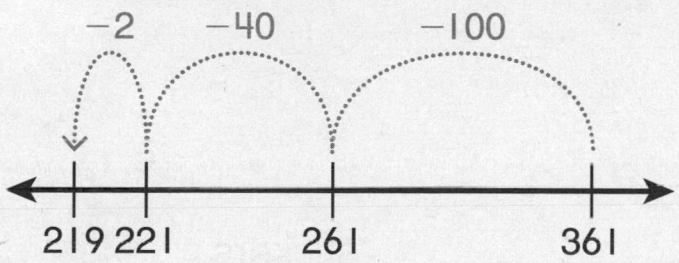

So, 361 − 142 = 219.

Another Way

Use easier numbers.

140 is easier to subtract than 142.
142 = 140 + 2

Subtract 140.
Then subtract 2 more.

$$\begin{array}{r} 361 \\ -\ 140 \\ \hline 221 \end{array} \qquad \begin{array}{r} 221 \\ -\ \ \ 2 \\ \hline 219 \end{array}$$

So, 361 − 142 = 219.

Use any strategy to subtract. Show your work.

1. 412 − 103 = _____

2. 398 − 235 = _____

3. 753 − 304 = _____

Make Sense Mrs. Anderson gives star stickers to her class. She starts with 989 stickers in September. Find out how many she has left as the months go by. Use any strategy. Show your work.

4. In September, Mrs. Anderson gives away 190 stickers.

989 − 190 = _____

_____ stickers

5. In October and November, Mrs. Anderson gives away 586 stickers.

_____ − _____ = _____

_____ stickers

6. In December, Mrs. Anderson gives away 109 more stickers.

_____ − _____ = _____

_____ stickers

7. **Higher Order Thinking** Kelly cuts out 265 strips of paper for an art project. She glues some strips of paper to her piece of art. Now she has 138 strips of paper left. How many strips of paper did Kelly use?

265 − _____ = 138

_____ strips of paper

8. **Assessment** Jimmy's hive has 528 bees. Julie's hive has 204 bees. How many more bees does Jimmy's hive have than Julie's hive?

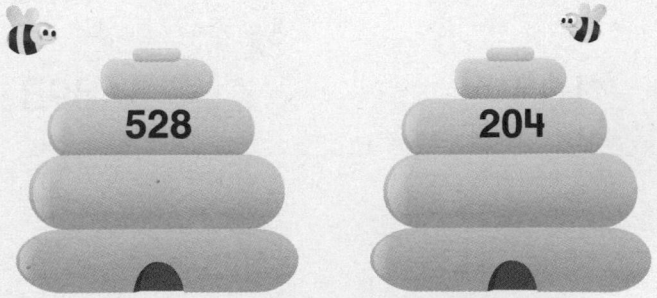

Ⓐ 224

Ⓑ 304

Ⓒ 314

Ⓓ 324

Copyright © Savvas Learning Company LLC. All Rights Reserved.

Name _____

Solve

Lesson 11-5

Use Models to Subtract

I can ...

use models to subtract 3-digit numbers.

SOL 2.6b, 2.6c

Solve & Share

427 people are at the beach. 182 people are swimming. How many people are **NOT** swimming?

Use place-value blocks to help. Draw your blocks below and solve.

Hundreds	Tens	Ones
−		

Hundreds	Tens	Ones

Digital Resources at SavvasRealize.com

Learn Glossary

Use models to find 328 − 133.
First, subtract the ones.

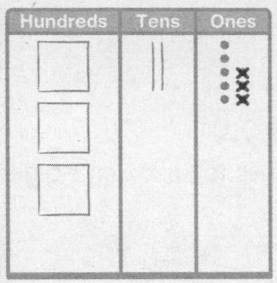

	Hundreds	Tens	Ones
	3	2	8
−	1	3	3
			5

Regroup 1 hundred as 10 tens.

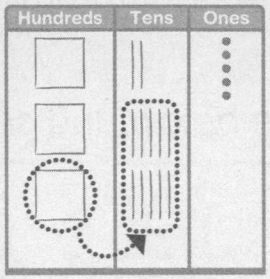

	Hundreds	Tens	Ones
	2	12	
	~~3~~	~~2~~	8
−	1	3	3
			5

Subtract the tens and the hundreds.

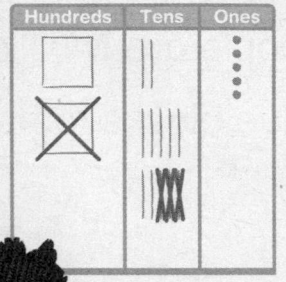

	Hundreds	Tens	Ones
	2	12	
	~~3~~	~~2~~	8
−	1	3	3
	1	9	5

So, 328 − 133 = 195.

Do You Understand?

Show Me! Explain why regrouping works in the problem above.

Guided Practice

Subtract. Draw place-value blocks to show your work. Regroup if needed.

1.

	Hundreds	Tens	Ones
	2	12	
	~~3~~	~~2~~	6
−	1	4	3
	1	8	3

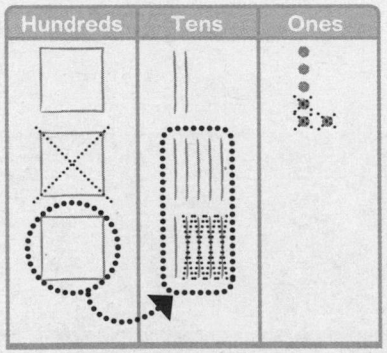

2.

	Hundreds	Tens	Ones
	3	6	3
−	1	2	7

Hundreds	Tens	Ones

3.

	Hundreds	Tens	Ones
	5	4	6
−	2	7	1

Hundreds	Tens	Ones

Copyright © Savvas Learning Company LLC. All Rights Reserved.

Name _____

Tools Assessment

Independent Practice

Subtract. Draw place-value blocks to show your work. Regroup if needed.

4.

	Hundreds	Tens	Ones
	☐	☐	☐
	3	1	4
−	1	5	2

Hundreds	Tens	Ones

5.

	Hundreds	Tens	Ones
	☐	☐	☐
	6	5	3
−	4	1	9

Hundreds	Tens	Ones

6.

	Hundreds	Tens	Ones
	☐	☐	☐
	4	3	8
−	1	6	2

Hundreds	Tens	Ones

7.

	Hundreds	Tens	Ones
	☐	☐	☐
	6	6	2
−	4	8	0

Hundreds	Tens	Ones

8. **Higher Order Thinking** Find the missing numbers. Explain your steps for solving.

	Hundreds	Tens	Ones
	☐	☐	☐
	8	5	4
−	2	9	
			2

Hundreds	Tens	Ones

_____

_____

_____

_____

_____

Problem Solving

Solve each problem below.
Draw place-value blocks to help.

9. **Model** Jeff has 517 baseball cards. He has 263 football cards. How many more baseball cards than football cards does he have?

Hundreds	Tens	Ones
−		

Hundreds	Tens	Ones

_____ more baseball cards

10. **Higher Order Thinking** Choose a number between 330 and 336. Subtract 180 from your number. Draw place-value blocks to show the difference.

11. **Assessment** There were 342 adults at the movie. There were 526 children at the movie. How many more children than adults were at the movie?

Ⓐ 184
Ⓑ 224
Ⓒ 284
Ⓓ 868

Copyright © Savvas Learning Company LLC. All Rights Reserved.

Name _____

Help Tools Games

Homework & Practice 11-5

Use Models to Subtract

HOME ACTIVITY Have your child draw place-value blocks to model and find 583 − 274.

Another Look! You can follow these steps to subtract three-digit numbers.

Find 327 − 164.

Step 1: Subtract the ones. Regroup if needed.
Step 2: Subtract the tens. Regroup if needed.
Step 3: Subtract the hundreds.

	Hundreds	Tens	Ones
	2	12	
	~~3~~	~~2~~	7
−	1	6	4
	1	6	3

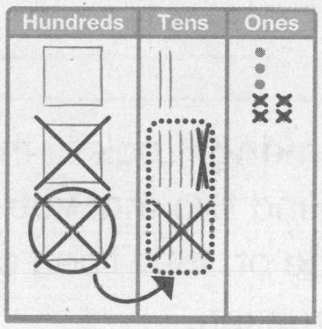

327 − 164 = 163

Subtract to find each difference. Draw place-value blocks to help.

1.

	Hundreds	Tens	Ones
	4	14	
	~~5~~	~~4~~	9
−	2	9	5
	2	5	4

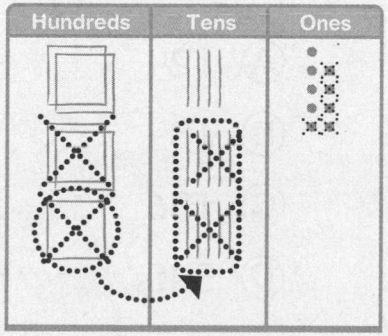

2.

	Hundreds	Tens	Ones
	8	3	5
−	5	1	6

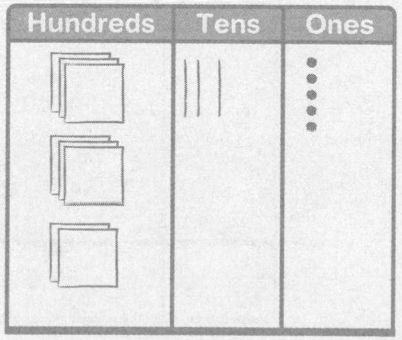

Solve the problems below. Remember to regroup when you need to.

3. **Generalize** Subtract. Then circle the problems where you regrouped to solve.

	Hundreds	Tens	Ones
	☐	☐	☐
	4	3	7
−	1	6	4

	Hundreds	Tens	Ones
	☐	☐	☐
	5	7	8
−	2	6	4

	Hundreds	Tens	Ones
	☐	☐	☐
	3	8	1
−	1	9	0

	Hundreds	Tens	Ones
	☐	☐	☐
	9	8	9
−	3	6	2

	Hundreds	Tens	Ones
	☐	☐	☐
	6	2	3
−	3	7	1

4. **Higher Order Thinking** Look at the differences in the problems above. Find two that you can use to subtract and get a difference of 354. Then complete the workmat to show your subtraction.

	Hundreds	Tens	Ones
	☐	☐	☐
−			

5. **Assessment** A farm has 319 animals. 136 of the animals are pigs. How many animals are **NOT** pigs?

	Hundreds	Tens	Ones
	☐	☐	☐
−			

Hundreds	Tens	Ones

_____ animals are **NOT** pigs.

6. **Assessment** An office building is 332 feet tall. An apartment building is 208 feet tall. How many feet taller is the office building?

Ⓐ 124

Ⓑ 134

Ⓒ 136

Ⓓ 540

Copyright © Savvas Learning Company LLC. All Rights Reserved.

Name _____

Solve

Lesson 11-6
Explain Subtraction Strategies

I can ...
explain why subtraction strategies work using models, place value, and mental math.

SOL 2.6b, 2.6c

Solve & Share

Find 532 – 215. Use any strategy. Then explain why your strategy works.

_____

_____

_____

Digital Resources at SavvasRealize.com

Find 437 – 245. Use any strategy.

One way Draw place-value blocks to show 437. Regroup 1 hundred as 10 tens. Then subtract.

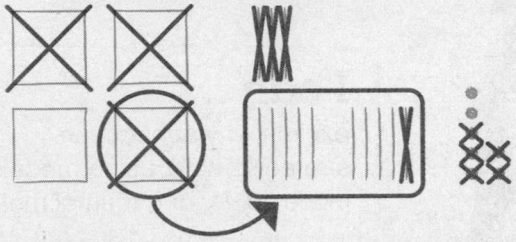

So, 437 – 245 = 192.

Another way is to use an open number line to subtract.

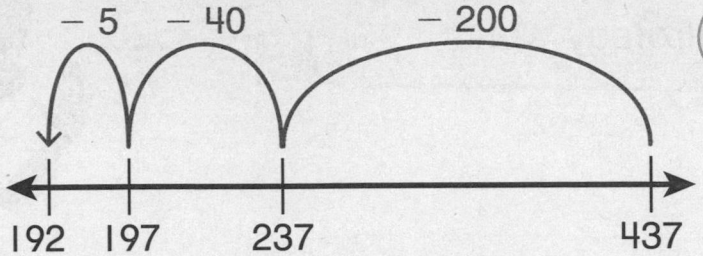

So, 437 – 245 = 192.

Do You Understand?

Show Me! Do you think both of these strategies are good for finding 437 – 245? Explain.

☆ Guided Practice ☆

Subtract any way you choose. Show your work. Then explain why the strategy works.

1. 345 – 116 = 229

Copyright © Savvas Learning Company LLC. All Rights Reserved.

Name _____

Tools Assessment

Independent Practice

Choose any strategy to solve each subtraction problem. Show your work. Then explain why the stategy works.

2. 312 − 179 = _____

3. 464 − 155 = _____

4. 612 − 478 = _____

5. **Number Sense** Use place value to find 748 − 319. Complete the equations.

319 = 300 + _____ + 9

Hundreds: 748 − _____ = _____

Tens: _____ − 10 = _____

Ones: _____ − _____ = _____

Problem Solving Solve each problem.

6. **Explain** Ava wants to use mental math to find 352 − 149. Show how she could find the difference. Is this a good strategy for Eva to use? Explain why or why not.

7. **Higher Order Thinking** Kristin found 562 − 399 = 163 using an open number line. She added up to subtract. First she added 1, then 100, and then 62.

   Draw Kristin's number line. Do you think Kristin's strategy was helpful? Explain.

8. **Assessment** Jeff counted back on this open number line to find 812 − 125.

   Use the numbers on the cards to find the missing numbers in the open number line. Write the missing numbers.

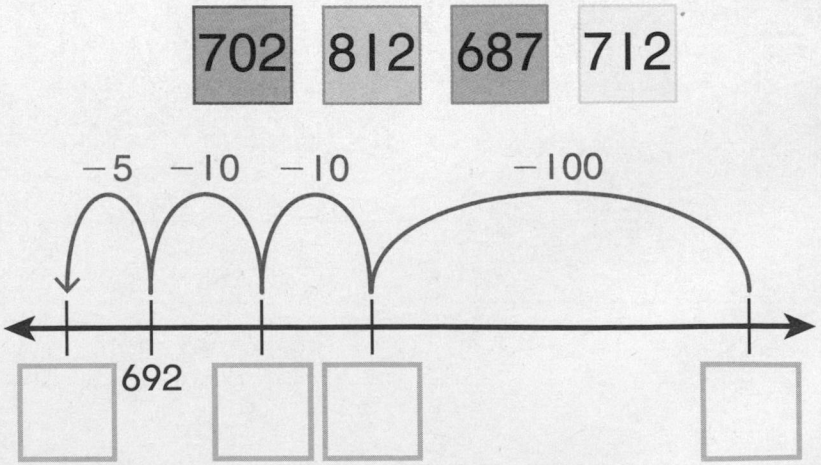

Copyright © Savvas Learning Company LLC. All Rights Reserved.

Name _____

Help Tools Games

Homework & Practice 11-6

Explain Subtraction Strategies

HOME ACTIVITY Ask your child to find 597 − 217 using a subtraction strategy he or she chooses. Then have your child explain why he or she thinks the strategy works.

Another Look! Find 725 − 592.

One Way Add up to subtract.

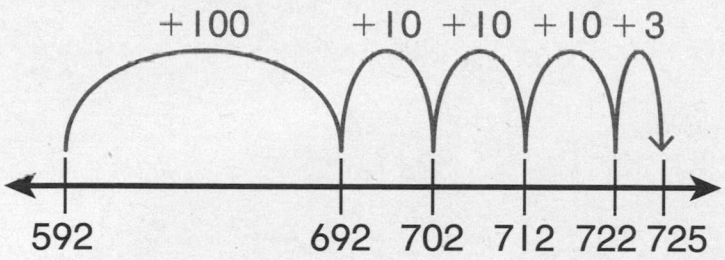

Add hundreds, tens, and ones.

100 + 10 + 10 + 10 + 3 = 133

So, 725 − 592 = 133.

Another Way It is easy to subtract 725 − 600 mentally. So, add 8 to 592 to make 600.

$$\begin{array}{r} 725 \\ -\ 600 \\ \hline 125 \end{array} \qquad \begin{array}{r} {}^{1}125 \\ +\ \ 8 \\ \hline 133 \end{array}$$

Since you added 8 to 592, you need to add 8 to 125 to get the difference.

So, 725 − 592 = 133.

Choose any strategy to solve each subtraction problem. Show your work. Then explain why the strategy works.

1. 926 − 407 = _____

2. 532 − 241 = _____

Solve each problem.

3. **Explain** Tanner wants to count back on an open number line to find 577 − 479. Marci wants to use mental math to find the difference. Which strategy do you think works better? Why? Show how you would find 577 − 479.

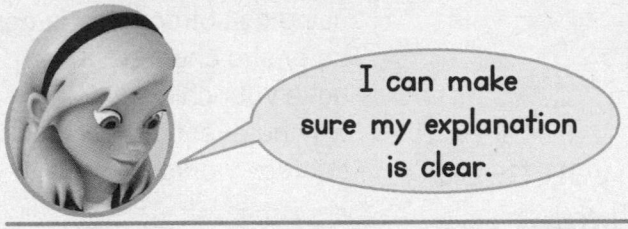

4. **Higher Order Thinking** Danny wants to draw place-value blocks to find 342 − 127. Draw the blocks he would use. Explain why this strategy works.

5. **Assessment** Landon counted back on this open number line to find 898 − 133.

Use the numbers on the cards to find the missing numbers in the open number line. Write the missing numbers.

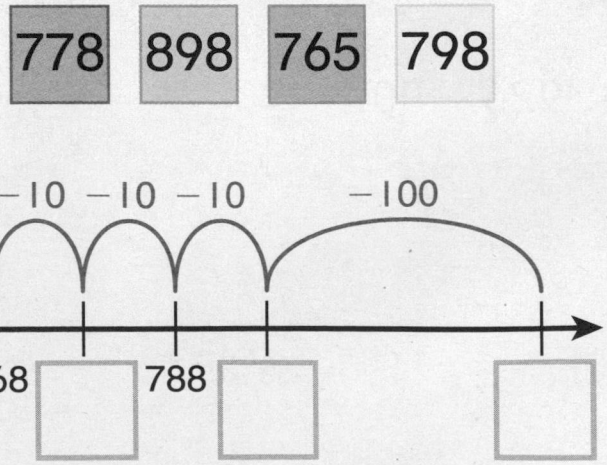

Copyright © Savvas Learning Company LLC. All Rights Reserved.

Name _____

Solve

Problem Solving

Lesson 11-7
Persevere

I can ...
solve problems that take more than one step.

SOL 2.6b, 2.6c, 2.6a

Solve & Share

Jody wants to bake 350 muffins. She bakes one batch of 160 muffins and one batch of 145 muffins. How many more muffins does Jody need to bake?

Solve any way you choose. Show your work.

Thinking Habits

What do I know?

What do I need to find?

How can I check that my solution makes sense?

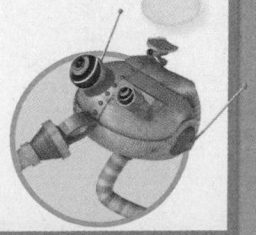

Learn Glossary

Grade 2 wants to sell 10 more tickets to the school play than Grade 1.

Grade 1 sold 476 tickets. Grade 2 sold 439 tickets.

How many more tickets does Grade 2 have to sell to reach their goal?

How can I make sense of the problem?

I can see what I know. I can find hidden questions. I can choose a strategy to solve the problem.

An easy first step is to answer the hidden question.

What is the Grade 2 goal?

Grade 2 Goal

476 + 10 = 486 tickets

Now I can subtract the number of tickets Grade 2 sold from their goal.

$$\begin{array}{r} {}^{7}4\,{}^{1}8\,{}^{1}6 \\ -\,4\;3\;9 \\ \hline 4\;7 \end{array}$$

Grade 2 needs to sell 47 more tickets to reach their goal.

Do You Understand?

Show Me! What questions can you ask yourself when you get stuck? Be ready to explain how questions can help.

Guided Practice

Solve the problem. Remember to ask yourself questions to help. Show your work.

1. Kim had 455 shells. First, she gives 134 of the shells to a friend. Then she finds 54 more shells. How many shells does Kim have now?

What will you find first? Which operation will you use?

Copyright © Savvas Learning Company LLC. All Rights Reserved.

Name _____

Tools Assessment

Independent Practice

Use the table to solve each problem. Show your work.

Weights of Wild Animals (in pounds)					
Animal	Arctic Wolf	Black Bear	Grizzly Bear	Mule Deer	Polar Bear
Weight	176	270	990	198	945

2. How much heavier is a grizzly bear than an arctic wolf and a black bear together?

3. How much less does a black bear weigh than the weight of 2 mule deer?

4. How much more does a polar bear weigh than an arctic wolf, a black bear, and a mule deer together?

Problem Solving

Performance Assessment

Big Truck

The picture at the right shows the height of a truck and the height of a smokestack on top of the truck. The height of a bridge is 144 inches.

Use the information at the right.
Can the truck travel under the bridge?

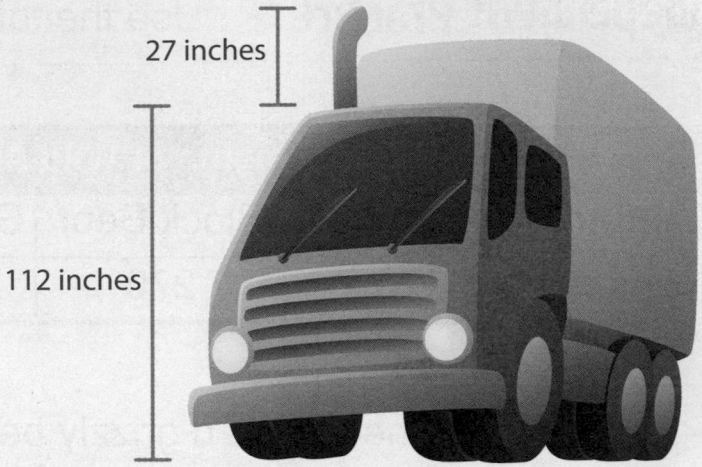

5. **Make Sense** What do you know? What are you trying to find?

_____

_____

_____

_____

_____

6. **Make Sense** What hidden question do you need to answer first? Find the answer to the hidden question.

7. **Explain** Can the truck travel under the bridge? Show your work.Why does your solution make sense?

Copyright © Savvas Learning Company LLC. All Rights Reserved.

Name _____

Help Tools Games

Homework & Practice 11-7
Make Sense and Persevere

HOME ACTIVITY Ask your child to make up a math story that can be solved by adding or subtracting. Then have your child make up a new math story that can be solved using the answer to the first problem.

Another Look! You need to use more than one step to solve some problems.

Read the problem. Complete the steps to solve.

Carl has 254 baseball cards.
He gives 145 cards to John and 56 to Amy.
How many cards does Carl have left?

Step 1 Add to find the number of cards Carl gives to John and Amy.

145 + 56 = 201

Step 2 Subtract the number of cards Carl gives away from the number of cards he has.

254 − 201 = 53 53 cards left

Solve the problem. Show your work.
Be ready to explain why your answer makes sense.

1. Mr. Wu buys a box of 300 nails. He uses 156 nails to build a deck. He uses 98 nails to build stairs. How many nails are left?

Performance Assessment

A School of Fish

Some fish travel in large groups called schools. Swimming in schools helps keep fish safe.

375 fish are swimming in a school. First, 47 fish swim away. Then 116 more fish join the school. How many fish are in the school now?

2. **Reasoning** Which operations will you use to find how many fish are in the school now? Explain.

3. **Generalize** Are there now more or less than 375 fish in the school? Explain how you know.

4. **Make Sense** How many fish are in the school now? Show your work.

Copyright © Savvas Learning Company LLC. All Rights Reserved.

Name _____

TOPIC 11 **Fluency Practice Activity**

Color a path from **Start** to **Finish**. Follow the sums and differences that are even numbers. You can only move up, down, right, or left.

I can ...
add and subtract within 20.

Start

6 + 6	10 + 8	16 − 8	9 − 0	14 − 4	6 − 2	10 + 10	8 − 3	2 + 7
5 + 4	9 − 4	11 − 9	10 + 5	13 − 5	2 − 1	7 + 9	10 − 9	10 + 9
15 − 8	3 + 10	5 + 1	9 + 8	6 + 8	12 − 5	7 + 7	16 − 9	13 − 8
12 − 9	14 − 7	14 − 6	16 − 7	9 + 9	5 + 6	8 − 6	2 + 5	4 + 7
8 + 9	9 + 6	7 + 5	12 − 8	1 + 7	18 − 9	6 − 0	17 − 9	15 − 7

Finish

TOPIC 11 Vocabulary Review

A-Z Glossary

Word List
- bar diagram
- difference
- hundreds
- mental math
- open number line
- regroup

Understand Vocabulary

Draw a line from each term to its example.

1. hundreds
2. bar diagram
3. regroup

63 = 5 tens and 13 ones

823

---

4. This open number line is incomplete. It needs to show counting back to find 538 − 115. Write in the missing numbers and labels.

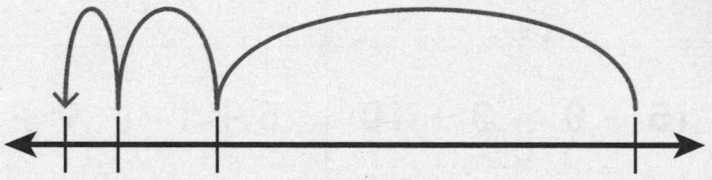

Use Vocabulary in Writing

5. Find 205 − 121. Use terms from the Word List to explain your work.

$$\begin{array}{r} 205 \\ -\ 121 \\ \hline \end{array}$$

Copyright © Savvas Learning Company LLC. All Rights Reserved.

Name _____

TOPIC 11

Reteaching

Set A

You can subtract 10 or 100 mentally.

549 − 10 = ?

The tens digit goes down by 1.

549 − 10 = 539

549 − 100 = ?

The hundreds digit goes down by 1.

549 − 100 = 449

Subtract using mental math.

1. 426 − 10 = _____

   426 − 100 = _____

2. 287 − 10 = _____

   287 − 100 = _____

3. 800 − 10 = _____

   800 − 100 = _____

Set B

Find 673 − 458. Start at 458 on an open number line. Add up to 673.

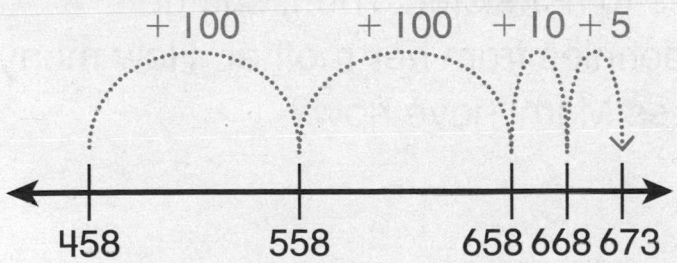

Add 100 + 100 + 10 + 5 = 215

So, 673 − 458 = 215.

Use an open number line to subtract.

4. 449 − 217 = _____

5. 903 − 678 = _____

Set C

You can draw place-value blocks to show subtraction. Find 327 − 219.

	Hundreds	Tens	Ones
		1	17
	3	~~2~~	~~7~~
−	2	1	9
	1	0	8

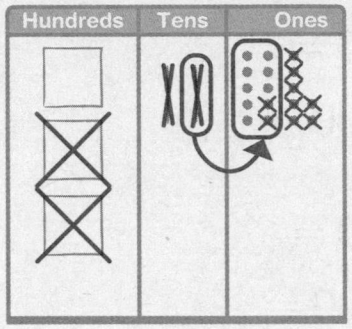

Subtract. Draw models and regroup if needed.

6.

	Hundreds	Tens	Ones
	6	5	3
−	4	2	7

Hundreds	Tens	Ones

Set D

Thinking Habits

Persevere

What do I know?

What do I need to find?

How can I check that my solution makes sense?

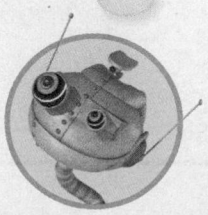

Solve the problem.
Ask yourself questions to help.

7. Marni has 354 pennies. First, she gives 149 pennies to her sister. Then, she gets 210 more pennies from her mother. How many pennies does Marni have now?

Copyright © Savvas Learning Company LLC. All Rights Reserved.

Name _____

TOPIC 11 Assessment

1. Which equals 100 less than 763? Choose all that apply.

- ☐ 663
- ☐ 600 + 60 + 3
- ☐ 863
- ☐ 800 + 60 + 3

2. The open number line below shows subtraction.

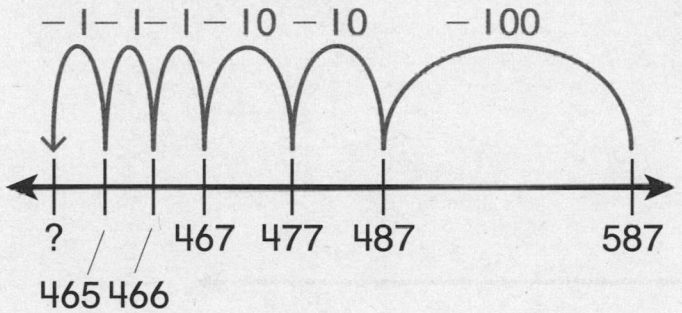

Complete the equation. Write the numbers being subtracted and the difference.

_____ – _____ = _____

3. Is the difference equal to 462? Choose Yes or No. Use different strategies to subtract.

998 – 536 = ?	○ Yes	○ No
842 – 380 = ?	○ Yes	○ No
687 – 125 = ?	○ Yes	○ No
924 – 462 = ?	○ Yes	○ No

4. There are 537 boys and 438 girls at the concert. How many more boys than girls are at the concert?

Ⓐ 89
Ⓑ 99
Ⓒ 101
Ⓓ 109

5. Show how to add up on an open number line to find 740 – 490. Then write the difference below.

740 – 490 = _____

6. Look at your work in Item 5. Why can you use adding up on an open number line to find 740 – 490? Choose all that apply.

- ☐ You can always add up to subtract on an open number line.
- ☐ You can't always add up to subtract on an open number line.
- ☐ An open number line helps you break apart numbers to subtract.
- ☐ An open number line should be used for any type of problem.

7. Use the numbers on the cards to find the missing numbers in the subtraction problem. Use the place-value models to help. Write the missing numbers.

7	6	1	2

	Hundreds	Tens	Ones
	☐	☐	14
	3	~~7~~	~~4~~
–	1	5	7

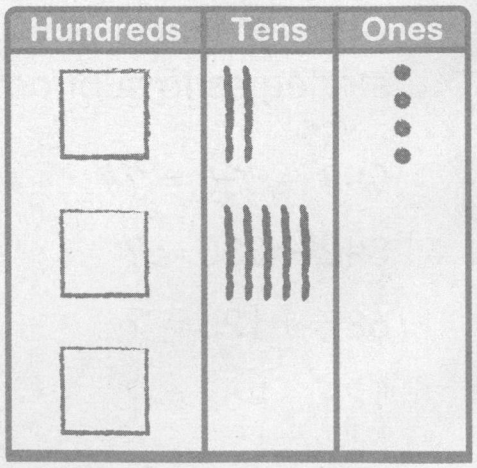

Copyright © Savvas Learning Company LLC. All Rights Reserved.

Name _____

TOPIC 11 Performance Assessment

Bead It!

The chart shows the number of beads sold at Betty's craft store for 4 weeks.

Number of Beads Sold	
Week 1	400
Week 2	536
Week 3	675
Week 4	289

1. How many more beads did Betty sell in Week 2 than in Week 1? Use mental math to solve. Write the missing numbers in the equation.

_____ − _____ = _____

_____ more beads

2. 458 glass beads were sold in Week 3. The other beads sold in Week 3 were plastic. How many plastic beads were sold in Week 3?

Use the open number line to solve.

_____ _____ = _____

Explain how you solved the problem. Tell how you know your answer is correct.

3. Dex buys 243 beads at Betty's store. He uses 118 of them to make a bracelet. How many beads does Dex have left?

Solve the problem. Show your work. Explain which strategy you used.

_____ – _____ = _____

_____ beads

4. Ginny buys 958 beads. 245 beads are blue. 309 beads are orange. 153 beads are white. The rest are red. How many red beads does Ginny buy?

Part A

What is the hidden question in the problem?

_____

_____

Part B

Solve the problem. Show your work. Explain which strategy you used.

_____ red beads

Copyright © Savvas Learning Company LLC. All Rights Reserved.

TOPIC 12

Measuring Length

Essential Question: What are ways to measure length?

Digital Resources

Solve Learn Glossary

Tools Assessment Help Games

Math and Science Project: Growing and Measuring

Find Out Grow bean plants. Give them numbers. Put some in sunlight. Put some in a dark place. Water some of the plants. Do not water some of the plants. See how the plants in each group grow.

Journal: Make a Book Show what you learn in a book. In your book, also:

- Tell if plants need sunlight and water to grow.
- Find plants to measure. Draw pictures of the plants. Tell how tall each plant is.

Name _____

Review What You Know

Vocabulary

1. Draw a line to show the **length** of the bat.

2. School is getting out. Circle **a.m.** or **p.m.**

a.m.

p.m.

3. Draw clock hands to show **quarter past** 10.

Estimating and Measuring Length

4. Use snap cubes.

Estimate the length.

about _____ cubes

Measure the length.

about _____ cubes

5.

Estimate the length.

about _____ cubes

Measure the length.

about _____ cubes

Skip Counting

6. Write the missing numbers.

5, 10, _____, 20, _____

210, 220, _____, 240

400, _____, 600, 700

Copyright © Savvas Learning Company LLC. All Rights Reserved.

My Word Cards

Study the words on the front of the card.
Complete the activity on the back.

A-Z Glossary

estimate

inch (in.)

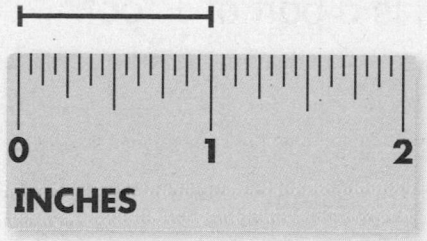

foot (ft)

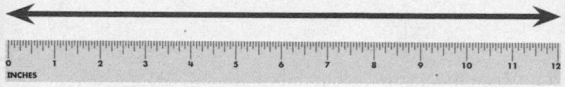

yard (yd)

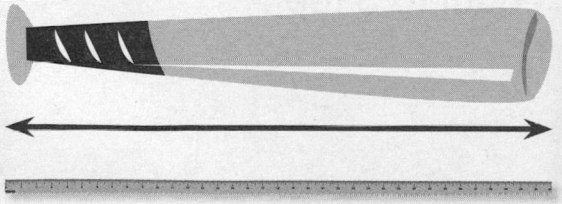

length

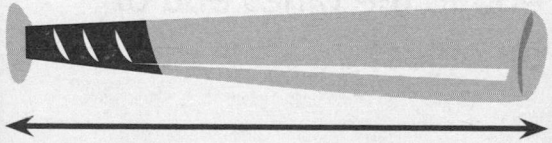

distance across

height

My Word Cards

Use what you know to complete the sentences.
Extend learning by writing your own sentence using each word.

A _____

is a standard unit of length equal to 12 inches.

An _____

is a standard unit of length that is a part of 1 foot.

When you

_____,

you make a good guess.

_____

is how tall an object is from bottom to top.

_____

is the distance from one end to the other end of an object.

A _____

is a standard unit of length equal to 3 feet.

Copyright © Savvas Learning Company LLC. All Rights Reserved.

My Word Cards

Study the words on the front of the card.
Complete the activity on the back.

A-Z Glossary

nearest inch

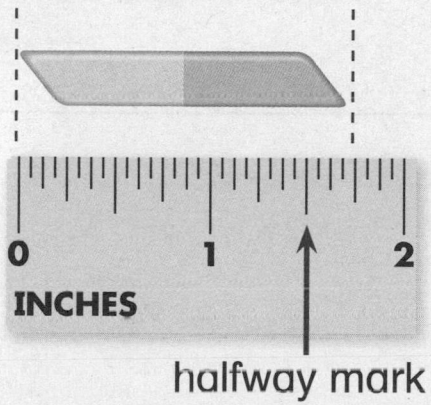

centimeter (cm)

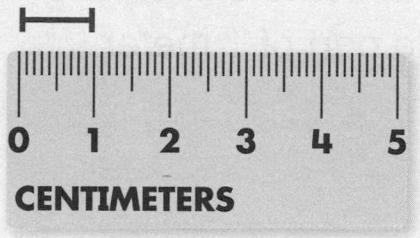

meter (m)

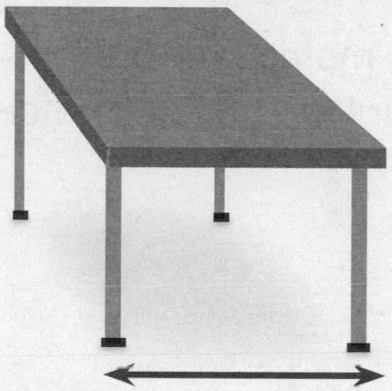

nearest centimeter

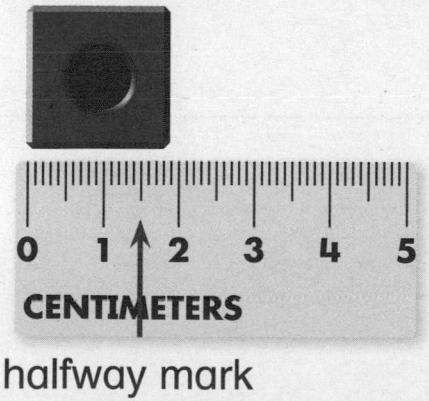

My Word Cards

Use what you know to complete the sentences.
Extend learning by writing your own sentence using each word.

A _____

is a metric unit of length equal to 100 centimeters.

A _____

is a metric unit of length that is a part of 1 meter.

The inch closest to the measure is the

_____.

The closest centimeter to the measure is the

_____.

Copyright © Savvas Learning Company LLC. All Rights Reserved.

Name _____

Solve

Lesson 12-1
Estimating Length

I can ...
estimate the length of an object by relating the length of the object to a measurement I know.

SOL 2.8a

Solve & Share

Your thumb is about 1 inch long. Use your thumb to find three objects that are each about 1 inch long. Draw the objects.

From your elbow to your fingers is about 1 foot long. Use this part of your arm to find three objects that are each about 1 foot long. Draw the objects.

about 1 inch	about 1 foot

Digital Resources at SavvasRealize.com

You can use the length of objects you know to **estimate** the length of other objects.

Use a small paperclip to estimate how long the eraser is.

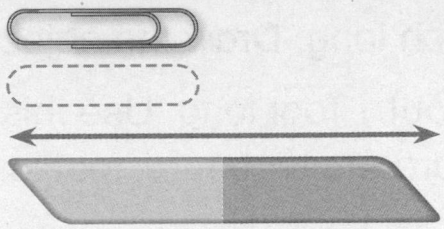

The eraser is about 2 paper clips long. So, it is about 2 inches long.

Do You Understand?

Show Me! Is your height closer to 4 feet or 4 yards? How do you know?

☆ Guided Practice ☆

Write the name and length of an object whose length you know. Then use that object to help you estimate the length of the object shown.

Object	Object Whose Length I Know	Estimate
1. 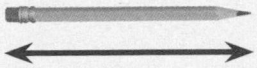	My paper clip is 1 inch long.	My pencil is about _____ long.
2. 	My book is _____ long.	My desk is about _____ long.

Copyright © Savvas Learning Company LLC. All Rights Reserved.

Name _____

Tools Assessment

Independent Practice

Write the name and length of an object whose length you know. Then use that object to help you estimate the length of the object shown.

Object	Object Whose Length I Know	Estimate
3. 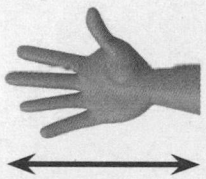	My _____ is _____ long.	My hand is about _____ long.
4. 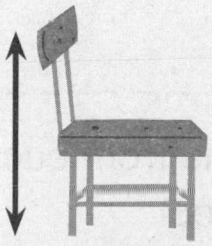	My _____ is _____ long.	My chair is about _____ high.

5. **Higher Order Thinking** Would you estimate the distance from your classroom to the principal's office in inches, feet or yards? Explain.

_____

_____

_____

_____

_____

Problem Solving Solve each problem.

6. **Vocabulary** Complete the sentence using one of the words below.

exact **estimated** **inch**

An _____ measurement is a good guess.

7. **Reasoning** Joy and Kyle estimate the height of their classroom. Joy estimates the height to be 10 feet. Kyle estimates the height to be 10 yards. Who has the better estimate? Explain.

_____

_____

_____

_____

8. **Higher Order Thinking** A city wants to build a bridge over a river. Should they plan out an exact length of the bridge or is an estimated length good enough? Explain.

_____

_____

_____

_____

_____

9. **Assessment** Draw a line from each estimate to a matching object.

About 1 inch	About 1 foot	About 3 feet

Copyright © Savvas Learning Company LLC. All Rights Reserved.

Name _____

Help Tools Games

Homework & Practice 12-1 Estimating Length

HOME ACTIVITY Have your child identify three objects that are about 1 inch, 1 foot, and 1 yard in length or height.

Another Look!

A small paper clip is about 1 inch long.

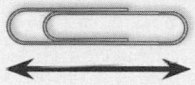

about 1 inch

A tablet computer is about 1 foot long. There are 12 inches in 1 foot.

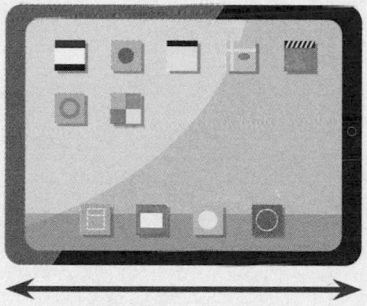

about 1 foot

A scarf is about 1 yard long. There are 3 feet in 1 yard.

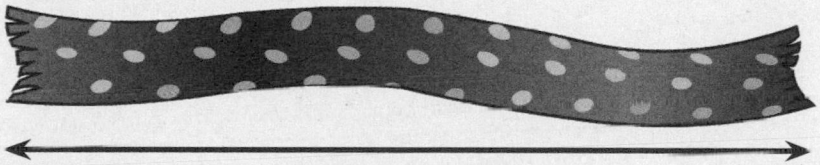

about 1 yard

About how long or tall is each object? Circle the answer.

1. 

about 1 inch

about 1 foot

about 1 yard

2. 

about 1 inch

about 1 foot

about 1 yard

3. 

about 1 inch

about 1 foot

about 1 yard

Reasoning Choose three objects and estimate their length or height in inches, feet, or yards. Draw a picture and write the name of each object. Write the estimated length or height next to each object.

4.

5.

6.

7. **Higher Order Thinking** Mia has 4 tiles. Jake has 5 tiles. Each tile is about 1 inch long. They use all of their tiles to measure the height of this water bottle. What is the height of the water bottle?

About _____ inches

8. **Assessment** Draw a line from each estimate to a matching object.

About 1 inch	About 1 foot	About 3 feet

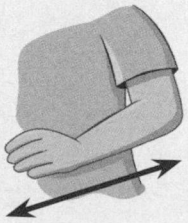

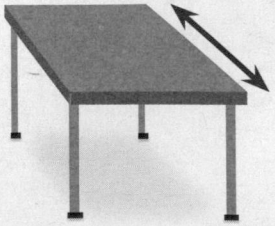

Copyright © Savvas Learning Company LLC. All Rights Reserved.

Name _____

Solve

Lesson 12-2

Measure with Inches

I can ...

estimate measures and use a ruler to measure length and height to the nearest inch.

SOL 2.8a

Solve & Share

The orange square is 1 inch long. How can you use 1 inch squares to find the length of the line in inches? Measure the line and explain.

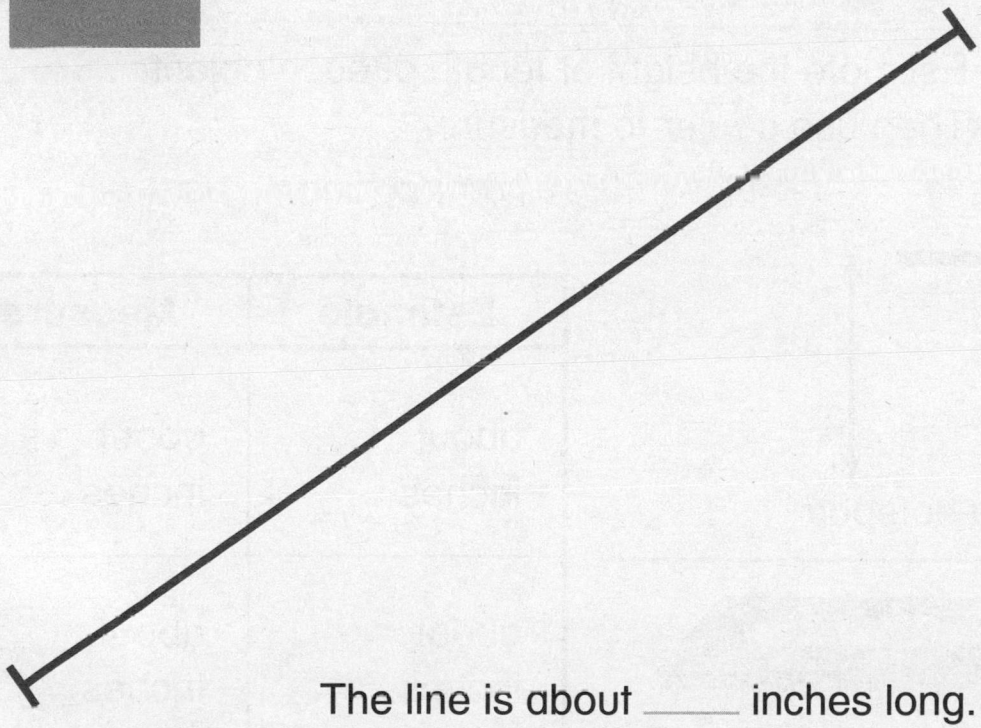

The line is about _____ inches long.

Digital Resources at SavvasRealize.com

You can measure the length and **height** of an object in inches (in.).

To measure to the **nearest inch**, look for the halfway mark.

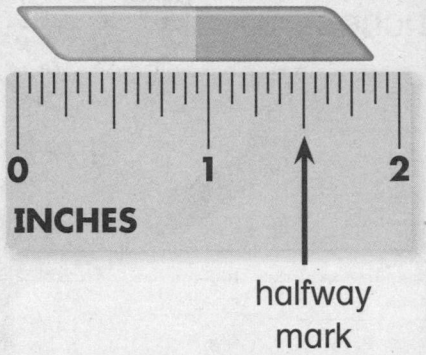

If the object is longer than the halfway mark, use the greater number.

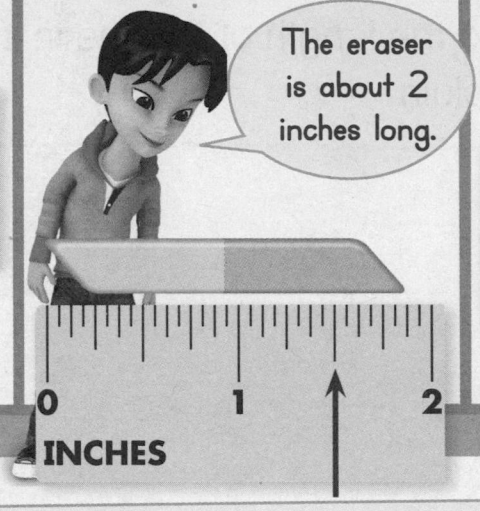

If the object is shorter than the halfway mark, use the smaller number.

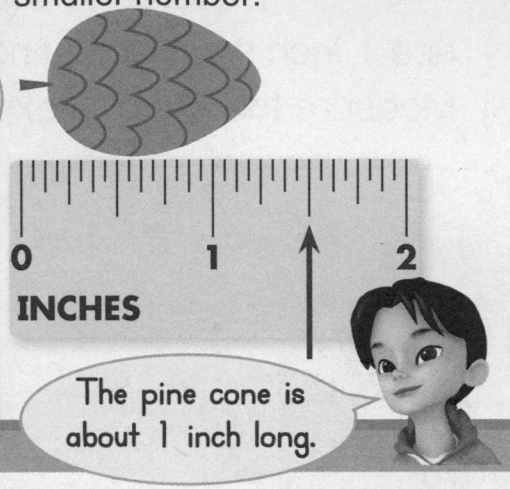

Do You Understand?

Show Me! Use a ruler to measure. What classroom objects are about 12 inches long?

Guided Practice

Estimate the height or length of each object. Then use a ruler to measure.

1.

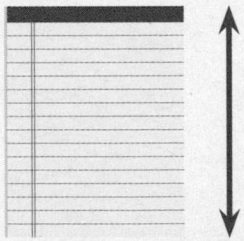

height of a notepad

2.

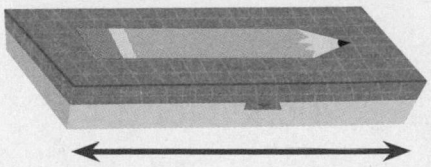

length of a pencil case

Estimate	Measure
about 12 inches	about 11 inches
about ____ inches	about ____ inches

Copyright © Savvas Learning Company LLC. All Rights Reserved.

Name _____

Tools Assessment

Independent Practice

Estimate the height or length of each object. Then use a ruler to measure.

3. 

length of a book bag

Estimate	Measure
about ____ inches	about ____ inches

4. 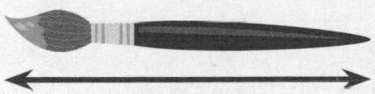

length of a paintbrush

Estimate	Measure
about ____ inches	about ____ inches

5. 

height of a cup

Estimate	Measure
about ____ inches	about ____ inches

6. 

length of a crayon box

Estimate	Measure
about ____ inches	about ____ inches

Higher Order Thinking Think about how to use a ruler to solve each problem.

7. Jason measures an object. The object is just shorter than the halfway mark between 8 and 9 on his inch ruler. How long is the object?

about _____ inches

8. Gina measures an object. The object is just longer than the halfway mark between 9 and 10 on her inch ruler. How long is the object?

about _____ inches

Problem Solving Solve each problem.

9. **Explain** Pam says that each cherry is about 1 inch wide. Is she correct? Explain.

10. **Vocabulary** Find an object in the classroom that measures about 6 inches. Write a sentence to describe the object. Use these words.

estimate **inches**

11. **Higher Order Thinking** Explain how to use an inch ruler to measure the length of an object.

12. **Assessment** Use a ruler. About how many inches long are the two stamps together?

Ⓐ 4 inches Ⓒ 2 inches

Ⓑ 3 inches Ⓓ 1 inch

Copyright © Savvas Learning Company LLC. All Rights Reserved.

Name _____

Help Tools Games

Homework & Practice 12-2

Measure with Inches

HOME ACTIVITY Ask your child to find items at home that are about 1 inch, about 6 inches, and about 12 inches long.

Another Look! You can use a ruler to measure inches.

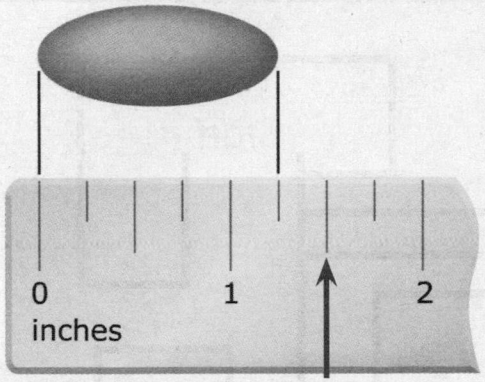

This bead is about 1 inch long.

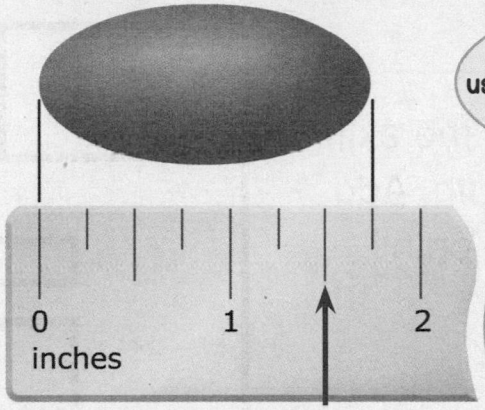

This bead is about 2 inches long.

Estimate the height or length. Then use a ruler to measure.

1. height of a book

2. length of a pencil

Estimate	Measure
about ____ inches	about ____ inches
about ____ inches	about ____ inches

3. **Number Sense** Estimate how long the path is to get out of this maze.

about _____ inches

4. **Make Sense** Draw a path from the start to the exit. Use a ruler to measure each part of your path. Add the lengths together. About how long is the path?

about _____ inches

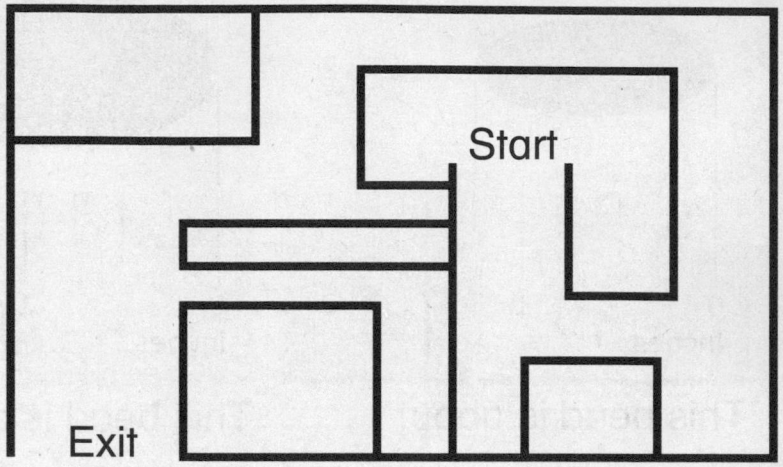

5. How close to the answer was your estimate?

_____

6. **Higher Order Thinking** Gina says this straw is about 2 inches long. Sal says it is about 3 inches long. Who is correct? Explain.

_____

_____

_____

_____

7. **Assessment** Use a ruler. Measure the length of the pencil in inches. Which is the correct measurement?

Ⓐ about 2 inches

Ⓑ about 3 inches

Ⓒ about 4 inches

Ⓓ about 5 inches

Copyright © Savvas Learning Company LLC. All Rights Reserved.

Name _____

Solve

Lesson 12-3
Inches, Feet, and Yards

I can ...
estimate measures and use tools to measure the length and height of objects to the nearest inch, foot, and yard.

SOL 2.8a

Solve & Share

Which objects in the classroom are about 1 inch, about 1 foot, and about 1 yard long? Show these objects below.

about 1 inch

about 1 foot

about 1 yard

Digital Resources at SavvasRealize.com

You can use a ruler to measure length.

The paper clip is about 1 inch (in.).

The book is about 1 foot (ft).

1 foot is 12 inches long.

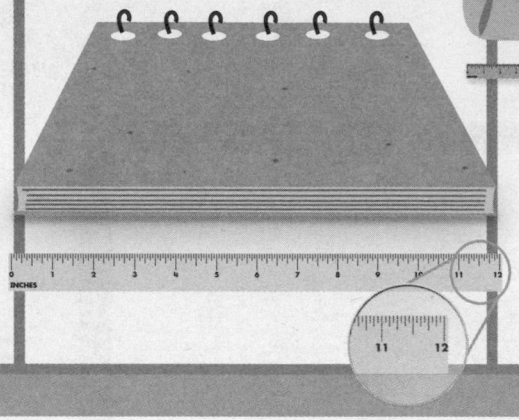

You can use a yardstick to measure length, too!

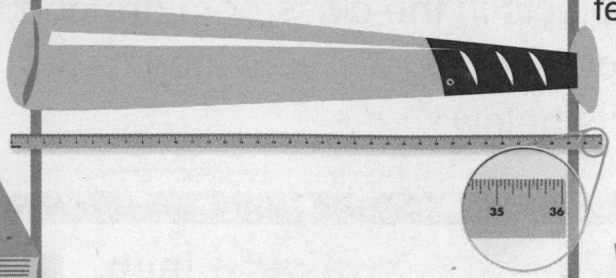

The bat is about 1 yard (yd).

A yardstick is 3 feet or 36 inches long.

You can use a measuring tape to measure inches, feet, or yards.

Do You Understand?

Show Me! Would you measure the length of a school building in inches or yards? Why?

Guided Practice

Match each object with a reasonable estimate of its length.

1. 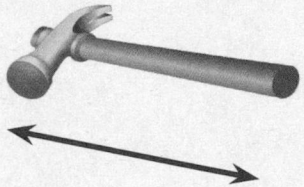 about 1 yard

2.  about 1 inch

3.  about 1 foot

Copyright © Savvas Learning Company LLC. All Rights Reserved.

Name _____

Tools Assessment

Independent Practice

Estimate the length of each object. Choose a ruler, yardstick, or measuring tape to measure. Write the tool you used.

	Estimate	Measure	Tool
4. 	about _____ inches	about _____ inches	_____
5. 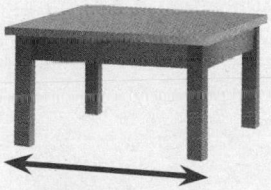	about _____ feet	about _____ feet	_____
6. 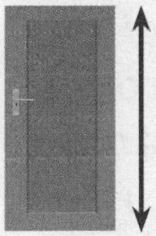	about _____ yards	about _____ yards	_____

7. **Higher Order Thinking** Explain how you could use a foot ruler to measure the length of a room in feet.

_____

_____

_____

_____

Problem Solving Solve each problem.

8. **Generalize** Circle the real object that is about 4 feet in length.

9. **Number Sense** Explain how to use a yardstick to measure the length of an object.

10. **Higher Order Thinking** Find an object in the classroom that you estimate measures about 2 feet. Draw the object.

What tool would you use to measure it? Explain why you chose the tool you did.

11. **Assessment** Jon sets two of the same real objects next to each other. Together, they have a length of about 4 feet. Which is the object Jon uses?

Ⓐ 

Ⓒ 

Ⓑ 

Ⓓ 

Copyright © Savvas Learning Company LLC. All Rights Reserved.

Name _____

Help Tools Games

Homework & Practice 12-3

Inches, Feet, and Yards

HOME ACTIVITY Have your child identify three objects at home that are about 1 inch, 1 foot, and 1 yard in length.

Another Look! You can use a yardstick to measure objects to the nearest foot.

Remember, 1 foot is 12 inches long.
So 2 feet are 24 inches long.
1 yard is 36 inches long
or 3 feet long.

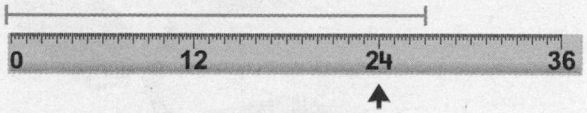

This string is about
2 feet long.

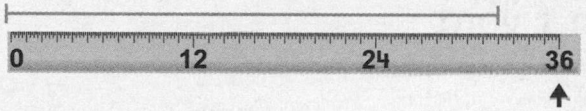

This string is about
3 feet long.

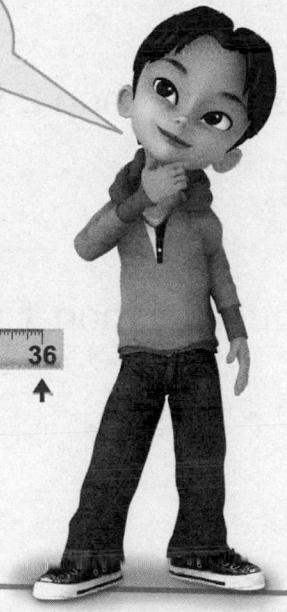

Estimate the height or length of each object. Then measure.

1. the height of the doorway
   Estimate: about _____ feet
   Measure: about _____ feet

2. the height of a chair
   Estimate: about _____ feet
   Measure: about _____ feet

3. the width of a window
   Estimate: about _____ feet
   Measure: about _____ feet

4. **Reasoning** Draw a picture of and name objects that have these lengths.

more than 6 inches but less than 1 foot

more than 1 foot but less than 2 feet

more than 2 feet but less than 1 yard

5. **Math and Science** Jay planted sunflowers in a sunny spot. He gave them water and watched them grow to be taller than he is. He measured the heights of the plants when they were full-grown. Were they 8 inches or 8 feet tall? Explain.

_____

_____

_____

_____

6. **Higher Order Thinking** Which tool would you choose to measure the number of inches around your waist? Explain.

_____

_____

_____

_____

_____

7. **Assessment** Use a ruler. About how long is the crayon?

Ⓐ about 1 inch

Ⓑ about 2 inches

Ⓒ about 4 inches

Ⓓ about 6 inches

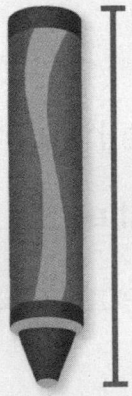

Copyright © Savvas Learning Company LLC. All Rights Reserved.

Name _____

Solve

Lesson 12-4

Measure Length Using Different Customary Units

I can ...

estimate and measure the length and height of objects in inches, feet, and yards.

SOL 2.8a

Solve & Share

Choose an object. Measure your object in feet. Then measure it in inches.

Do you need more feet or more inches to measure your object? Why?

about ____ feet long

about ____ inches long

more feet more inches

Do You Understand?

Show Me! Would you use a ruler, a yardstick, or measuring tape to measure the height of a door? Why?

Guided Practice

Measure each object using different units. Circle the unit you use more of to measure each object.

1. 

about _____ feet about _____ yards

more feet

more yards

2. 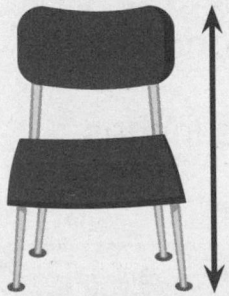

about _____ inches about _____ feet

more inches

more feet

Copyright © Savvas Learning Company LLC. All Rights Reserved.

Name _____

Tools Assessment

Independent Practice

Measure each object using different units.
Circle the unit you use fewer of to measure each object.

3. 

about _____ inches about _____ feet

fewer inches

fewer feet

4. 

about _____ feet about _____ yards

fewer feet

fewer yards

5. 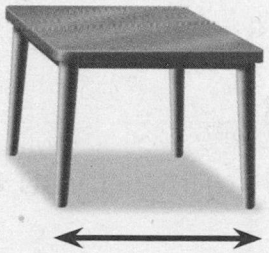

about _____ feet

about _____ yards

fewer feet

fewer yards

Number Sense

Circle the best estimate for the length of each object.

6. About how long is a key?

2 inches 2 feet 2 yards

Which tool would you use to measure the length of a key?

_____

7. About how long is a suitcase?

2 inches 2 feet 2 yards

Which tool would you use to measure the length of a suitcase?

_____

Problem Solving Solve each problem.

8. **Use Tools** Measure the length of an object in your classroom using two different units.

Object: _____

about _____ about _____

Which unit did you use more of? _____

Circle which tool you used.

ruler yardstick measuring tape

9. **Higher Order Thinking** Andrew wants to measure the length of a football field. Should he use feet or yards to measure it? Explain.

_____

_____

_____

_____

10. **Assessment** Which unit would you need fewest of to measure the length of the table?

Ⓐ inches Ⓒ yards

Ⓑ feet Ⓓ all the same

11. **Assessment** Which is the best estimate for the length of a vegetable garden?

Ⓐ about 1 inch Ⓒ about 5 yards

Ⓑ about 1 foot Ⓓ about 20 inches

Copyright © Savvas Learning Company LLC. All Rights Reserved.

Name _____

Help Tools Games

Homework & Practice 12-4

Measure Length Using Different Customary Units

Another Look! You can measure using different units.

Derrick measured the gift box in inches and in feet.

The gift box is about ____ inches long.

The gift box is about ____ foot long.

It takes more inches than feet to measure the gift box because an inch is a smaller unit.
If you use smaller units, you need to use more units.

HOME ACTIVITY Have your child use a foot ruler to measure objects in both inches and in feet. Then ask your child if he or she used more inches or more feet to measure each object.

Measure each object using different units.
Circle the unit you need more of to measure each object.

1. 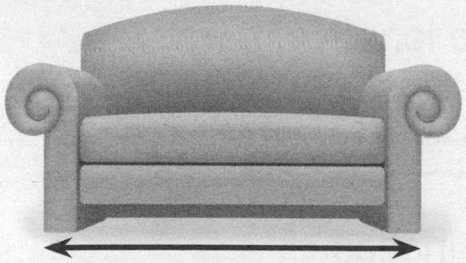

about ____ feet about ____ yards

more feet

more yards

2. 

about ____ inches about ____ feet

more inches

more feet

3. **Explain** Trina says that her dollhouse is about 8 yards tall. Is Trina's estimate a good estimate? Explain.

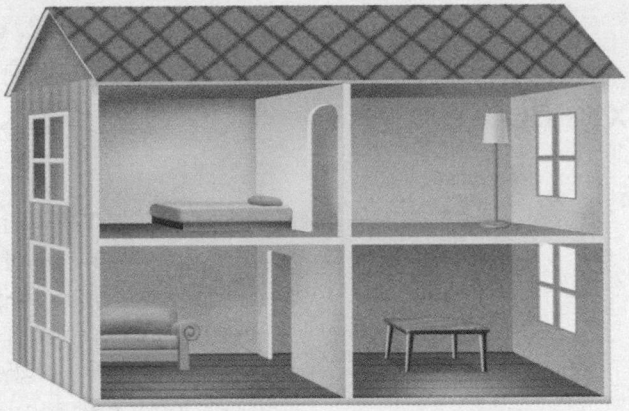

4. **Higher Order Thinking** Sarah wants to measure the length of her math book. Should she use inches, feet, or yards? Explain.

5. **Assessment** Which unit would you need the most of to measure the height of the umbrella?

Ⓐ inches

Ⓑ feet

Ⓒ yards

Ⓓ all the same

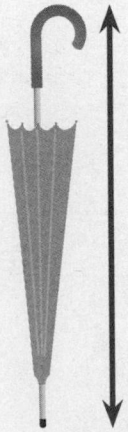

6. **Assessment** Which is the best estimate for the length of a pen?

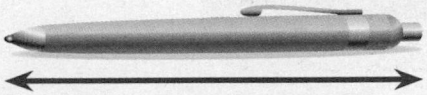

Ⓐ about 10 inches

Ⓑ about 6 inches

Ⓒ about 5 feet

Ⓓ about 10 yards

Copyright © Savvas Learning Company LLC. All Rights Reserved.

Name _____

Solve

Lesson 12-5
Measure with Centimeters

I can ...
estimate measures and use a ruler to measure length and height to the nearest centimeter.

SOL Prepares for 3.7a

Solve & Share

The green cube is 1 centimeter long. How can you use 1 centimeter cubes to find the length of the line in centimeters? Measure the line and explain.

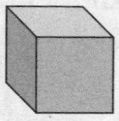

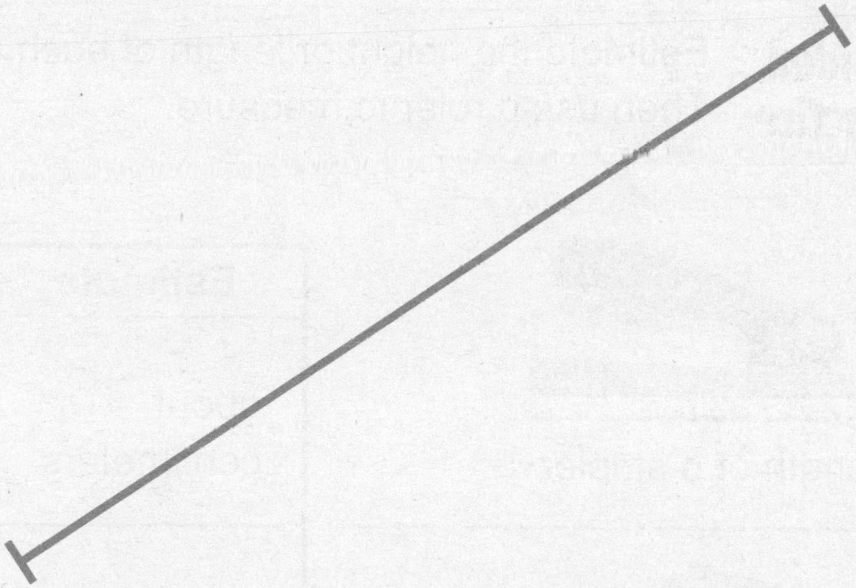

The line is _____ centimeters long.

Digital Resources at SavvasRealize.com

1 **centimeter (cm)** is smaller than 1 inch.

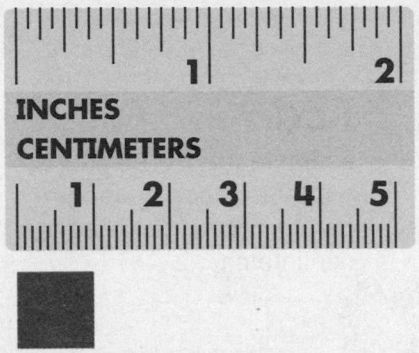

To measure to the **nearest centimeter,** look for the halfway mark.
If the object is longer than the halfway mark, use the greater number.

If the object is shorter than the halfway mark, use the smaller number.

Do You Understand?

Show Me! Explain how you know the length of the paper clip above is about 3 centimeters long.

Guided Practice

Estimate the height or length of each object. Then use a ruler to measure.

1.

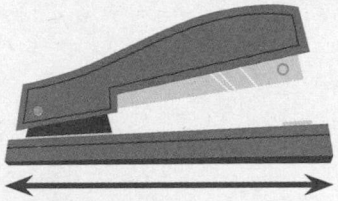

length of a stapler

2.

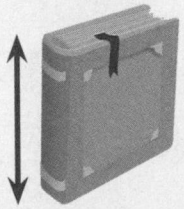

height of a book

Estimate	Measure
about 15 centimeters	about 18 centimeters
about ____ centimeters	about ____ centimeters

Copyright © Savvas Learning Company LLC. All Rights Reserved.

Name _____

Tools Assessment

Independent Practice

Estimate the width, height, or length of each real object. Then use a ruler to measure.

3. 

width of a shoelace

Estimate	Measure
about _____ centimeters	about _____ centimeters

4. 

width of a chair

Estimate	Measure
about _____ centimeters	about _____ centimeters

5. 

length of a pencil

Estimate	Measure
about _____ centimeters	about _____ centimeters

6. 

height of scissors

Estimate	Measure
about _____ centimeters	about _____ centimeters

Higher Order Thinking Explain whether each estimate is reasonable or not.

7. Josh estimated that the length of his reading book is about 6 centimeters.

_____

_____

8. Shae estimated that the height of her desk is about 10 centimeters.

_____

_____

Problem Solving Solve each problem.

9. **Vocabulary** Find an object that is about 10 centimeters long. Write a sentence to describe your object using these words.

centimeters **estimate**

_____

_____

_____

10. **Look for Patterns** Nick wants to put another pen end to end with this one. About how long would the two pens be together?

about _____ centimeters

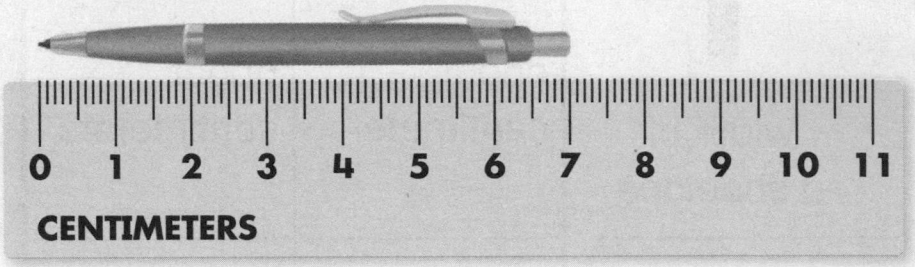

11. **Higher Order Thinking** Paul says that a toothbrush is about 19 centimeters long. Sarah says it is about 50 centimeters long. Who is correct? Explain.

_____

_____

_____

12. **Assessment** Mary measures the length of her eraser to the nearest centimeter. What is the length of her eraser to the nearest centimeter?

_____ centimeters

Copyright © Savvas Learning Company LLC. All Rights Reserved.

Name _____

Help Tools Games

Homework & Practice 12-5

Measure with Centimeters

Another Look! You can use a ruler to measure centimeters.

To measure to the nearest centimeter, look at the halfway mark between centimeters. If the object is longer, use the greater number. If the object is shorter, use the smaller number.

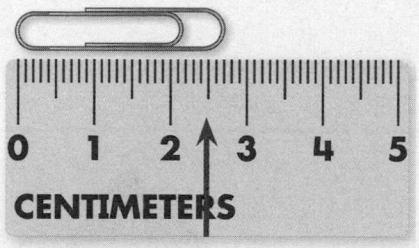

The paper clip is about 3 centimeters long.

This pencil is about 9 centimeters long.

HOME ACTIVITY Ask your child to find items at home that measure about 1 centimeter, about 10 centimeters, and about 100 centimeters. If possible, use a ruler to measure each object.

Estimate the height or length. Then use a ruler to measure.

1. length of a tape dispenser

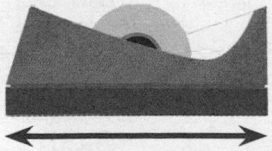

2. height of a book

Estimate	Measure
about _____ centimeters	about _____ centimeters
about _____ centimeters	about _____ centimeters

3. **Use Tools** Measure the length of this spoon in centimeters. About how long is the spoon?

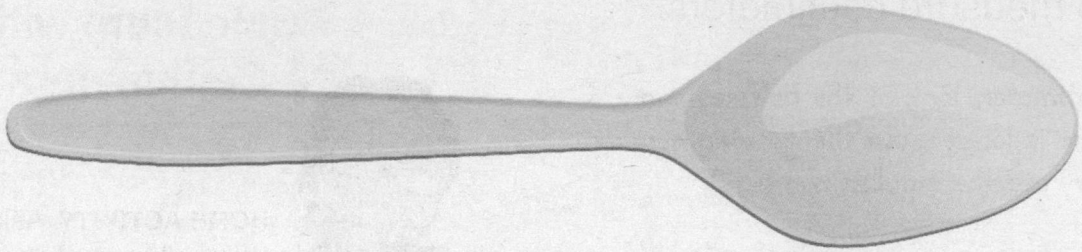

About _____ centimeters What tool did you use? _____

4. **Higher Order Thinking** Mia has a string that is shown below. Circle the shapes that Mia can make with part of her string.

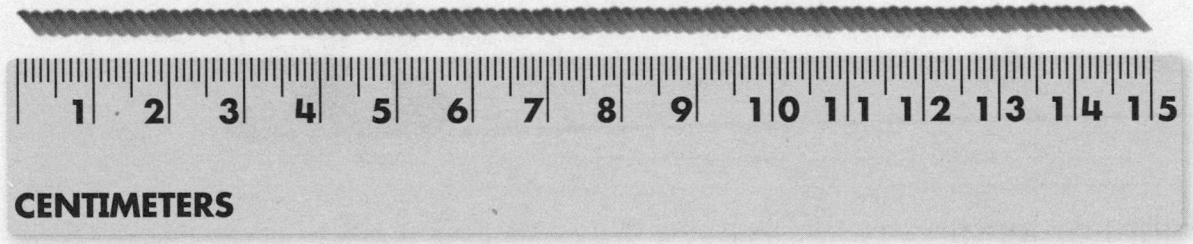

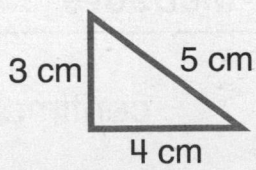

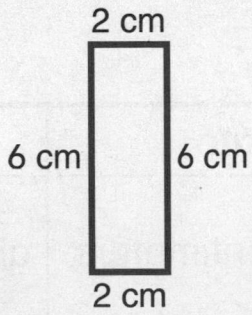

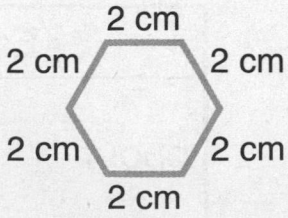

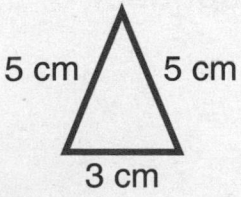

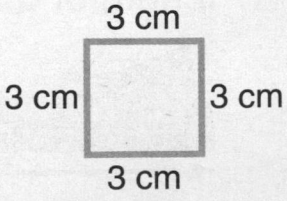

5. **Assessment** Measure this paper clip. How many centimeters long is the paper clip?

_____ centimeters

Copyright © Savvas Learning Company LLC. All Rights Reserved.

Name _____

Solve

Lesson 12-6
Centimeters and Meters

I can ...
estimate measures and use a ruler, meter stick, or tape measure to measure length and height to the nearest centimeter or meter.

SOL Prepares for 3.7a

Solve & Share

Which objects in the classroom are about 3 centimeters long?
Which objects are about 1 meter long?
Show these objects below.

about 3 centimeters

about 1 meter

Digital Resources at SavvasRealize.com

You can use a ruler or a meter stick to measure length.

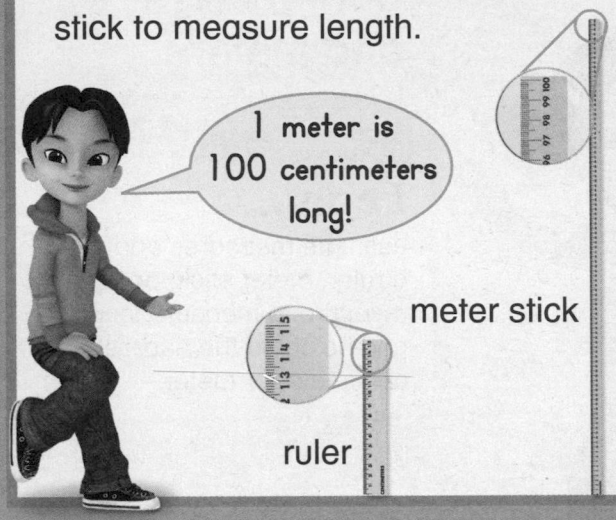

The button is about 1 centimeter (cm) long.

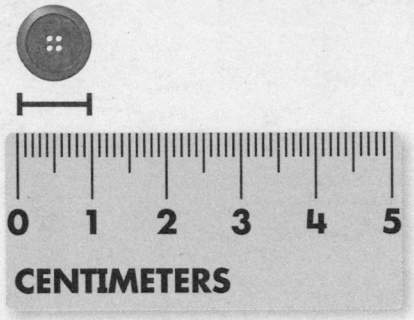

This table is about 1 meter (m) long.

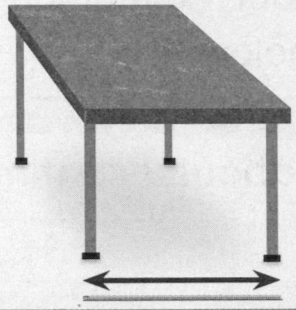

You can also use a measuring tape to measure centimeters and meters.

Do You Understand?

Show Me! Would you measure the length of a house in centimeters or meters? Why?

Guided Practice

Match each object with a reasonable estimate of its length.

1. 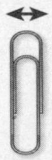 about 1 cm

2.  about 10 cm

3. 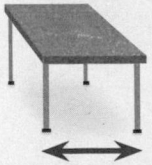 about 1 m

4.  about 10 m

Copyright © Savvas Learning Company LLC. All Rights Reserved.

Name _____

Tools Assessment

Independent Practice

Estimate the length or height of each real object shown. Then choose a tool and measure. Write the tool you used.

	Estimate	Measure	Tool
5. 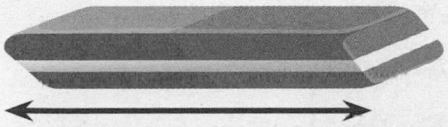	about _____ cm	about _____ cm	_____
6. 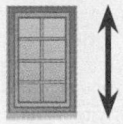	about _____ m	about _____ m	_____
7. 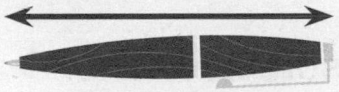	about _____ cm	about _____ cm	_____
8. 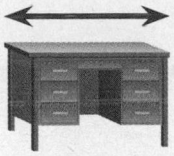	about _____ m	about _____ m	_____

9. Tom uses a meter stick to measure the length of a fence. He moves the meter stick 5 times to measure from one end to the other end. How long is the fence?

_____ meters

10. **Higher Order Thinking** Debbie says that her doll is about 30 meters long. Do you think this is a good estimate? Why or why not?

_____

_____

Problem Solving Solve each problem.

11. **Be Precise** Choose an object to measure. Use metric units. Draw the object and write your measurements.

12. Circle the real object that would be about 2 meters long.

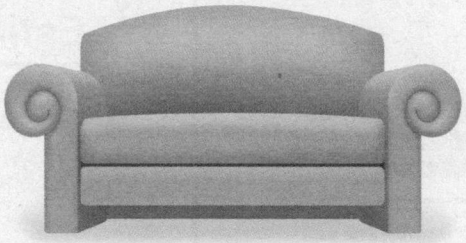

13. **Higher Order Thinking** Each side of a place-value cube is 1 centimeter long. Use a place value cube to draw a 5 centimeter ruler.

14. **Assessment** Measure each line. Which lines are at least 6 centimeters long? Choose all that apply.

- ☐ ———————————————
- ☐ ————————
- ☐ ————————
- ☐ ————————

Copyright © Savvas Learning Company LLC. All Rights Reserved.

Name _____

Help Tools Games

Homework & Practice 12-6

Centimeters and Meters

HOME ACTIVITY Have your child show you an object at home that is about a centimeter long and another object that is about a meter long.

Another Look! You can use a meter stick to measure length in meters.

Step 1: Line up a meter stick with one end of an object.

Step 2: Mark the spot where the other end of the meter stick sits on the object.

Step 3: Then move the meter stick so the 0 end starts where you marked.

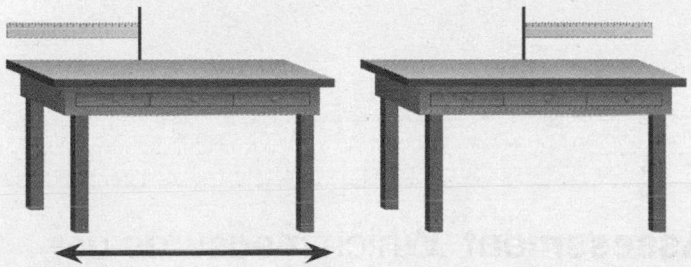

The table is about 2 meters long.

Estimate the height or length of each object. Then measure.

1. the length of a table

   Estimate:

   about _____ meters

   Measure:

   about _____ meters

2. the height of a chair

   Estimate:

   about _____ meters

   Measure:

   about _____ meters

3. the length of your room

   Estimate:

   about _____ meters

   Measure:

   about _____ meters

4. **Math and Science** Sarah put bean plants by a window with sunlight. She watered them every other day. Sarah measured the height of the plants after 3 weeks. Do you think they measured 12 centimeters or 12 meters? Explain.

_____

_____

_____

_____

5. **Reasoning** What would be a reasonable estimate for the length of a calculator?

about _____ centimeters

6. **Higher Order Thinking** Do you need fewer centimeters or fewer meters to measure the height of a doorway? Explain.

_____

_____

_____

_____

_____

_____

7. **Assessment** Which measures are reasonable estimates for the length of a bedroom? Choose all that apply.

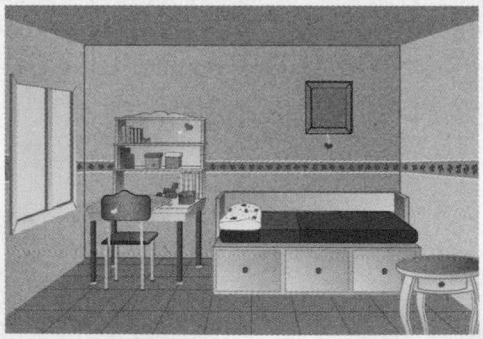

- ☐ 4 centimeters
- ☐ 3 meters
- ☐ 4 meters
- ☐ 30 centimeters

Copyright © Savvas Learning Company LLC. All Rights Reserved.

Name _____

Solve

Lesson 12-7

Measure Length Using Different Metric Units

I can ...

measure the length and height of objects using different metric units.

SOL Prepares for 3.7a

Solve & Share

Measure this pencil in inches. Then measure it again in centimeters. Which measurement has more units?

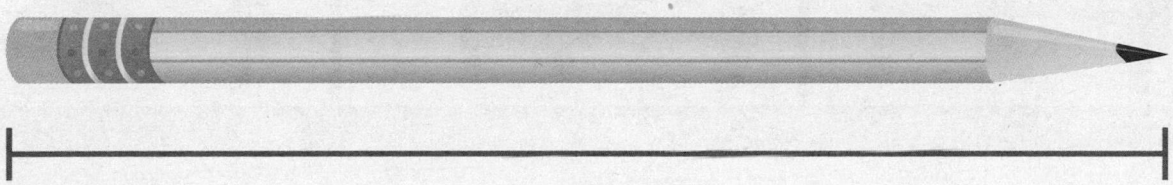

about _____ inches about _____ centimeters

Which has more units? _____

Digital Resources at SavvasRealize.com

Do You Understand?

Show Me! Would it take more centimeters or more meters to measure the height of a wall? Why?

Guided Practice

Measure each object using different units. Circle the unit you need more of to measure each object.

1. 

about _____ centimeters more centimeters

about _____ meters more meters

2. 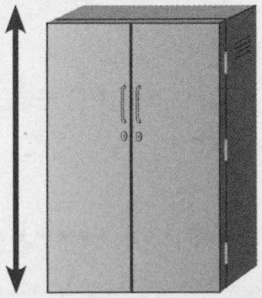

about _____ centimeters more centimeters

about _____ meters more meters

Copyright © Savvas Learning Company LLC. All Rights Reserved.

Name _____

Tools Assessment

Independent Practice

Measure each object using different units.
Circle the unit you need fewer of to measure each object.

3. 

about _____ meters

about _____ centimeters

fewer centimeters

fewer meters

4. 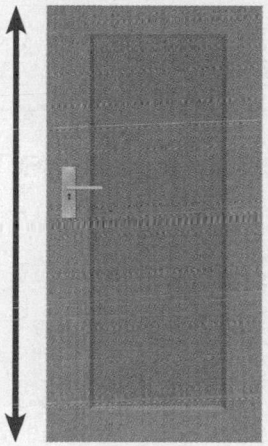

about _____ meters

about _____ centimeters

fewer centimeters

fewer meters

5. **Higher Order Thinking** Jay measured the height of his bedroom in both centimeters and meters. Did he use fewer centimeters or fewer meters? Explain.

_____

_____

_____

_____

Problem Solving Solve each problem.

6. **Explain** If you had to measure the length of the hallway outside of your classroom, would you use centimeters or meters? Explain.

7. **Higher Order Thinking** A meter stick is about 39 inches long. Is a meter longer or shorter than a yard? Explain.

8. **Assessment** Estimate the length of a baseball bat in centimeters and meters.

_____ centimeters

_____ meters

Which number must be greater? Explain.

9. **Assessment** Tina measures the length of a jump rope using different units. How will her measurements compare?

Choose Yes or No.

more meters than centimeters	○ Yes	○ No
more centimeters than inches	○ Yes	○ No
more inches than feet	○ Yes	○ No
more yards than feet	○ Yes	○ No

Copyright © Savvas Learning Company LLC. All Rights Reserved.

Name _____

Help Tools Games

Homework & Practice 12-7

Measure Length Using Different Metric Units

Another Look! You can measure using different units.

Andy measures the length of the television using both centimeters and meters.

The television is about

1 meter long.

The television is about

88 centimeters long.

It takes fewer meters than centimeters to measure the television. If you use larger units, you will use fewer of them.

HOME ACTIVITY Select two objects in your home, such as a table or a window. Ask your child if he or she would use more centimeters or meters to measure each object.

Measure each object using centimeters and meters. Circle the unit you need fewer of to measure each object.

1.

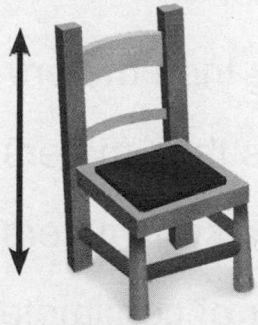

about _____ centimeters fewer centimeters

about _____ meters fewer meters

2.

about _____ centimeters fewer centimeters

about _____ meters fewer meters

3. **Make Sense** Circle the objects that are easier to measure using centimeters. Cross out the objects that are easier to measure using meters.

4. **Higher Order Thinking** Shane and Karen want to measure the length of a soccer field.
Should they use centimeters or meters to measure it? Explain.

_____

_____

_____

_____

5. **Assessment** Carlos measures the length of a couch in centimeters and meters. How will his measurements compare?

Choose Yes or No.

more centimeters than meters	○ Yes	○ No
fewer centimeters than meters	○ Yes	○ No
fewer meters than centimeters	○ Yes	○ No
the same number of centimeters and meters	○ Yes	○ No

Copyright © Savvas Learning Company LLC. All Rights Reserved.

Name _____

Solve & Share

Circle two paths. Estimate which one is longer. How can you check if your estimate is correct?

Solve

Lesson 12-8

Compare Lengths

I can ...

tell how much longer one object is than another.

SOL Prepares for 3.7a

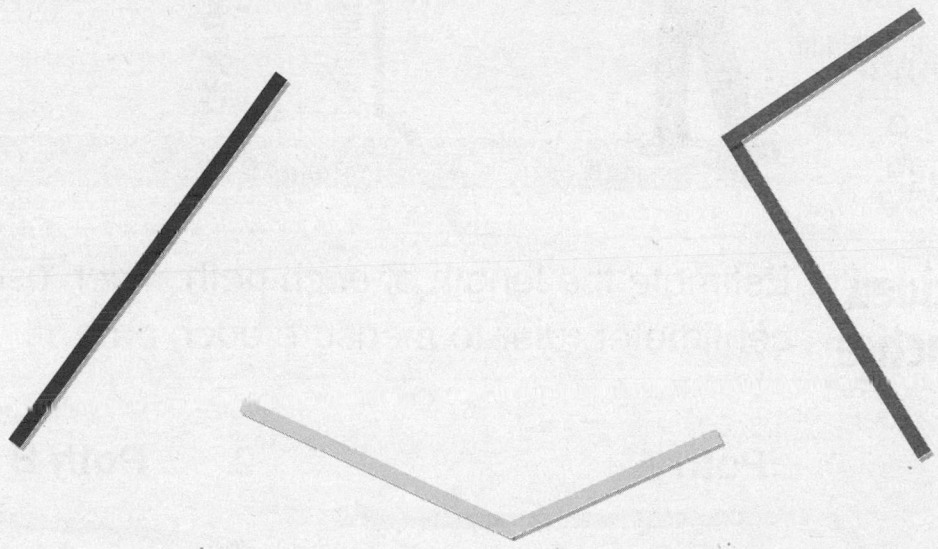

Estimate: The _____ path is longer.

Measure: The _____ path is longer.

Which path is longer?
How much longer?

Think about both parts of the path when you estimate and measure.

Estimate: 5 cm

Estimate: 6 cm

One part of the blue path is about 2 cm. The other part is about 2 cm. Add to find the length.

$2 + 2 = 4$
The blue path is about 4 cm long.

0 1 2 3 4
CENTIMETERS

One part of the red path is about 1 cm. The other part is about 4 cm. Add to find the length.

$1 + 4 = 5$
The red path is about 5 cm long.

0 1 2 3 4
CENTIMETERS

Subtract to compare lengths.
$5 - 4 = 1$

The red path is about 1 cm longer than the blue path.

Do You Understand?

Show Me! How can you find the length of a path that is not straight?

Guided Practice

Estimate the length of each path. Then use a centimeter ruler to measure each path.

1. Path A

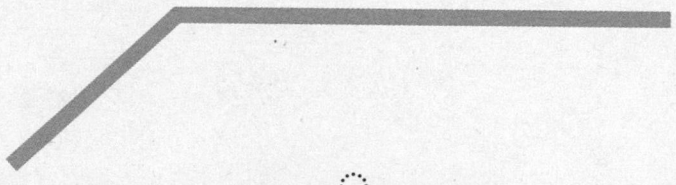

Estimate: about 9 cm

Measure: about 10 cm

2. Path B

Estimate: about _____ cm

Measure: about _____ cm

3. Which path is longer?

_____

4. How much longer?

about _____ cm longer

Copyright © Savvas Learning Company LLC. All Rights Reserved.

Name _____

Tools Assessment

Independent Practice

Estimate the length of each path.
Then use a centimeter ruler to measure each path.

5. **Path C**

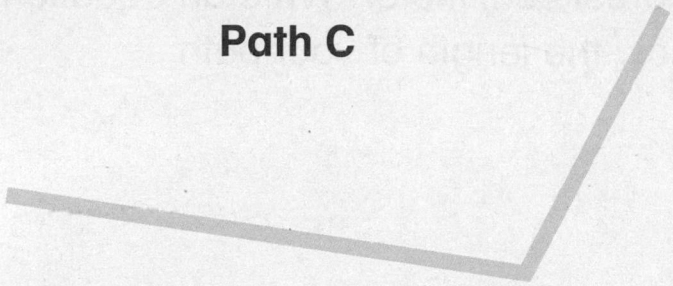

Estimate: about _____ centimeters

Measure: about _____ centimeters

6. **Path D**

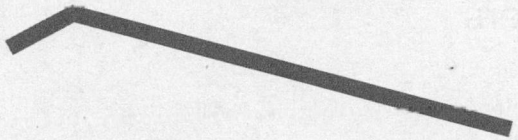

Estimate: about _____ centimeters

Measure: about _____ centimeters

7. Which path is longer?

_____

8. How much longer?

about _____ centimeters longer

Higher Order Thinking Think about the length of each object. Circle the best estimate of its length.

9. a key

about 1 cm about 6 cm about 20 cm

10. a pen

about 2 cm about 4 cm about 15 cm

Use your estimates to complete:

A pen is about _____ cm longer than a _____.

Problem Solving Solve each problem.

11. **Explain** A path has two parts. The total length of the path is 12 cm. If one part is 8 cm, how long is the other part? Explain.

_____ centimeters

12. **Higher Order Thinking** Draw a path with two parts. Measure the length to the nearest centimeter. Write an equation to show the length of your path.

13. **Higher Order Thinking** Beth drew a picture of a bike path. Use tools. Measure the length of the path below. Write the total length.

Beth's Path

about _____ centimeters

14. **Assessment** Peter measures a path that has a total length of 12 cm. Janna measures a path that has two parts. Each part measures 7 cm.

How much longer is Janna's path than Peter's path? Show your work.

_____

_____

_____

Copyright © Savvas Learning Company LLC. All Rights Reserved.

Name _____

Help Tools Games

Homework & Practice 12-8

Compare Lengths

Another Look! You can write an equation to help you find the total length of a path. What is the total length of Path A?

Path A

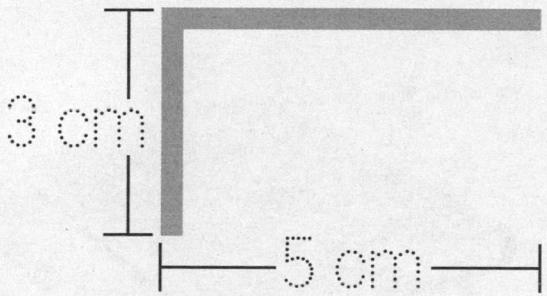

3 + 5 = 8

Path A is about 8 centimeters long.

HOME ACTIVITY Draw a path that is made up of two parts. Have your child use a centimeter ruler to measure each part and then find the total length.

Use a centimeter ruler to measure Path B. Answer each question.

1. **Path B**

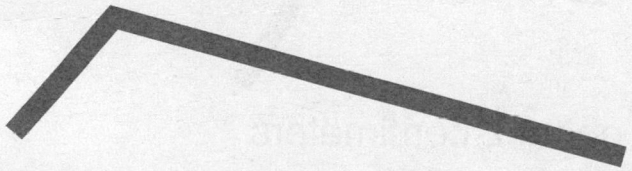

____ + ____ = ____

about ____ centimeters long

2. Which path is longer, Path A or Path B?

Path A

Path B

3. How much longer is the longer path than the shorter path?

about ____ centimeter longer

4. **Model** Joanna drew a path that is 8 cm shorter than Liam's path. Joanna's path is 19 cm long. How long is Liam's path? Write an equation.

_____ + _____ = _____ centimeters

5. **Model** Nadine drew a path that is 7 cm longer than Nancy's path.Nadine's path is 15 cm long. How long is Nancy's path? Write an equation.

_____ − _____ = _____ centimeters

Use the pictures on the right to solve each problem.

6. Kristin cleans out her desk. Write the items she finds in order from longest to shortest. Then fill in the blanks for each sentence below.

_____ _____ _____ _____

longest shortest

7. **Higher Order Thinking** Fill in the missing words.

The pencil is _____ than the ruler, and the ruler is shorter than the _____. So, the pencil is _____ than the _____.

8. **Assessment** Use a ruler. What is the total length of the purple path?

Ⓐ about 2 centimeters

Ⓑ about 4 centimeters

Ⓒ about 6 centimeters

Ⓓ about 8 centimeters

Copyright © Savvas Learning Company LLC. All Rights Reserved.

Name _____

Solve

Problem Solving

Lesson 12-9
Precision

I can ...
choose tools, units, and methods that help me be precise when I measure.

SOL 2.8a, Prepares for 3.7a

Solve & Share

Zeke measures the snake and says it is about 4 inches long. Jay says it is about 5 inches long.

Who measures the snake more precisely? Measure and explain.

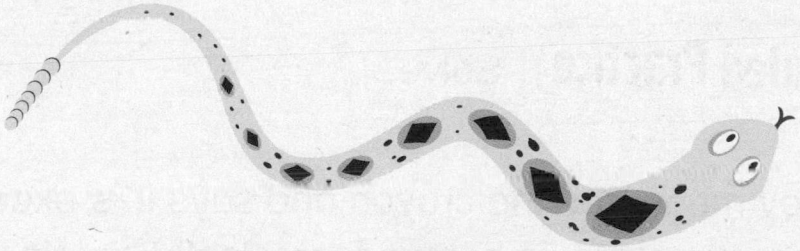

Length: _____

_____

_____

_____

_____

Thinking Habits

Which unit of measure will I use?

Is my work precise?

Learn Glossary

Anna uses a string to help measure the worm.

Is her work precise? Why or why not?

What can I do to measure precisely?

I can choose units and tools that will help me measure precisely.

Measure Precisely
Estimate first.
Choose a tool.
Start at 0.
Measure twice.
Write the unit.

Anna lines up the string along a ruler to measure the length.

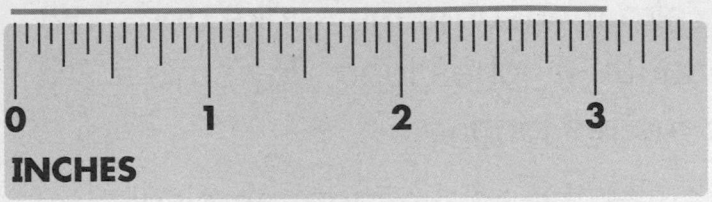

Then Anna measures the worm again to check her work. Then she writes the length.

The worm is about 3 inches long.

Anna uses precision to measure and write the units.

Do You Understand?

Show Me! How does using a string help Anna use precision to measure the worm?

Guided Practice Solve.

1. Bev measures the crayon and says it is exactly 5 centimeters. Is her work precise? Explain.

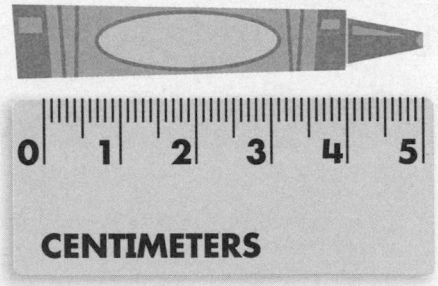

_____

_____

Copyright © Savvas Learning Company LLC. All Rights Reserved.

Name _____

Tools Assessment

Independent Practice

Solve each problem.

2. Traci measures the length of her pencil. She uses a centimeter ruler. Traci writes 17 for the length. Is her answer precise? Explain.

3. Steve uses centimeter cubes. He says the pencil is 9 centimeters long. Is his work precise? Explain.

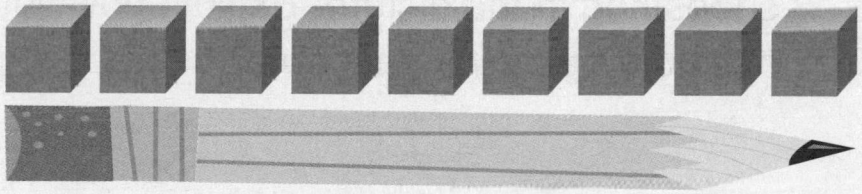

4. Use a centimeter ruler to measure the pencil yourself. How long is the pencil? Explain what you did to make sure your work is precise.

Performance Assessment

Shoestring

Katie lost a shoestring.
The shoestring has the same length as the shoestring at the right.
What is the length of the shoestring Katie lost?

5. **Make Sense** Estimate the length of the shoestring in the picture. Explain how your estimate helps you measure.

6. **Use Tools** What tools can you use to measure the shoestring? Explain.

7. **Be Precise** Measure the shoestring. Tell why your work is precise.

Copyright © Savvas Learning Company LLC. All Rights Reserved.

Name _____

Help Tools Games

Homework & Practice 12-9
Precision

HOME ACTIVITY Have your child measure the length of a household item. Have your child choose the unit to use. Ask your child to explain how he or she knows the measurement is precise.

Another Look! Amy uses a button to measure the length of a glue stick. She knows one button is 1 centimeter. She finds that the glue stick is 5 cm.

Amy used a ruler to check her work. She started at the 0 mark.

First time: 5 cm **Second time: 5 cm**

Solve the problem. You can use string or buttons to help.

1. Find the length of the chain at the right. Estimate and use tools to measure.

   Estimate: _____

   Actual measurement: _____

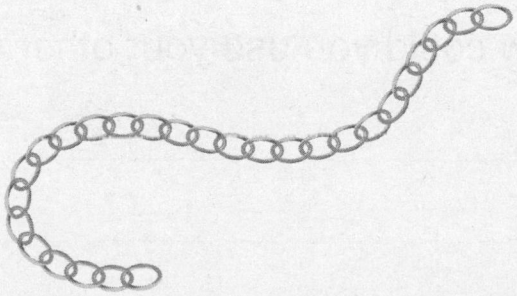

Performance Assessment

Distance Around Your Shoe

Shoes have different sizes and shapes. The picture shows the bottom of a shoe. What is the total distance around the bottom of one of your shoes?

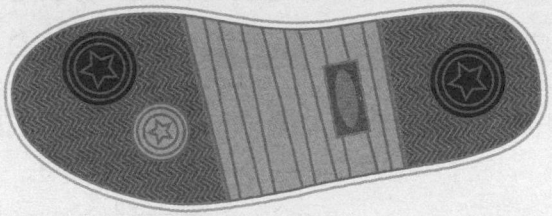

2. **Reasoning** What units of measure will you use? Explain.

3. **Be Precise** What is the distance around one of your shoes? Explain how you found it.

4. **Explain** How could you use your other shoe to check your work?

Copyright © Savvas Learning Company LLC. All Rights Reserved.

Name _____

TOPIC 12 **Fluency Practice Activity**

Find a Match

Find a partner. Point to a clue. Read the clue.

Look below the clues to find a match. Write the clue letter in the box next to the match.

Find a match for every clue.

I can ...
add and subtract within 100.

Clues

A The sum is between 47 and 53.

B The difference equals 56 − 20.

C The sum equals 100.

D The difference equals 79 − 27.

E The difference is between 25 and 35.

F The sum equals 41 + 56.

G The difference is less than 20.

H The sum equals 26 + 19.

☐ 81 − 29	☐ 60 − 24	☐ 34 + 11	☐ 23 + 27
☐ 63 − 34	☐ 32 + 65	☐ 56 + 44	☐ 47 − 31

TOPIC 12 Vocabulary Review

A-Z Glossary

Understand Vocabulary

1. Circle the unit that has the *greatest* length.

foot meter inch

2. Circle the unit that has the *shortest* length.

yard inch centimeter

3. Cross out the unit you would **NOT** use to measure the length of a book.

inch centimeter yard

4. Cross out the unit you would **NOT** use to measure the height of a house.

inch foot meter

Word List

- centimeter (cm)
- estimate
- foot (ft)
- height
- inch (in.)
- length
- meter (m)
- nearest centimeter
- nearest inch
- yard (yd)

Estimate the length of each item.

5. pencil _____

6. paper clip _____

7. school desk _____

Use Vocabulary in Writing

8. Use words to tell how to find the height of a table. Use terms from the Word List.

_____

_____

_____

_____

_____

Copyright © Savvas Learning Company LLC. All Rights Reserved.

Name _____

TOPIC 12

Reteaching

Set A

There are 12 inches in 1 foot.
There are 3 feet in 1 yard.
You can use lengths of objects you know to estimate lengths of other objects.

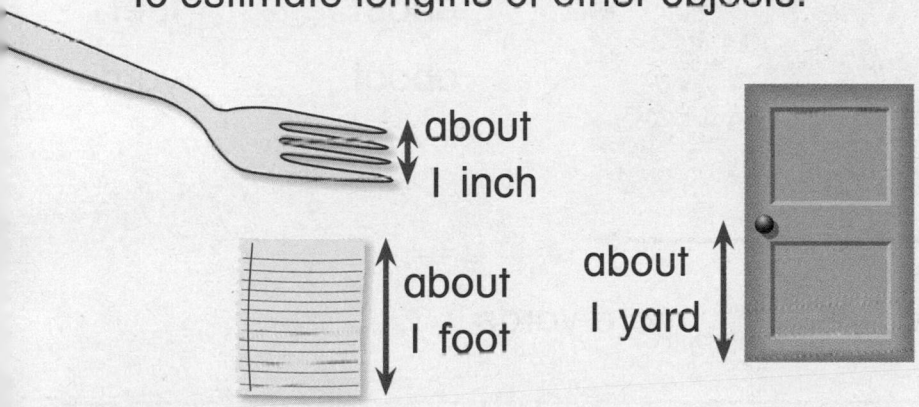

Estimate the lengths of two classroom objects in feet. Name each object and write your estimate.

1. Object: _____
   about _____ feet
2. Object: _____
   about _____ feet

Set B

You can measure the length of an object to the nearest inch.

The string is longer than halfway between 1 and 2.
So, use the greater number.
The string is about 2 inches.

Find objects like the ones shown. Use a ruler to measure their lengths.

3. 

   about _____ inches

4. 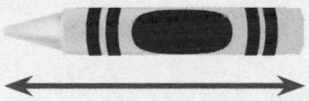

   about _____ inches

Set C

The measure of the height of a window takes *more* feet than yards.

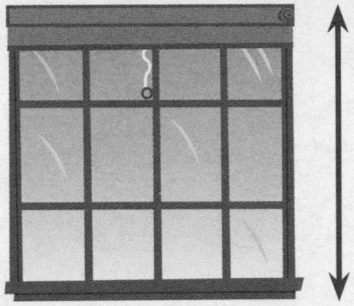

about 3 feet

about 1 yard

Measure the object in inches and feet.
Circle the unit you needed *more* of.

5.

about _____ feet

about _____ yards

more feet more yards

Set D

You can measure the length of an object to the nearest centimeter.

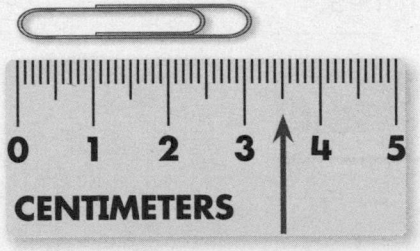

The paper clip is less than halfway between 3 and 4.
So, use the lesser number.
The paper clip is about 3 cm.

Find objects like the ones shown.
Use a ruler to measure their lengths.

6.

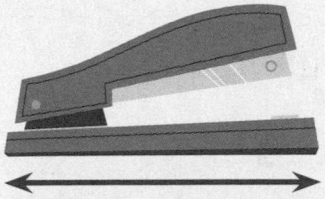

about _____ cm

7.

about _____ cm

Copyright © Savvas Learning Company LLC. All Rights Reserved.

Name _____

TOPIC 12

Reteaching
Continued

Set E

There are 100 centimeters in 1 meter.

about 1 centimeter

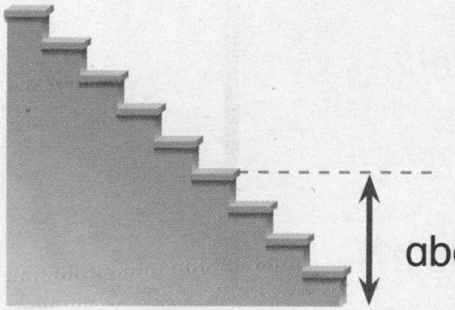

about 1 meter

Circle the picture of the object that is about each length or height.

8. about 1 centimeter

9. about 1 meter

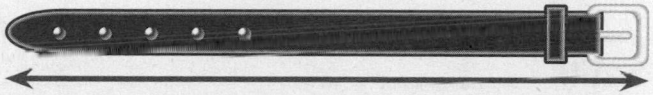

Set F

The measure of the height of this cart takes *fewer* meters than centimeters.

about 93 centimeters

about 1 meter

Measure the object in centimeters and meters. Circle the unit you needed *fewer* of.

10.

about _____ centimeters

about _____ meters

fewer centimeters

fewer meters

Set G

Which path is longer? How much longer? Measure each part. Then add the lengths.

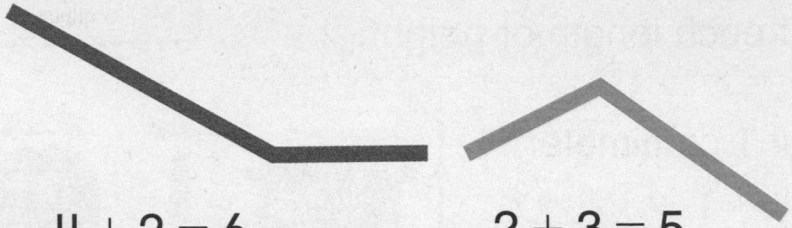

$4 + 2 = 6$

The purple path is 6 cm.

$2 + 3 = 5$

The green path is 5 cm.

Subtract the lengths to compare.

$6 - 5 = 1$

The purple path is about 1 centimeter longer.

Use a centimeter ruler. Measure each path.

11. Red path: _____ centimeters

12. Blue path: _____ centimeters

13. Which path is longer?

_____

How much longer is it?

about _____ centimeters longer

Set H

Thinking Habits

Attend to Precision

Which unit of measure will I use?

Is my work precise?

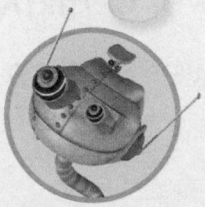

14. Measure the length of the bottom of this page in feet and in inches.

about _____ ft about _____ in.

15. Which measure in Item 14 is more precise? Explain.

_____

_____

_____

Copyright © Savvas Learning Company LLC. All Rights Reserved.

Name _____

TOPIC 12 Assessment

1. Estimate. About how tall is the flower?

Ⓐ about 5 cm

Ⓑ about 10 cm

Ⓒ about 15 cm

Ⓓ about 1 meter

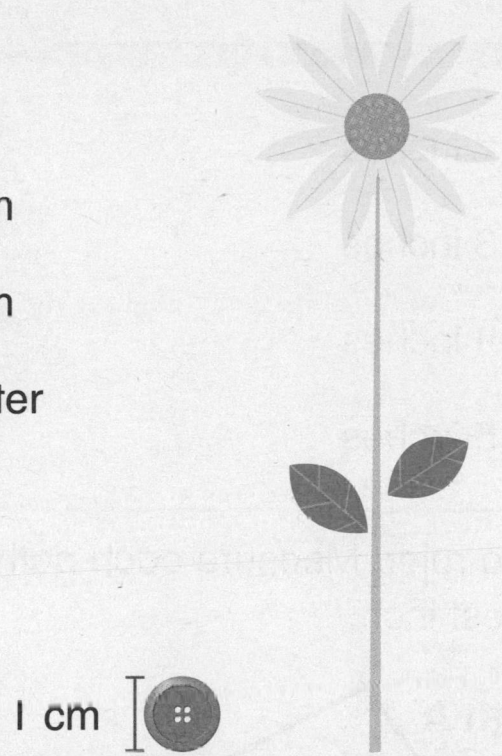

2. Draw a line from each estimate to a matching object.

about 1 inch

about 1 foot

about 1 yard

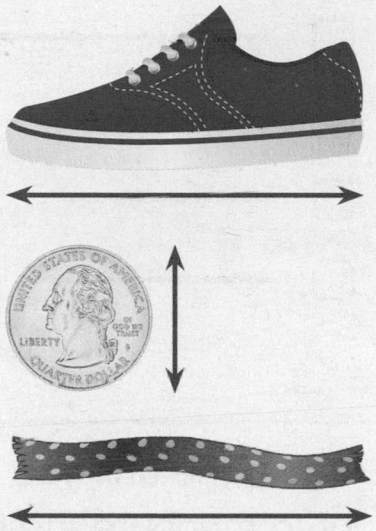

3. Which units would you need the fewest of to measure the height of a fence?

Ⓐ inches

Ⓑ feet

Ⓒ yards

Ⓓ all the same

4. Dan measures the width of the window with a yardstick. He says it measures 3. Is his answer precise? Explain.

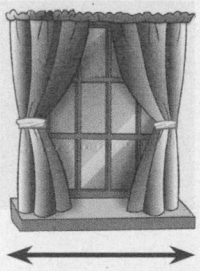

_____

_____

_____

_____

5. Use a ruler to measure each line to the nearest centimeter.
Which are about 3 centimeters long?
Choose all that apply.

☐ _____

☐ _____

☐ _____

☐ _____

6. Use a ruler to measure the length of the pencil in inches.
Which is the correct measurement?

Ⓐ 2 inches

Ⓑ 3 inches

Ⓒ 4 inches

Ⓓ 5 inches

7. Circle the unit you need fewer of to measure the length of a kitchen.

fewer centimeters fewer meters

Circle the unit you need fewer of to measure the length of a table.

fewer feet fewer yards

8. Use a ruler. Measure each path to the nearest inch.

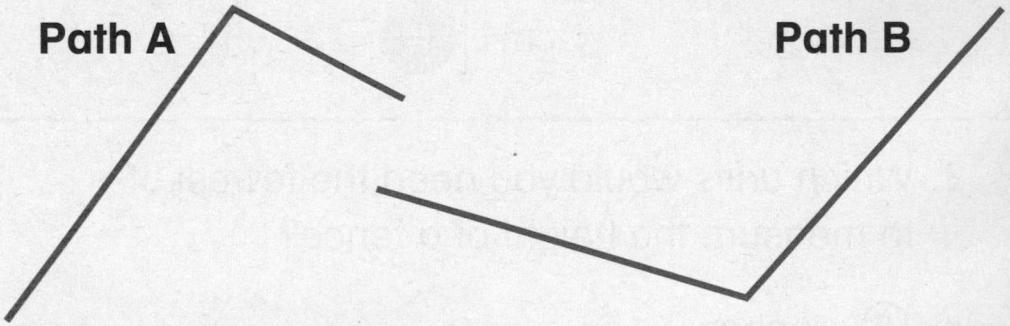

Which path is longer? _____

How much longer? about _____ longer

Copyright © Savvas Learning Company LLC. All Rights Reserved.

Name _____

TOPIC 12 Assessment Continued

9. Use a ruler. Measure the length of the marker to the nearest centimeter. How long is the marker?

Ⓐ 6 centimeters

Ⓑ 9 centimeters

Ⓒ 12 centimeters

Ⓓ 15 centimeters

10. A path has two parts. The total length of the path is 15 cm. One part of the path is 9 cm long. How long is the other part?

Ⓐ 24 cm

Ⓑ 15 cm

Ⓒ 9 cm

Ⓓ 6 cm

11. Use a ruler. Measure each path to the nearest centimeter.

Path A

Path B

Which path is longer? _____

How much longer?

about _____ longer

12. Measure the gray line with tools you need to be precise. Choose all the measurements that are precise.

☐ 4 centimeters

☐ 4 inches

☐ 10

☐ 10 centimeters

13. Juan uses different units to measure a jump rope. Compare the measurements.

Choose Yes or No.

more inches than feet	○ Yes	○ No
fewer inches than feet	○ Yes	○ No
more centimeters than meters	○ Yes	○ No
fewer centimeters than meters	○ Yes	○ No

14. Kendra measures her crayon to the nearest centimeter.
What is the length of her crayon to the nearest centimeter?

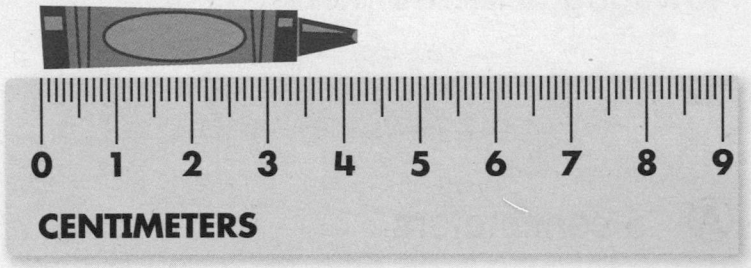

_____ centimeters

15. Kim's softball bat is 1 yard long.
She uses 3 bats to measure the length of the classroom whiteboard.
About how long is the whiteboard?

3 inches Ⓐ 3 feet Ⓑ 1 yard Ⓒ 3 yards Ⓓ

16. Kevin measured the length of a car in inches and in feet.
Why is the number of feet less than the number of inches?

96 inches or 8 feet

_____

_____

_____

_____

Copyright © Savvas Learning Company LLC. All Rights Reserved.

Name _____

TOPIC 12

Performance Assessment

Happy Hiking!

The Torres family loves to hike.
They use this map to plan their hiking trip.

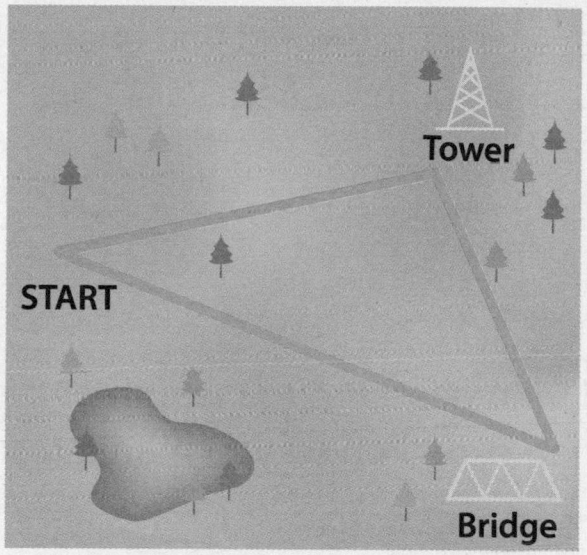

1. Use a centimeter ruler.
   Find the total length of the triangle hiking path shown on the map.

   about ____ centimeters

   Explain how you found the length.

   _____

   _____

   _____

   _____

2. Debbie Torres uses a backpack for hiking.
   She wants to measure its length.
   She wants to be precise. Should she use inches, feet, or yards?
   Explain your answer.

Length of a backpack

_____

_____

_____

_____

3. Daniel Torres estimates the height of his water bottle. Is his estimate reasonable? Explain.

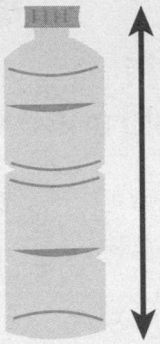

about
20 meters

4. Maria Torres says that it would take more yards than feet to measure the height of the tower. Do you agree? Circle Yes or No. Then explain why.

Yes No

5. On the hike, the Torres family sees a caterpillar. Use the picture below to answer the questions.

Part A

To be precise, which unit would you choose to measure the length of the caterpillar?

Part B

Estimate and then measure the length of the caterpillar. Then explain how you measured.

Estimate: _____

Measurement: _____

Copyright © Savvas Learning Company LLC. All Rights Reserved.

TOPIC 13 More Addition, Subtraction, and Length

Essential Question: How can you add and subtract lengths?

Digital Resources

Solve Learn Glossary

Tools Assessment Help Games

Math and Science Project: Modeling Land, Water, and Length

Find Out Find and share books and other sources that show the shapes and kinds of land and water in an area. Draw a picture or make a model to show the land or water in an area.

Journal: Make a Book Show what you learn in a book. In your book, also:

- Draw a picture to show the shape of some land or water in your area.
- Make up a math story about lengths. Draw a picture to show how to solve the problem in your story.

Name _____

Review What You Know

Vocabulary

1. Circle the measuring unit that is better to **estimate** the **length** of a room.

meter

centimeter

2. Circle the number of feet in 1 **yard**.

2 feet

3 feet

4 feet

12 feet

3. The clock shows the time a math class begins. Circle **a.m.** or **p.m.**

a.m.

p.m.

Estimate

4. **Estimate** the length of the eraser in centimeters.

About _____ centimeters

Compare

5. A sidewalk is 632 yards long. A jogging trail is 640 yards long.

Use <, >, or = to compare the lengths.

632 ◯ 640

Rectangles

6. Label the 2 missing lengths of the sides of the rectangle.

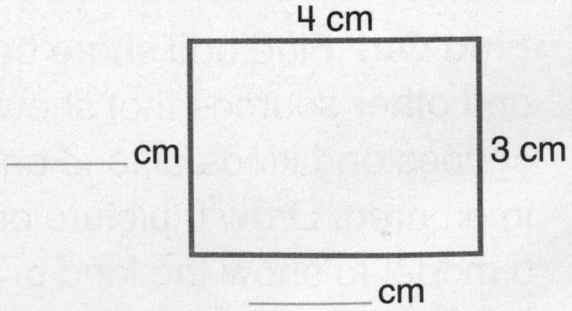

Copyright © Savvas Learning Company LLC. All Rights Reserved.

Name _____

Solve

Lesson 13-1

Add and Subtract with Measurements

I can ...

solve problems by adding or subtracting length measurements.

SOL 2.6c

Solve & Share

What is the total distance around the blue rectangle in centimeters? Show your work. Did you add or subtract?

_____ ○ _____ ○ _____ ○ _____ = _____

The distance around the blue rectangle is _____ centimeters.

The book is 9 inches long and 6 inches wide.

What is the distance around the front cover of the book?

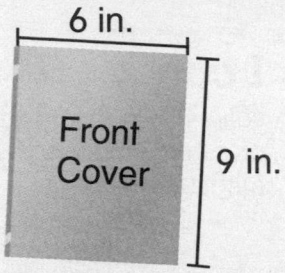

Add the lengths of all four sides to find the distance around the cover.

$9 + 6 + 9 + 6 = ?$

$18 + 12 =$

$10 + 10 + 8 + 2 =$

$20 + 10 = 30$

The distance around the cover is 30 inches.

How much longer is the teacher's arm than the child's arm?

Arm Length in Centimeters	
Teacher	66
Child	47

Subtract to compare measurements.

$66 - 47 = ?$

$$\begin{array}{r} 5\,16 \\ \cancel{6}\,\cancel{6} \\ -\,4\,7 \\ \hline 19 \end{array}$$

The teacher's arm is 19 centimeters longer than the child's arm.

Do You Understand?

Show Me! Explain how to find the distance around a square park that is 2 miles long on each side.

Guided Practice

Decide if you need to add or subtract. Then write an equation to help solve each problem.

1. What is the distance around the baseball card?

10 cm

7 cm

$10 + 7 + 10 + 7 = 34$

Distance around: 34 cm

2. What is the distance around the puzzle?

15 in.

12 in.

Distance around: _____ in.

Copyright © Savvas Learning Company LLC. All Rights Reserved.

Name _____

Tools Assessment

Independent Practice

Decide if you need to add or subtract.
Then write an equation to help solve each problem.

3. What is the distance around the door?

_____

Distance around: _____ ft

4. What is the distance around the cell phone?

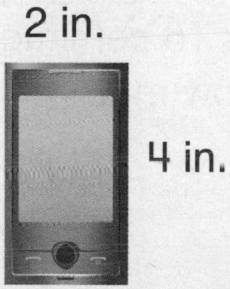

_____

Distance around: _____ in.

5. How much longer is the red scarf than the blue scarf?

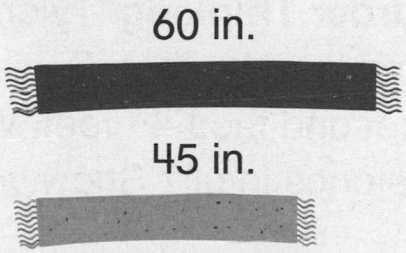

_____

_____ in. longer

6. **Algebra** What is the length of the shorter side of the rectangle? Complete the equation to solve.

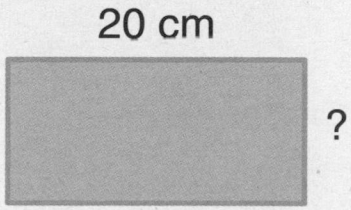

20 + _____ + 20 + _____ = 60

The shorter side is _____ centimeters.

Problem Solving

Decide if you need to add or subtract.
Then write an equation to help solve each problem.

7. **Model** Ashley's sunflower is 70 inches tall. Kwame's sunflower is 60 inches tall. How much taller is Ashley's sunflower than Kwame's sunflower?

_____ _____ inches taller

8. **Model** Ben measures the length of a leaf and a plant. The leaf is 15 centimeters. The plant is 37 centimeters. How much shorter is the leaf than the plant?

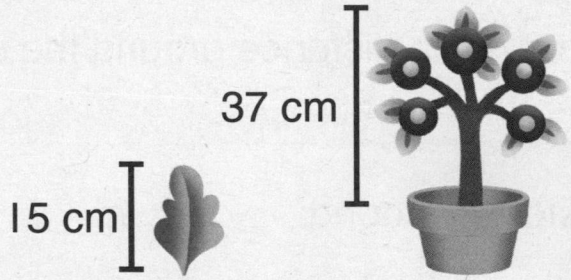

_____ _____ centimeters shorter

9. **Higher Order Thinking** Tyler threw a ball 42 feet and then 44 feet. Sanjay threw a ball 38 feet and then 49 feet. Who threw the longer distance in all? Show your work.

10. **Assessment** What is the distance around the placemat?

Ⓐ 28 in.
Ⓑ 39 in.
Ⓒ 56 in.
Ⓓ 66 in.

Copyright © Savvas Learning Company LLC. All Rights Reserved.

Name _____

Help Tools Games

Homework & Practice 13-1

Add and Subtract with Measurements

Another Look!

You can use addition or subtraction to solve problems with measurements. How much longer is the snake than the worm?

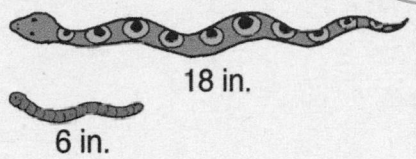

18 − 6 = 12

The snake is 12 inches longer than the worm.

HOME ACTIVITY Ask your child to find a rectangular object (*a book, piece of paper, tile, etc.*). Have your child measure each side in inches and write an equation to find the distance around the object.

Decide if you need to add or subtract. Then write an equation to help solve each problem.

1. How much shorter is the feather than the ribbon?

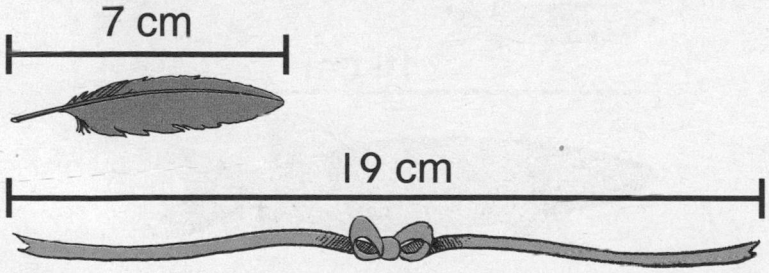

_____ centimeters shorter

2. What is the distance around the rug?

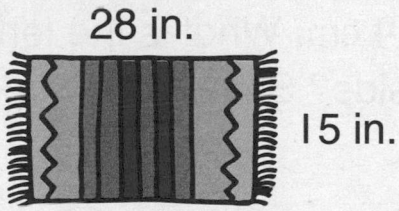

_____ inches

Decide if you need to add or subtract.
Then write an equation to help solve each problem.

3. **Model** What is the distance around the front cover of the game box?

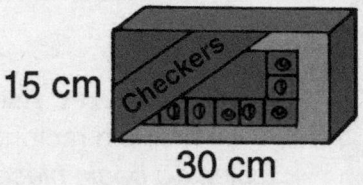

_____

The distance around the game box is _____.

4. **Higher Order Thinking** The distance around Tim's rectangular book is 48 centimeters. The length of each longer side is 14 cm. What is the length of each shorter side? Show your work.

_____

_____

Each shorter side of the book is _____ long.

5. **Assessment** How much longer is the green fish than the blue fish?

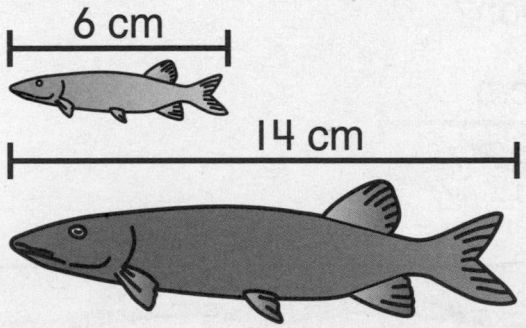

Ⓐ 7 cm
Ⓑ 8 cm
Ⓒ 20 cm
Ⓓ 40 cm

Copyright © Savvas Learning Company LLC. All Rights Reserved.

Name _____

Solve

Lesson 13-2
Find Unknown Measurements

I can ...
add or subtract to solve problems about measurements.

SOL 2.6b, 2.6c

Solve & Share

Julie and Steve each cut a piece of yarn.
The total length of both pieces is 12 cm.

Use centimeter cubes to measure each piece of yarn.
Circle Julie and Steve's pieces. Then explain your thinking.

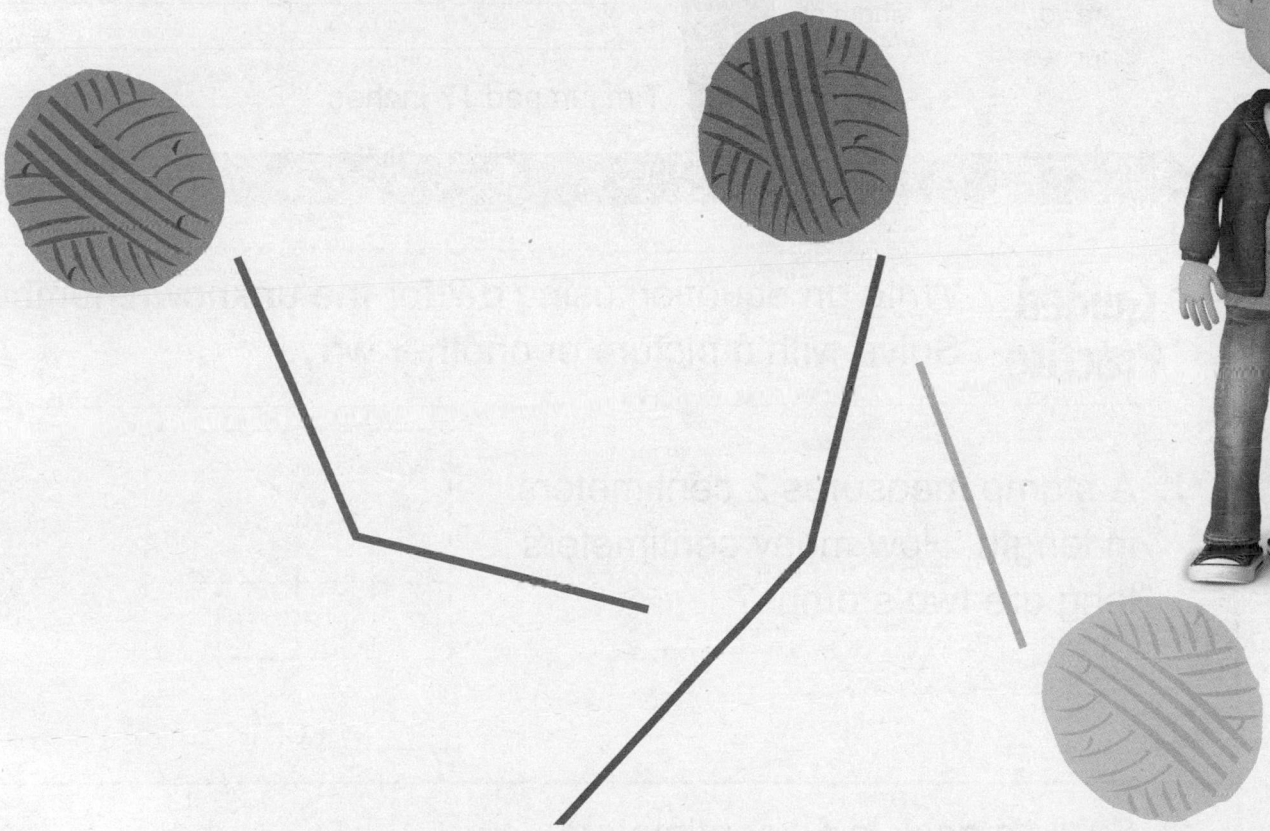

_____

_____

_____

Digital Resources at SavvasRealize.com

Michelle jumped 24 inches. Tim jumped 7 fewer inches than Michelle. How far did Tim jump?

What operation should I use?

You can write a subtraction equation to show the problem.

The length of Tim's jump is unknown.

24	–	7	=	?
↑		↑		↑
length of Michelle's jump		fewer inches		length of Tim's jump

You can draw a picture, such as a yardstick. Then count back to solve the problem.

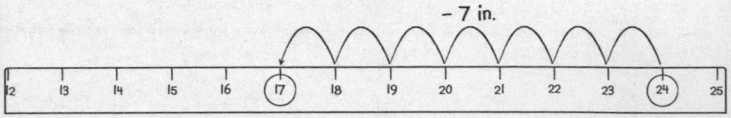

Tim jumped 17 inches.

Do You Understand?

Show Me! How does drawing a yardstick help you solve the problem above?

Guided Practice

Write an equation using a ? for the unknown number. Solve with a picture or another way.

1. A stamp measures 2 centimeters in length. How many centimeters long are two stamps?

   2 + 2 = ?

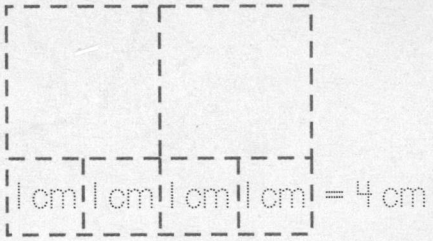

   _____ cm

2. Stuart's desk is 64 centimeters long. His dresser is 7 centimeters longer than his desk. How long is Stuart's dresser?

   _____ _____ cm

Copyright © Savvas Learning Company LLC. All Rights Reserved.

Name _____

Tools Assessment

Independent Practice

Write an equation using a ? for the unknown number. Solve with a picture or another way.

3. Filipe's pencil box is 24 centimeters long. Joe's pencil box is 3 centimeters shorter than Filipe's. How long is Joe's pencil box?

_____ _____ cm

4. Clark threw a red ball and a blue ball. He threw the red ball 17 feet. He threw the blue ball 7 feet farther. How far did Clark throw the blue ball?

_____ _____ ft

5. **Math and Science** Ashlie's map shows where animals, land, and water are at a zoo.

The distance around her map is 38 inches. What is the length of the missing side?

_____

_____ inches

8 in.

11 in.

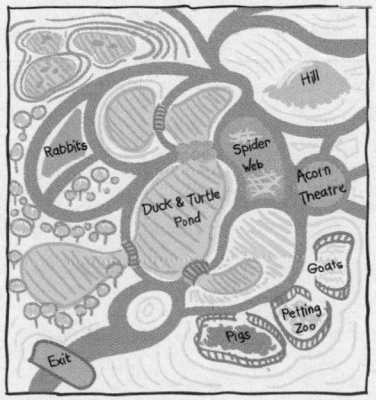

? in.

8 in.

Problem Solving Solve each problem.

6. **Make Sense** A brown puppy is 43 centimeters tall. A spotted puppy is 7 centimeters shorter than the brown puppy. A white puppy is 14 centimeters taller than the brown puppy. How tall is the spotted puppy? Think about what you need to find.

_____ cm

7. **Vocabulary** Complete the sentences using the terms below.

foot **yard** **inch**

A paper clip is about 1 _____ long.

My math book is about 1 _____ long.

A baseball bat is about 1 _____ long.

8. **Higher Order Thinking** Jack jumped 15 inches. Tyler jumped 1 inch less than Jack and 2 inches more than Randy. Who jumped the farthest? How far did each person jump?

9. **Assessment** Kim was 48 inches tall in January. She grew 9 inches during the year. How tall is Kim at the end of the year? Write an equation with an unknown and then draw a picture to solve.

_____

_____ in.

Copyright © Savvas Learning Company LLC. All Rights Reserved.

Name _____

Help Tools Games

Homework & Practice 13-2

Find Unknown Measurements

HOME ACTIVITY Have your child draw a picture to solve this problem. *A building is 24 meters tall. The tree next to the building is 5 meters tall. How much shorter is the tree than the building?*

Another Look!

Lance's boat is 13 meters long.
Cory's boat is 7 meters longer.
How long is Cory's boat?

You can follow these steps to solve word problems.

Step 1 Write an equation to show the problem. 13 + 7 = ?

Step 2 Draw a picture to help solve.

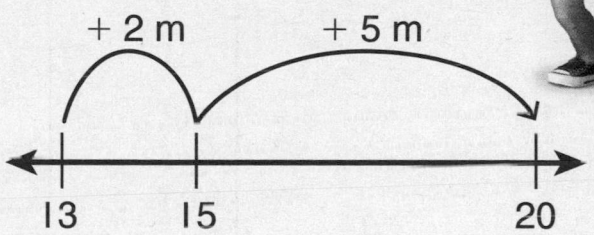

Step 3 Solve the problem. Cory's boat is 20 meters long.

Write an equation using a ? for the unknown number. Solve with a picture or another way.

1. Suzy's ribbon is 83 centimeters long. She cuts off 15 centimeters. How long is Suzy's ribbon now?

_____ _____ cm

Solve each problem.

2. Jackie's shoelaces are 13 inches, 29 inches, and 58 inches long. What is the total length of all of Jackie's shoelaces? Draw a picture and write an equation to solve.

_____ in.

3. **Reasoning** Mary is 2 inches taller than Bill. Bill is 48 inches tall. How tall is Mary?

4. **Higher Order Thinking** Kyle's bedroom is 11 feet long. Garrett's bedroom is 2 feet longer than Kyle's room. Priya's bedroom is 3 feet shorter than Garrett's room. What is the sum of the lengths of Garrett and Priya's bedrooms?

_____ ft

5. **Assessment** Ryan's desk is 25 inches tall. His floor lamp is 54 inches tall. How many inches taller is Ryan's floor lamp? Write an equation and draw a picture to solve.

_____

_____ inches taller

Copyright © Savvas Learning Company LLC. All Rights Reserved.

Name _____

Solve

Lesson 13-3

Continue to Find Unknown Measurements

I can ...

add and subtract to solve measurement problems by using drawings and equations.

SOL 2.6b, 2.6c

Solve & Share

Alex has a piece of ribbon that is 45 feet long. He cuts the ribbon. Now he has 39 feet of ribbon. How many feet of ribbon did Alex cut off?

Draw a picture and write an equation to solve. Show your work.

_____ ◯ _____ = _____

A string is 28 cm.
Alex cuts off a piece.
Now the string is 16 cm.
How long is the piece of string Alex cut off?

You can write an addition or subtraction equation.

28	−	?	=	16
↑		↑		↑
length at first		length cut		length now

16	+	?	=	28
↓		↓		↓
length now		length cut		length at first

You can draw a picture for 28 − ? = 16 or 16 + ? = 28.

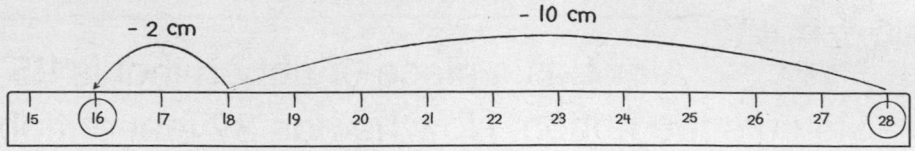

28 − 12 = 16

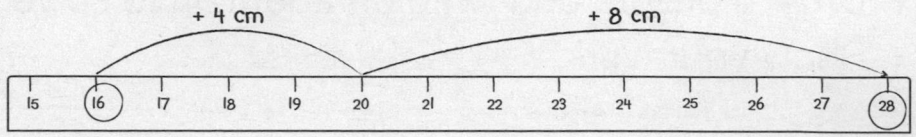

16 + 12 = 28

Alex cut off 12 cm of string.

Do You Understand?

Show Me! How does writing an equation help you solve the problem above?

Guided Practice

Write an equation using a ? for the unknown number. Solve with a picture or another way.

1. A plant was 15 inches tall. It grew and is now 22 inches tall. How many inches did the plant grow?

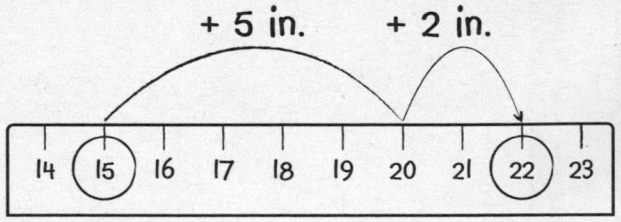

15 + ? = 22

2. Each bus is 10 meters long. Each boat is 7 meters long. What is the total length of two buses and two boats?

Copyright © Savvas Learning Company LLC. All Rights Reserved.

Name _____

Tools Assessment

Independent Practice

Write an equation using a ? for the unknown number. Solve with a picture or another way.

3. Brent's rope is 49 inches long. He cuts off some of the rope and now it is 37 inches long. How much rope did Brent cut off?

_____ _____

4. Sue ran for some meters and stopped. Then she ran another 22 meters for a total of 61 meters in all. How many meters did she run at first?

_____ _____

5. **Algebra** Solve each equation. Use the chart.

○	=	12
☆	=	39
△	=	42
□	=	57

○ + ☆ = _____

□ − ☆ = _____

☆ + △ + ○ = _____

Problem Solving Solve each problem.

6. **Make Sense** The yellow boat is 15 feet shorter than the green boat. The green boat is 53 feet long. How long is the yellow boat? Think about what you are trying to find.

Write an equation to solve. Show your work.

_____ ft

7. **Vocabulary** Steve measured the length of his desk. It measured 2 units.

Circle the unit Steve used.

meter **foot** **centimeter** **inch**

Lori measured the length of her cat. It measured 45 units.

Circle the unit Lori used.

centimeter **yard** **inch** **foot**

8. **Higher Order Thinking** Lucy's ribbon is 1 foot long. Kathleen's ribbon is 15 inches long. Whose ribbon is longer and by how many inches? Explain your thinking.

_____

_____

_____

_____

_____

9. **Assessment** Mary's water bottle is 25 cm long. Joey's water bottle is 22 cm long. Ella's water bottle is 17 cm long.

Which statements are correct? Choose all that apply.

- ☐ Mary's bottle is 8 cm longer than Ella's.
- ☐ Joey's bottle is 6 cm longer than Ella's.
- ☐ Joey's bottle is 3 cm shorter than Mary's.
- ☐ Ella's bottle is 8 cm longer than Mary's.

Copyright © Savvas Learning Company LLC. All Rights Reserved.

Name _____

Help Tools Games

Homework & Practice 13-3

Continue to Find Unknown Measurements

HOME ACTIVITY Have your child draw a picture and write an equation to solve this problem. *Paul has 45 feet of string. Sal cuts some string off. Now Paul has 38 feet of string. How many feet of string did Sal cut off?*

Another Look!

Kelsey is 59 inches tall.
She grows and is now 73 inches tall.
How many inches did Kelsey grow?

Show the problem with an equation: $59 + ? = 73$.

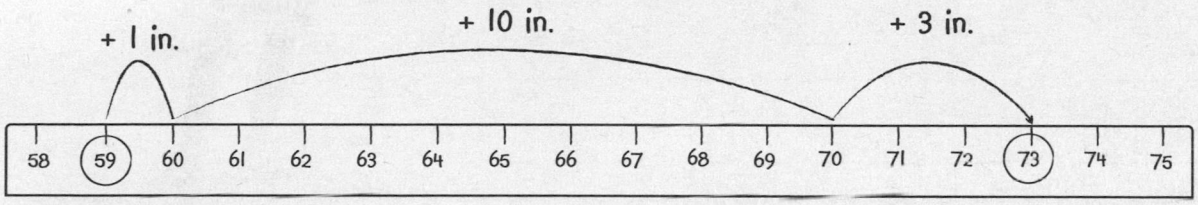

Kelsey grew 14 inches.

Write an equation using a ? for the unknown number. Solve with a picture or another way.

1. Brigit has a piece of rope. She ties 18 more meters of rope to her rope. Now the rope is 27 meters long. How long was the rope to begin with?

_____ _____

Solve each problem.

2. **Explain** Elizabeth ran 36 meters. Haruki ran 8 fewer meters than Elizabeth. Delilah ran 3 fewer meters than Haruki. How many meters did Delilah run? Explain your thinking.

_____

_____

_____

3. **Higher Order Thinking** The lengths of the pencils are given at the right.

Write and solve a two-step problem about the pencils.

_____

_____

_____

_____

_____

_____

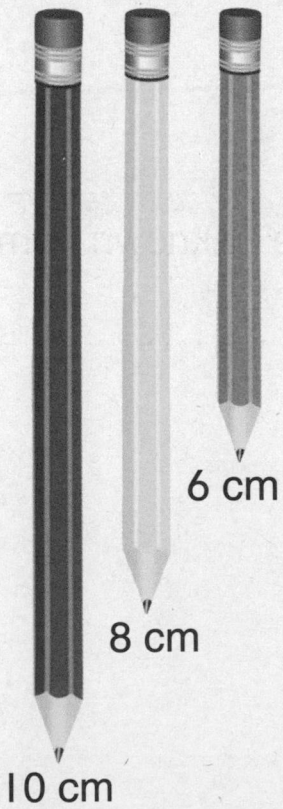

4. **Assessment** A hammer is 1 foot long. A car is 15 feet long. A shovel is 4 feet long.

Which statements are correct? Choose all that apply.

- ☐ The car is 9 ft longer than the hammer.
- ☐ The hammer is 14 ft shorter than the car.
- ☐ The shovel is 3 ft longer than the hammer.
- ☐ The car is 11 feet longer than the shovel.

Copyright © Savvas Learning Company LLC. All Rights Reserved.

Name _____

Solve

Lesson 13-4

Add and Subtract on a Number Line

I can ...
add and subtract on a number line.

SOL 2.6b, 2.6c

Solve & Share

Amelia walks 18 blocks on Monday and 5 blocks on Tuesday. How many blocks does she walk in all?

Use the number line to show how many blocks Amelia walks. Then write an equation to show your work.

_____ ◯ _____ = _____

Amelia walks 17 blocks before dinner. She walks 8 blocks after dinner. How many blocks does she walk in all?

You can use a number line to add lengths.
First, show the 17 blocks Amelia walks before dinner.
Then, add the 8 blocks she walks after dinner.

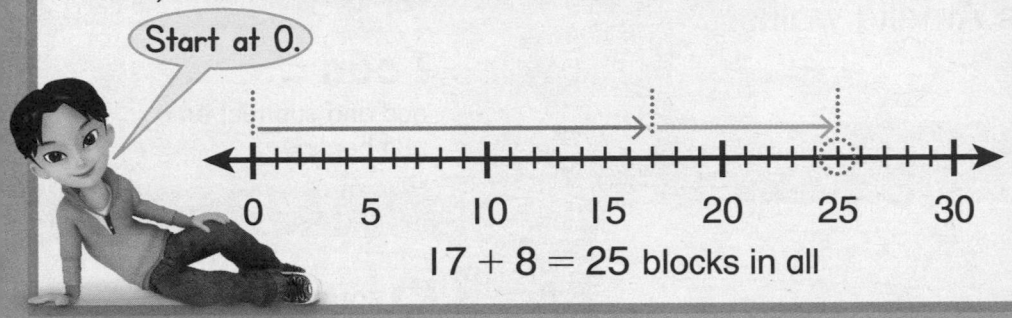

$17 + 8 = 25$ blocks in all

Amelia buys 17 feet of rope. She cuts off 8 feet of rope to make a jump rope. How many feet of rope does she have left?

You can also use a number line to subtract lengths.
First, show the 17 feet of rope.
Then, subtract the 8 feet of rope she cuts off.

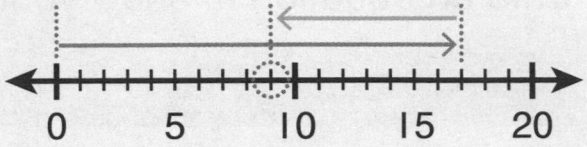

$17 - 8 = 9$ feet of rope left

Do You Understand?

Show Me! Explain how to add 14 inches and 11 inches using a number line.

Guided Practice

Use the number lines to add or subtract.

1. $21 + 7 =$ 28

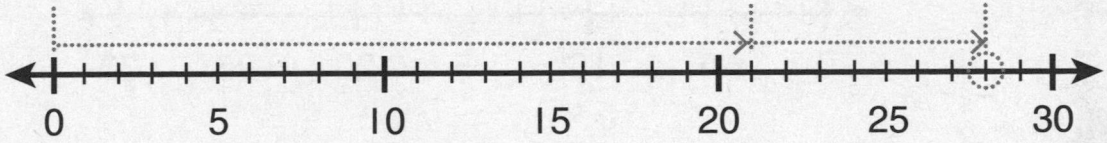

2. $28 - 14 =$ _____

Copyright © Savvas Learning Company LLC. All Rights Reserved.

Name _____

Tools Assessment

Independent Practice

Use the number lines to add or subtract.

3. 80 − 35 = _____

4. 19 + 63 = _____

5. **Higher Order Thinking** Use the number line to show 15 inches plus 0 inches. Explain your thinking.

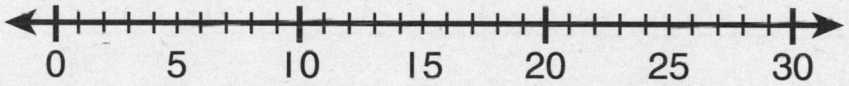

_____

6. **Number Sense** Show each number below as a length from 0 on the number line. Draw four separate arrows.

9 | 14 | 24 | 28

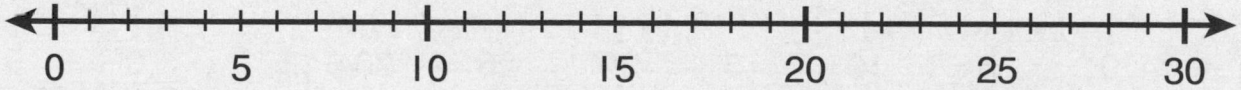

Problem Solving

Use the number line to solve each problem.

7. **Use Tools** A football team gains 15 yards on its first play. The team gains 12 yards on its second play. How many yards does the team gain in two plays?

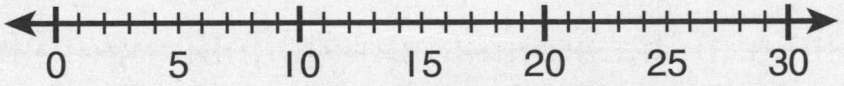

_____ yards

8. **Use Tools** Mia buys 25 feet of board. She uses 16 feet of board for a sandbox. How many feet of board does she have left?

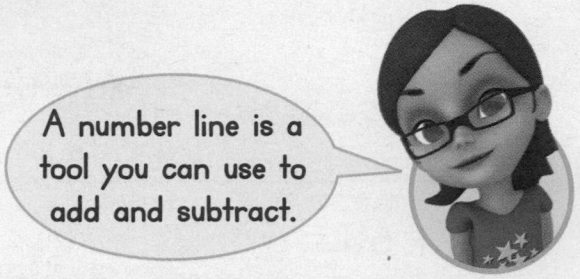

_____ feet

9. **Higher Order Thinking** The runners on the track team ran 12 miles on Monday. On Tuesday, they ran 6 more miles than they ran on Monday. How many miles did they run in all on both days?

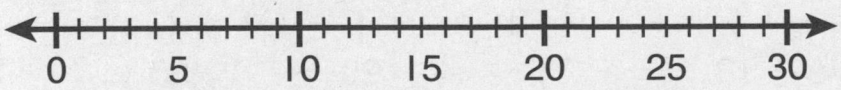

_____ miles

10. **Assessment** Deb has two pencils. One pencil is 9 cm long and the other pencil is 13 cm long. What is the total length of both pencils?

Use the number line to show your work.

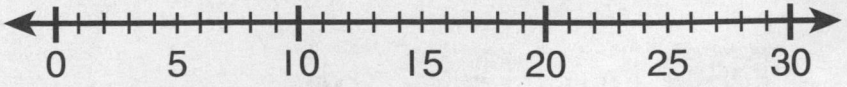

_____ centimeters

Copyright © Savvas Learning Company LLC. All Rights Reserved.

Name _____

Help Tools Games

Homework & Practice 13-4

Add and Subtract on a Number Line

HOME ACTIVITY Measure the length of a fork and a spoon in centimeters. Then draw a number line to show how you would find the total length of the two objects.

Another Look!

$10 + 19 = ?$

Start at 0. Draw an arrow to show the first length.

Then draw a second arrow that points right to add or left to subtract.

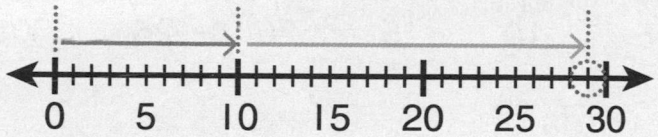

$10 + 19 =$ 29

$19 - 13 = ?$

You can add or subtract on a number line.

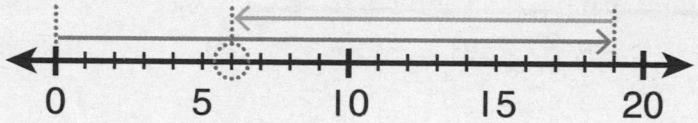

$19 - 13 =$ 6

Use the number lines to add or subtract.

1. $31 - 24 =$ _____

2. $18 + 23 =$ _____

3. **Number Sense** Look at the number line. Write the equation that it shows.

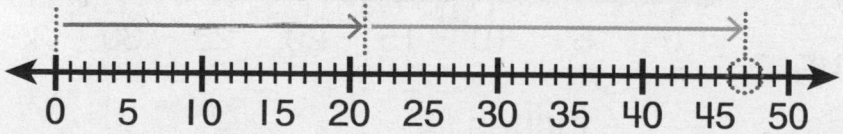

_____ ◯ _____ = _____

Use Tools Use a number line to solve each problem.

4. One box has 15 centimeters of ribbon. Another box has 14 centimeters of ribbon. How many centimeters of ribbon are in both boxes?

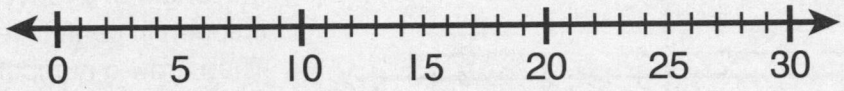

_____ centimeters

5. Susan kicks a ball 26 yards to Joe. Then, Joe kicks the ball 18 yards straight back to Susan. How far is the ball from Susan now?

_____ yards

6. **Higher Order Thinking** Henry is painting a 38 foot fence. He paints 17 feet in the morning. He paints 16 more feet after lunch. How many feet of fence are still left to paint?

_____ feet

7. **Assessment** Sam has 38 inches of yarn. He gives 23 inches of yarn to Lars. How many inches of yarn does Sam have now? Show your work on the number line.

_____ inches

Copyright © Savvas Learning Company LLC. All Rights Reserved.

Name _____

Solve

Problem Solving

Lesson 13-5
Use Appropriate Tools

I can ...
choose the best tool to use to solve problems.

SOL 2.6b, 2.6c, 2.8a

Solve & Share

Choose a tool to solve each part of the problem. Be ready to explain which tools you used and why.

Which line is longer? How much longer?
Draw a line that is that length.

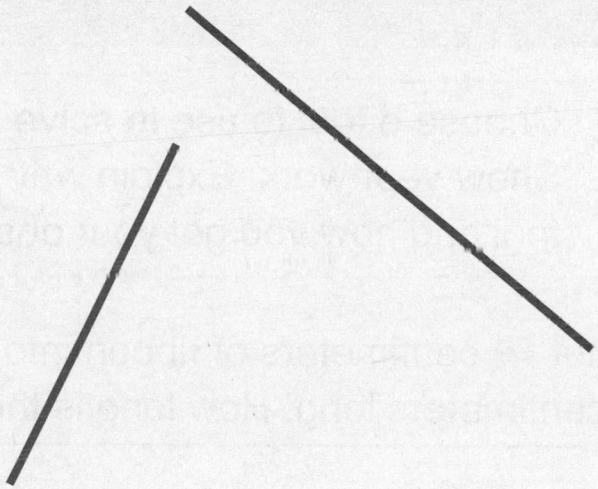

Thinking Habits

Which of these tools can I use?

counters	paper and pencil
cubes	place-value blocks
measuring tools	technology
number line	

Am I using the tool correctly?

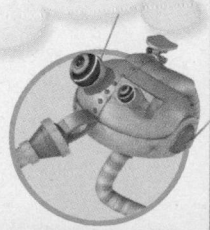

Sara plays soccer. She is 56 feet away from the goal. Then she runs 24 feet straight towards the goal.

How many feet from the goal is Sara now?

How can I use a tool to help me solve the problem?

I can think of tools that could help me. Then I can choose the best tool to use.

Tools

counters	paper and pencil
cubes	place-value blocks
measuring tools	technology
number line	

I don't need a measuring tool. The units are given in feet. I need to subtract. I will draw a number line.

$56 - 24 = ?$

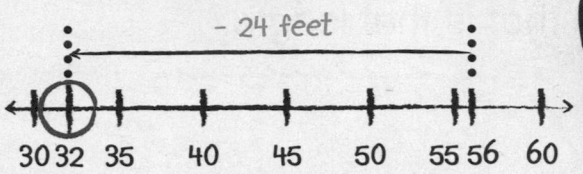

Sara is 32 feet from the goal.

I can use paper and pencil to check my work.

$$\begin{array}{r} 56 \\ -\ 24 \\ \hline 32 \end{array}$$

Do You Understand?

Show Me! Explain why counters are **NOT** the best tool to use to solve the problem above.

Guided Practice

Choose a tool to use to solve the problem. Show your work. Explain why you chose that tool and how you got your answer.

1. Sara cut 19 centimeters of ribbon into two pieces. One piece is 11 centimeters long. How long is the other piece?

_____ ◯ _____ = _____ _____

Copyright © Savvas Learning Company LLC. All Rights Reserved.

Name _____

Tools Assessment

Independent Practice

Solve each problem. Show your work.

2. Work with a partner. Measure each other's arm from the shoulder to the tip of the index finger. Measure to the nearest inch. Whose arm is longer and by how much?

   Choose a tool to use to solve the problem. Explain why you chose that tool and how you got your answer.

_____ ◯ _____ = _____

_____

3. Marcel jumped 39 centimeters high. Jamal jumped 48 centimeters high. How much higher did Jamal jump than Marcel?

   Which tool would you **NOT** use to solve this problem? Explain.

_____ ◯ _____ = _____

_____

Problem Solving

Performance Assessment

Sailboats

Zak is measuring sailboats at the dock.
Mr. Lee's sailboat is 64 feet long.
Ms. Flint's sailboat is 25 feet shorter than Mr. Lee's boat.

Help Zak find the length of Ms. Flint's boat.

4. **Use Tools** Which tool would you **NOT** use to solve this problem? Explain.

_____

_____

_____

_____

5. **Be Precise** Will you add or subtract to solve the problem? _____

Write an equation. Use ? for the unknown.

What unit of measure will you use?

_____

6. **Explain** What is the length of Ms. Flint's boat? Did you use a tool to solve the problem? Explain.

_____

_____

_____

Copyright © Savvas Learning Company LLC. All Rights Reserved.

Name _____

Help Tools Games

Homework & Practice 13-5
Use Appropriate Tools

Another Look! What tool would you use to solve this problem?

Valerie drives 21 miles on Monday and 49 miles on Tuesday. How many miles does she drive in all?

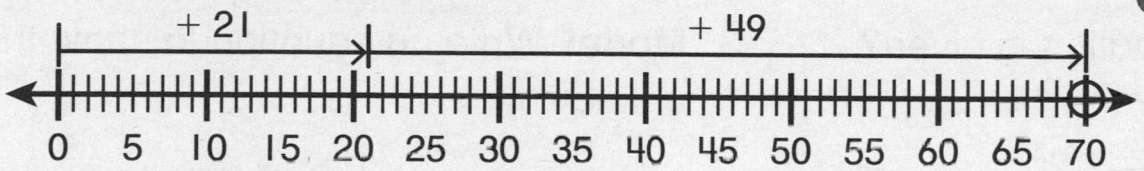

21 + 49 = 70

Valerie drives 70 miles in all.

HOME ACTIVITY Ask your child to explain what tool he or she would use to solve this problem: *Measure the length of a door and a window to the nearest foot. How much longer is the door than the window?*

Choose a tool to help you solve the problem. Show your work. Explain why you chose that tool and how you got your answer.

1. Aaron was 38 inches tall when he was 4 years old. Aaron is 8 years old and 47 inches tall. How many inches did Aaron grow?

Performance Assessment

Trains

Mr. Bolt needs to measure the length of a train. The first car is the engine car. It is 8 meters long. There are also four boxcars. Each boxcar is 12 meters long.

Help Mr. Bolt find the total length of the train.

2. **Make Sense** What information is given? What do you need to find?

_____

_____

_____

_____

_____

3. **Model** Write an equation to show the unknown.

_____

What unit of measure will you use?

_____

4. **Use Tools** What is the total length of the train? Choose a tool to solve the problem. Show your work. _____

Copyright © Savvas Learning Company LLC. All Rights Reserved.

Name _____

TOPIC 13 **Fluency Practice Activity**

Follow the Path

Color a path from **Start** to **Finish**. Follow the sums and differences that are odd numbers. You can only move up, down, right, or left.

I can ...
add and subtract within 100.

Start

80 − 23	94 − 73	21 + 22	45 + 36	19 + 24	86 − 53	14 + 15	25 − 17	35 + 49
65 − 21	97 − 35	35 + 23	12 + 20	98 − 12	74 − 48	27 + 48	54 + 46	53 − 31
51 + 21	35 + 52	28 + 43	18 + 31	51 − 38	79 − 24	95 − 30	61 − 29	30 + 24
55 − 27	60 − 17	27 + 39	29 + 49	62 − 28	36 + 56	59 − 31	42 − 26	87 − 45
36 + 16	38 + 25	88 − 53	33 + 18	34 + 49	45 − 32	62 − 23	97 − 38	19 + 74

Finish

TOPIC 13 Vocabulary Review

A-Z Glossary

Word List
- centimeter (cm)
- foot (ft)
- height
- inch (in.)
- length
- mental math
- meter (m)
- yard (yd)

Understand Vocabulary

Choose a term from the Word List to complete each sentence.

1. The length of your finger can best be measured in centimeters or _____.
2. 100 _____ equals 1 meter.
3. _____ is how tall an object is from bottom to top.

Write T for *true* or F for *false*.

4. _____ 1 yard is 5 feet long.
5. _____ 12 inches is 1 foot long.
6. _____ A centimeter is longer than a meter.
7. _____ You can do mental math in your head.

Use Vocabulary in Writing

8. Tell how to find the total length of two pieces of string. One piece of string is 12 inches long. The other piece is 9 inches long. Use terms from the Word List.

_____

_____

_____

_____

Copyright © Savvas Learning Company LLC. All Rights Reserved.

Name _____

TOPIC 13

Reteaching

Set A

What is the distance around the front of the bookcase?

Add the lengths. Write an equation.

$4 + 3 + 4 + 3 =$ 14

Distance around: 14 feet

Write an equation to help solve.

1. What is the distance around the front of the crayon box?

_____

Distance around: _____ cm

Set B

A kite string is 27 feet long.
Some of the string is cut off.
Now the kite string is 18 feet long.
How many feet of kite string were cut off?

Write an equation and draw a picture.

$27 - ? = 18$ or $18 + ? = 27$

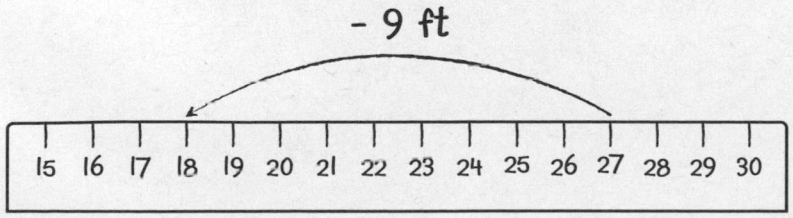

27 − 9 = 18 9 feet

Write an equation using a symbol, ?, for the unknown number. Then draw a picture to solve.

2. A piece of yarn is 42 inches long. Mia cuts some of it off. It is now 26 inches long. How much yarn did Mia cut off?

_____

Set C

A book measures 10 inches long. Another book measures 13 inches long. What is the total length of both books?

You can show 10 + 13 on a number line.

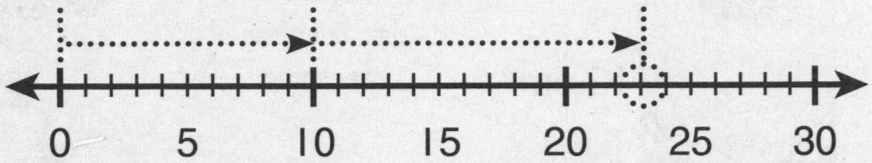

23 inches

Solve the problem using the number line.

3. One room in Jackie's house is 15 feet long. Another room is 9 feet long. What is the total length of both rooms?

_____

Set D

Thinking Habits

Use Tools

Which of these tools can I use?

counters
cubes
measuring tools
number line
paper and pencil
place-value blocks
technology

Am I using the tool correctly?

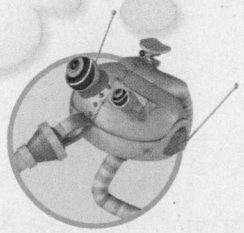

Choose a tool to solve the problem.

4. Damon's shoelace is 45 inches long. His shoelace breaks. One piece is 28 inches long. How long is the other piece?

Explain your solution and why you chose the tool you used.

_____ ◯ _____ = _____ _____

Copyright © Savvas Learning Company LLC. All Rights Reserved.

Name _____

TOPIC 13 Assessment

1. What is the distance around the cover of the notepad?

7 in.

5 in.

Distance around: _____ in.

2. Kate is 48 inches tall. Tom is 2 inches taller than Kate. James is 3 inches shorter than Tom.

How tall is James?

Ⓐ 45 inches

Ⓑ 47 inches

Ⓒ 50 inches

Ⓓ 53 inches

3. Alexis has a rope that is 7 feet long. Mariah's rope is 9 feet long. Sam's rope is 3 feet longer than Mariah's rope.

Use the measurements on the cards to complete each sentence.

2 feet	5 feet	12 feet

Sam's rope is _____ long.

Alexis's rope is _____ shorter than Mariah's rope.

Sam's rope is _____ longer than Alexis's rope.

4. Joe rides his bike 18 miles. Then he rides 7 more miles.

Use the number line to find how far Joe rides. Then explain your work.

_____

_____

_____

_____

5. Pat says that each unknown equals 25 cm. Do you agree? Choose Yes or No.

47 cm + ? = 72 cm	○ Yes	○ No
? + 39 cm = 54 cm	○ Yes	○ No
99 cm − 64 cm = ?	○ Yes	○ No
93 cm − ? = 68 cm	○ Yes	○ No

6. Grace got a plant that was 34 cm tall. The plant grew and now it is 42 cm tall. How many centimeters did the plant grow?

Ⓐ 8 cm
Ⓑ 12 cm
Ⓒ 42 cm
Ⓓ 76 cm

7. Claire rides her bike 26 miles on Saturday and Sunday. She rides 8 miles on Sunday. How many miles does she ride on Saturday?

Write an equation to show the unknown.
Then use the number line to solve the problem.

_____ ○ _____ = _____

_____ miles

8. Chris had a string that is 18 cm long. He cut off 7 cm. How much string is left?

Part A Which of these tools could you use to solve the problem? Choose all that apply.

- ☐ centimeter ruler
- ☐ paper and pencil
- ☐ number line
- ☐ inch ruler

Part B Write an equation to show the unknown. Then draw a number line to solve.

_____ ○ _____ = _____

_____ cm

Copyright © Savvas Learning Company LLC. All Rights Reserved.

Name _____

TOPIC 13 Performance Assessment

Fishing Fun

Jim and his family go on a fishing trip. They use a boat and fishing gear to help them catch fish.

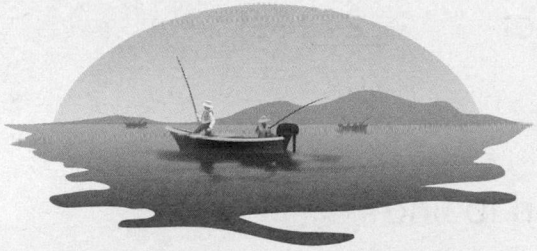

1. Jim takes this fishing box with him. What is the distance around the front of the fishing box? Write an equation to help solve the problem.

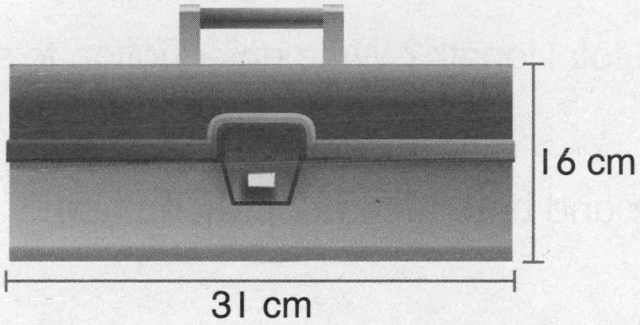

_____

Distance around: _____ centimeters

2. Jim's fishing pole is 38 inches long. His dad's fishing pole is 96 inches long. How much shorter is Jim's pole than his dad's pole?

Part A Write a subtraction equation that shows the problem.

_____

Part B Solve the problem.

_____ inches shorter

3. Jim catches a fish 49 yards away from the shore. Later, he helps row the boat closer to the shore. Now he is 27 yards away from the shore. How many yards closer to shore is Jim now than when he caught the fish?

Part A Write an addition equation that shows the problem.

_____

Part B Solve the problem.

_____ yards

4. Jim catches a silver fish that is 12 inches long. His sister catches a green fish that is 27 inches long.

What is the total length of both fish? Use the number line to solve.

_____ inches

5. Jim has 27 yards of fishing line. He gives 12 yards of line to a friend. How many yards of line does Jim have left?

_____ yards

Tools

counters	paper and pencil
cubes	place-value blocks
measuring tools	technology
number line	

6. Jim's family meets a man with a big boat. A parking spot at the dock is 32 feet long. Will the man's car and boat fit in the parking spot?

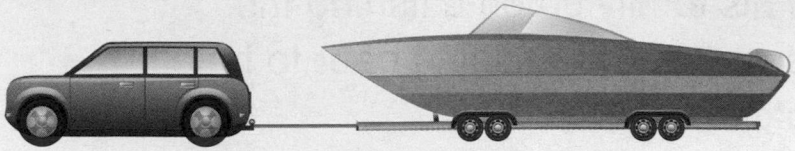

Part A

What do you need to find? _____

_____

_____

_____

Part B

What is the total length? Write an equation to solve.

_____ _____

Will the car and boat fit in the parking spot? Explain.

_____

_____

What tool did you use? _____

Copyright © Savvas Learning Company LLC. All Rights Reserved.

TOPIC 14 Graphs and Data

Essential Question: How can line plots, bar graphs, and picture graphs be used to show data and answer questions?

Digital Resources

Solve Learn Glossary Tools Assessment Help Games

These backpacks look cool!

But which one would work better for you?

Wow! Let's do this project and learn more.

Math and Science Project: Comparing Objects and Data

Find Out Work with a partner.
Compare two backpacks.
Which one holds more?
Which one has more parts?
Which one is easier to put on?
Think of other ways to compare.

Journal: Make a Book Show what you learn in a book. In your book, also:

- Tell one good thing and one bad thing about each backpack.
- Draw line plots, picture graphs, and bar graphs to show and compare data.

Name _____

Review What You Know

Vocabulary

1. Circle the number that has a 6 in the **tens** place.

406

651

160

2. Circle the **tally marks** that show 6.

Favorite Toy	
Car	~~||||~~ ||
Blocks	||||
Doll	~~||||~~	

3. Circle the **difference**.

$22 - 9 = 13$

$34 + 61 = 95$

Comparing Numbers

4. A zoo has 405 snakes. It has 375 monkeys. Compare the number of snakes to the number of monkeys.

Write > or <.

405 ◯ 375

Interpret Data

5.

Picnic Tickets Sold	
Jean	16
Paulo	18
Fatima	12

Who sold the most picnic tickets?

_____

Addition and Subtraction

6. Byron scores 24 points in a game.
Ava scores 16 points in the same game.
How many more points does Byron score than Ava?

_____ more points

Copyright © Savvas Learning Company LLC. All Rights Reserved.

My Word Cards

Study the words on the front of the card.
Complete the activity on the back.

A-Z Glossary

data

Favorite Fruit	
Apple	7
Peach	4
Orange	5

line plot

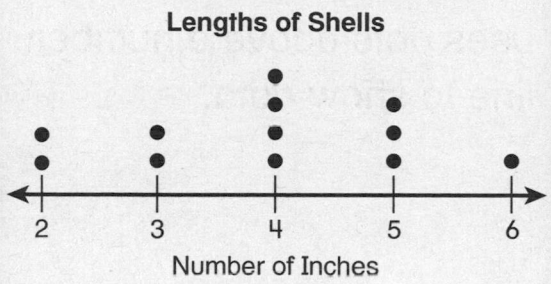

bar graph

symbol

A 🧍 stands for 1 student.

Some math symbols: = + −

picture graph

Favorite Ball Games	
Baseball	🧍🧍
Soccer	🧍🧍🧍🧍🧍🧍🧍🧍
Tennis	🧍🧍🧍🧍

Each 🧍 = 1 student

My Word Cards

Use what you know to complete the sentences.
Extend learning by writing your own sentence using each word.

A _____

uses bars to show data.

A _____

uses dots above a number line to show data.

_____

are information you collect.

A _____

_____

uses pictures to show data.

A _____

is a picture or character that stands for something.

Copyright © Savvas Learning Company LLC. All Rights Reserved.

Name _____

Solve

Lesson 14-1
Line Plots

I can ...
measure the lengths of objects, then make a line plot to organize the data.

SOL 2.8a

Solve & Share

Find four objects that are each shorter than 9 inches. Measure the length of each object to the nearest inch. Record the measurements in the table.

Then plot the data on the number line.

Which object is longest? Which is shortest?

Object	Length in Inches

Lengths of Objects

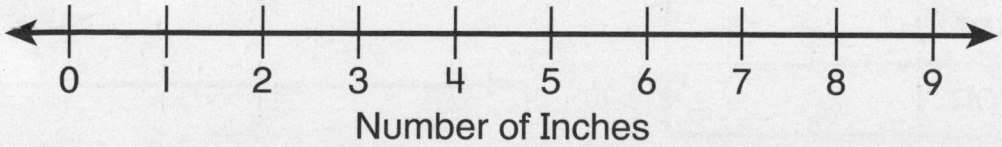

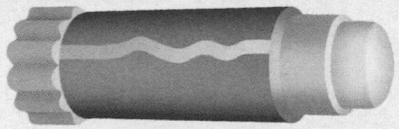

2 inches long

You can measure the length of objects. This large glue stick is 2 inches long.

You can use a table to record the measurement **data**.

Object	Length in Inches
Glue stick	2
String	4
Feather	6
Scissors	4

You can make a **line plot** to show the data. Place a dot over the number that shows each length.

The two dots above the 4 tell me that two objects are 4 inches long.

Lengths of Objects

Number of Inches

Do You Understand?

Show Me! Measure the length of your pencil to the nearest inch. Record your measurement on the line plot above. How does it change the data?

Guided Practice

Measure each object in inches. Record each length in the table. Then make a line plot. Show each length on the line plot.

1. 4 inches long

____ inches long

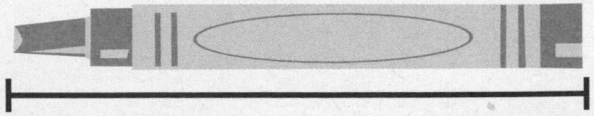

2.

Object	Length (in.)
Marker	4
Crayon	

Lengths of Objects

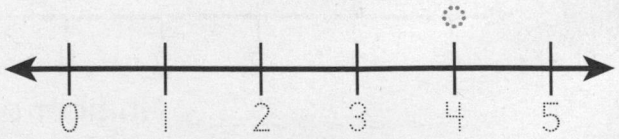

Number of Inches

Copyright © Savvas Learning Company LLC. All Rights Reserved.

Name _____

Tools Assessment

Independent Practice

Measure each object in inches. Record each length in the table. Show each length on the line plot.

3. The paintbrush is _____ inches long.

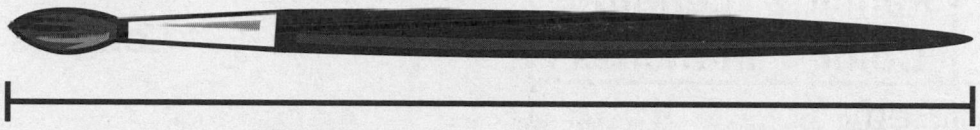

4. The chalk is _____ inches long.

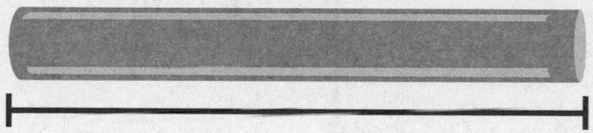

5. The straw is _____ inches long.

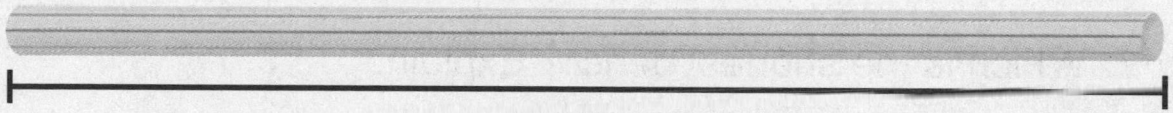

6. The glue stick is _____ inches long.

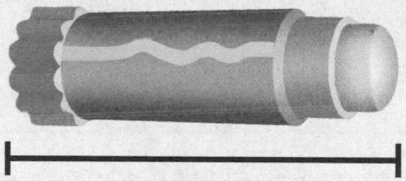

7.

Object	Length in Inches
Paintbrush	
Chalk	
Straw	
Glue Stick	

Lengths of Objects

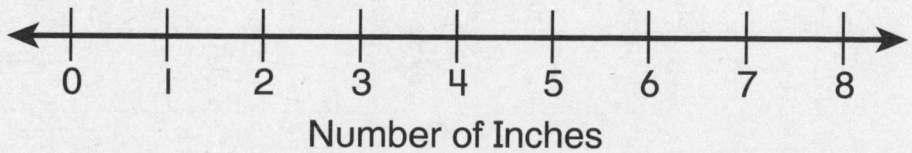

Problem Solving Solve each problem.

8. **Model** Sophia measured the length of her colored pencils and made a table. Use the data to make a line plot.

Pencil Color	Length in Inches
Red	4
Blue	3
Green	7
Yellow	9

Lengths of Pencils

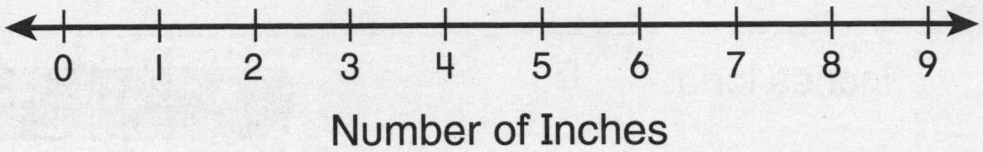

Number of Inches

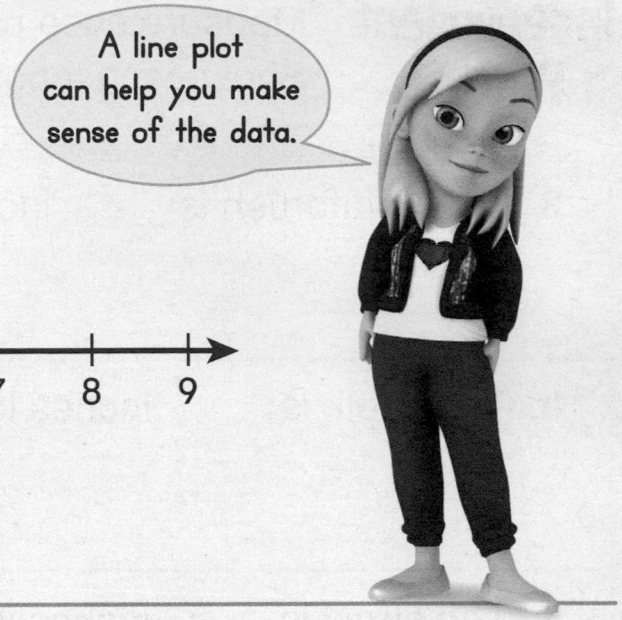

9. Which is the shortest pencil? Explain.

_____

_____

10. **Higher Order Thinking** Which two pencils have a total length of 16 inches? Explain.

_____

_____

_____

11. **Assessment** Measure the length of the purple pencil in inches. Write the length below. Record your measurement on the line plot above in Item 8.

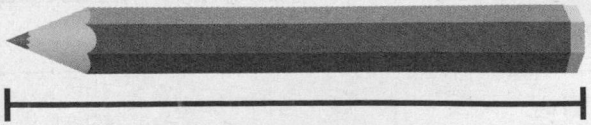

_____ inches

Copyright © Savvas Learning Company LLC. All Rights Reserved.

Name _____

Help Tools Games

Homework & Practice 14-1
Line Plots

HOME ACTIVITY Use the line plot to ask your child questions about the data. Encourage your child to explain each answer.

Another Look! You can make a line plot to show data.

The table shows the lengths of objects in inches.
Use the data from the table to make a line plot.

Object	Length in Inches
Pencil	5
Scissors	8
Stapler	6

Lengths of Objects

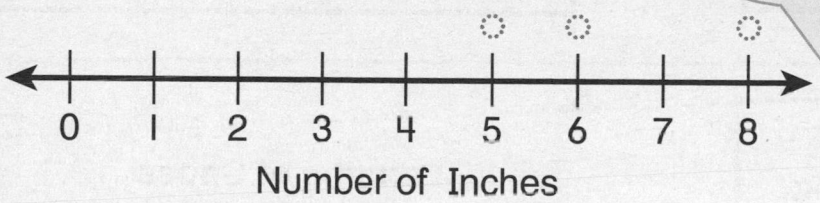

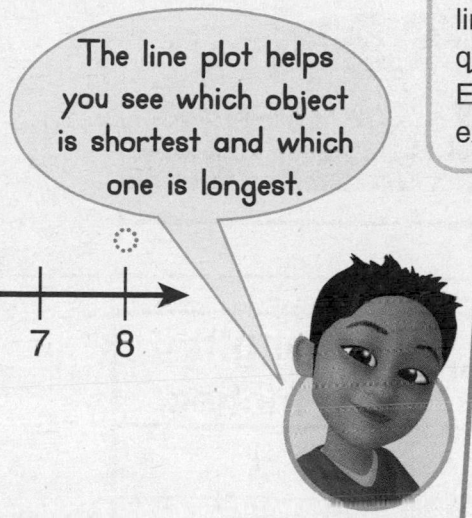

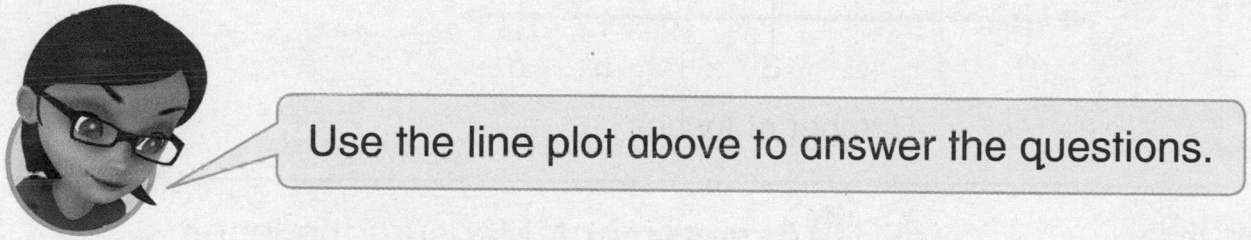

1. Which object is longest? _____

2. Which object is shortest? _____

3. How much shorter is the stapler than the scissors? _____

4. How much longer is the scissors than the pencil? _____

Be Precise Measure each shoe in inches. Then record each length in the table. Show each length on the line plot.

5. The green shoe is _____ long.

6. The purple shoe is _____ long.

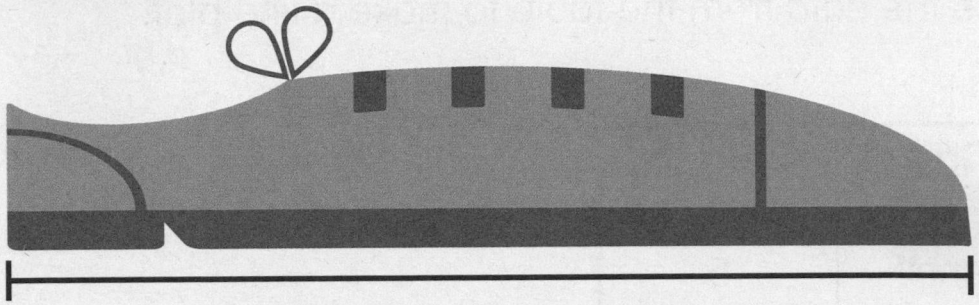

7.

Shoe Color	Length in Inches
Blue	4
Red	5
Green	
Purple	

Lengths of Shoes

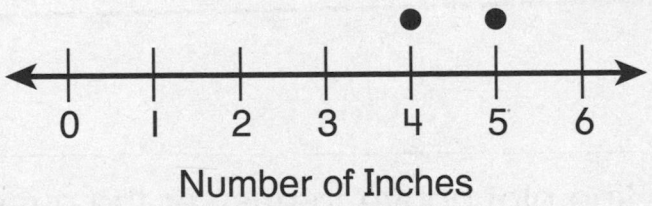

8. **Higher Order Thinking** Which three shoes have a total length of 13 inches? Explain.

_____

_____

_____

9. **Assessment** Measure the length of the yellow shoe in inches. Write the length below. Record your measurement on the line plot above.

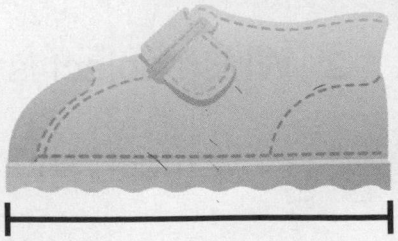

_____

Copyright © Savvas Learning Company LLC. All Rights Reserved.

Name _____

Solve

Lesson 14-2
More Line Plots

I can ...
measure the lengths of objects, then make a line plot to organize the data

SOL 2.8a, Prepares for 3.7a

Solve & Share

Measure the length of your shoe. Then use your data and data from your class to make a line plot.

Tell one thing you learn from the data.

Shoe Lengths

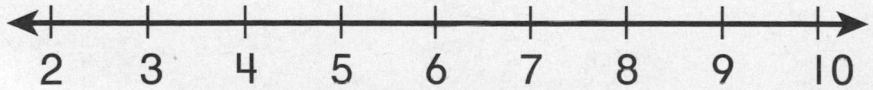

Number of Inches

Digital Resources at SavvasRealize.com

Some students measure their heights. They record the data in a table. Are there any patterns in the data?

Student Heights in Inches			
46	48	47	49
49	47	46	48
48	49	50	47
49	48	49	51

To make a line plot, draw a number line, and write a title and labels to fit your data.

Students' Heights

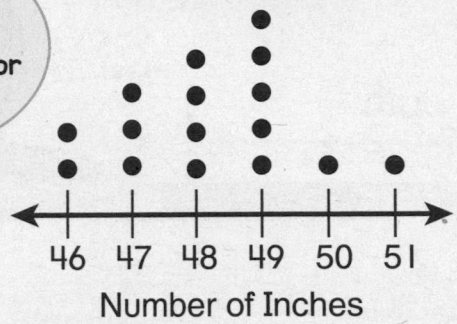

Do You Understand?

Show Me! How many students measured their height? Tell how you know.

Guided Practice

Use the table to make a line plot. Then use the line plot to answer each question.

1.

Feather Lengths (cm)			
7	5	6	4
9	4	7	6
6	8	6	4
7	5	8	6

Feather Lengths

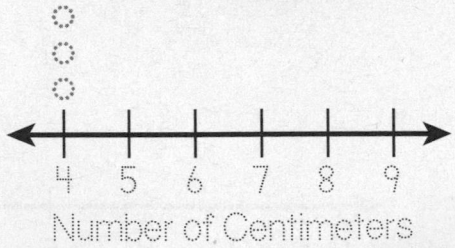

2. What is the most common feather length? 6 cm

3. Why does the number line use the numbers 4 through 9?

Copyright © Savvas Learning Company LLC. All Rights Reserved.

Name _____

Tools Assessment

Independent Practice

Collect data and use the data to complete the line plot. Then use the line plot to solve the problems.

4. Measure the length of your pencil in centimeters. Collect pencil-length data from your classmates. Make a line plot with the data.

Title: _____

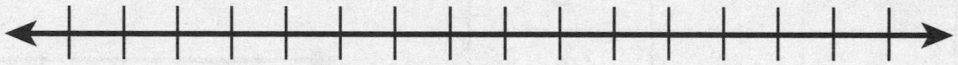

Label: _____

5. What is the length of the longest pencil?

_____

6. What is the length of the shortest pencil?

_____

7. What is the difference in length between the shortest and longest pencil?

_____

8. What is the most common pencil length?

_____

9. **Vocabulary** Use these words to complete the sentences. **longest** **line plot** **order**

A _____ can help you see the data in _____.

A line plot makes it easy to see the shortest and _____ objects.

Problem Solving

Model Use the data in the table to complete the line plot. Then use the line plot to solve the problems.

10.

Crayon Lengths in Centimeters			
6	7	5	6
7	5	7	6
7	8	6	5
5	6	7	6
8	8	6	8

Title: _____

Label: _____

11. **Higher Order Thinking** How many crayons are longer than 5 centimeters? Explain.

_____

_____

_____

_____

_____

12. **Assessment** Measure the length of the blue crayon to the nearest centimeter. Write the length below.

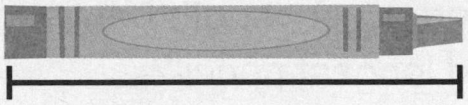

_____

Then record your measurement on the line plot above that you made in Item 10.

Copyright © Savvas Learning Company LLC. All Rights Reserved.

Name _____

Help Tools Games

Homework & Practice 14-2
More Line Plots

HOME ACTIVITY Have your child measure the lengths of three windows in your home. The windows should have different lengths. Then ask your child to make a line plot of the data.

Another Look! 7 students measured the length of the scissors to the nearest centimeter. The results are shown in the table below.

Length of Scissors in Centimeters			
8	7	7	6
7	6	7	7

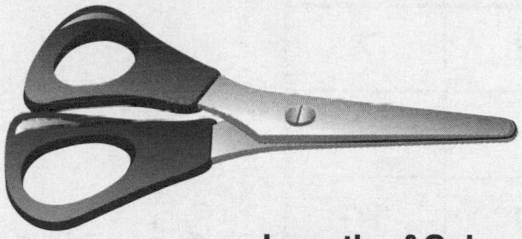

Step 1 Measure the length of the scissors to the nearest centimeter.

Step 2 Write your measurement in the table above.

Step 3 Record your measurement on the line plot at the right.

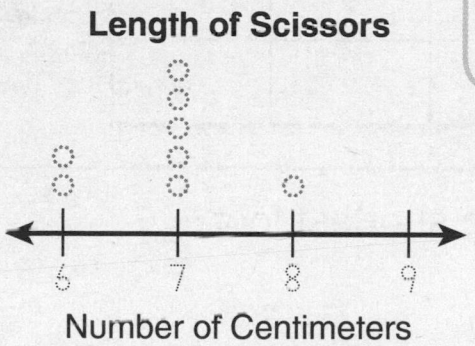

Use the line plot above to answer each question.

1. Which measurement of the length of the scissors is most common?

   _____ centimeters

2. Why did people get different measurements? Write Yes or No.

   _____ The object has a shape that is **NOT** flat.

   _____ The measurement is halfway between two units.

   _____ The ruler is not aligned with 0 when used.

Model Measure the foot length of 3 friends or family members. Write the measurements in the table below. Then use the data to complete the line plot.

3.

Foot Lengths in Inches			
8	7	8	7
6	9	6	7
10	7	9	10
7			

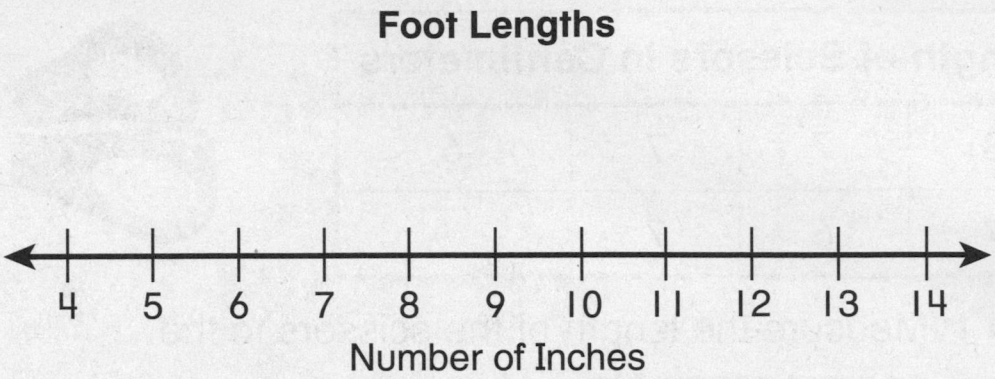

4. How long is the shortest foot?

_____

5. What is the most common foot length?

_____

6. **Higher Order Thinking** How many people have a foot length that is an even number of inches? Explain.

_____

_____

_____

_____

_____

7. **Assessment** Measure the length of this foot to the nearest inch. Write the length below. Record your measurement on the line plot you made in Item 3.

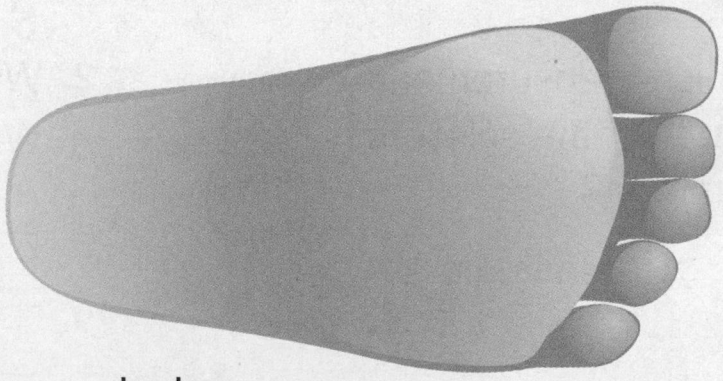

_____ inches

Copyright © Savvas Learning Company LLC. All Rights Reserved.

Name _____

Solve

Lesson 14-3
Bar Graphs

I can ...
draw bar graphs and use them to solve problems.

SOL 2.15a, 2.15b

Solve & Share

The graph shows the number of birthdays in each season for a class.
How can you use the graph to write the number of birthdays in this table? Tell how you know.

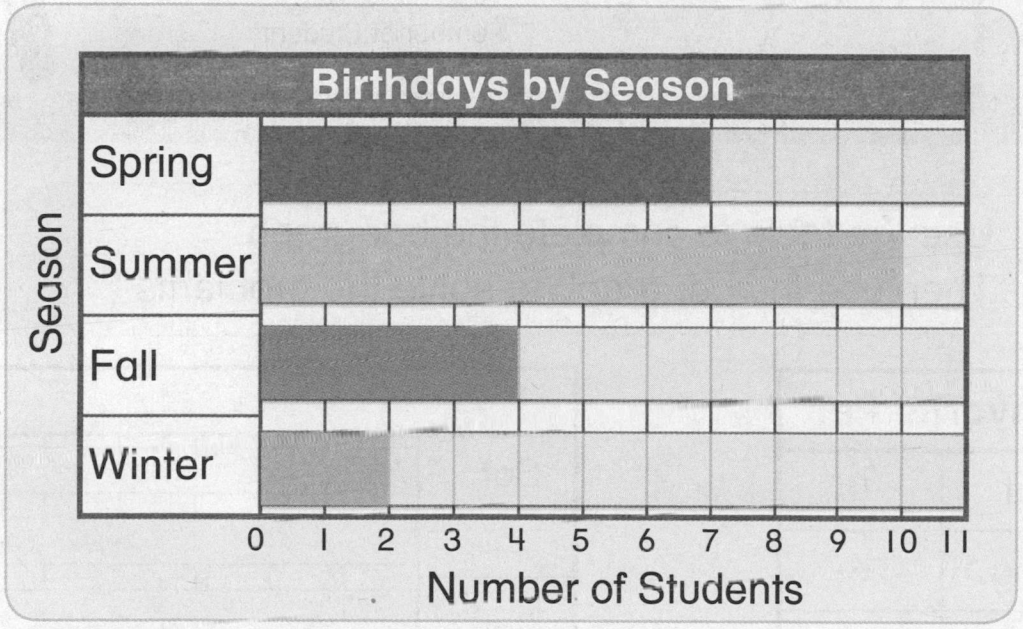

Birthdays by Season	
Spring	
Summer	
Fall	
Winter	

Digital Resources at SavvasRealize.com

Use the table to make a **bar graph**. First, write a title and label the graph.

Favorite Activities	
Music	3
Dance	4
Art	1
Drama	6

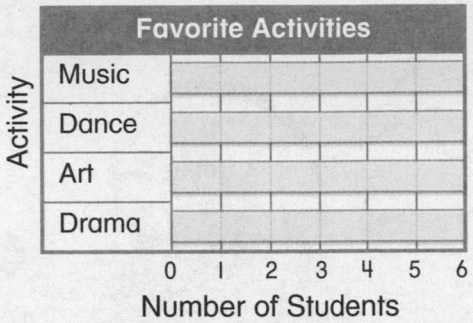

Then color boxes for each activity to match the data.

Favorite Activities	
Music	3
Dance	4
Art	1
Drama	6

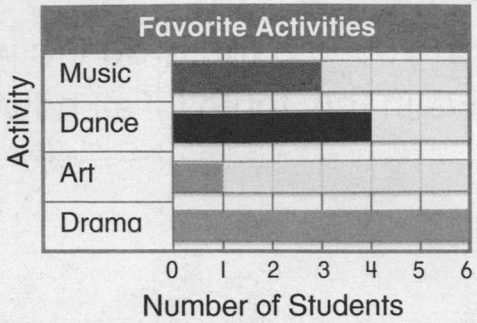

Do You Understand?

Show Me! Which activity did the most students choose? Explain how you know.

Guided Practice

Use the table to complete the bar graph. Then use the bar graph to solve the problems.

Favorite Pet	
Cat	4
Dog	6
Bird	2
Turtle	3

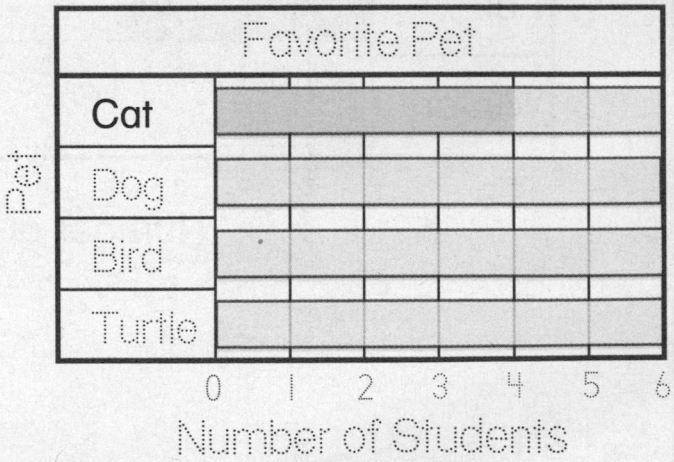

1. How many students chose cat?

4

2. Which pet did the most students choose?

Copyright © Savvas Learning Company LLC. All Rights Reserved.

Name _____

Tools Assessment

Independent Practice

Use the bar graph to solve the problems.

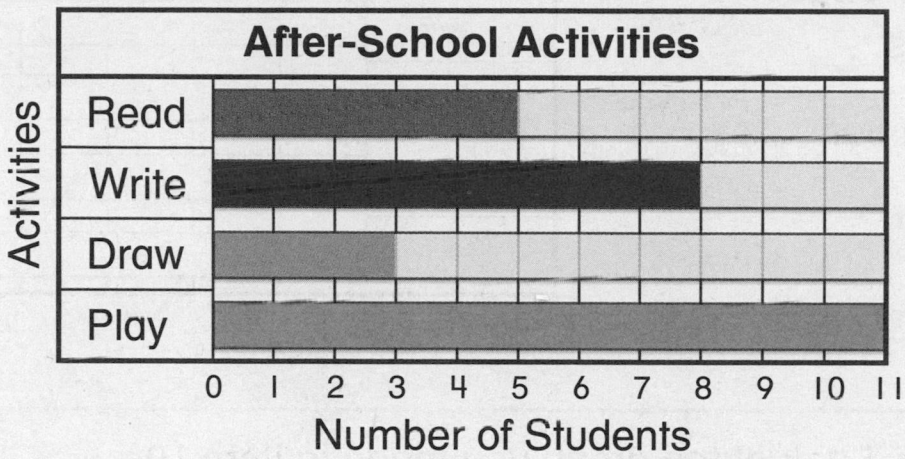

3. How many students write after school? _____

4. Which activity do exactly 5 students do after school? _____

5. Which activity do the fewest students do after school? _____

6. How many students read or draw after school? _____

7. Which activity do the most students do after school? _____

8. How many more students play than read after school? _____

9. **Higher Order Thinking** How would the graph be different if 2 students changed their after-school activity from Play to Read?

_____

_____

_____

Problem Solving Solve the problems below.

10. **Model** Wanda went to the farm. She bought 8 pears, 5 oranges, 2 apples, and 9 peaches.

Use this data to make a bar graph.

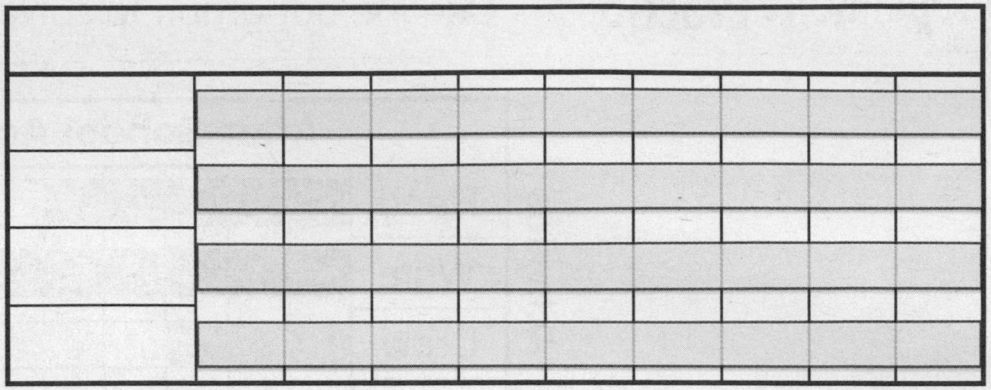

11. **Higher Order Thinking** Look at the graph you made in Item 10. How would the graph change if Wanda bought 3 more pears?

12. **Assessment** Look at the bar graph you made in Item 10. Which is correct? Choose all that apply.

- ☐ Wanda bought the same number of pears and peaches.
- ☐ Wanda bought 3 more oranges than apples.
- ☐ Wanda bought 24 pieces of fruit in all.
- ☐ Wanda bought 4 more peaches than oranges.

Copyright © Savvas Learning Company LLC. All Rights Reserved.

Name _____

Help Tools Games

Homework & Practice 14-3
Bar Graphs

HOME ACTIVITY Gather three small groups of objects, such as 3 pens, 4 rubber bands, and 6 buttons. Make a table and a bar graph with your child to show how many of each object you have.

Another Look! The table shows how students voted to name the class goldfish.

Use the data from the table to make a bar graph.

Goldfish Names	
Flash	5
Goldie	3
Rocky	6
Bubbles	8

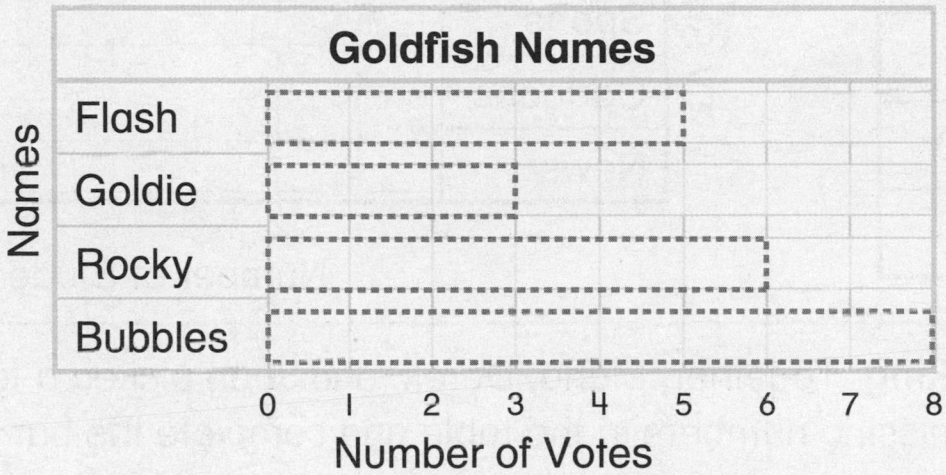

Use the bar graph above to solve the problems.

1. How many students voted for the name Goldie or the name Rocky?

_____

2. How many fewer students voted for the name Flash than voted for the name Rocky?

_____

3. Which name did the most students vote for? _____

4. Which name did the fewest students vote for? _____

Complete the bar graphs and solve the problems.

5. **Model** Use the data in the table to complete the bar graph.

Favorite TV Shows	
Animals	6
Sports	8
Cartoons	10
News	3

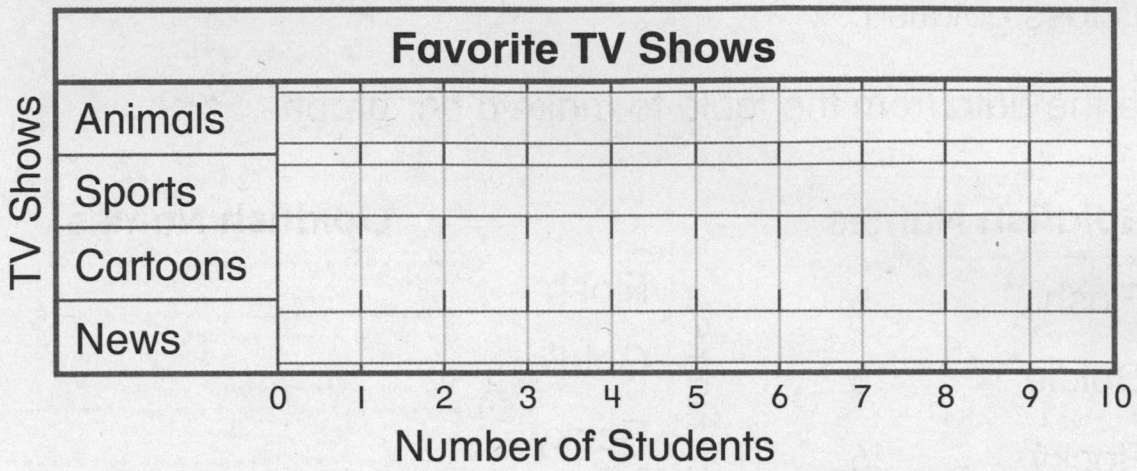

6. **Higher Order Thinking** Together, Marla, Derek, and Juan picked a total of 19 apples. Write the possible missing numbers in the table and complete the bar graph.

Apple Picking	
Marla	3
Derek	
Juan	

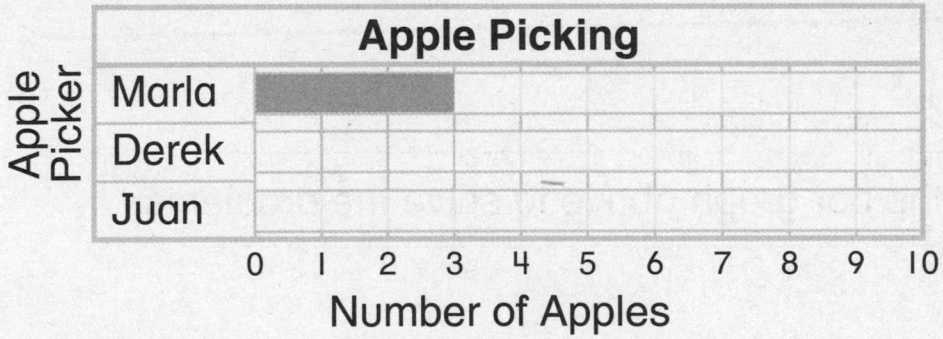

7. **Assessment** Look at the bar graph in Item 5. Which statements are correct? Choose all that apply.

- ☐ 2 fewer students chose sports than animals.
- ☐ 10 students chose news or animals.
- ☐ 5 more students chose sports than news.
- ☐ 27 students in all were counted.

Copyright © Savvas Learning Company LLC. All Rights Reserved.

Name _____

Solve

Lesson 14-4
Picture Graphs

I can ...
draw picture graphs and use them to solve problems.

SOL 2.15a, 2.15b

Solve & Share

The graph shows the favorite subjects for a class. How can you use the graph to write the data in this table? Tell how you know.

Favorite School Subject	
Reading	
Math	
Science	
Social Studies	

The tally chart shows the favorite ball games of Ms. Green's class.

Favorite Ball Games	
Baseball	II
Soccer	~~IIII~~ III
Tennis	IIII

You can show the same data in another way.

Choose a **symbol** to represent the data.

The symbol will be 🧍. Each 🧍 represents 1 student.

A **picture graph** uses pictures to show data.

You can draw the symbols to show the data.

8 students chose soccer!

Favorite Ball Games	
Baseball	🧍🧍
Soccer	🧍🧍🧍🧍🧍🧍🧍🧍
Tennis	🧍🧍🧍🧍

Each 🧍 = 1 student

Do You Understand?

Show Me! How are the tally chart and picture graph for the favorite ball games of Ms. Green's class alike?

☆ Guided Practice ☆

Use the tally chart to complete the picture graph. Then use the picture graph to solve the problems.

Favorite Colors	
Blue	~~IIII~~
Red	~~IIII~~ I
Purple	III

Favorite Colors	
Blue	
Red	
Purple	

Each ✏️ = 1 vote

1. How many students like blue best?

   5

2. Which color is the favorite of most students?

   _____

Copyright © Savvas Learning Company LLC. All Rights Reserved.

Name _____

Tools Assessment

Independent Practice

Use the tally chart to complete the picture graph. Then use the picture graph to solve the problems.

3.

Favorite Season	
Spring	IIII
Summer	~~IIII~~ ~~IIII~~
Fall	~~IIII~~ I
Winter	II

Favorite Season	
Spring	
Summer	
Fall	
Winter	

Each = 1 vote

4. How many students like fall best? _____

5. Which season do exactly 4 students like best? _____

6. Which season do the fewest students like? _____

7. How many students like the season with the fewest votes? _____

8. Which season do the most students like? _____

9. How many students like the season with the most votes? _____

10. **Higher Order Thinking** Look at the picture graph above. How would the graph change if 2 students changed their votes from Summer to Fall?

_____

_____

Problem Solving

Use the tally chart to complete the picture graph.
Use the picture graph to solve the problems.

11. Model Bob made a tally chart to show the trees in a park.

Trees in the Park	
Birch	III
Oak	~~IIII~~ I
Maple	~~IIII~~
Pine	II

Trees in the Park	
Birch	
Oak	
Maple	
Pine	

Each = 1 tree

12. Math and Science Birch, oak, maple, and pine trees are common in North America. Which type of tree is most common in the park? _____

13. Higher Order Thinking How many birch and maple trees are there in all?

_____

14. Assessment Draw a picture graph to show the data in the table.

Favorite Drink	
Milk	III
Juice	IIII
Water	I

Each = 1 vote

Copyright © Savvas Learning Company LLC. All Rights Reserved.

Name _____

Help Tools Games

Homework & Practice 14-4
Picture Graphs

Another Look! A picture graph uses pictures or symbols to show information.

The number at the right tells how many students chose each snack. Complete the picture graph.

Favorite Snacks		
Popcorn	☺☺☺☺☺☺☺☺☺	9
Fruit Cup	☺☺☺☺	4
Yogurt	☺☺☺☺☺☺☺	7
Cheese and Crackers	☺☺☺☺☺☺☺☺☺☺	10

Each ☺ = 1 student

HOME ACTIVITY Tell your child which snack shown in the picture graph is your favorite. Ask him or her to explain how the Favorite Snacks picture graph would change if your response was added to the picture graph.

Use the picture graph above to solve the problems.

1. How many students like cheese and crackers best?

_____

2. How many students like yogurt best?

_____

3. Which snack is the least favorite?

_____

4. Which snack is most students' favorite?

_____

Solve each problem.

5. **Model** The tally chart shows how many tickets each student has. Use the tally chart to complete the picture graph.

Tickets We Have	
Denise	IIII
Steve	II
Tom	~~IIII~~ IIII
Lisa	~~IIII~~ I

Tickets We Have	
Denise	
Steve	
Tom	
Lisa	

Each TICKET = 1 ticket

6. **Higher Order Thinking** Lisa gives 2 tickets to Steve. How many tickets does Steve have now? Explain.

_____

_____

_____

7. **Assessment** The tally chart shows the favorite pets of a class of second graders. Use the tally chart to draw a picture graph.

Favorite Pets	
Cat	~~IIII~~ I
Dog	~~IIII~~ II
Fish	~~IIII~~
Hamster	II

♥ = 1 Vote

Copyright © Savvas Learning Company LLC. All Rights Reserved.

Name _____

Solve

Lesson 14-5

Draw Conclusions from Graphs

I can ...
draw conclusions from graphs.

SOL 2.15b, 2.15a

Solve & Share

7 students voted for Turtle as their favorite pond animal. 10 students voted for Frog. 4 students voted for Fish. Make a picture graph to show the data. Write two things you notice about the data.

Favorite Pond Animals

Turtle	
Frog	
Fish	

Each ★ = 1 vote

1. _____

2. _____

Digital Resources at SavvasRealize.com

Look at the bar graph. What does it show?

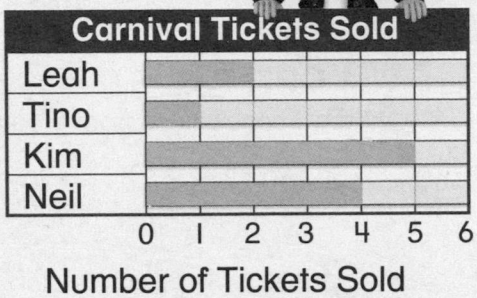

The length of each bar shows how many tickets each person sold.

Leah has sold 2 tickets. Who has sold the most tickets?

You can also compare information and solve problems.

Kim sold the most tickets.

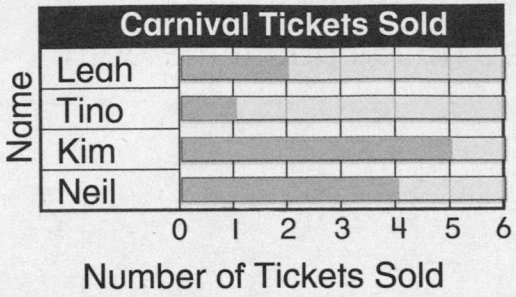

$5 - 1 = 4$ Kim sold 4 more tickets than Tino.

$5 - 4 = 1$ Neil sold 1 less ticket than Kim.

Do You Understand?

Show Me! Look at the graph above. How many tickets did Kim and Neil sell in all? How do you know?

Guided Practice

Use the bar graph to solve the problems.

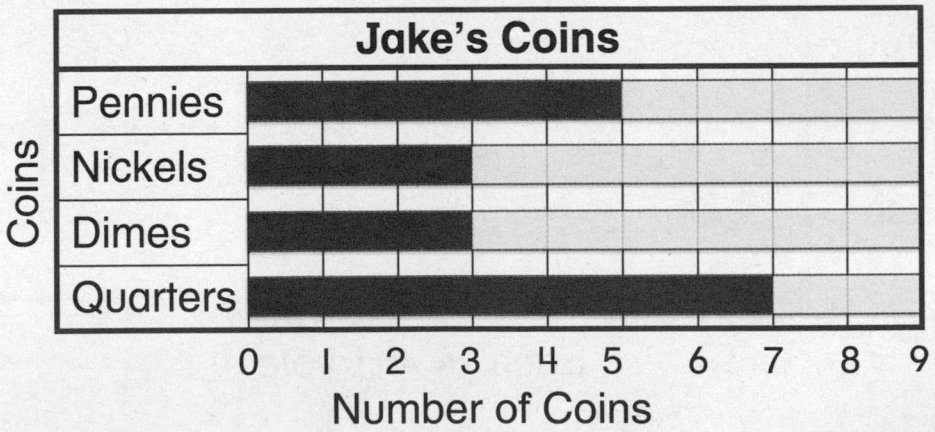

1. How many pennies does Jake have?

5

2. Jake spends 3 of his quarters. How many does he have left?

Copyright © Savvas Learning Company LLC. All Rights Reserved.

Name _____

Tools Assessment

Independent Practice

Use the bar graph to solve the problems.

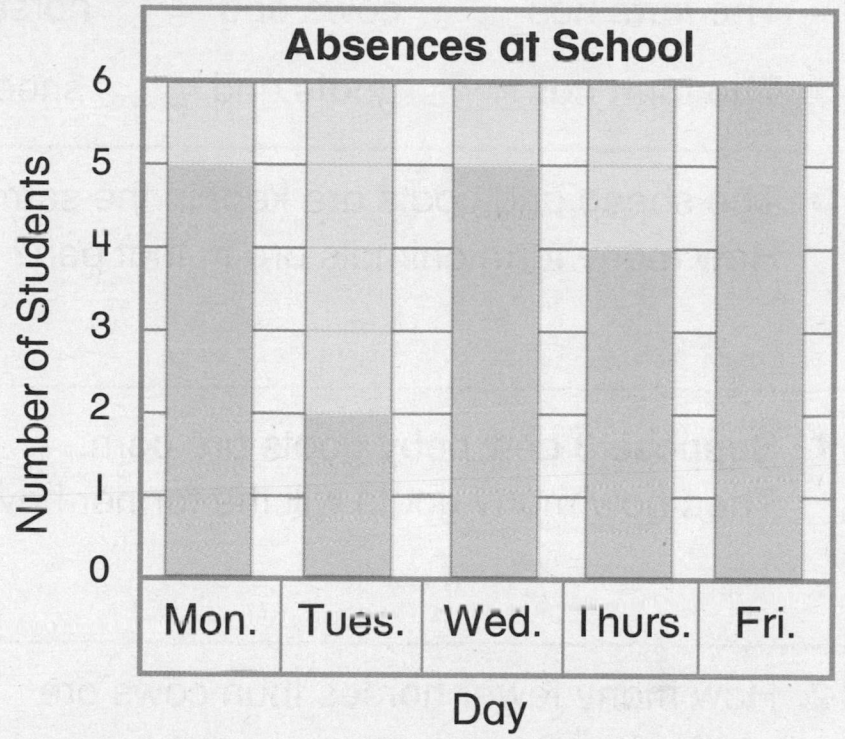

3. How many students in all were absent on Tuesday and Thursday?

_____

4. Were fewer students absent on Monday or Friday? How many fewer?

_____

5. Three of the students absent on Friday were boys. How many girls were absent on Friday?

_____

6. On which two days were the same number of students absent?

_____

7. Were more students absent on Wednesday or Thursday? How many more?

_____

8. Higher Order Thinking The graph shows the number of students absent last week. This week, 19 students were absent. Compare the number of students absent this week to the number of students absent last week.

_____

_____

_____

Problem Solving

Use the bar graph to solve each problem.

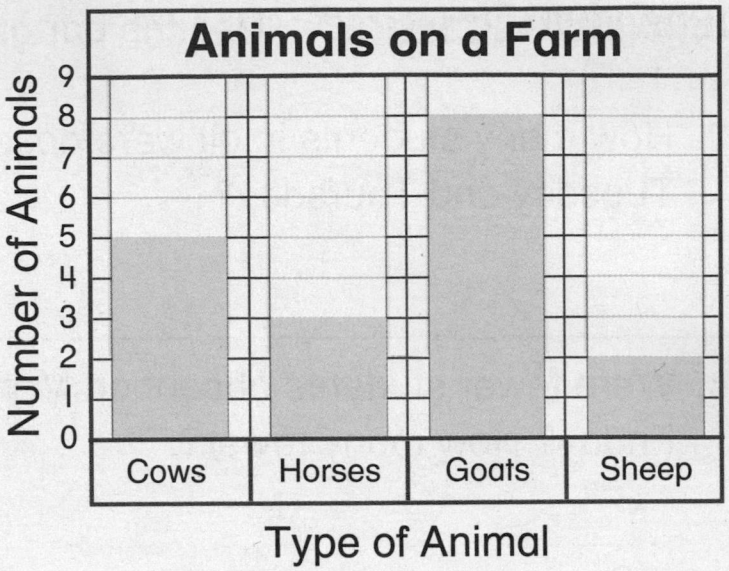

9. **Make Sense** Complete each sentence.

The farm has _____ cows and _____ horses.

The farm has _____ goats and _____ sheep.

10. The sheep and goats are kept in the same pen. How many farm animals are in that pen?

_____

11. Suppose 3 new baby goats are born. Then how many goats will the farmer have?

_____

12. How many fewer horses than cows are on the farm?

_____

13. Write the order of animals on the farm from the greatest number to the least number.

_____

14. **Higher Order Thinking** Do you think the bars on a bar graph should all be the same color? Explain.

_____

_____

15. **Assessment** The farmer wants to buy some sheep. He wants to have as many sheep as cows. How many more sheep should the farmer buy?

_____

Copyright © Savvas Learning Company LLC. All Rights Reserved.

Name _____

Help Tools Games

Homework & Practice 14-5

Draw Conclusions from Graphs

Another Look! You can draw conclusions from data in a graph.

This picture graph shows students' favorite types of books.
Write how many students chose each type of book.

	Favorite Type of Book
7	Biography
5	Adventure
4	Science
9	Mystery

Each = 1 vote

HOME ACTIVITY Use the Favorite Type of Book picture graph to ask your child questions about the data. Encourage your child to explain each answer.

Use the picture graph above to answer the questions.

1. Which was the least favorite type of book?

_____

2. Which type of book did most students vote for? _____

3. How many more students voted for biography than for adventure?

_____

4. If each student voted one time only, how many students voted in all?

_____

Use the bar graph to solve each problem.

5. **Make Sense** Complete each sentence.

The fruit basket has _____ apples and _____ pears.

The fruit basket has _____ oranges and _____ plums.

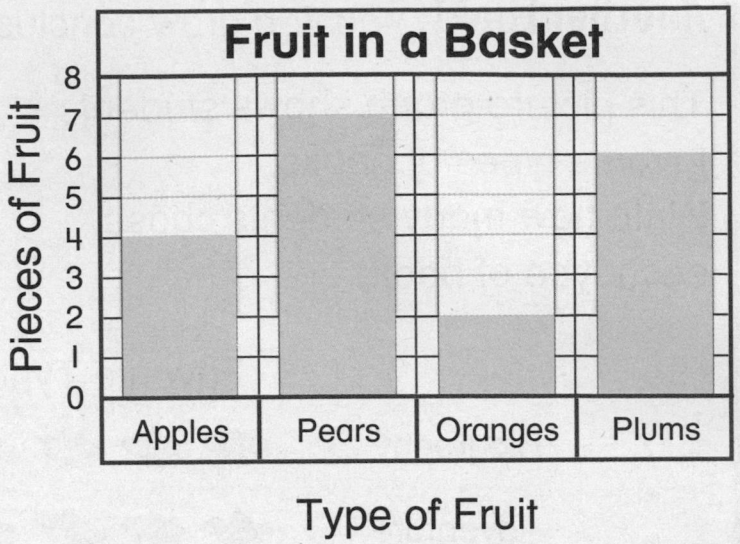

6. Write the order of the type of fruit from the least number to the greatest number.

_____

7. How many apples and oranges in all are in the basket?

_____

8. Maria uses 4 of the pears to make a pie. How many pears are left in the basket?

_____

9. **Higher Order Thinking** Does it matter how you order the data in a bar graph? Explain.

_____

_____

_____

_____

10. **Assessment** How many fewer apples than plums are in the basket?

_____

Copyright © Savvas Learning Company LLC. All Rights Reserved.

Name _____

Solve

Problem Solving

Lesson 14-6
Reasoning

I can ...
reason about data in bar graphs and picture graphs to write and solve problems.

SOL 2.15b, 2.15a, 2.6c

Solve & Share

Make a picture graph to show how many connecting cubes, counters, and ones cubes you have. Then write and solve a problem about your data.

Math Tools	
Connecting Cubes	
Counters	
Ones Cubes	

Thinking Habits

What do the symbols mean?

How are the numbers in the problem related?

Each _____ = 1 math tool

_____

_____

_____

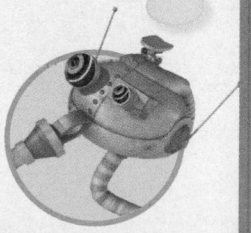

Digital Resources at SavvasRealize.com

The bar graph shows the number of stamps each student has collected.

Write and solve a problem about the data in the bar graph.

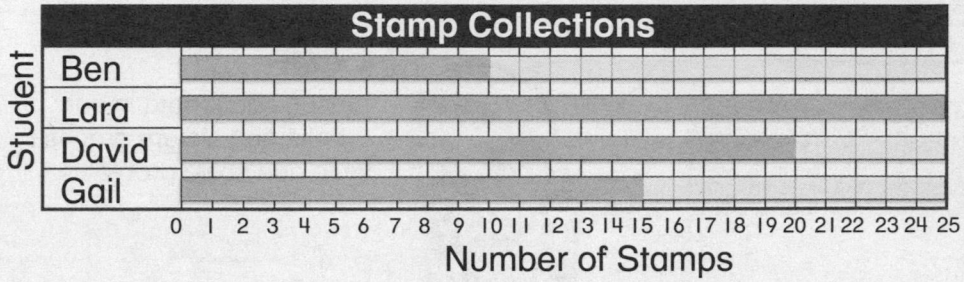

How can I use reasoning to write and solve a problem?

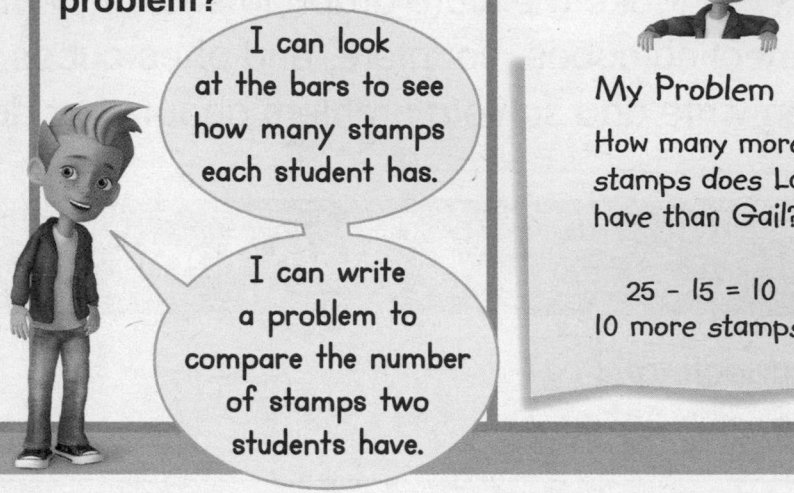

My Problem

How many more stamps does Lara have than Gail?

25 - 15 = 10
10 more stamps

Do You Understand?

Show Me! Use reasoning to write your own problem about the data in the graph. Then solve it.

Guided Practice

Use the bar graph to write and solve problems.

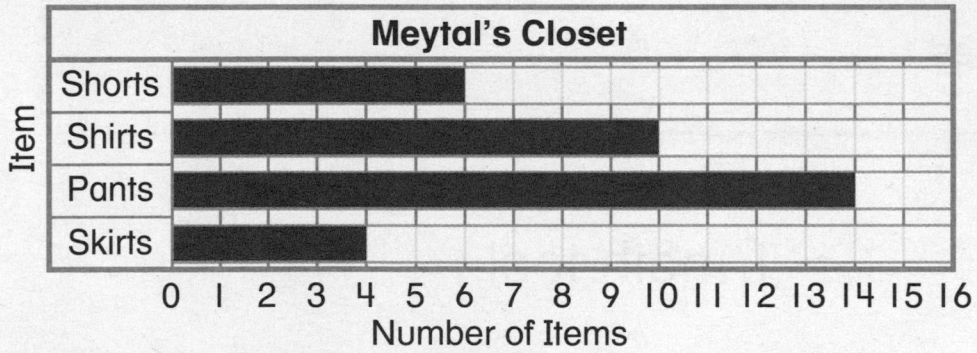

1. How many shirts and skirts are there in all?

10 + 4 = 14

2. _____ ◯ _____ = _____

Copyright © Savvas Learning Company LLC. All Rights Reserved.

Name _____

Tools Assessment

Independent Practice

Use the bar graph to write and solve problems.

3. _____

_____

_____

_____ ◯ _____ = _____

_____

_____

4. _____

_____

_____

_____ ◯ _____ = _____

_____

_____

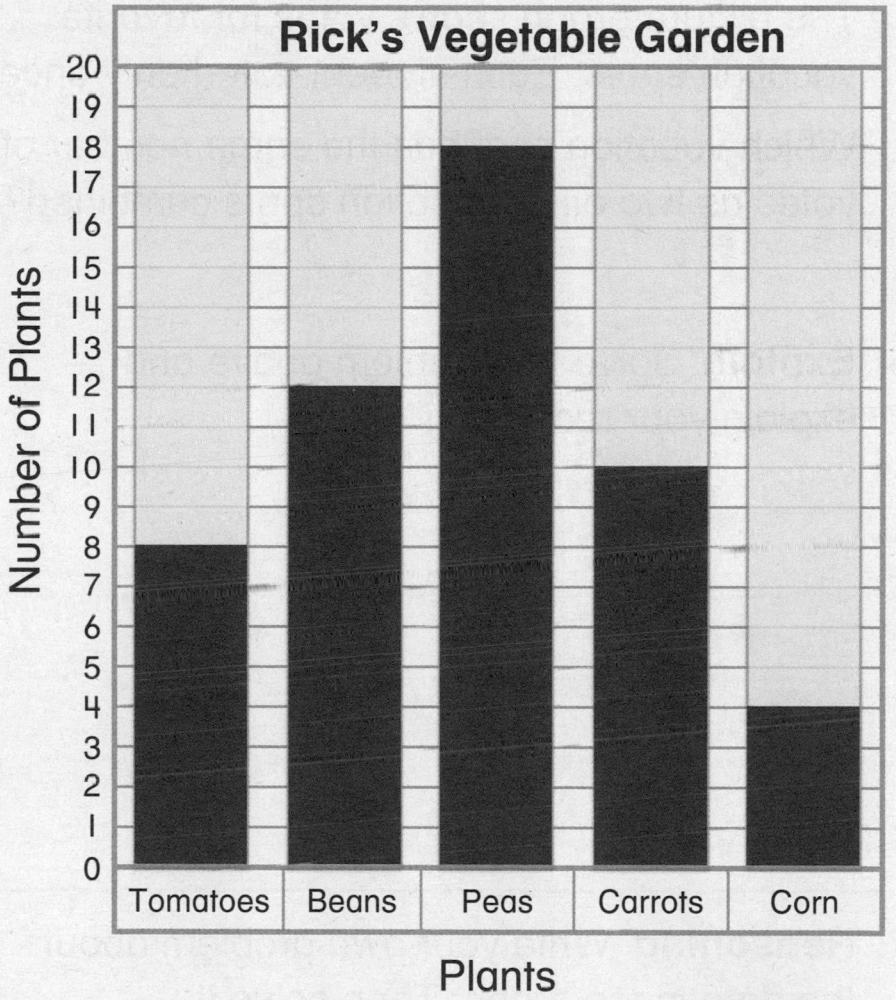

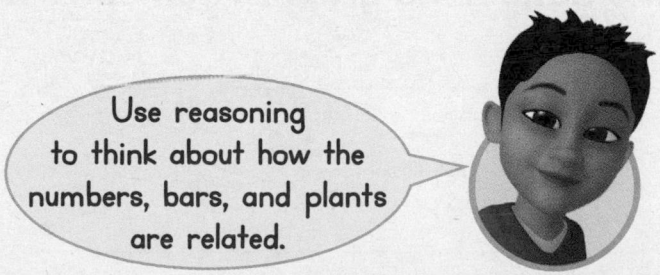

Problem Solving

Performance Assessment

Vacation Time!

The picture graph shows votes for favorite vacation spots. Each student voted only once.

Which vacation spot has the same number of votes as two other vacation spots combined?

Votes for Favorite Vacation Spot	
Beach	✓✓✓✓✓✓✓✓✓✓✓
Mountains	✓✓✓✓✓✓✓
City	✓✓✓✓
Theme Park	✓✓✓✓✓✓✓✓✓✓✓✓

Each ✓ = 1 vote

5. **Explain** Solve the problem above and explain your reasoning.

6. **Make Sense** How many students voted in all? Tell how you know.

7. **Reasoning** Write your own problem about the data in the graph. Then solve it.

____ ◯ ____ = ____

Copyright © Savvas Learning Company LLC. All Rights Reserved.

Name _____

Help Tools Games

Homework & Practice 14-6
Reasoning

Another Look! You can reason about data in the picture graph to write and solve problems.

How many more votes did the Tigers get than the Lions?

Votes for Team Name	
Wolves	
Tigers	
Lions	

Each = 1 vote

Count the symbols for the votes for Tigers and Lions on the picture graph. Then subtract.

Tigers 10 Lions 8

10 − 8 = 2

The Tigers got 2 more votes than the Lions.

HOME ACTIVITY Look at the picture graph for team names together. Ask your child to find how many more votes there are for Wolves and Lions combined than there are for Tigers. Have your child explain how to find the answer.

Write and solve problems about the data in the picture graph above.

1. _____

_____

___ ◯ ___ = ___

_____

2. _____

_____

___ ◯ ___ = ___

_____

Performance Assessment

Gym Games

Ms. Winn has to cut one game from gym class. So, she asked students to choose their favorite game. The bar graph shows the results. Each student voted only once. Which game should she cut and why?

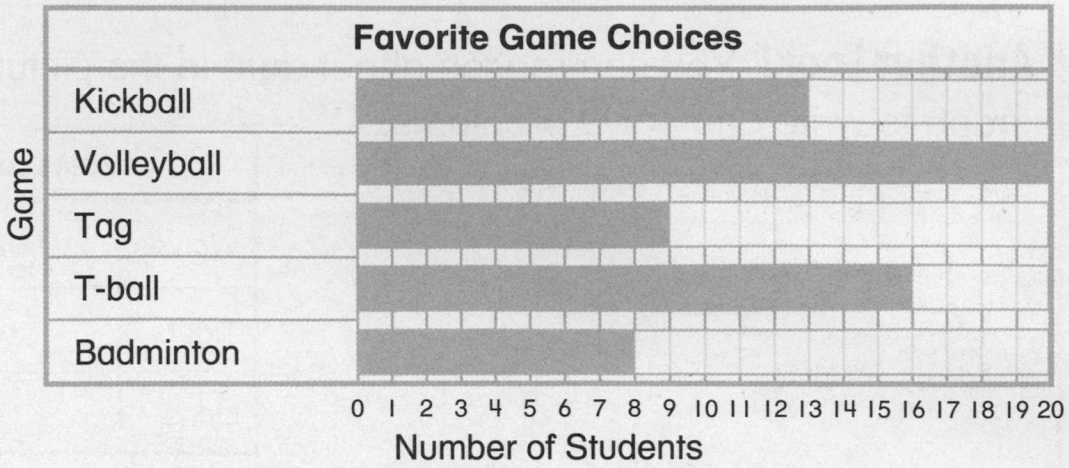

3. **Make Sense** How many students voted for each game? Tell how you know.

4. **Explain** Ms. Winn wants to cut tag from gym class. Do you agree? Explain.

5. **Reasoning** How many fewer students chose tag and badminton combined than volleyball? Explain your reasoning.

Copyright © Savvas Learning Company LLC. All Rights Reserved.

Name _____

TOPIC 14 **Fluency Practice Activity**

Find a Match

Find a partner. Point to a clue. Read the clue.

Look below the clues to find a match. Write the clue letter in the box next to the match.

Find a match for every clue.

I can ...
add and subtract within 100.

Clues

A The difference is less than 16.

B The sum equals 43 + 25.

C The difference equals 75 − 46.

D The sum equals 53 + 20.

E The difference equals 96 − 19.

F The sum equals 75.

G The sum is between 60 and 65.

H The difference is between 25 and 28.

☐ 39 + 24	☐ 81 − 52	☐ 33 + 42	☐ 35 + 38
☐ 73 − 59	☐ 67 − 40	☐ 88 − 11	☐ 17 + 51

TOPIC 14 Vocabulary Review

A-Z Glossary

Word List
- bar graph
- data
- line plot
- picture graph
- symbol

Understand Vocabulary

Label each data display. Write *line plot, bar graph,* or *picture graph.*

1.

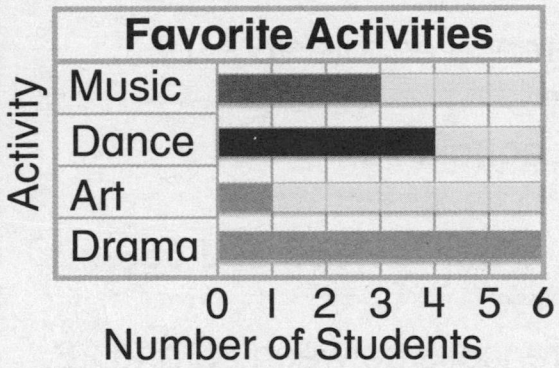

_____

2.

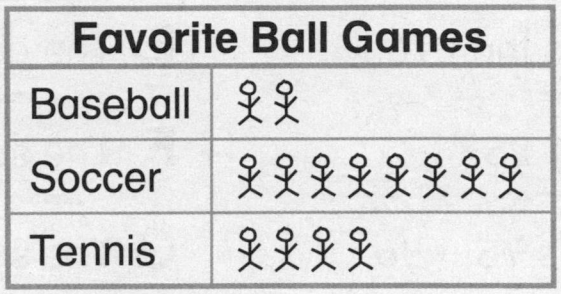

Each ☺ = 1 student

_____

3.

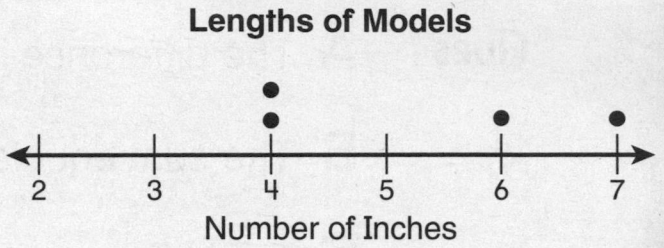

_____

Use Vocabulary in Writing

4. Look at the graph in Item 2. Use words to tell how to find which ball game is the most popular. Use terms from the Word List.

_____

_____

_____

_____

_____

Copyright © Savvas Learning Company LLC. All Rights Reserved.

Name _____

TOPIC 14

Set A _____

Reteaching

Line plots show and organize data.
Use an inch ruler. Measure the length of the toy car. Then record the measurement in the table.

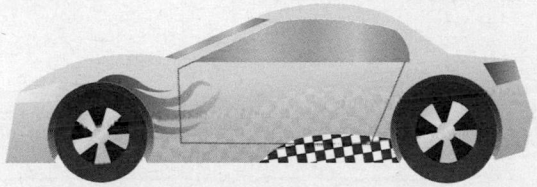

Toy	Length in Inches
Car	3
Airplane	5
Doll	5
Block	1

Place a dot over the number that shows the length of each toy.

Length of Toys

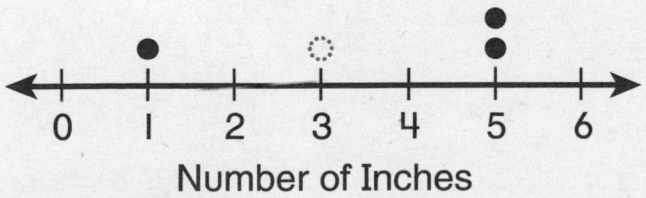

Complete the table and show the data on a line plot.

1. Use an inch ruler. Measure the length of the pencil. Then record the measurement in the table.

Object	Length in Inches
Pencil	
Stapler	6
Scissors	6
Eraser	3

2. Make a line plot to show each length.

Length of Objects

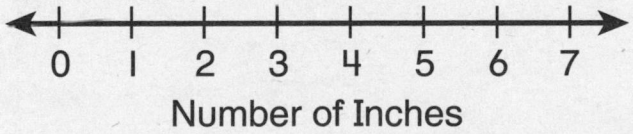

Set B

You can make a bar graph to show the data in a table.

Students voted for their favorite nut. The table shows the number of votes.

Favorite Nut	
Peanut	7
Almond	4
Cashew	5

Color one space for each vote in the bar graph.
Then use the graph to solve the problem.

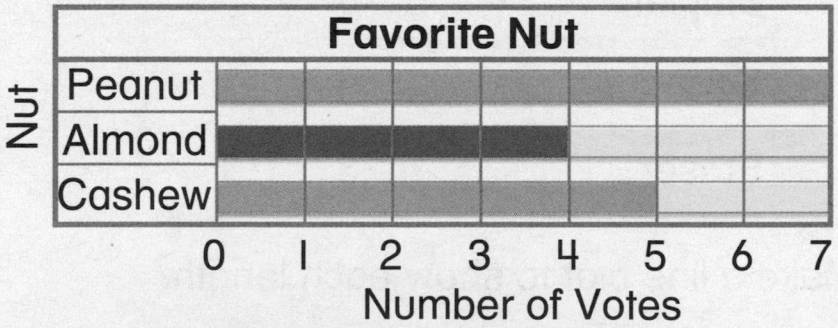

How many students voted? 16

Use the table to complete the bar graph. Then solve each problem.

3.

Favorite Yogurt	
Lemon	3
Vanilla	7
Banana	6

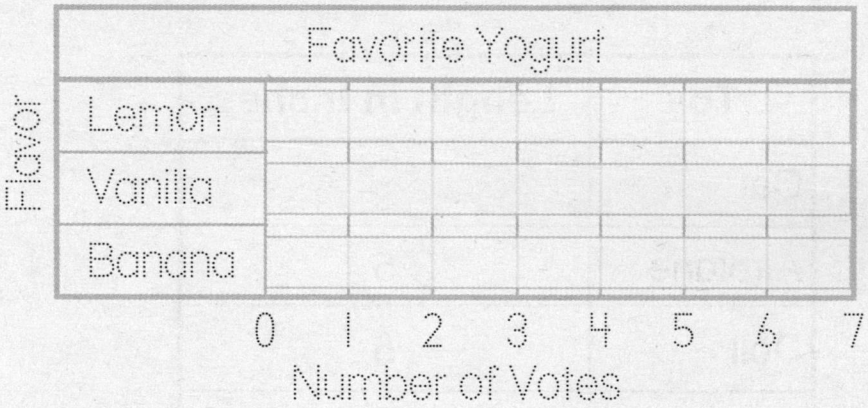

4. How many more students voted for vanilla than banana? ____

5. How many fewer students voted for lemon than vanilla? ____

Copyright © Savvas Learning Company LLC. All Rights Reserved.

Name _____

TOPIC 14

Reteaching Continued

Set C

A picture graph uses pictures or symbols to show data.

The tally chart shows votes for favorite sea animals.

Favorite Sea Animals	
Whale	𝍸 I
Dolphin	II
Seal	IIII

Use the data to make a picture graph.
Each 🧍 stands for 1 vote.

Favorite Sea Animals	
Whale	🧍🧍🧍🧍🧍🧍
Dolphin	🧍🧍
Seal	🧍🧍🧍🧍

🧍 = 1 vote

Which sea animal has the fewest votes?

dolphin

Use the tally chart to complete the picture graph.
Then solve each problem.

6.

Favorite Birds	
Blue Jay	𝍸
Robin	𝍸 III
Seagull	𝍸 𝍸

Favorite Birds	
Blue Jay	
Robin	
Seagull	

🐦 = 1 vote

7. How many votes did seagull get?

_____

8. Which bird had the fewest votes?

_____

Thinking Habits

Reasoning

What do the symbols mean?

How are the numbers in the problem related?

How can I write a word problem using the information that is given?

How do the numbers in my problem relate to each other?

How can I use a word problem to show what an equation means?

Use the picture graph to solve each problem. Each student voted once.

Favorite Winter Sport	
Skiing	❄ ❄ ❄ ❄ ❄ ❄ ❄
Snowboarding	❄ ❄ ❄ ❄ ❄ ❄ ❄ ❄ ❄ ❄
Skating	❄ ❄ ❄ ❄ ❄ ❄ ❄ ❄
Ice Fishing	❄ ❄ ❄ ❄

Each ❄ = 1 vote

9. How many fewer students chose ice fishing than snowboarding? ____

10. Write and solve your own problem about the data.

_____

_____

____ ◯ ____ = ____

_____

Copyright © Savvas Learning Company LLC. All Rights Reserved.

Name _____

TOPIC 14 Assessment

1. Pam has 5 pennies, 2 nickels, 8 dimes, and 9 quarters. Show this data in the bar graph below. Draw the bars.

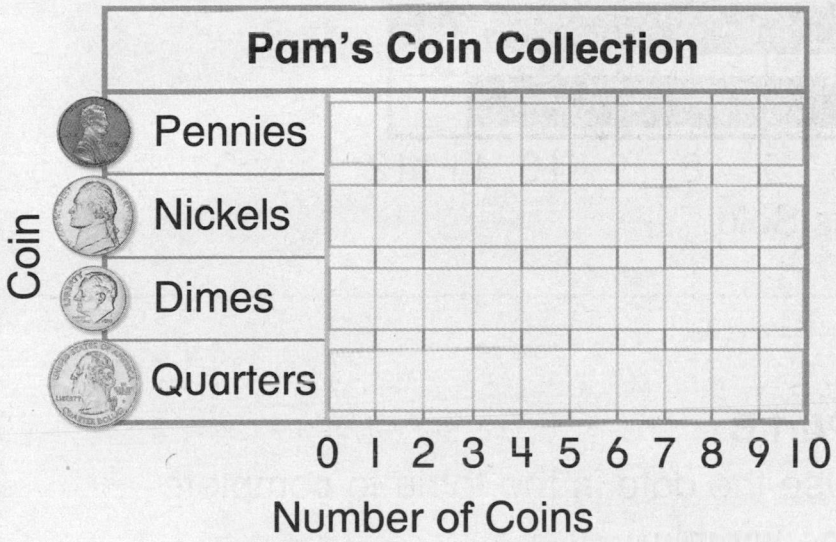

2. Use the bar graph you made above. Pam spends 5 of her dimes to buy an apple. Now how many dimes does Pam have left?

Ⓐ 13

Ⓑ 5

Ⓒ 3

Ⓓ 0

3. Is each sentence about the picture graph correct? Choose Yes or No.

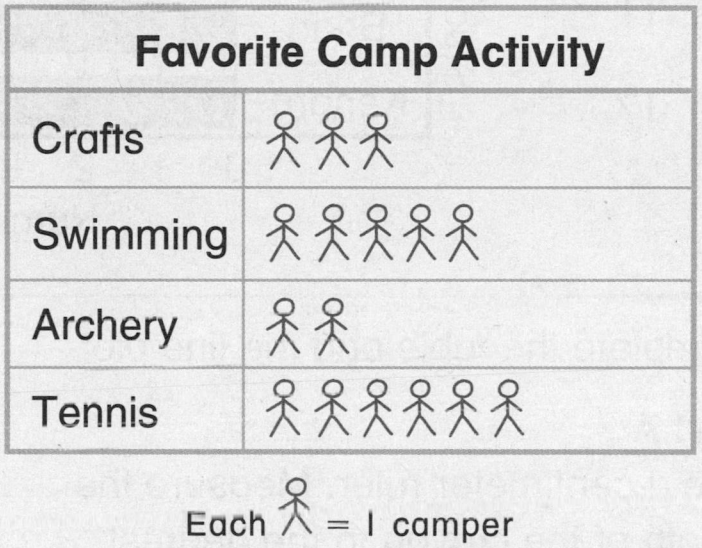

7 students voted for tennis. ○ Yes ○ No

16 students voted in all. ○ Yes ○ No

2 more students voted for swimming than for crafts. ○ Yes ○ No

3 fewer students voted for tennis than for crafts. ○ Yes ○ No

4. How many more tickets did Kendra sell than Leon?

Ⓐ 5

Ⓑ 6

Ⓒ 11

Ⓓ 17

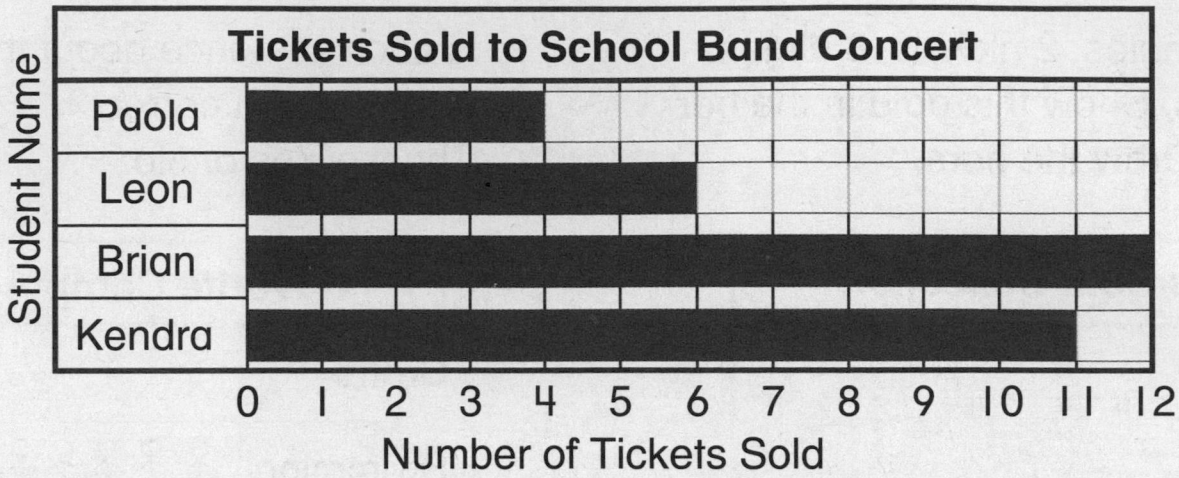

5. Complete the table and the line plot.

Part A

Use a centimeter ruler. Measure the length of the crayon to the nearest centimeter. Write the length in the table below.

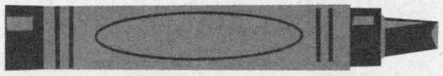

Crayon Lengths in Centimeters			
5	7	7	8
4	7	5	

Part B

Use the data in the table to complete the line plot.

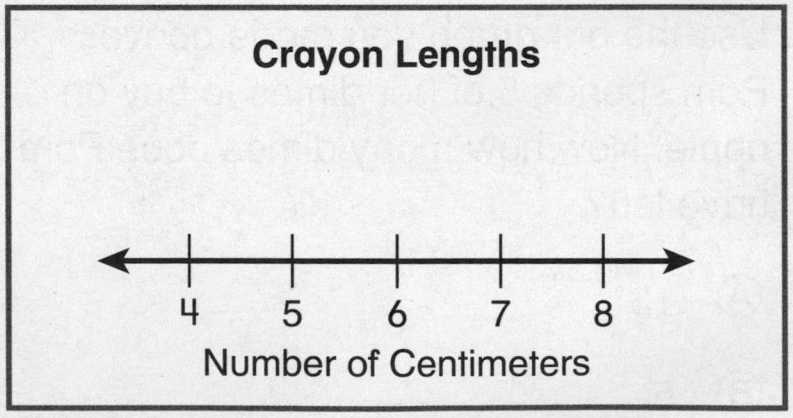

What is the difference in length between the shortest and longest crayon?

_____

Copyright © Savvas Learning Company LLC. All Rights Reserved.

6. Scott is making a picture graph from the data in the tally chart. How many symbols should he draw in the bottom row?

Favorite Fruit	
Apple	IIII
Banana	~~IIII~~ I
Pear	I
Orange	~~IIII~~

Favorite Fruit	
Apple	☺ ☺ ☺ ☺
Banana	☺ ☺ ☺ ☺ ☺ ☺
Pear	☺
Orange	

Each ☺ = 1 student

Ⓐ 3 Ⓑ 4 Ⓒ 5 Ⓓ 6

---

7. Mary gets new stamps every month. The bar graph shows the number of stamps she collects each month.

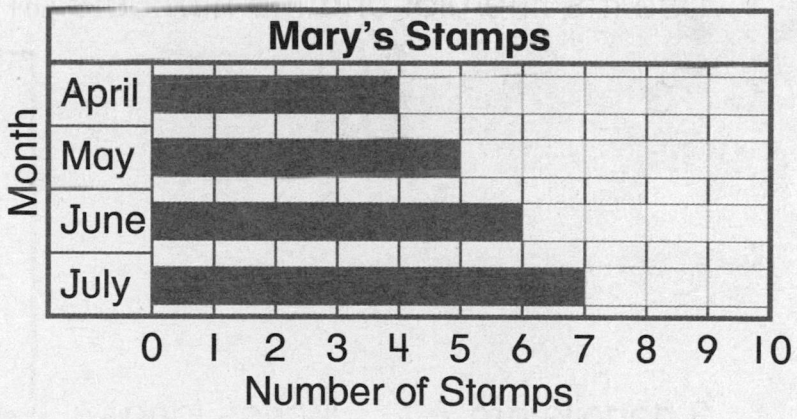

Which statements are true? Choose all that apply.

- ☐ Mary collects 1 more stamp in May than she does in April.
- ☐ Mary collects 2 fewer stamps in June than she does in July.
- ☐ Mary collects a total of 11 stamps in May and June.
- ☐ Mary collects one additional stamp each month from May to July.

8. Use the tally chart to complete the picture graph.
Then use the picture graph to solve the problems.

Favorite Flower	
Rose	~~IIII~~ I
Daisy	III
Tulip	~~IIII~~
Lily	~~IIII~~ III

Favorite Flower	
Rose	
Daisy	
Tulip	
Lily	

Each = 1 vote

How many students voted for Lily? _____

Which flower is the least favorite? _____

---

9. Use the line plot and the numbers on the cards to complete each sentence.

3 4 5 7

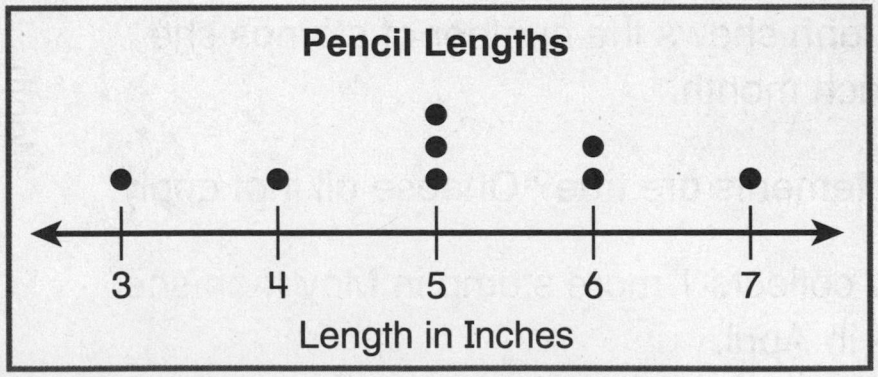

3 pencils are _____ inches long.

The longest pencil is _____ inches long.

The shortest pencil is _____ inches long.

The difference between the shortest and longest pencil is _____ inches.

Copyright © Savvas Learning Company LLC. All Rights Reserved.

Name _____

TOPIC 14 Performance Assessment

School Surveys

Some students asked their classmates different questions.

George asked his classmates to vote on their favorite lunch. This table shows the results.

Favorite Lunch	
Taco	5
Pizza	8
Hamburger	9
Salad	6

1. Use the table to complete the bar graph.

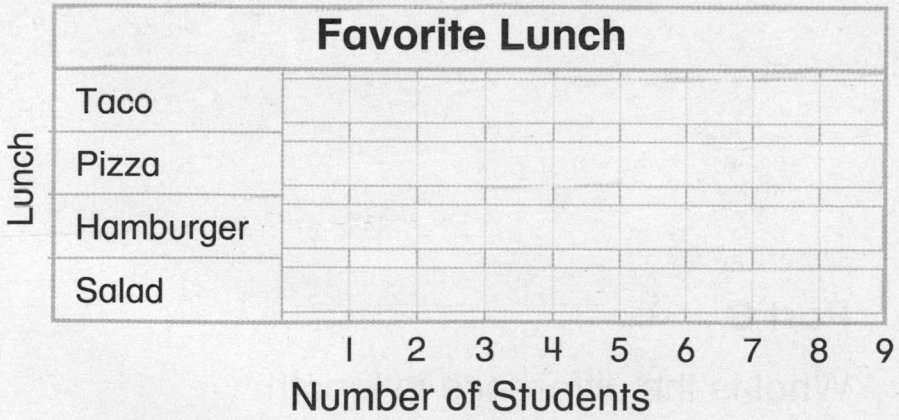

2. Use the Favorite Lunch table to complete the picture graph.

Favorite Lunch	
Taco	
Pizza	
Hamburger	
Salad	

Each ✔ = 1 student

3. Use the graphs you made to answer these questions.

How many students chose salad as their favorite lunch? _____

Which lunch is the favorite of the most students? _____

How would the bar graph change if two more students chose Taco?

_____

_____

4. Write and solve a math story about the Favorite Lunch graphs you made.

Part A

Use the bar graph or the picture graph about favorite lunches to write a math story problem. The problem should include addition or subtraction.

_____

_____

_____

_____

Part B

Solve your math story problem. Explain how you solved the problem.

_____

_____

_____

_____

_____

_____

5. Gina asked her classmates to measure the length of their favorite storybook in inches. She recorded their measurements in this table.

Lengths of Books in Inches			
12	9	8	10
6	10	11	9
10	9	9	12
12	10	7	7

Part A

Use the table to make a line plot.

Part B

What is the difference in length between the longest and shortest books?

_____ inches

Copyright © Savvas Learning Company LLC. All Rights Reserved.

TOPIC 15 Shapes and Their Attributes

Essential Question: How can shapes be described, compared, and broken into parts?

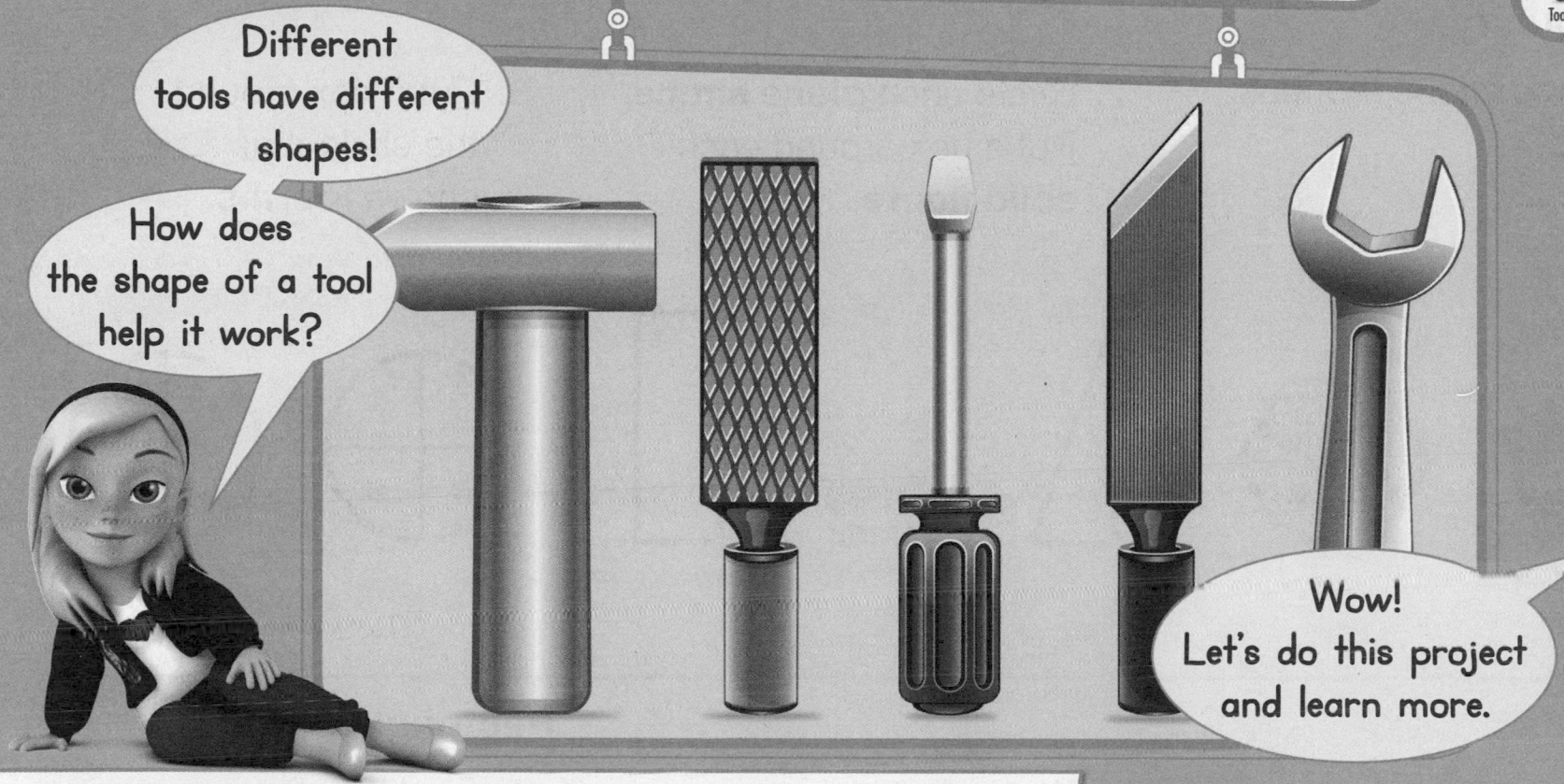

Math and Science Project: All About Shape

Find Out Draw pictures of tools used for gardening, cooking, or fixing. Describe the shape of each tool. Tell how the shape of each tool helps it work.

Journal: Make a Book Show your work in a book. In your book, also:

- Choose a tool that you use at school. Tell how the shape of the tool helps it work.
- Draw and describe polygon shapes.

Name _____

Review What You Know

Vocabulary

1. Circle the shape that has 6 **sides**.

2. Circle each **plane shape**. Put a box around each **solid figure**.

3. Put a box around the circle that shows **fourths**.

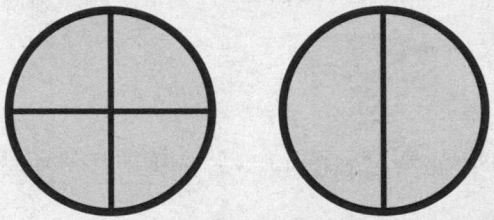

Basic Facts

4. Write each sum.

5	7	10
+ 8	+ 7	+ 10

5. Write each difference.

17	15	12
− 9	− 6	− 8

Rectangles

6. Find the distance around.

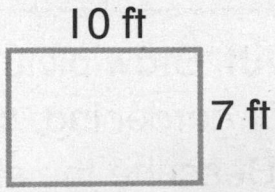

_____

Copyright © Savvas Learning Company LLC. All Rights Reserved.

My Word Cards

Study the words on the front of the card.
Complete the activity on the back.

A-Z Glossary

vertices (vertex)

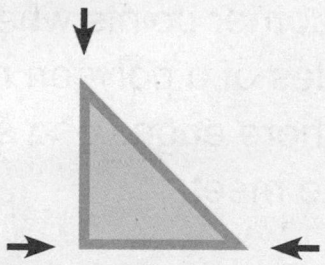

quadrilateral

pentagon

hexagon

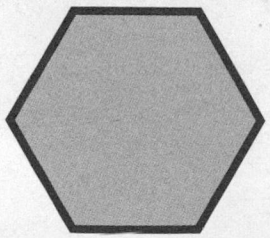

polygon

angle

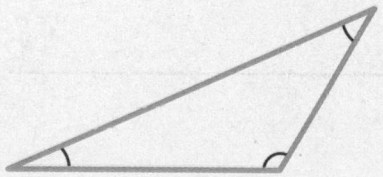

My Word Cards

Use what you know to complete the sentences.
Extend learning by writing your own sentence using each word.

A _____

is a polygon that has 5 sides.

A _____

is a polygon that has 4 sides.

_____

are corner points where 2 sides of a polygon meet or where edges of a solid figure meet.

One corner point is called a

_____.

The corner shape formed by two sides that meet is called an

_____.

A closed plane shape with 3 or more sides is called a

_____.

A _____

is a polygon that has 6 sides.

Copyright © Savvas Learning Company LLC. All Rights Reserved.

My Word Cards

Study the words on the front of the card.
Complete the activity on the back.

A-Z Glossary

right angle

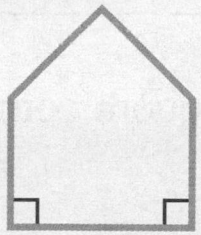

cube

face

edge

equal shares

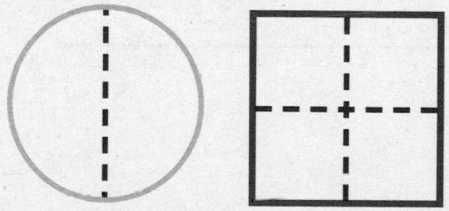

halves

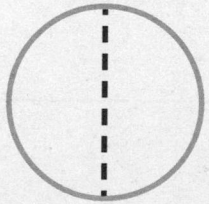

My Word Cards

Use what you know to complete the sentences.
Extend learning by writing your own sentence using each word.

A flat surface of a solid that does not roll is called a

_____.

A _____

is a solid figure with six faces that are matching squares.

A _____

_____

forms a square corner.

When a whole is divided into 2 equal shares, the shares are called

_____.

Parts of a whole that are the same size are called

_____.

A line formed where two faces of a solid figure meet is called an

_____.

Copyright © Savvas Learning Company LLC. All Rights Reserved.

My Word Cards

Study the words on the front of the card.
Complete the activity on the back.

A-Z Glossary

thirds

fourths

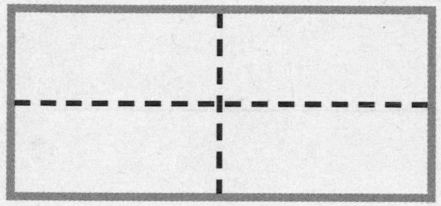

My Word Cards

Use what you know to complete the sentences.
Extend learning by writing your own sentence using each word.

When a whole is divided into 4 equal shares, the shares are called

_____.

When a whole is divided into 3 equal shares, the shares are called

_____.

Copyright © Savvas Learning Company LLC. All Rights Reserved.

Name _____

Solve

Lesson 15-1
2-Dimensional Shapes

I can ...
recognize shapes by how they look.

SOL 2.13

Solve & Share

Draw some closed plane shapes that have 3 vertices.
Write the name for one of your shapes.
Is this name correct for all of the shapes you made?

3 vertices

Digital Resources at SavvasRealize.com

Triangles	Quadrilaterals	Pentagons	Hexagons
3 sides, 3 **vertices**	4 sides, 4 vertices	5 sides, 5 vertices	6 sides, 6 vertices
Not Triangles	Not Quadrilaterals	Not Pentagons	Not Hexagons

Do You Understand?

Show Me! How do sides and vertices help you name a plane shape?

Guided Practice

Match each shape to its name.

1.

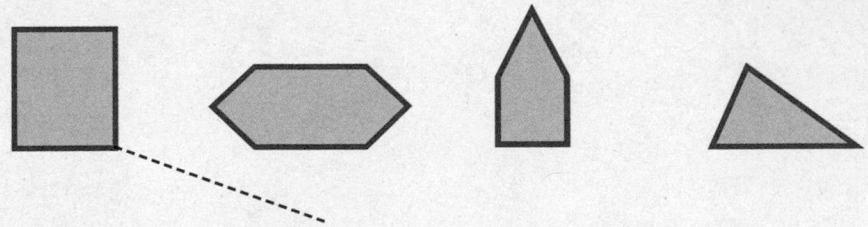

triangle quadrilateral pentagon hexagon

Tell how many sides and vertices. Name each shape.

2.

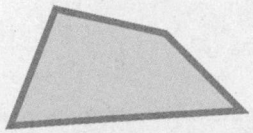

_____ sides

_____ vertices

Shape: _____

3.

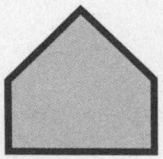

_____ sides

_____ vertices

Shape: _____

Copyright © Savvas Learning Company LLC. All Rights Reserved.

Name _____

Tools Assessment

Independent Practice

Match each shape to its name.

4. 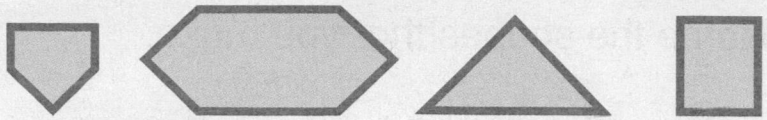

triangle quadrilateral pentagon hexagon

5. 

triangle quadrilateral pentagon hexagon

Draw the shape. Tell how many sides and vertices.

6. Quadrilateral

_____ sides

_____ vertices

7. Hexagon

_____ sides

_____ vertices

8. Triangle

_____ sides

_____ vertices

9. **Higher Order Thinking** Bianca drew a triangle and a pentagon. How many sides and vertices did she draw in all? Draw the shapes.

_____ sides _____ vertices

Problem Solving Solve each problem.

10. **Model** Marcos has 4 toothpicks. He places them as shown. What shape can Marcos make if he adds one more toothpick?

_____

11. **Vocabulary** Connect all the dots to make two shapes that have **vertices.** Name the shapes that you make.

_____ _____

12. **Higher Order Thinking** Randall said that a square is a quadrilateral. Susan said that a square is a square, so it is not a quadrilateral. Who is correct? Explain.

_____

_____

_____

_____

_____

_____

13. **Assessment** Which polygon is **NOT** a hexagon?

Ⓐ 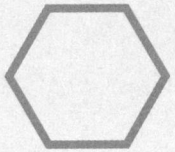

Ⓑ 

Ⓒ 

Ⓓ 

Copyright © Savvas Learning Company LLC. All Rights Reserved.

Name _____

Help Tools Games

Homework & Practice 15-1

2-Dimensional Shapes

Another Look! You can name shapes by their number of sides and vertices.

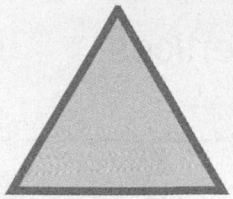

A triangle has

3 sides and

3 vertices.

A quadrilateral has

4 sides and

4 vertices.

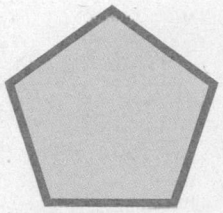

A pentagon has

5 sides and

5 vertices.

A hexagon has

6 sides and

6 vertices.

HOME ACTIVITY Look around your home for items that are shaped like triangles, quadrilaterals, pentagons, or hexagons. Ask your child to tell the number of sides and vertices for each shape.

Name each shape.
Write the number of sides and vertices.

1.

Shape: _____

_____ sides

_____ vertices

2.

Shape: _____

_____ sides

_____ vertices

3.

Shape: _____

_____ sides

_____ vertices

Tell how many sides or vertices each student drew.

4. **Algebra** Leona drew 2 pentagons.

She drew _____ vertices.

5. **Algebra** Nestor drew 3 quadrilaterals.

He drew _____ sides.

6. **Algebra** Kip drew a hexagon and a triangle.

He drew _____ vertices.

7. **Model** Draw 2 hexagons that look different from the one shown.

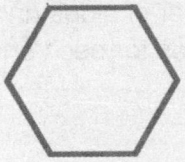

8. **Model** Draw 2 quadrilaterals that look different from the one shown.

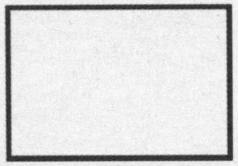

9. **Higher Order Thinking** Tami traced the flat sides of this wooden block. What shapes did she draw? Name and draw the shapes.

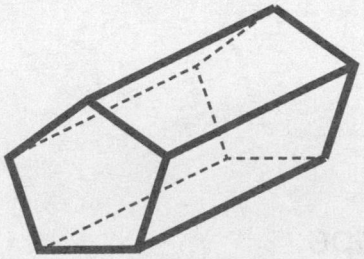

10. **Assessment** Jin drew two polygons. One of the polygons is shown below. If Jin drew 9 sides and 9 vertices in all, which other polygon did he draw?

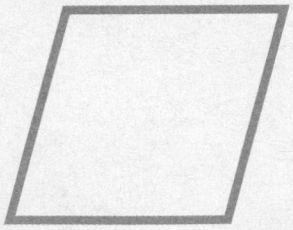

Ⓐ triangle

Ⓑ rhombus

Ⓒ rectangle

Ⓓ pentagon

Copyright © Savvas Learning Company LLC. All Rights Reserved.

Name _____

Solve

Lesson 15-2
Polygons and Angles

I can ...
describe plane shapes by how they look.

SOL 2.13

Solve & Share

Look at the two plane shapes below. How are they alike? How are they different? What is a name for both shapes?

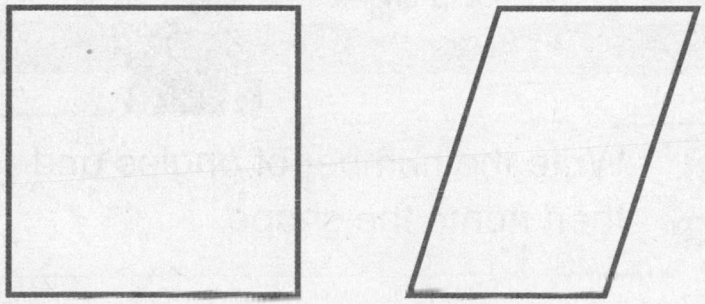

_____

_____

_____

_____

_____

Polygon

A closed plane shape with 3 or more sides is called a polygon.

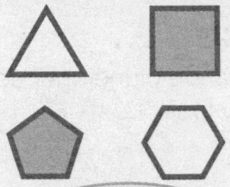

You know the names of these polygons.

Not Polygons

Polygons are not open shapes. Polygons do not have curved sides.

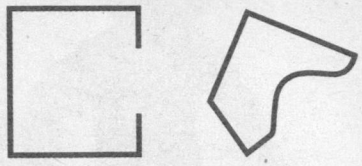

A circle is not a polygon.

Angle

Polygons have angles. They have the same number of angles as sides and vertices.

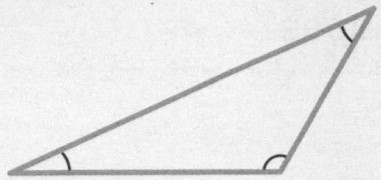

A triangle has 3 angles.

Right Angle

A right angle forms a square corner. A square has 4 right angles. The pentagon below has 2 right angles.

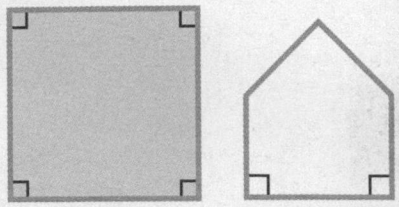

Do You Understand?

Show Me! How many angles does this shape have? How many right angles? Name the shape.

Guided Practice

Write the number of angles and then name the shape.

1.

_____ angles

Shape: _____

2. 

_____ angles

Shape: _____

3. 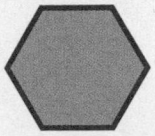

_____ angles

Shape: _____

4. 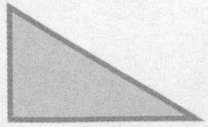

_____ angles

Shape: _____

Copyright © Savvas Learning Company LLC. All Rights Reserved.

Name _____

Tools Assessment

Independent Practice

Write the number of angles and then name the shape.

5.  _____ angles

Shape: _____

6. 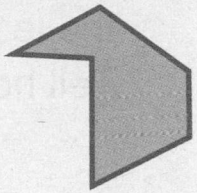 _____ angles

Shape: _____

7.  _____ angles

Shape: _____

8. 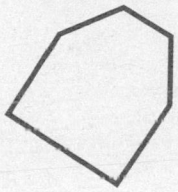 _____ angles

Shape: _____

9.  _____ angles

Shape: _____

10.  _____ angles

Shape: _____

11. **Higher Order Thinking** Draw a polygon with 2 right angles and 2 angles that are not right angles. Name the shape you draw.

Problem Solving Solve each problem.

12. **Be Precise** Which plane shapes are sewn together in the soccer ball?

_____

_____

13. **Math and Science** Bees make honeycomb. The honeycomb shape uses the least amount of wax. Name the shape. Tell how many angles the shape has.

_____

14. **Higher Order Thinking** Draw a polygon shape that has 7 angles.
How many sides does the polygon have?
How many vertices does it have?

_____

15. **Assessment** Name the shape of the sign below. Write 3 things that describe the shape.

_____

_____

_____

_____

Copyright © Savvas Learning Company LLC. All Rights Reserved.

Name _____

Help Tools Games

Homework & Practice 15-2
Polygons and Angles

Another Look! Polygons are closed plane shapes with 3 or more sides. Polygons have the same number of angles and vertices as sides.

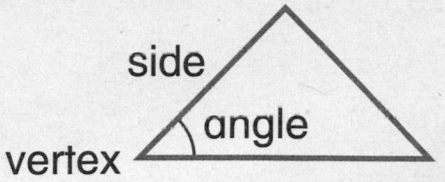

Name and describe this polygon.

Pentagon 5 sides 5 vertices 5 angles

HOME ACTIVITY Ask your child to find objects that have polygon shapes. Have your child name each shape and tell how many angles it has.

Write the number of angles and then name the shape.

1. 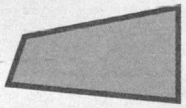 _____ angles

   Shape: _____

2. 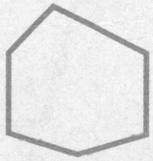 _____ angles

   Shape: _____

3.  _____ angles

   Shape: _____

Solve each problem.

4. **Be Precise** The sign below tells drivers to yield. This means to wait for other cars or people to go first.
Which polygon shape do you see in the sign?

_____

5. **Vocabulary** The outside edges of this nut for a bolt form a **polygon** shape. Name that shape.

_____

6. **Higher Order Thinking** Look at the design below. Write three names for the shape that has right angles.

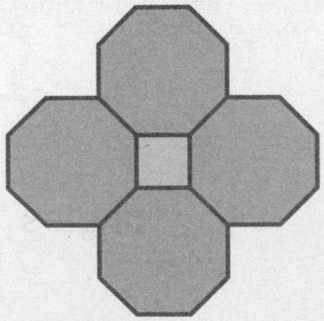

_____

_____

7. **Assessment** Name the shape below. Write 3 things that describe the shape.

_____

_____

_____

_____

Copyright © Savvas Learning Company LLC. All Rights Reserved.

Name _____

Solve

Lesson 15-3

Draw 2-Dimensional Shapes

I can ...
draw polygon shapes.

SOL 2.13

Solve & Share

Draw a polygon with 3 sides that are the same length. Then draw a polygon with 3 sides that are different lengths. Then tell 4 ways they are alike.

Sides: Same Length	Sides: Different Lengths

_____

_____

_____

_____

Digital Resources at SavvasRealize.com

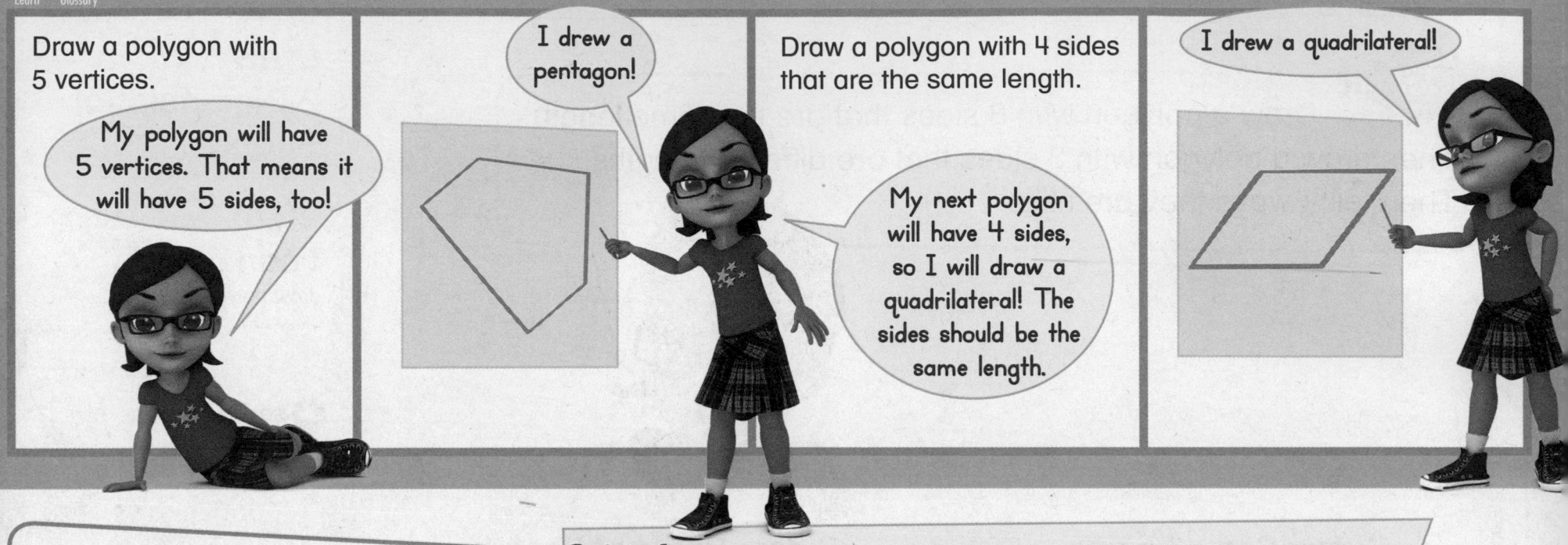

Do You Understand?

Show Me! Draw a quadrilateral with 4 sides that are the same length and with 4 right angles. Write 2 names for the quadrilateral.

☆ Guided Practice ☆

Draw each shape. Complete the sentences.

1. Draw a polygon with 3 vertices.

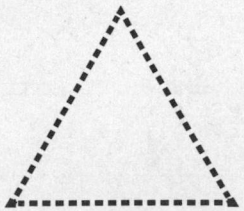

The polygon also has _____ sides.

The polygon is a _____.

2. Draw a polygon with 6 sides.

The polygon also has _____ angles.

The polygon is a _____.

Copyright © Savvas Learning Company LLC. All Rights Reserved.

Name _____

Tools Assessment

Independent Practice

Draw each shape. Complete the sentences.

3. Draw a polygon with 3 vertices and 1 right angle.

The polygon also has _____ sides.

The polygon is a _____.

4. Draw a quadrilateral with opposite sides that are the same length.

The polygon also has _____ vertices.

The polygon is a _____.

5. Draw a polygon with 4 sides that are the same length.

The polygon also has _____ angles.

The polygon is a _____.

6. Draw a polygon with 4 sides that are different lengths.

The polygon also has _____ angles.

The polygon is a _____.

7. Draw a polygon with 5 vertices and 3 sides that are the same length.

The polygon also has _____ sides in all.

The polygon is a _____.

8. Higher Order Thinking Can you draw a polygon with 3 vertices and 4 sides? Explain.

Problem Solving Solve the problems below.

9. **Be Precise** Draw a rectangle with 4 equal sides.

What is another name for this shape?

_____

10. Draw 3 shapes. The first shape is a quadrilateral. The number of vertices in each shape increases by one.

Name the third shape. _____

11. **Higher Order Thinking** The owner of Joe's Fish Market wants a new sign. He wants the sign to have curved sides. Draw a sign for Joe's Fish Market.

Is the sign a polygon? Explain.

_____

_____

12. **Assessment** David drew two different polygons. One of the polygons was a square. If David drew 9 sides and 9 vertices in all, what other polygon did David draw?

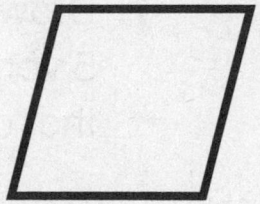

Ⓐ

Ⓒ

Ⓑ

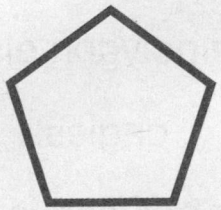

Ⓓ

Copyright © Savvas Learning Company LLC. All Rights Reserved.

Name _____

Help Tools Games

Homework & Practice 15-3

Draw 2-Dimensional Shapes

HOME ACTIVITY Ask your child to draw a polygon with 4 vertices. Then ask your child to tell you the name of the polygon and how many sides and angles it has.

Another Look! The number of sides in a polygon is the same as the number of vertices and the number of angles.

Draw a polygon with 6 vertices.

The sides can be the same length.

The sides can be different lengths.

Each polygon has 6 vertices.

Each polygon also has 6 sides and 6 angles.

Both polygons are hexagons.

Draw two different polygons for each number of vertices.

1. 4 vertices

Each polygon has _____ sides.

Both polygons are _____.

2. 5 vertices

Each polygon has _____ angles.

Both polygons are _____.

Draw each polygon. Then complete the sentences.

3. It has 2 fewer sides than a pentagon.

The shape is a _____.

4. It has 3 more vertices than a triangle.

The shape is a _____.

5. **Make Sense** It has 1 less vertex than a hexagon and 2 more angles than a triangle.

The shape is a _____.

6. **Higher Order Thinking** Tanika has 7 toothpicks. She uses them all to create two polygons. Draw two polygons that Tanika could have created. Write the names of your shapes.

7. **Assessment** Kit drew a polygon that has 4 vertices. Which could **NOT** be Kit's polygon?

quadrilateral Ⓐ

rectangle Ⓒ

triangle Ⓑ

square Ⓓ

8. **Assessment** Reg drew a polygon with more sides than a square and fewer vertices than a hexagon. Which could Reg have drawn?

triangle Ⓐ

quadrilateral Ⓒ

rectangle Ⓑ

pentagon Ⓓ

Copyright © Savvas Learning Company LLC. All Rights Reserved.

Name _____

Solve

Lesson 15-4
Cubes

I can ...
draw cubes and describe how they look.

SOL 2.13

Solve & Share

Describe this shape in 3 or more ways.

_____

_____

_____

_____

Digital Resources at SavvasRealize.com

A **cube** is a solid figure with 6 equal **faces**, 12 **edges**, and 8 vertices.

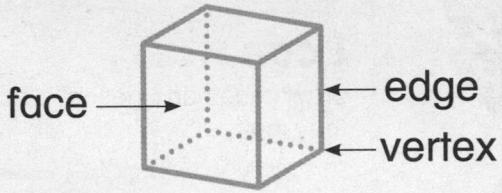

Each face is a square, with 4 equal edges and 4 right angles.

These are cubes.

These are **NOT** cubes.

You can use dot paper to draw a cube. The dashed lines show the edges that you can't see when you look at a solid cube.

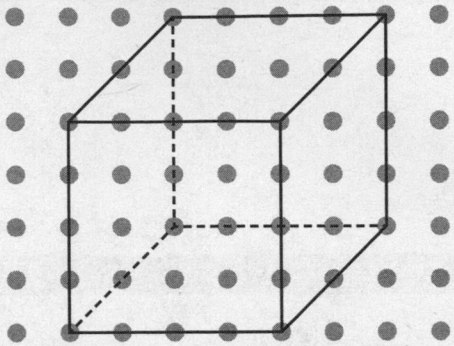

Do You Understand?

Show Me! What solid figure has 6 equal faces?

_____

What is the shape of each face?

_____

Guided Practice

Circle the cubes in the group of shapes. Be ready to explain how you know they are cubes.

1.

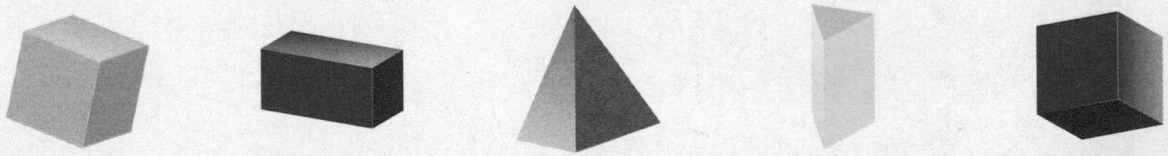

2. Use the dot paper. Draw a cube.

Copyright © Savvas Learning Company LLC. All Rights Reserved.

Name _____

Tools Assessment

Independent Practice

Decide if the shape is a cube. Then draw a line from each shape to *cube* or ***NOT** a cube*.

3.

cube

NOT a cube

4. Trace the cube shown below.

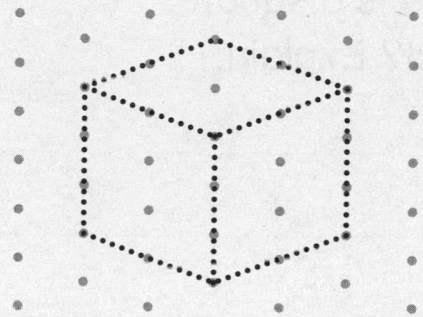

How many faces can you see?

_____ faces

Algebra Use what you know about cubes to write an equation and solve each problem.

5. How many vertices do these two cubes have in all?

_____ + _____ = _____

_____ vertices

6. How many faces do these two cubes have in all?

_____ + _____ = _____

_____ faces

Problem Solving

Use what you know about cubes to solve each problem.

7. **Explain** Scott is holding a solid figure with 6 equal faces, 12 edges, and 8 vertices. Scott says the figure is a cube. Carmen says the figure is a square. Who is correct? Explain.

_____

_____

_____

8. **Vocabulary** Circle the vocabulary word that completes the sentence.

vertices **faces** **edges**

A cube has 6 _____.

9. **Higher Order Thinking** Use a place-value ones cube or another solid cube. Look at the cube as you turn it. Turn the cube in any direction.

What is the greatest number of faces you can see at one time? Explain.

_____

_____

_____

10. **Assessment** Complete the sentences about a cube.

A cube is a solid _____.

A cube has _____ equal faces,

_____ vertices, and _____ edges.

Copyright © Savvas Learning Company LLC. All Rights Reserved.

Name _____

Help Tools Games

Homework & Practice 15-4
Cubes

Another Look! You can tell if a shape is a cube by counting its faces, vertices, and edges. Number cubes are examples of real-life objects that are cubes.

These real-life objects are **NOT** cubes.

HOME ACTIVITY Have your child find an object at home that has a cube shape. Ask your child to describe the object including the number of faces, vertices, and edges.

Tell whether each shape or object is a cube. If it is not a cube, tell what shape it is. Then explain how you know.

1. 

_____

_____

_____

_____

_____

2. 

_____

_____

_____

_____

_____

Use what you know about cubes to solve each problem.

3. **Look for Patterns** You can make two squares to draw a cube.

   1. Connect the 4 blue dots to make one square.
   2. Connect the 4 green dots to make another square.
   3. Connect each corner of the blue square to a like corner of the green square.

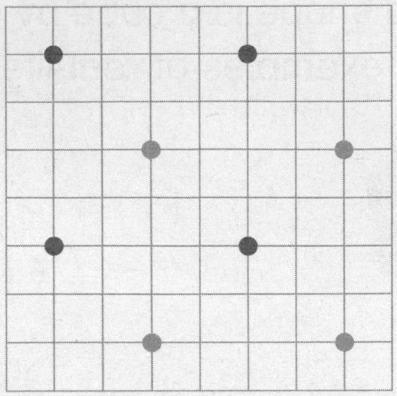

4. **Higher Order Thinking** Look at the solid figure below. Count the number of faces, vertices, and edges it has. Why is this figure **NOT** a cube?

_____ faces

_____ vertices

_____ edges

5. **Assessment** Circle the shapes that are **NOT** cubes. Explain how you know.

Copyright © Savvas Learning Company LLC. All Rights Reserved.

Name _____

Solve

Lesson 15-5

Divide Rectangles into Equal Squares

I can ...
divide rectangles into equal squares.

SOL Prepares for 3.4a, 3.4b

Solve & Share

How many equal squares cover this rectangle?
How could you show this with an addition equation?

Columns

Rows

_____ equal squares

Equation: _____

How many red squares can cover this rectangle?

Begin like this:

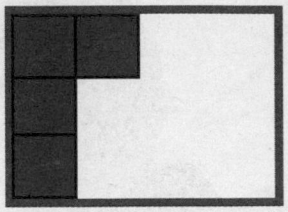

NOT like this:

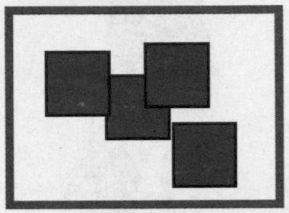

Count. Each row has 4 squares. You can add the squares by rows.

4 + 4 + 4 = 12

Count. Each column has 3 squares. You can add the squares by columns.

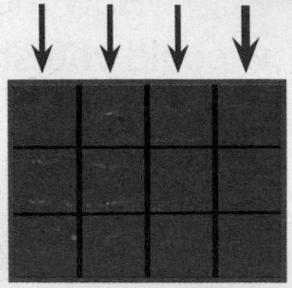

3 + 3 + 3 + 3 = 12

Do You Understand?

Show Me! Explain how you can divide a rectangle into equal squares.

Guided Practice Solve.

1. Use square tiles to cover the rectangle. Trace the tiles. Column 1 is done for you.

2. Count and add. How many squares cover the rectangle?

Add by rows: ____ + ____ + ____ = ____

Add by columns:

____ + ____ + ____ + ____ + ____ + ____ = ____

Copyright © Savvas Learning Company LLC. All Rights Reserved.

Name _____

Tools Assessment

Independent Practice

Use square tiles to cover each rectangle. Trace the tiles. Count the squares.

3.

Add by rows:

____ + ____ + ____ + ____ = ____

Add by columns:

____ + ____ + ____ + ____ + ____ = ____

4.

Add by rows:

____ + ____ + ____ + ____ = ____

Add by columns:

____ + ____ + ____ + ____ = ____

5. **Number Sense** Draw a rectangle that is divided into 6 equal squares.

Problem Solving Solve each problem.

6. **Look for Patterns** Lisa bakes corn bread. She cuts it into equal square pieces. How many equal squares do you see? Write two equations to show the total number of square pieces.

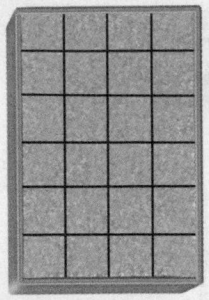

Rows: ____ + ____ + ____ + ____ + ____ + ____ = ____ pieces

Columns: ____ + ____ + ____ + ____ = ____ pieces

7. **Vocabulary** Label the **columns** and the **rows** for the large square below.

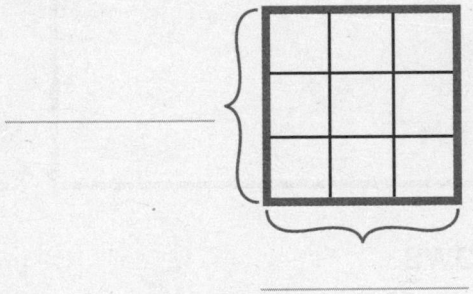

8. **Higher Order Thinking** Look at the large square in Item 7. What do you notice about the number of rows and the number of columns? Explain.

_____

_____

_____

_____

9. **Assessment** Count the equal squares in the rows and columns of the rectangle. Then use the numbers on the cards to write the missing numbers in the equations.

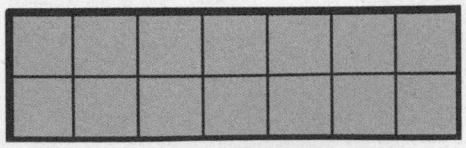

14	2	7

Rows: ____ + ____ = ____

Columns: ____ + ____ + ____ + ____ + ____ + ____ + ____ = ____

Copyright © Savvas Learning Company LLC. All Rights Reserved.

Name _____

Help Tools Games

Homework & Practice 15-5

Divide Rectangles into Equal Squares

Another Look! How many squares cover this rectangle?

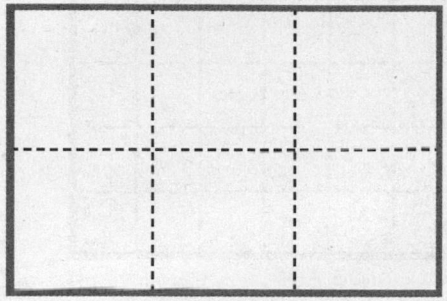

Add the rows: 3 + 3 = 6

Add the columns: 2 + 2 + 2 = 6

HOME ACTIVITY Ask your child to draw a rectangular section of a floor made of square tiles. Then ask your child to count how many squares make up that rectangle.

Use square tiles to cover the rectangle. Trace the tiles. Count the squares.

1.

2. How many squares cover the rectangle?

Add by rows:

____ + ____ + ____ = ____

Add by columns:

____ + ____ + ____ + ____ + ____

= ____

Solve each problem.

3. **Look for Patterns** Mr. Cory puts square tiles on the kitchen floor. The square tiles are all the same size. How many equal squares are there? Write two equations to show the total number of square tiles.

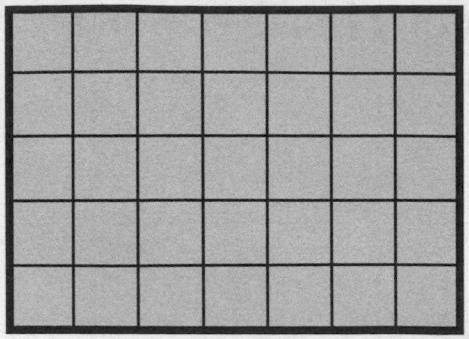

Rows:

____ + ____ + ____ + ____ + ____ = ____ tiles

Columns:

____ + ____ + ____ + ____ + ____ + ____ + ____ = ____ tiles

4. **Higher Order Thinking** 10 friends want to equally share a rectangular pan of granola bars. Show how to divide the rectangle into 10 equal pieces.

5. **Assessment** Count the equal squares in the rows and columns of the rectangle. Then use the numbers on the cards to write the missing numbers in the equations.

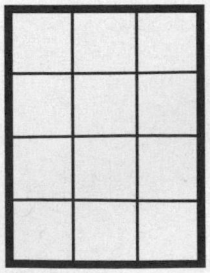

4	12	3

Rows: ____ + ____ + ____ + ____ = ____

Columns: ____ + ____ + ____ = ____

Copyright © Savvas Learning Company LLC. All Rights Reserved.

Name _____

Solve

Lesson 15-6
Partition Shapes

I can ...
divide circles and rectangles into halves, thirds, and fourths.

SOL 2.4a, 2.4b

Solve & Share

Use one type of pattern block to cover this shape.
Draw lines to show how you placed the pattern blocks.
How many equal shares does the shape have now?
What do you notice about the equal shares?

_____ shares

_____

_____

_____

Digital Resources at SavvasRealize.com

Are these shares equal?

2 **equal shares**

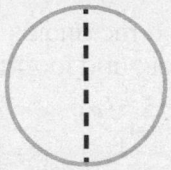

These shares are **halves**.

NOT equal shares

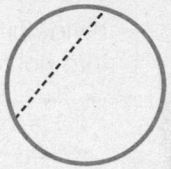

These shares are not halves.

Are these shares equal?

3 equal shares

These shares are **thirds**.

NOT equal shares

These shares are not thirds.

Are these shares equal?

4 equal shares

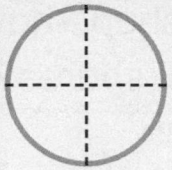

These shares are **fourths**.

NOT equal shares

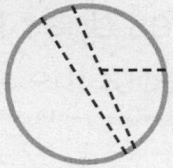

These shares are not fourths.

You can show equal shares in different ways.

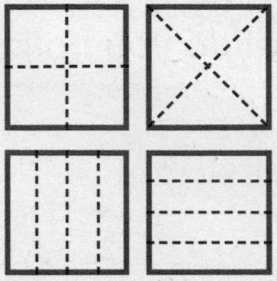

Do You Understand?

Show Me! Divide this rectangle into three equal shares. How many thirds is one share? How many thirds is the whole rectangle?

Guided Practice

Solve each problem.

1. Describe each equal share.
   Write *a half of, a third of,* or *a fourth of.*

_____ _____ _____

2. Divide each square into halves. Show four different ways.

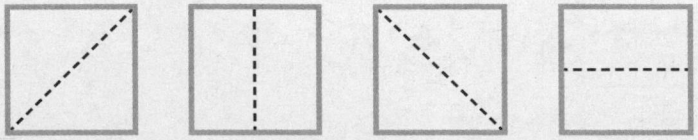

Copyright © Savvas Learning Company LLC. All Rights Reserved.

Name _____

Tools Assessment

Independent Practice Divide each shape into the number of equal shares given. Show 2 ways. Then complete the sentences.

3. 3 equal shares

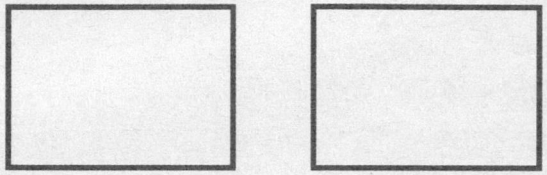

Each share is _____ the whole.

Each whole is _____.

4. 4 equal shares

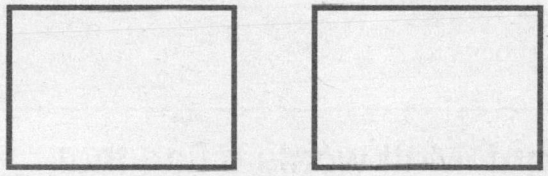

Each share is _____ the whole.

Each whole is _____.

5. 2 equal shares

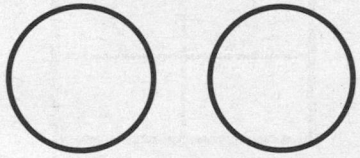

Each share is _____ the whole.

Each whole is _____.

6. Higher Order Thinking Draw what comes next.

Problem Solving Solve each problem.

7. **Model** Leon cut a waffle into halves. Draw lines to show 3 different ways he could have cut the waffle.

8. **Math and Science** Tina is planting a garden. She wants to have equal parts for beans, for tomatoes, and for peppers. Draw a picture of how she could divide her garden.

9. **Higher Order Thinking** Draw lines on the picture to solve the problem.

4 friends want to share a watermelon. How could they cut the watermelon so each friend gets an equal share?

Each friend will get _____.

10. **Assessment** Matt wants a flag that shows fourths. Which flags could Matt use? Choose all that apply.

☐

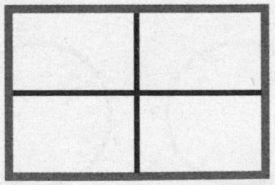

☐

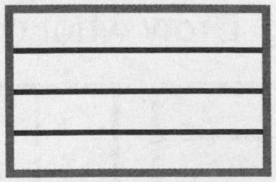

☐

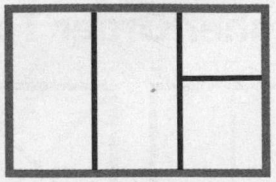

☐

Copyright © Savvas Learning Company LLC. All Rights Reserved.

Name _____

Help Tools Games

Homework & Practice 15-6
Partition Shapes

Another Look! Equal shares are the same size.

2 equal shares

halves

thirds

fourths

3 equal shares

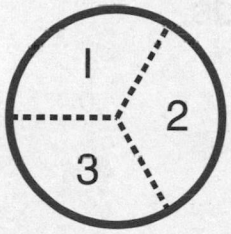

halves

thirds

fourths

4 equal shares

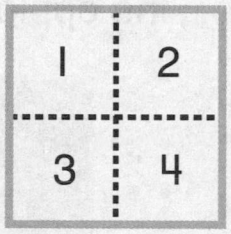

halves

thirds

fourths

HOME ACTIVITY Draw three squares. Ask your child to draw lines in one square to show halves. Then have your child draw lines in the second square to show thirds, and draw lines in the third square to show fourths.

Draw the number of equal shares given for each shape. Then circle the word that describes the shares.

1. 4 equal shares

halves

thirds

fourths

2. 3 equal shares

halves

thirds

fourths

3. 2 equal shares

halves

thirds

fourths

4. 4 equal shares

halves

thirds

fourths

Model Divide the shapes into equal shares.

5. Two students want to equally share a small pizza. Draw how to split the pizza into halves.

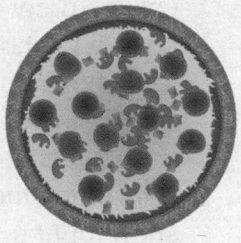

6. Three students want to equally share a tray of apple crisp. Draw two ways to split the apple crisp into thirds.

7. Four students want to share an apple pie. Draw lines to split the pie into fourths.

8. **Higher Order Thinking** This shape is divided into four pieces. Ryan says this shape is divided into fourths. Is he correct? Explain.

_____

_____

_____

9. **Assessment** Tom cut his muffin in half to share it with his brother. Which pictures do **NOT** show halves? Choose all that apply.

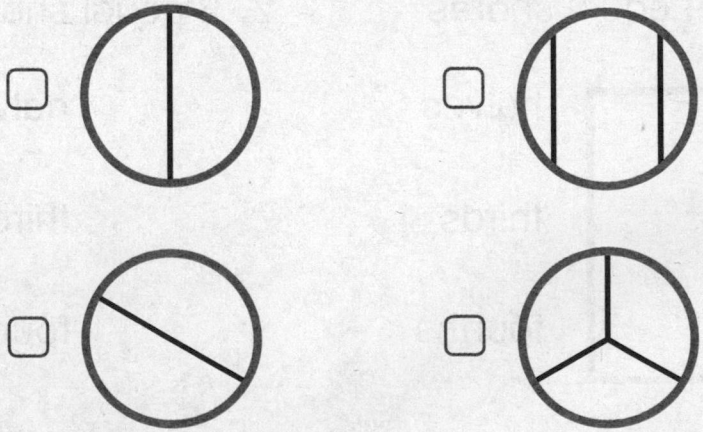

Copyright © Savvas Learning Company LLC. All Rights Reserved.

Name _____

Solve

Lesson 15-7

Equal Shares, Different Shapes

I can ...

make equal shares that do not have the same shape.

SOL 2.4a, 2.4b

Solve & Share

Divide this pizza into 4 equal shares. Compare your answer with a partner. Do you both have 4 equal shares? Did you both get the same answer?

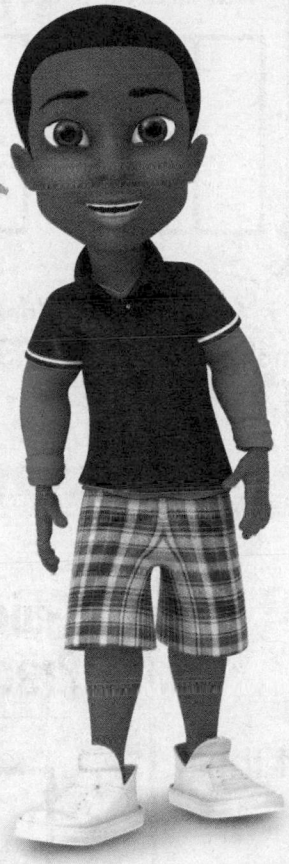

How can this square be divided into 3 equal shares?

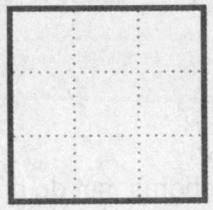

You can use the smaller squares to help.

These show equal shares that are all the same shape.

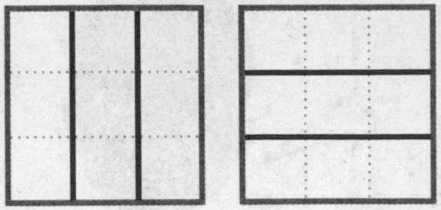

You can draw lines to make 3 columns or 3 rows.

These show equal shares that are **NOT** all the same shape.

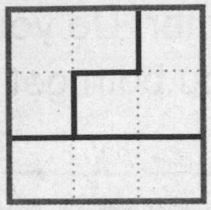

Each share is 3 squares. The shares are equal.

Each way shows 3 equal shares.

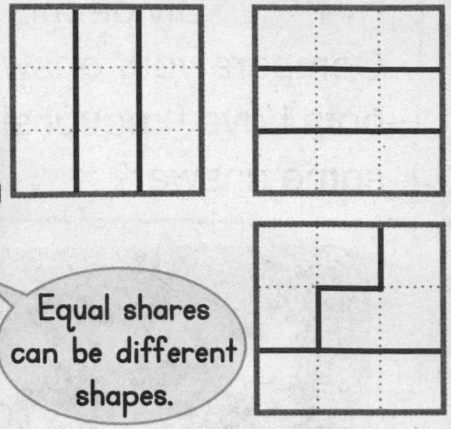

Equal shares can be different shapes.

Do You Understand?

Show Me! How can you check to make sure all of the shares are equal?

Guided Practice

Draw lines to show two different ways to divide the same rectangle into 2 equal shares.

1.

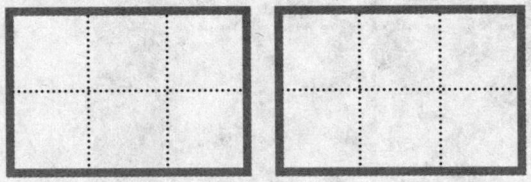

2. How many squares are in each equal share of the rectangles?

____

3. Describe the equal shares and the whole.

Each share is a half of the whole.

Each whole is two halves.

Copyright © Savvas Learning Company LLC. All Rights Reserved.

Name _____

Tools Assessment

Independent Practice

Draw lines to show two different ways to divide the same rectangle into 4 equal shares. Then answer the questions.

4. Show equal shares that are the **same shape**.

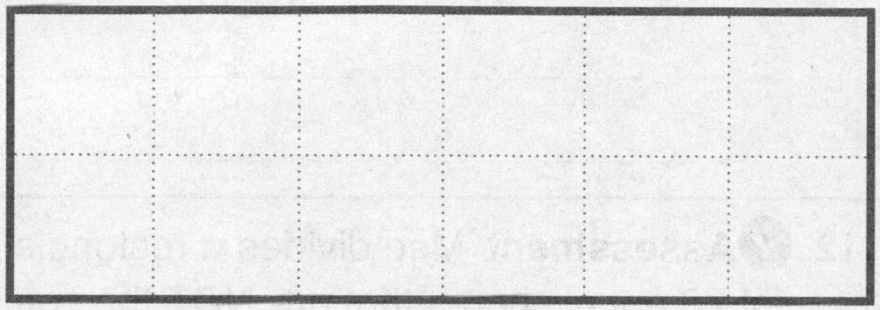

Show equal shares that are **different shapes**.

5. How many squares are in each equal share in Item 4? _____

6. Describe the equal shares and the whole in Item 4.

Each share is _____ the whole.

Each whole is _____.

Draw lines to show two different ways to divide the same rectangle into 3 equal shares.

7.

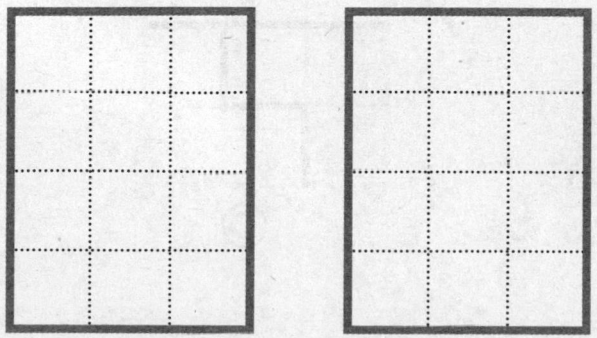

8. **Higher Order Thinking** How can equal shares in a rectangle have different shapes?

_____

_____

_____

Problem Solving Solve each problem.

9. Allen wants to share this pan of corn bread with 3 friends. Allen and his friends will each get an equal share.

How many pieces will be in each share?

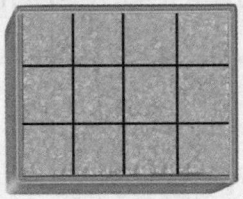

_____ pieces

10. **Explain** Greg says that equal shares can be different in shape and size. Is Greg correct? Explain.

_____

_____

_____

11. **Higher Order Thinking** Donna drew the line in this rectangle to make 2 equal shares. Are the shares equal? Why or why not?

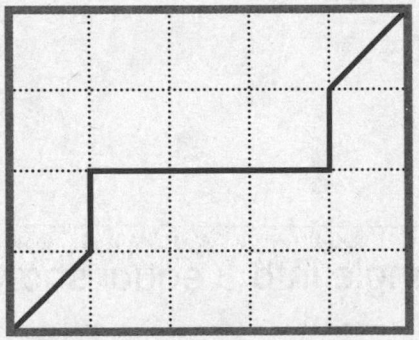

_____

_____

_____

_____

12. **Assessment** Meg divides a rectangle into 3 equal shares that are **NOT** the same shape. Which could be Meg's rectangle?

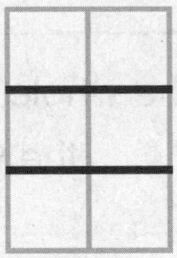

Ⓐ

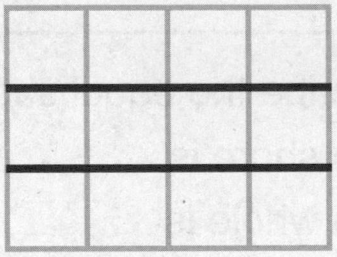

Ⓒ

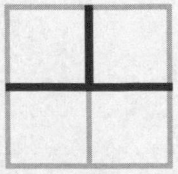

Ⓑ

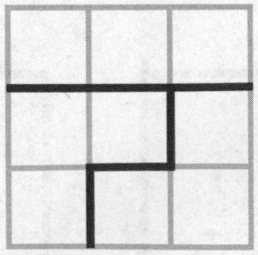

Ⓓ

Copyright © Savvas Learning Company LLC. All Rights Reserved.

Name _____

Help Tools Games

Homework & Practice 15-7

Equal Shares, Different Shapes

HOME ACTIVITY Draw a rectangle. Ask your child to divide it into two equal shares that have different shapes.

Another Look!

You can divide a rectangle into equal shares in different ways.

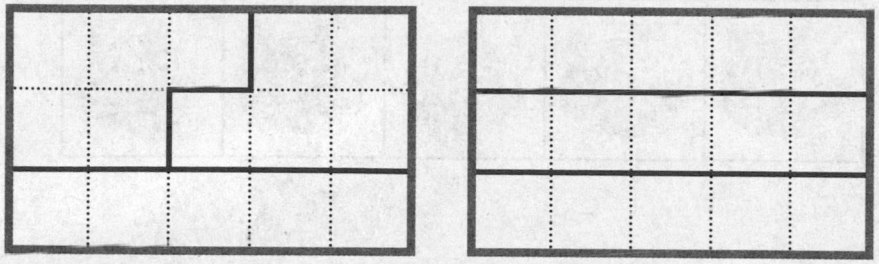

Each rectangle has 3 equal shares. Each equal share has 5 squares.

Draw lines to show three different ways to divide the same rectangle into 2 equal shares.

1.

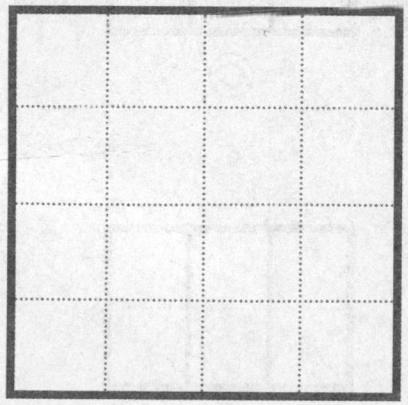

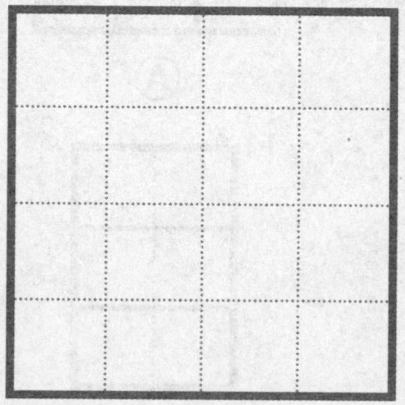

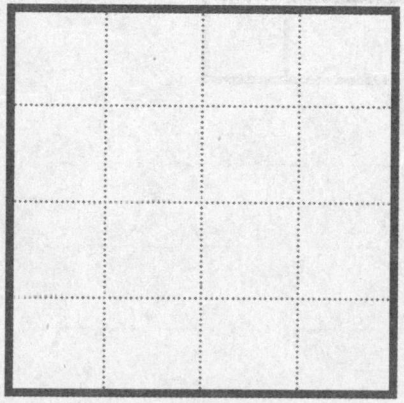

Solve each problem.

2. **Explain** Lexi wants to share the sheet of tiger stickers with two friends. Are there enough stickers to make equal shares for Lexi and her two friends? Explain.

3. **Higher Order Thinking** Corbin drew lines in this rectangle to make equal shares. How do you know that each share is **NOT** a third of the whole rectangle?

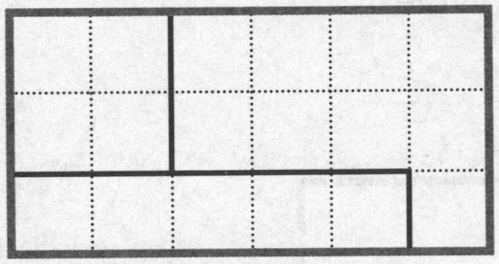

4. **Assessment** Lynn divides a rectangle into 3 equal shares. Which could **NOT** be Lynn's rectangle?

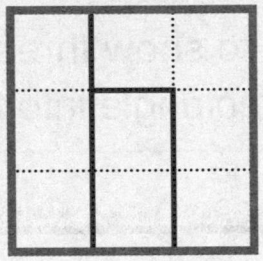

Ⓐ

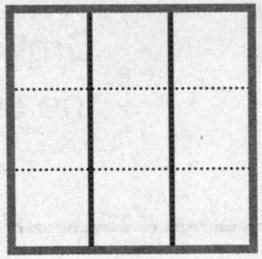

Ⓒ

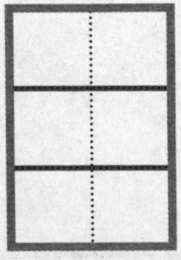

Ⓑ

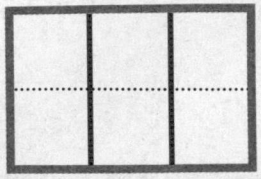

Ⓓ

Copyright © Savvas Learning Company LLC. All Rights Reserved.

Name _____

Solve

Problem Solving

Lesson 15-8
Repeated Reasoning

I can ...
use repeated reasoning to divide rectangles into rows and columns and to create designs with equal shares.

SOL 2.4b

Solve & Share

Design a flag made of 15 equal squares. Use rows and columns. Draw two possible flag designs. Then write an equation for each flag to show the total number of squares.

Divide each flag to make three equal shares. Color each share differently.

My Flag Designs

Equation: _____

Equation: _____

Thinking Habits

Does something repeat in the problem?

How can the solution help me solve another problem?

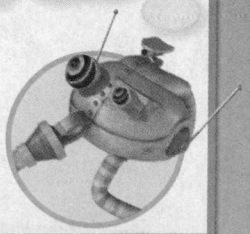

Digital Resources at SavvasRealize.com

Sam is designing a square quilt. The quilt must have 4 colors with an equal share for each color.

Help Sam make two designs.

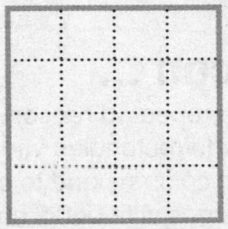

How can I look for things that repeat in the problem?

I can count the small squares in each share in my first design. That will help me draw the shares in my second design.

Here, I used the same shape for each share. Each share is 4 small squares.

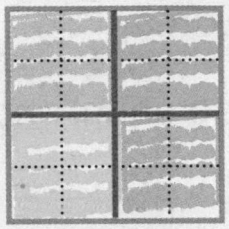

Design 1

In both designs, each colored share is one fourth of the whole.

Here, I used different shapes for the shares.

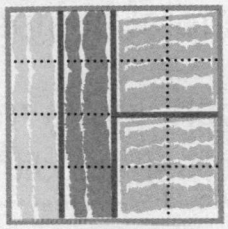

Design 2

Do You Understand?

Show Me! How do you know each share in Design 2 is a fourth of the whole square?

Guided Practice

Solve the problem. Use crayons to color.

1. Hamal is painting a design. The design must have 3 colors with an equal share for each color. Create two possible designs for Hamal.

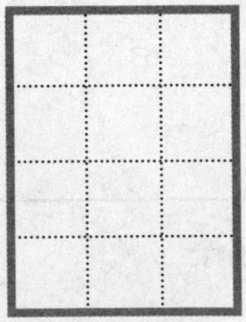

Design 1

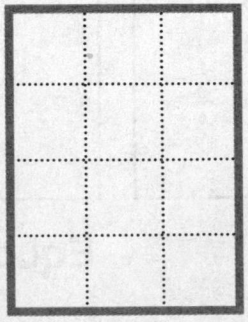

Design 2

Be ready to explain how you used repeated reasoning to help you solve the problem.

Copyright © Savvas Learning Company LLC. All Rights Reserved.

Name _____

Tools Assessment

Independent Practice

Solve each problem. Use crayons to color. Explain your work.

2. Marie wants to put a rectangular design on a T-shirt. The design must have 4 colors with an equal share for each color. Create two possible designs for Marie.

Design 1

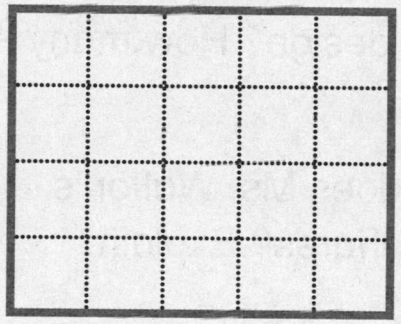

Design 2

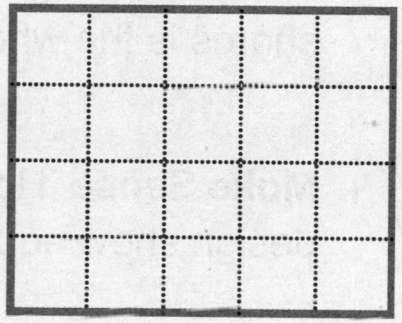

3. Grant wants to put a circle design on his toy car. The design must have 3 colors with an equal share for each color. Create two possible designs for Grant.

Design 1

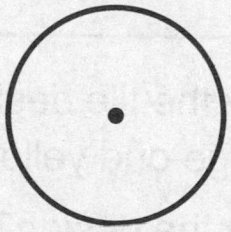

Design 2

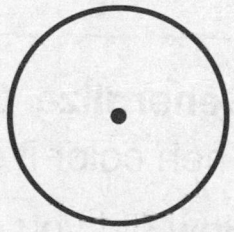

Problem Solving

Performance Assessment

Tile Design

Ms. Walton created this rectangular tile design. What share of the design is orange? What share of the design is yellow? How many shares is the whole design? How many thirds is the whole?

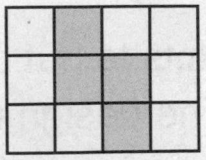

4. **Make Sense** How does Ms. Walton's design show equal shares? Explain.

5. **Reasoning** What share of the design is orange? What share of the design is yellow? How many shares is the whole design? How many thirds is the whole?

6. **Generalize** Copy the tile design above onto this grid. Then color it orange and yellow to match the design shown above.

How did you copy the design? Describe one or two shortcuts you used.

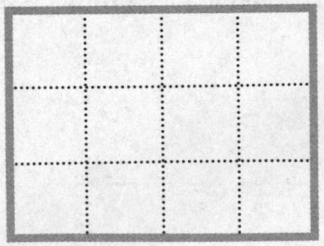

Copyright © Savvas Learning Company LLC. All Rights Reserved.

Name _____

Help Tools Games

Homework & Practice 15-8
Repeated Reasoning

Another Look! Create two different designs for these squares that are the same size. Each design needs to have 2 colors with an equal share for each color.

I can draw a line down the center to make equal shares.

I can draw a line from opposite corners to make equal shares.

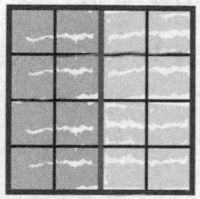

Design 1

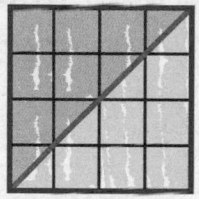

Design 2

HOME ACTIVITY Draw two identical rectangles. Have your child use crayons to draw a different design in each rectangle. Each rectangle should show 4 equal shares, each in a different color.

Solve the problem. Use crayons to color. Explain your solution.

1. Make two different designs. Each design must have 3 colors with an equal share for each color. One design should have shares that are NOT all the same shape.

_____

_____

_____

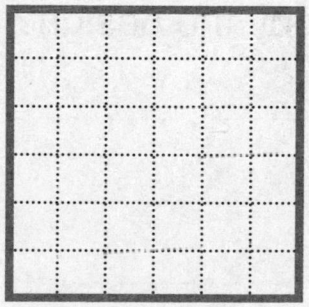

Design 1

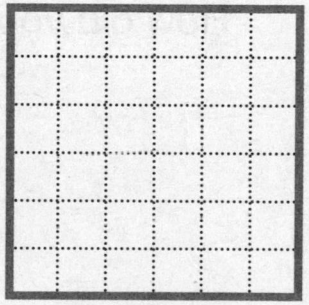

Design 2

Performance Assessment

A Design Repeated

Steven created this design on 4 squares of grid paper.
He wants to repeat this design 6 times on a larger grid.
Answer the questions to help Steven create the larger design.

2. **Look for Patterns** Look at each small square of Steven's design. How are they alike? How are they different?

3. **Explain** Describe Steven's design. Explain what it looks like. Use *half of, a third of*, or *a fourth of* when you describe it.

4. **Generalize** Copy Steven's design 4 times.
Use 2 colors. Put 2 designs next to each other in each row.

How did you copy the design? Describe a shortcut you used.

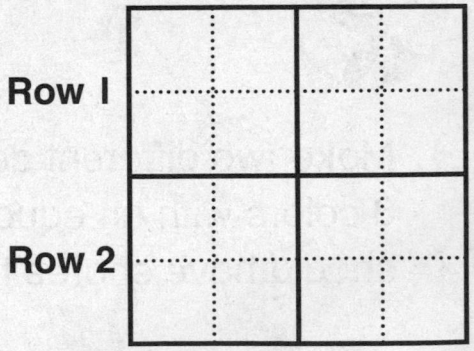

Copyright © Savvas Learning Company LLC. All Rights Reserved.

Name _____

TOPIC 15 **Fluency Practice Activity**

Follow the Path

Find each sum or difference. Then color a path from **Start** to **Finish**. Follow the sums and differences that are even numbers. You can only move up, down, right, or left.

I can ...
add and subtract within 100.

Start

69 − 23	31 + 25	78 − 47	97 − 49	72 + 12	76 − 38	67 − 47	48 + 24	46 + 37
84 − 61	73 − 55	68 + 29	11 + 17	37 + 58	86 − 51	21 + 38	82 − 18	81 − 62
43 + 42	27 + 49	35 + 48	46 − 32	73 − 26	30 + 31	46 − 28	47 + 41	62 − 39
25 + 16	60 − 36	50 − 29	39 + 43	60 − 45	64 + 23	29 + 35	56 + 41	94 − 61
35 + 42	85 − 23	24 + 56	58 + 36	97 − 38	25 − 16	38 + 62	79 − 49	59 + 23

Finish

TOPIC 15 Vocabulary Review

A-Z Glossary

Word List

- angle
- cube
- edge
- equal shares
- face
- fourths
- halves
- hexagon
- pentagon
- polygon
- quadrilateral
- right angle
- thirds
- vertex

Understand Vocabulary

Write *always*, *sometimes*, or *never*.

1. A cube has exactly 4 faces. _____
2. A right angle forms a square corner. _____
3. Quadrilaterals are squares. _____
4. A solid figure with faces has edges. _____

Draw a line from each term to its example.

5. hexagon
6. pentagon
7. vertex

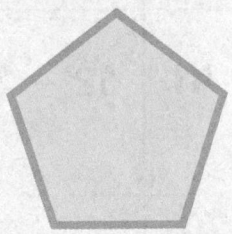

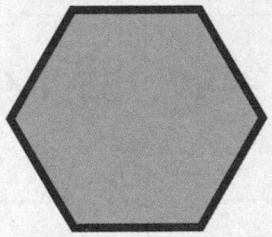

Use Vocabulary in Writing

8. Tell how you can divide a square into two equal shares. Then tell how you can divide that same square into 3 equal shares. Use terms from the Word List.

Copyright © Savvas Learning Company LLC. All Rights Reserved.

Name _____

TOPIC 15

Reteaching

Set A

You can name a plane shape by its number of sides and vertices.

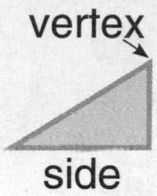

3 sides

3 vertices

Shape: triangle

4 sides

4 vertices

Shape: quadrilateral

Write the number of sides and vertices. Name the shape.

1. 

_____ sides

_____ vertices

Shape: _____

2. 

_____ sides

_____ vertices

Shape: _____

Set B

You can name a polygon by the number of its angles.

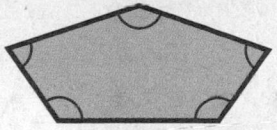

5 angles

pentagon

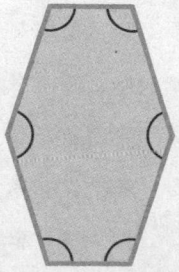

6 angles

hexagon

Write the number of angles. Then name the shape.

3. 

_____ angles

Shape: _____

4. 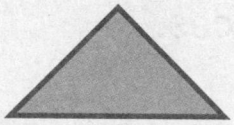

_____ angles

Shape: _____

Set C

You can draw a polygon with a given number of sides, vertices, or angles.

Draw a polygon with 4 sides that are different lengths.

Draw a polygon with 5 vertices.

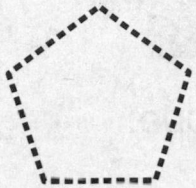

Draw a polygon with 3 angles. One angle is a right angle.

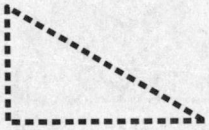

Draw each polygon described.

5. 6 sides

6. 3 vertices

7. 5 sides and 2 right angles

8. 8 angles

Set D

You can describe and draw cubes.

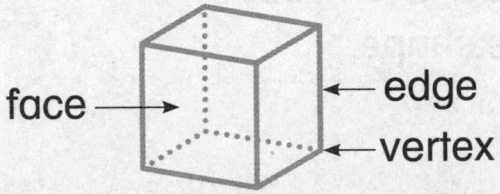

Every cube has 6 faces, 12 edges, and 8 vertices.

9. Cross out the shapes that are **NOT** cubes.

10. Draw a cube. Use the dots to help you.

Copyright © Savvas Learning Company LLC. All Rights Reserved.

Name _____

TOPIC 15

Reteaching
Continued

Set E

You can cover a rectangle with squares.

column

row →

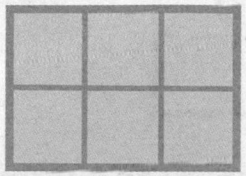

Count by rows: 3 + 3 = 6

Count by columns: 2 + 2 + 2 = 6

6 squares cover the rectangle.

Use square tiles to cover the rectangle. Trace the tiles. Then count the squares.

11.

_____ squares cover the rectangle.

Set F

You can divide circles and rectangles into equal shares.

2 equal shares are **halves**.

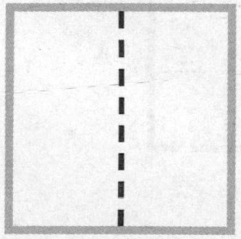

3 equal shares are **thirds**.

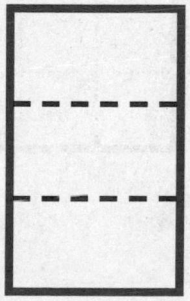

4 equal shares are **fourths**.

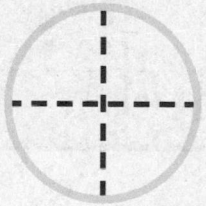

Divide each shape into the given number of equal shares. Show 2 ways.

12. halves

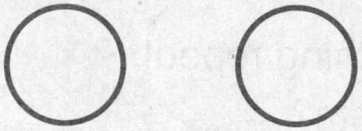

13. thirds

14. fourths

Set G

Equal shares can be different shapes.

This is one way to divide this rectangle into 3 equal shares.

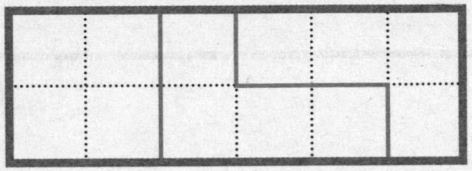

Each equal share is 4 squares.

Draw lines to show two more ways to divide the rectangle into 3 equal shares.

15. equal shares that are **NOT** all the same shape

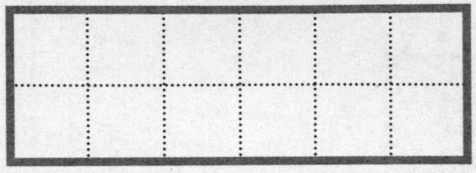

16. equal shares that are all the same shape

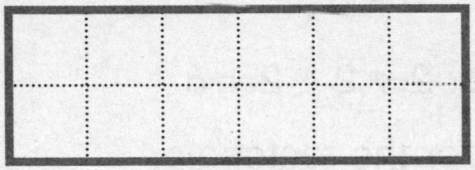

Set H

Thinking Habits

Repeated Reasoning

Does something repeat in the problem?

How can the solution help me solve another problem?

Use the design shown. Create a different design with 3 equal shares.

17.

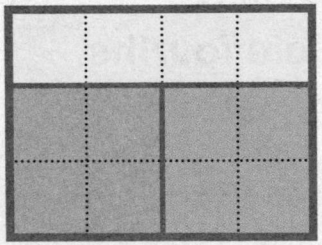

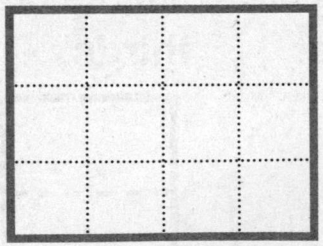

Copyright © Savvas Learning Company LLC. All Rights Reserved.

Name _____

TOPIC 15 Assessment

1. Which polygons are pentagons? Choose all that apply.

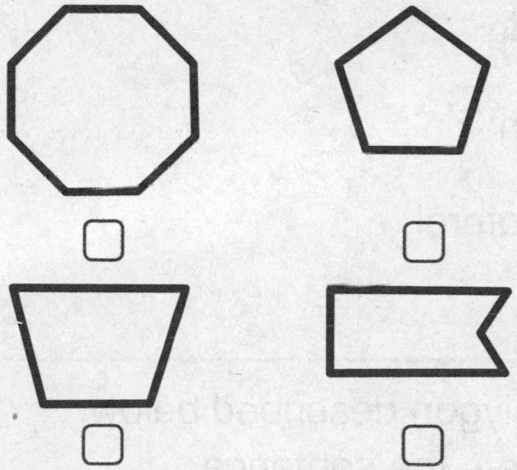

2. Rita draws a polygon. It has fewer than 8 sides and more angles than a square. Which shape did Rita draw?

Ⓐ triangle

Ⓑ rectangle

Ⓒ hexagon

Ⓓ quadrilateral

3. Which rectangles are divided into fourths? Choose all that apply.

4. Draw a polygon with 4 angles. Make one angle a right angle. Then name the polygon.

Name: _____

5. Is the polygon a quadrilateral? Choose Yes or No.

I have 3 sides and 3 angles. ○ Yes ○ No

I have 4 sides and 4 angles. ○ Yes ○ No

I am a square. ○ Yes ○ No

I am a rectangle. ○ Yes ○ No

6. Mandy draws a polygon with 6 sides and 6 angles. Which shape did she draw?

Ⓐ pentagon

Ⓑ hexagon

Ⓒ octagon

Ⓓ quadrilateral

7. Name the shape below. Write 3 things that describe the shape.

_____

_____

_____

_____

8. Draw the polygon described below. Then complete the sentence.

I have 2 fewer sides than a pentagon.
I have 1 less angle than a square.
I have one right angle.

The shape is a _____.

Copyright © Savvas Learning Company LLC. All Rights Reserved.

9. Complete the sentence to name and describe the solid figure below.

A _____ has ____ faces, ____ vertices, and ____ edges.

10. Divide the circle into 2 equal shares. Then complete the sentences.

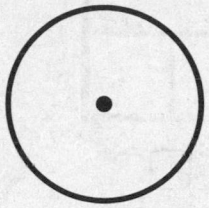

Each share is a _____ of the whole.

The whole is ____ halves.

11. Brad says there are only two ways to divide the same rectangle below into 3 equal shares. Do you agree? Use words and pictures to explain.

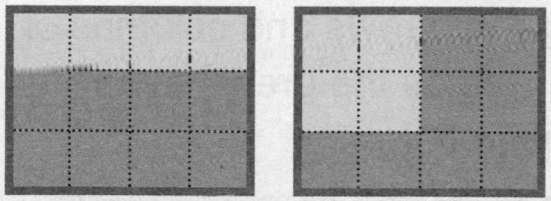

_____

_____

12. Count the number of squares in the rows and columns of the rectangle. Use the numbers on the cards to write the missing numbers in the equations.

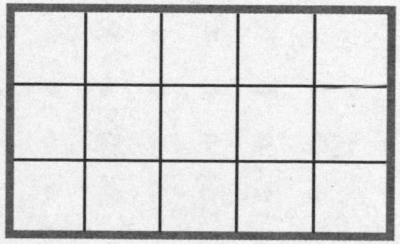

15	3	5

Rows: ____ + ____ + ____ = ____ squares

Columns: ____ + ____ + ____ + ____ + ____ = ____ squares

13. Kerry wants a design that shows thirds. Which designs could Kerry use? Choose all that apply.

☐

☐

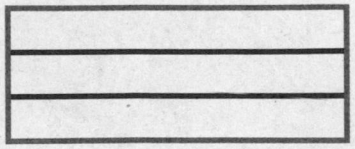

☐

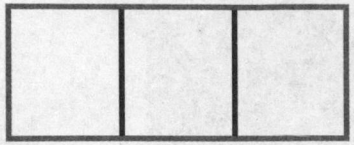

☐

14. Is the solid figure a cube? Choose Yes or No.

☐ Yes ☐ No

☐ Yes ☐ No

☐ Yes ☐ No

☐ Yes ☐ No

15. Use the dot paper. Draw a cube.

16. Divide the rectangle into rows and columns of squares the same size as the green square. Then count the squares.

_____ squares

Copyright © Savvas Learning Company LLC. All Rights Reserved.

Name _____

TOPIC 15 Performance Assessment

Happy Home

Tina and her family moved into a new home. They bought different things for each room.

1. They hang pictures on the wall. Name the shape of each picture frame.

_____

_____

2. The rug in the kitchen has 5 sides and 5 vertices. Draw the shape of the rug.

Name the shape. _____

3. The wallpaper uses this pattern.

Name the shape in the pattern.

_____

Write the number of sides, vertices, and angles in the shape.

_____ sides _____ vertices _____ angles

4. The living room has 2 end tables.

Circle the table that is a cube. Explain.

_____

_____

_____

_____

_____

5. Tina has a new quilt for her bed.
Her quilt has this design.

What share is green? _____

What share is yellow? _____

6. Tina's mother is making a quilt made of smaller squares. She wants the quilt to have 4 colors. Each color has an equal share.

Part A

Use 4 colors to make a possible quilt design below. Make the equal shares the same shape.

Design 1

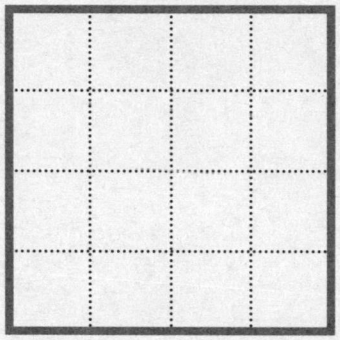

Part B

Use 4 colors to make a different quilt design below. Make the equal shares have different shapes.

Design 2

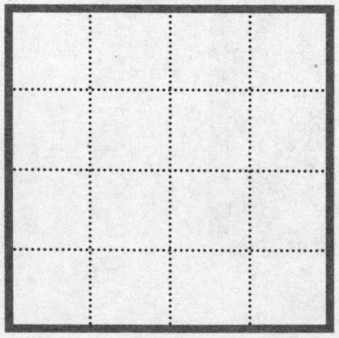

Copyright © Savvas Learning Company LLC. All Rights Reserved.

STEP UP to Grade 3

Lessons

1 Multiplication as Repeated Addition.....921
2 Arrays and Multiplication.....925
3 Division as Sharing.....929
4 Division as Repeated Subtraction.....933
5 Add with Partial Sums.....937
6 Models for Adding 3-Digit Numbers.....941
7 Subtract with Partial Differences.....945
8 Models for Subtracting 3-Digit Numbers.....949
9 Divide Regions into Equal Parts.....953
10 Fractions and Regions.....957

Grade 3 lessons look different. Rotate the pages so your name is at the top.

Name _____

Solve

Step Up to Grade 3

Lesson 1
Multiplication as Repeated Addition

I can ...
use addition or multiplication to join equal groups.

SOL 3.4a, 3.4b, 3.17

Solve & Share

Ms. Witt bought 3 boxes of paint with 5 jars of paint in each box. What is the total number of jars Ms. Witt bought? ***Solve this problem any way you choose.***

Look Back! Model with Math How can you use a picture to show the math you did in the problem?

Learn Glossary

Essential Question

How Can You Find the Total Number of Objects in Equal Groups?

A

Jessie used 3 bags to bring home the goldfish she won at the Fun Fair. She put the same number of goldfish in each bag. How many goldfish did she win?

I can use counters to show the groups.

8 goldfish in each bag

B

The counters show 3 groups of 8 goldfish.

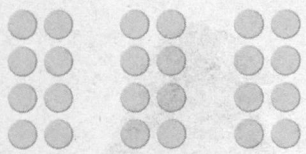

You can use addition to join equal groups.

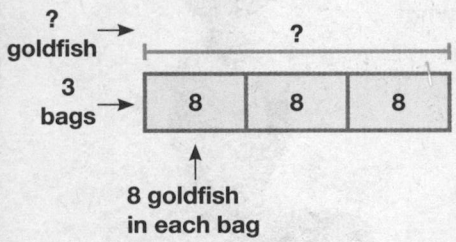

$8 + 8 + 8 = 24$

C

Multiplication is an operation that gives the total number when you join equal groups.

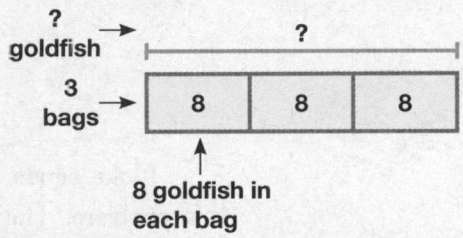

3 times 8 equals 24

$3 \times 8 = 24$

factor factor product

Factors are the numbers that are being multiplied. The product is the answer to a multiplication problem.

D

You can write equations.

Use a question mark for the unknown number that you find.

Addition equation:
$8 + 8 + 8 = ?$
$8 + 8 + 8 = 24$

Multiplication equation:
$3 \times 8 = ?$
$3 \times 8 = 24$

Jessie won 24 goldfish.

Convince Me! Model with Math Suppose Jessie won 5 bags of 8 goldfish. Draw a bar diagram and write an addition equation and a multiplication equation to represent the problem.

Copyright © Savvas Learning Company LLC. All Rights Reserved.

Name _____

Tools

Guided Practice

Do You Understand?

1. **Reasoning** Can you write $3 + 3 + 3 + 3 = 12$ as a multiplication equation? Explain.

2. **Reasoning** Can you write $1 + 5 + 7 = 13$ as a multiplication equation? Explain.

3. Write an addition equation and a multiplication equation to solve this problem.
Matt buys 3 bags of apples. There are 6 apples in each bag. How many apples does Matt buy?

Do You Know How?

Complete **4** and **5**. Use the pictures to help.

4.

2 groups of ____

$3 + 3 =$ ____

$2 \times$ ____ $=$ ____

5.

____ groups of 2

$2 +$ ____ $+$ ____ $=$ ____

$3 \times$ ____ $=$ ____

Independent Practice

Complete **6** and **7**. Use the pictures to help.

6.

2 groups of ____

$4 +$ ____ $=$ ____

$2 \times$ ____ $=$ ____

7.

3 groups of ____

$4 +$ ____ $+$ ____ $=$ ____

$3 \times$ ____ $=$ ____

In **8–11**, complete each equation. Use counters or draw a picture to help.

8. $5 + 5 + 5 + 5 = 4 \times$ ____

9. ____ $+$ ____ $= 2 \times 7$

10. $9 +$ ____ $= 2 \times$ ____

11. $6 + 6 + 6 + 6 =$ ____ $\times$ ____

Problem Solving

12. **Model with Math** Lily has 8 eggs. Draw pictures to show two different ways Lily can make equal groups using 8 eggs.

13. **Be Precise** Erin reads 54 pages of her book. The book has 93 pages in all. How many pages does Erin have left to read? Show your work.

____ pages

14. **Critique Reasoning** Chris says she can write two different equations to show 15 as repeated addition. Is Chris correct? Why or why not?

15. **Higher Order Thinking** George says you need equal groups to multiply. Is George correct? Why or why not?

Assessment

16. Zoey has 10 stickers. She puts them in 2 groups of 5. How can you represent this? Choose all that apply.

- ☐ $5 + 2$
- ☐ $2 + 2 + 2 + 2 + 2$
- ☐ $5 + 5$
- ☐ 2×5
- ☐ $10 + 2 + 5$

17. Drew earns \$6 each week. He wants to know how much money he will have saved after 5 weeks. How can you represent this? Choose all that apply.

- ☐ \$6 + \$6 + \$6 + \$6 + \$6
- ☐ \$6 × 6
- ☐ \$6 + \$5
- ☐ \$5 + \$5 + \$5 + \$5 + \$5
- ☐ \$6 × 5

Copyright © Savvas Learning Company LLC. All Rights Reserved.

Name _____

Solve

Step Up to Grade 3

Lesson 2
Arrays and Multiplication

I can ...
use arrays to show and solve multiplication problems.

SOL 3.4a, 3.4b, 3.17

Solve & Share

Mark put sports cards in an album. He put 4 rows of cards on each page. He put 3 cards in each row. How many cards are on each page? ***Solve this problem any way you choose.***

Look Back! Make Sense and Persevere Will your answer be the same if Mark puts 3 rows of 4 cards on each page? Explain.

Learn Glossary

Essential Question

How Does an Array Show Multiplication?

A

Dana keeps her swimming medal collection in a display on the wall.

The display has 4 rows. Each row has 5 medals. How many medals are in Dana's collection?

The medals are in an array. An array shows objects in equal rows and columns.

B The counters show 4 rows and 5 columns.

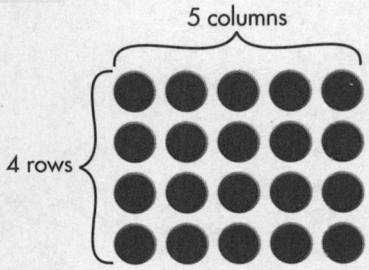

Each row is a group. You can use addition or skip counting to find the total.

Addition: $5 + 5 + 5 + 5 = 20$
Skip counting: 5, 10, 15, 20

C Multiplication can also be used to find the total in an array.

You say, "4 times 5 equals 20."

$$4 \times 5 = 20$$

number of rows — number in each row

There are 20 medals in Dana's collection.

Convince Me! Construct Arguments Jason also has a swimming medal collection. His display has 5 rows with 5 medals in each row. Who has more medals, Jason or Dana? Draw an array, then write an addition equation and a multiplication equation to show your work.

Copyright © Savvas Learning Company LLC. All Rights Reserved.

Name _____

Tools

Guided Practice

Do You Understand?

1. Look at page 926. What does the second factor tell you about the array?

2. Gina puts muffins in 4 rows with 8 muffins in each row. Draw an array to find the total number of muffins.

Do You Know How?

In **3** and **4**, write a multiplication equation for each array.

3. 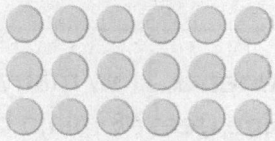

4. 

Independent Practice

In **5–7**, write a multiplication equation for each array.

5. 

6. 

7. 

In **8** and **9**, draw an array to show each equation. Write the product.

8. $5 \times 9 =$ ____

9. $2 \times 8 =$ ____

Problem Solving

10. Look for Relationships Lance draws these two arrays. How are the arrays alike? How are they different?

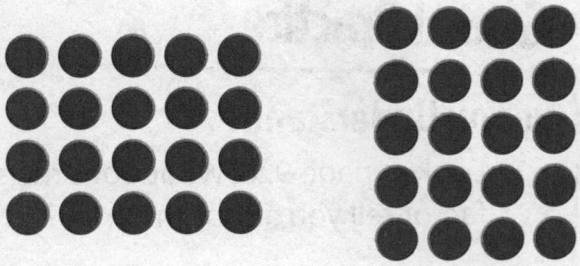

11. Construct Arguments How many more birch trees are there than pine trees? Explain how you know.

DATA

Trees in the Park	
Birch	~~////~~ /
Oak	///
Maple	~~////~~
Pine	//

12. Higher Order Thinking Rachel has 19 pictures. Can she use all the pictures to make an array with exactly 4 equal rows? Why or why not?

13. Larry puts 7 nickels in each of his 3 empty piggy banks. How many nickels does Larry put in the banks? Write a multiplication equation to show how you solved the problem.

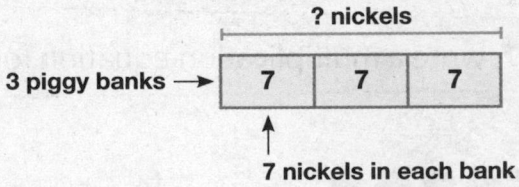

Assessment

14. Mr. Williams planted 6 rows of apple trees on his farm. The apple trees are in 8 columns. How many trees are there in all?

Ⓐ 6
Ⓑ 8
Ⓒ 14
Ⓓ 48

15. Tina bought the stickers shown below. Which of the following shows how many stickers Tina bought?

Ⓐ $5 + 2$
Ⓑ 5×2
Ⓒ 5×5
Ⓓ $5 - 2$

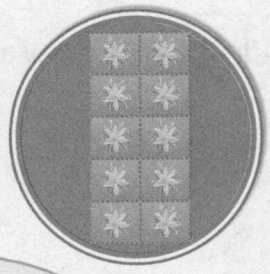

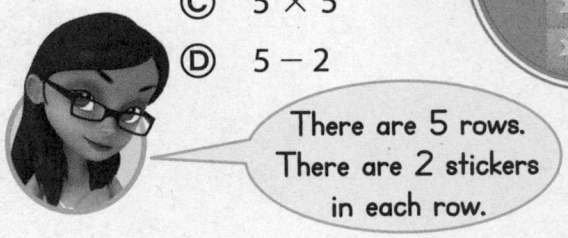

Copyright © Savvas Learning Company LLC. All Rights Reserved.

Name _____

Solve

Step Up to Grade 3

Lesson 3
Division as Sharing

I can ...
use objects or pictures to show how objects can be divided into equal groups.

SOL 3.4a, 3.4b

Solve & Share

Four friends picked 20 apples. They want to share them equally. How many apples should each person get? ***Solve this problem any way you choose.***

Look Back! Use Appropriate Tools Can you use counters to help you solve this problem? Explain.

Learn Glossary

Essential Question

How Many Are in Each Group?

A

Three friends have 12 toys to share equally. How many toys will each friend get?

Think of arranging 12 toys into 3 equal groups.

B

What You Think

Put one toy at a time in each group.

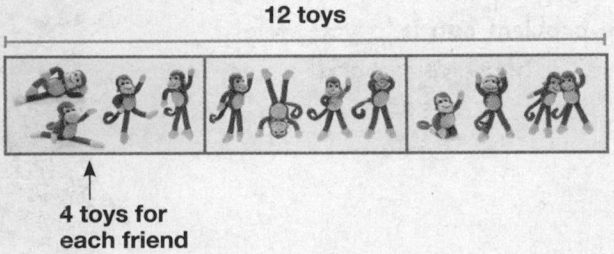

When all the toys are grouped, there will be 4 in each group.

C

What You Write

You can write a division equation to find the number in each group.

12	÷	3	=	4
↑ Total		↑ Number of equal groups		↑ Number in each group

Each friend will get 4 toys.

Convince Me! Be Precise What would happen if 3 friends wanted to share 13 toys equally?

Copyright © Savvas Learning Company LLC. All Rights Reserved.

Name _____

Tools

Guided Practice

Do You Understand?

1. 15 blocks are divided into 3 rows. How many blocks are in each row? Use the bar diagram to solve.

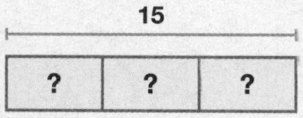

15 ÷ 3 = ____ blocks

2. **Be Precise** Can 11 apples be shared equally among 4 children with no apples remaining? Explain.

Do You Know How?

In **3** and **4**, draw a picture to solve.

3. 16 bananas are shared equally by 4 monkeys. How many bananas does each monkey get?

4. 21 marbles are divided equally into 3 jars. How many marbles are in each jar?

Independent Practice

In **5** and **6**, draw a picture to solve.

5. 24 sandwiches are divided equally into 6 bags. How many sandwiches are in each bag?

6. 12 pencils are shared equally by 2 people. How many pencils does each person have?

In **7–10**, complete each equation.

7. 14 ÷ 2 = ☐

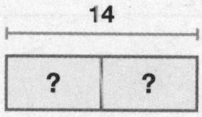

8. 24 ÷ 8 = ☐

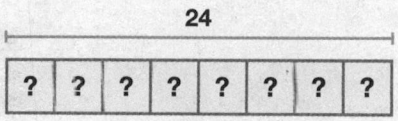

9. 12 ÷ 4 = ____

10. 28 ÷ 7 = ____

Problem Solving

11. **Critique Reasoning** Dean is putting 16 pens into equal groups. He says if he puts them into 2 equal groups he will have more pens in each group than if he puts them in 4 equal groups. Is Dean correct? Explain.

12. **Make Sense and Persevere** Ms. Baker's second grade class is divided into 4 teams. Each team has an equal number of students. Do you have enough information to find how many students are on each team? Explain.

13. Lily draws a rectangle. Sarah draws a pentagon. Who draws the shape with more sides? How many more sides does that shape have?

14. **Model with Math** The jazz band in a parade marches in 9 rows with 6 members in each row. Write an equation to show how many members there are.

15. **Number Sense** Joan equally shares 30 grapes with some friends. Is the number of grapes that each friend gets greater than 30 or less than 30? Explain.

16. **Higher Order Thinking** Lacie has 16 shells. She gives 6 shells to her mom. Then she and her sister share the other shells equally. How many shells does Lacie get? How many shells does her sister get? How do you know?

Assessment

17. Darren has the 12 stickers shown at the right. He wants to put an equal number of stickers on each of 2 books. Draw circles in each box to represent the stickers Darren puts on each book.

Book 1

Book 2

Copyright © Savvas Learning Company LLC. All Rights Reserved.

Name _____

Solve

Step Up to Grade 3

Lesson 4

Division as Repeated Subtraction

I can ...
use repeated subtraction to understand and solve division problems.

SOL 3.4a, 3.4b

Solve & Share

Li made 12 tacos. He wants to give some of his friends 2 tacos each. If Li does not get any of the tacos, how many of his friends will get tacos? ***Solve this problem any way you choose.***

Look Back! Use Appropriate Tools How can counters or other objects help you show your work?

Learn Glossary

Essential Question

How Can You Divide Using Repeated Subtraction?

A

June has 10 strawberries to serve to her guests. If each guest eats 2 strawberries, how many guests can June serve?

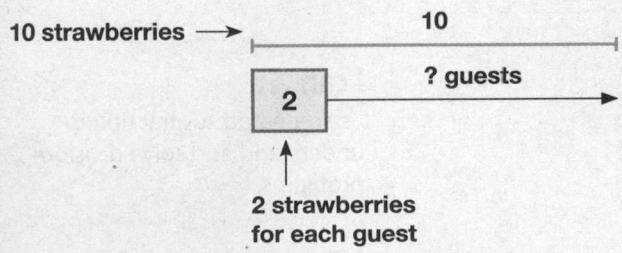

B

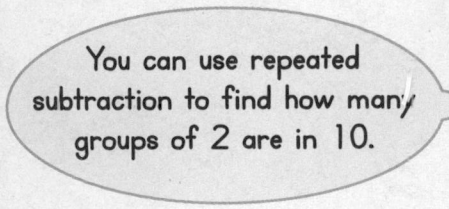

$10 - 2 = 8$
$8 - 2 = 6$
$6 - 2 = 4$
$4 - 2 = 2$
$2 - 2 = 0$

You can subtract 2 five times. There are five groups of 2 in 10.

There are no strawberries left.

June can serve 5 guests.

C

You can write a division equation to find the number of groups.

Write: $10 \div 2 = ?$

Read: Ten divided by 2 equals what number?

Solve: $10 \div 2 = 5$

June can serve 5 guests.

Convince Me! Model with Math In the example above, what if each guest eats 5 strawberries? Use the math you know to represent the problem and find how many guests June could serve.

Copyright © Savvas Learning Company LLC. All Rights Reserved.

Name _____

Tools

Guided Practice

Do You Understand?

1. Show how you can use repeated subtraction to find how many groups of 5 there are in 25. Then write a division equation to solve the problem.

Do You Know How?

In **2** and **3**, use counters or draw a picture to solve.

2. The basketball team has 14 shoes. There are 2 shoes in each pair. How many pairs of shoes are there?

3. Maya has 18 cat toys. She gives each of her cats 6 toys. How many cats does Maya have?

Independent Practice

In **4** and **5**, complete the equations.

4. Tanya picks 18 pears. She places 9 pears in each bag. How many bags does Tanya have?

   18 − 9 = __

   __ − 9 = __

   ____ ÷ 9 = __

   Tanya has __ bags.

5. The workers on a farm have 7 keys each. There are 21 keys. How many workers are on the farm?

   21 − 7 = ____

   ____ − 7 = __

   __ − __ = __

   ____ ÷ __ = __

   There are __ workers.

In **6** and **7**, use counters or draw a picture to solve.

6. Shawna bought 36 markers that came in packages of 4 markers each. How many packages did Shawna buy?

7. James has 16 pencils. He puts 2 pencils on each desk. How many desks are there?

Problem Solving

8. **Generalize** The chart shows the number of pennies each of three friends has in her pocket. Each friend divides her money into piles of 4 coins. Write division equations to show how many equal piles each friend can make. Explain what repeats in the equations and how it helps you solve.

DATA

Money in Pockets

Paige	20 pennies
Lexi	16 pennies
Nancy	12 pennies

9. If Lexi makes 8 columns of pennies, how many rows does she make? Write an equation to model and solve the problem.

10. **Model with Math** Tim has $45. He spends $21, then finds $28. How much money does Tim have now? Use math to represent the problem.

11. **Higher Order Thinking** A bakery plans to make 8 new muffins each year. How many years will it take for the store to make 40 new muffins? Write and solve an equation.

Assessment

12. Andy writes the following:

$8 - 4 = 4$

$4 - 4 = 0$

Which equation could Andy use to represent the same problem?

Ⓐ $4 \times 4 = 16$

Ⓑ $8 \div 8 = 1$

Ⓒ $8 \div 4 = 2$

Ⓓ $4 \div 2 = 2$

13. Rae writes the following:

$27 - 9 = 18$

$18 - 9 = 9$

$9 - 9 = 0$

Which problem is Rae trying to solve?

Ⓐ $27 \div 9$

Ⓑ $27 \div 3$

Ⓒ $27 - 9$

Ⓓ 27×3

Copyright © Savvas Learning Company LLC. All Rights Reserved.

Name _____

Solve

Step Up to Grade 3

Lesson 5
Add with Partial Sums

I can ...
add numbers using partial sums.

SOL 3.3a, 3.3b

Solve & Share

Find the sum of 327 + 241. Think about place value. ***Solve this problem any way you choose.***

Look Back! Reasoning How can using place value help you solve this 3-digit addition problem?

Learn Glossary

Essential Question

How Can You Break Large Addition Problems into Smaller Ones?

A

Find the sum of 243 + 179. Each digit in the numbers can be modeled with place-value blocks.

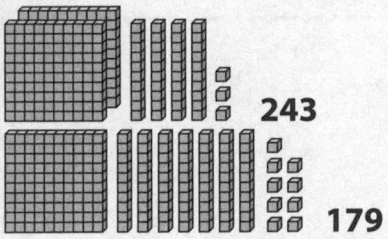

B

Step 1

Break 243 + 179 into smaller problems. Think about the place value of each number.

Hundreds	Tens	Ones
200	40	3
+ 100	+ 70	+ 9
300	110	12

C

Step 2

Then, add the sums of all the places.

$$\begin{array}{r} 300 \\ 110 \\ +\ 12 \\ \hline 422 \end{array}$$

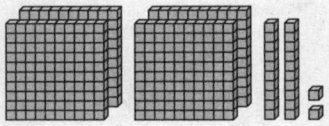

So, 243 + 179 = 422.

Convince Me! Construct Arguments Lexi says, "To solve 243 + 179, I can just count on with place-value blocks to find the answer: 100, 200, 300, another hundred from the 11 tens is 400, one more ten and 12 ones is 422!" How is Lexi's way like Steps 1 and 2 above?

Copyright © Savvas Learning Company LLC. All Rights Reserved.

Name _____

Tools

Guided Practice

Do You Understand?

1. **Reasoning** Suppose you are adding 824 + 106. What would the tens problem be? Why?

2. Write the smaller problems you could use to find 512 + 362. What is the sum?

Do You Know How?

In **3**, use place value to find the sum.

3.

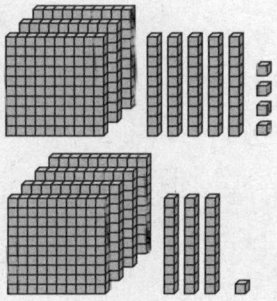

Find 354 + 431.

Hundreds	Tens	Ones	Total
300	50	4	
+ 400	+ 30	+ 1	

Independent Practice

In **4** through **11**, find each sum.

4.

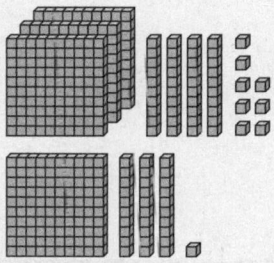

348 + 131

Hundreds	Tens	Ones	Total
300	40	8	
+ 100	+ 30	+ 1	

5.

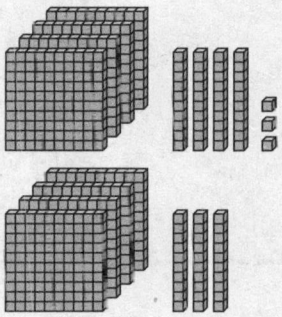

443 + 430

Hundreds	Tens	Ones	Total
400	40	3	
+ 400	+ 30	+ 0	

6. 264 + 524

7. 541 + 276

8. 249 + 180

9. 342 + 168

10. 191 + 502

11. 473 + 405

Problem Solving

12. Critique Reasoning Henry believes the sum of 345 + 124 is 479. Is Henry correct? Explain.

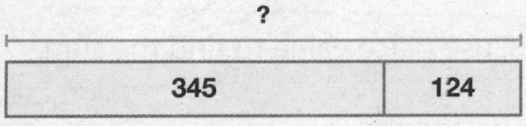

13. Construct Arguments Explain how the solids shown in Group A and Group B could have been sorted.

Group A **Group B**

14. Model with Math Bill needs to find 325 + 133. Into what three smaller problems can Bill break this addition? What is the sum?

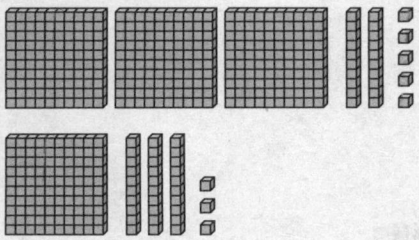

15. Higher Order Thinking A school cafeteria sells 215 lunches on Monday, 104 lunches on Tuesday, and 262 lunches on Wednesday. Did the cafeteria sell more lunches on Monday and Tuesday or on Tuesday and Wednesday? Explain.

Assessment

16. Jan read a book with 288 pages. Lara read a book with 416 pages. How many pages did Jan and Lara both read? Solve using partial sums.

Ⓐ 694
Ⓑ 704
Ⓒ 706
Ⓓ 716

17. Cody wants to add 482 + 315. He writes (400 + 300) + (80 + 10) + (2 + 5). Which shows the sum of the hundreds, tens, and ones?

Ⓐ 700 + 90 + 5
Ⓑ 700 + 90 + 7
Ⓒ 800 + 80 + 5
Ⓓ 800 + 60 + 7

Copyright © Savvas Learning Company LLC. All Rights Reserved.

Name _____

Solve

Step Up to Grade 3

Lesson 6
Models for Adding 3-Digit Numbers

I can ...
add 3-digit numbers using models, drawings, and place value.

SOL 3.3a, 3.3b

Solve & Share

Find the sum of 146 + 247.

Solve this problem any way you choose.

Look Back! Generalize When you add numbers, how do you know if you need to regroup?

Learn Glossary

Essential Question

How Can You Add 3-Digit Numbers with Place-Value Blocks?

A

Find 143 + 285.

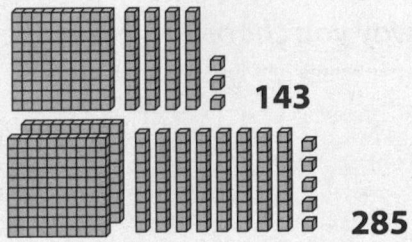

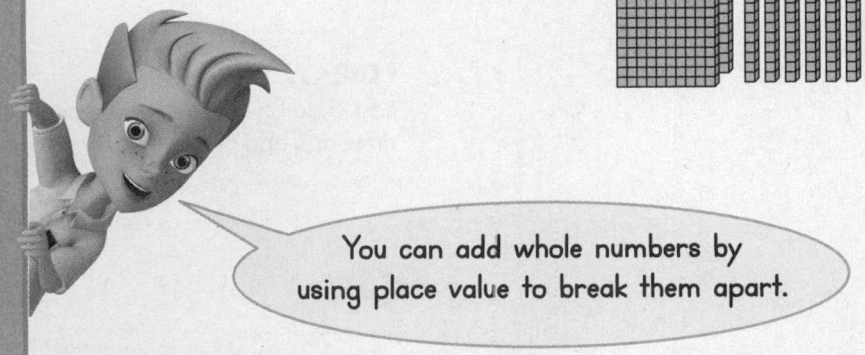

Add the ones, tens, and hundreds.

B

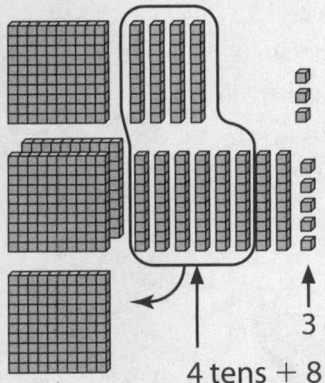

3 ones + 5 ones = 8 ones

4 tens + 8 tens = 12 tens

12 tens = 1 hundred 2 tens ← Regroup.

1 hundred + 2 hundreds + 1 hundred = 4 hundreds ← Add the hundreds.

C

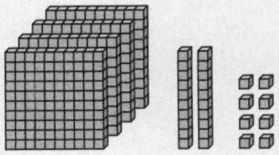

4 hundreds 2 tens 8 ones

428

143 + 285 = 428

Convince Me! Model with Math Mr. Wu drove 224 miles yesterday. He drove 175 miles today. Use place-value blocks or draw pictures of blocks to find how many miles Mr. Wu drove.

Copyright © Savvas Learning Company LLC. All Rights Reserved.

Name _____

Tools

Another Example!

You may have to regroup twice when you add. Find 148 + 276.

Step 1

Add the ones.
8 ones + 6 ones = 14 ones

Regroup.
14 ones = 1 ten 4 ones

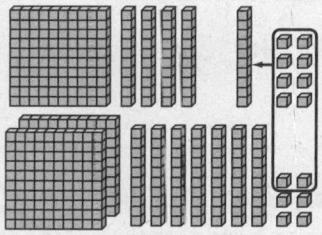

Step 2

Add the tens.
1 ten + 4 tens + 7 tens = 12 tens

Regroup.
12 tens = 1 hundred 2 tens

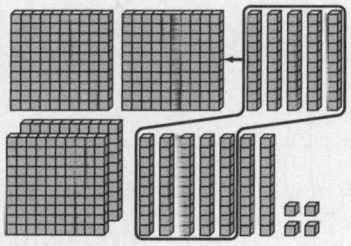

Step 3

Add the hundreds.
1 hundred + 1 hundred + 2 hundreds = 4 hundreds

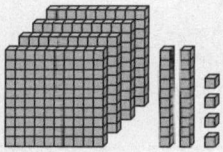

So, 148 + 276 = 424.

Guided Practice

Do You Understand?

1. **Generalize** How do you know when you need to regroup?

2. **Use Appropriate Tools** Use place-value blocks to find 136 + 279.

Do You Know How?

In **3**, use the model to write the problem and find the sum.

3.

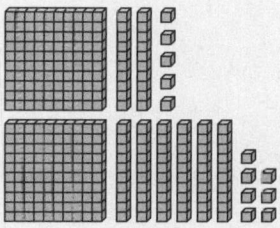

Independent Practice

In **4** through **6**, write the problem and find the sum.

4.

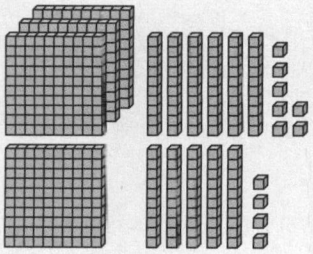

5.

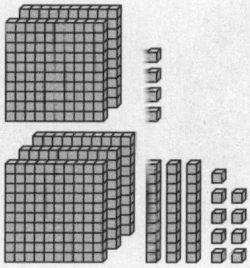

6.

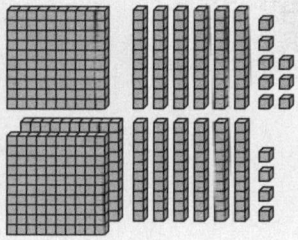

Problem Solving

7. **Model with Math** Juan wants to use place-value blocks to show 148 + 256. Draw a picture of the blocks Juan should use. What is the sum?

8. **Use Appropriate Tools** Manuel plays basketball and scores 15 points in game one, 8 points in game two, and 17 points in game three. How many points did Manuel score? Use the number line to solve the problem.

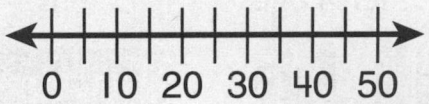

9. **Construct Arguments** Al and Mark were playing a computer game. Al scored 265 points in the first round and 354 points in the second round. Mark scored 352 points in the first round and 237 points in the second round. Who scored more points and won the game? Explain.

10. **Higher Order Thinking** Paula is saving money to buy a new computer that costs $680. Last month she saved $415, and this month she saved $298. Does Paula have enough money saved to buy the computer? Use place-value blocks to help you solve the problem. Explain.

Assessment

11. Write an equation that represents what the place-value blocks show.

12. Mrs. Samuels bought a $526 plane ticket in May and a $194 plane ticket in June. Use place-value blocks or draw pictures to find out how much Mrs. Samuels spent on both of the plane tickets.

Copyright © Savvas Learning Company LLC. All Rights Reserved.

Name _____

Solve

Step Up to Grade 3

Lesson 7

Subtract with Partial Differences

I can ...
subtract numbers using partial differences.

SOL 3.3a, 3.3b

Solve & Share Find the difference of 534 − 108. Think about place value. ***Solve this problem any way you choose.***

Look Back! Reasoning How can using place value help you solve this subtraction problem?

Learn Glossary

Essential Question

How Can You Break Large Subtraction Problems into Smaller Ones?

A

At the end of the fourth round of a game of Digit Derby, *Marco's score was 462 points. During the fifth round of the game, Marco loses points. What is Marco's score at the end of the fifth round?*

Find 462 − 181.

End of Round 4

Marco has 462 points.

End of Round 5

Marco loses 181 points.

B

Step 1

Start with 462.

Subtract the **hundreds**.
462 − 100 = 362

So far, 100 has been subtracted.

C

Step 2

Next, start with 362.

Subtract the **tens**.

You need to subtract 8 tens, but there are not enough tens. So, subtract the 6 tens.
362 − 60 = 302

Then, subtract the 2 tens that are left.
302 − 20 = 282

So far, 100 + 60 + 20 = 180 has been subtracted.

D

Step 3

That leaves just 1 to subtract.

Subtract the **ones**.
282 − 1 = 281

100 + 60 + 20 + 1 = 181 has been subtracted.

At the end of the fifth round, Marco's score is 281 points.

Convince Me! **Use Structure** Find 453 − 262. Use place value to help break the problem into smaller problems. Show your work.

Copyright © Savvas Learning Company LLC. All Rights Reserved.

Name _____

Tools

Guided Practice

Do You Understand?

1. **Construct Arguments** Why do you need to record the numbers you subtract at each step?

2. **Reasoning** Carmella is trying to find 784 − 310. She decides to start by subtracting 10 from 784. Do you agree with Carmella? Explain.

Do You Know How?

In **3** and **4**, use place value to help break the problem into smaller problems.

3. Find 564 − 346.

564 − 300 = ____

264 − 40 = ____

224 − 4 = ____

220 − 2 = ____

4. Find 769 − 375.

769 − 300 = ____

469 − 60 = ____

409 − 10 = ____

399 − 5 = ____

Independent Practice

In **5** through **10**, follow the steps to find each difference. Show your work.

5. 728 − 413

First, subtract 400.

____ − ____ = 328

Then, subtract 10.

____ − ____ = ____

Then, subtract 3.

____ − 3 = ____

6. 936 − 524

First, subtract 500.

936 − ____ = ____

Then, subtract 20.

____ − 20 = ____

Then, subtract 4.

____ − ____ = ____

7. 854 − 235

First, subtract 200.

____ − 200 = ____

Then, subtract 30.

____ − 30 = ____

Then, subtract 4.

____ − ____ = ____

Then, subtract 1.

____ − 1 = ____

8. 955 − 283

9. 946 − 507

10. 984 − 356

Problem Solving

11. Use Appropriate Tools Write the time shown on the clock in 2 different ways.

/

12. Use Structure There are 96 boys and 83 girls in the school lunchroom. Near the end of lunch, 127 students leave. How many students are left in the lunchroom? Show how you can break part of the problem into smaller problems.

13. Model with Math Yuki had a necklace with 131 beads. The string broke, and she lost 43 beads. How many beads does Yuki have left?

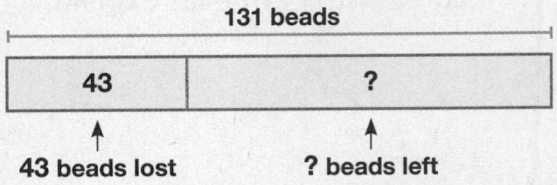

14. Higher Order Thinking Which weighs more, two adult male Basset Hounds or one adult male Great Dane? Show the difference in pounds between the two Basset Hounds and the Great Dane. Draw bar diagrams to represent and help you solve the problem.

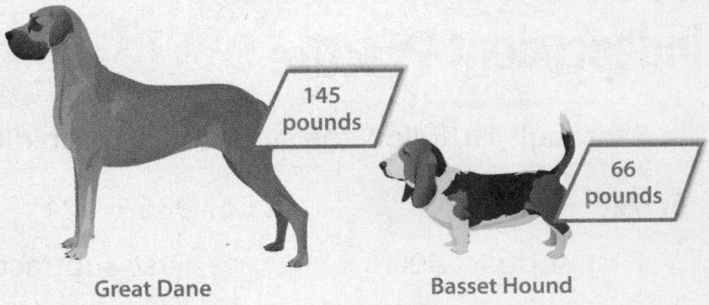

Assessment

15. Karl's book has 416 pages. He read 50 pages last week. He read another 31 pages this week. How many more pages does Karl have left to read?

Ⓐ 125 Ⓒ 335

Ⓑ 245 Ⓓ 345

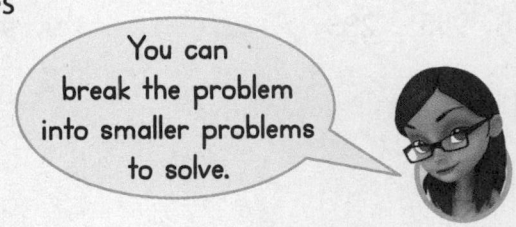

Copyright © Savvas Learning Company LLC. All Rights Reserved.

Name _____

Solve

Step Up to Grade 3

Lesson 8

Models for Subtracting 3-Digit Numbers

I can ...
subtract 3-digit numbers using models, drawings, and place value.

SOL 3.3a, 3.3b

Solve & Share

Find the difference of 246 − 153.

Solve this problem any way you choose.

Look Back! **Generalize** How can you check your answer for 246 − 153?

Learn Glossary

Essential Question

How Can You Subtract 3-Digit Numbers with Place-Value Blocks?

A

Fish caught near the Hawaiian Islands can be very large. How many more pounds does a broadbill swordfish weigh than a blue marlin?

Find 237 − 165.

DATA

Wild Hawaiian Fish Weights

Type of Fish	Weight (in lb)
Blue Marlin	165
Broadbill Swordfish	237

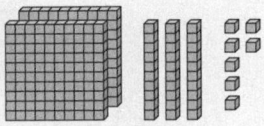

Show 237 with place-value blocks.

B Subtract the ones.

7 ones > 5 ones, so no regrouping.

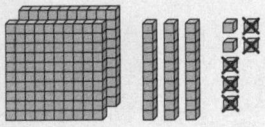

7 ones − 5 ones = 2 ones

$$\begin{array}{r} 237 \\ -\ 165 \\ \hline 2 \end{array}$$

C Subtract the tens.

3 tens < 6 tens, so regroup.
1 hundred = 10 tens

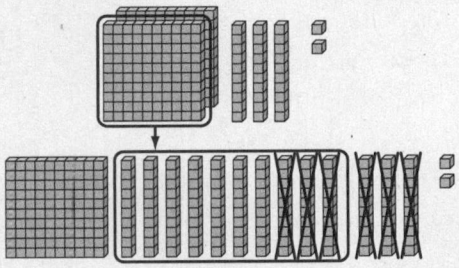

13 tens − 6 tens = 7 tens

$$\begin{array}{r} {}^{1}\cancel{2}\,{}^{13}\cancel{3}7 \\ -\ 165 \\ \hline 72 \end{array}$$

D Subtract the hundreds.

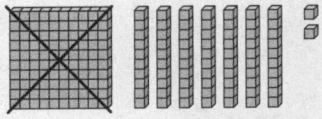

1 hundred − 1 hundred = 0 hundreds

$$\begin{array}{r} {}^{1}\cancel{2}\,{}^{13}\cancel{3}7 \\ -\ 165 \\ \hline 72 \end{array}$$

So, 237 − 165 = 72.
A broadbill swordfish weighs 72 more pounds than a blue marlin.

Convince Me! Model with Math Anderson needs $231 to buy a new bike. He saved $144 from his summer job. How much more does Anderson need to save to buy the bike? Write a subtraction equation that models the problem. Use place-value blocks to help you solve the problem using the same steps shown above.

Copyright © Savvas Learning Company LLC. All Rights Reserved.

Name _____

Tools

Guided Practice

Do You Understand?

1. **Generalize** In the example on page 950, for 237 − 165, why do you need to regroup 1 hundred into 10 tens?

2. **Model with Math** Gary saved $287 doing jobs in his neighborhood. He bought a computer printer for $183. How much money did Gary have left? Draw a picture of place-value blocks to help you subtract.

Do You Know How?

In **3** through **10**, use place-value blocks or draw pictures to subtract.

3. 859 − 768

4. 361 − 124

5. 285 − 49

6. 684 − 482

7. 384 − 358

8. 352 − 214

9. 512 − 101

10. 999 − 889

Independent Practice

In **11** through **22**, use place-value blocks or draw pictures to subtract.

11. 651 − 543

12. 492 − 138

13. 690 − 481

14. 508 − 137

15. 168 − 39

16. 618 − 476

17. 419 − 59

18. 192 − 108

19. 573 − 468

20. 596 − 128

21. 819 − 124

22. 438 − 283

Problem Solving

For **23** and **24**, use the table at the right.

Think:
What do I know?
What do I know?
What do I need to find?

23. How many more miles is it from Cleveland to Chicago than from Cincinnati to Cleveland?

24. **Make Sense and Persevere** Mr. Sousa is driving from Washington, D.C., to Cleveland and then to Cincinnati. He has traveled 182 miles. How many miles are left in his trip?

DATA

Trip Distances

Trip	Miles
Cleveland to Chicago	346
Cincinnati to Cleveland	249
Washington, D.C., to Cleveland	372

25. **Make Sense and Persevere** Which girl got more votes? How many more votes did that girl get?

DATA

Student Council President Votes

	7th Grade Votes	8th Grade Votes
Claudia	183	157
Jasmine	162	156

26. Kendra got $20 for her birthday. She earned $62 babysitting. Then she earned $148 shoveling snow. How much money does Kendra have?

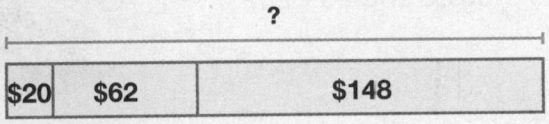

27. **Higher Order Thinking** Kim needs to find 437 − 258. Will she need to regroup to find the answer? If so, explain how she will need to regroup. What will Kim's answer be?

Assessment

28. It is 239 miles from Dallas to Houston and 275 miles from Dallas to San Antonio. How many fewer miles is it from Dallas to Houston than from Dallas to San Antonio?

Ⓐ 34 fewer miles
Ⓑ 36 fewer miles
Ⓒ 44 fewer miles
Ⓓ 45 fewer miles

29. An amusement park ride can hold 120 people. There are already 104 people on the ride. Which equation shows how many more people the ride can hold?

Ⓐ 120 − 104 = 16
Ⓑ 120 − 100 = 20
Ⓒ 120 − 94 = 26
Ⓓ 120 + 104 = 224

Copyright © Savvas Learning Company LLC. All Rights Reserved.

Name _____

Solve

Step Up to Grade 3

Lesson 9
Divide Regions into Equal Parts

I can ...
read and write a unit fraction.

SOL 2.4a

Solve & Share

Show two different ways to divide a 2×6 region into 6 equal parts. Color the 6 parts of each region a different color. How do you know the parts are equal?

Look Back! **Use Structure** How are the parts of the regions alike? How are they different?

Learn Glossary

Essential Question

How Can You Name the Equal Parts of a Whole?

A

Divide a whole into halves. What fraction can you write to represent one half of a whole?

B

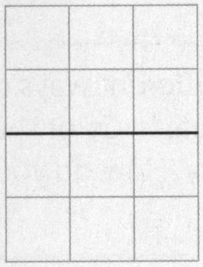

Each part is made up of 6 unit squares. Both parts have equal areas.

C

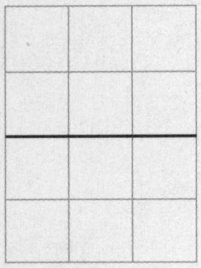

Each part is **one** half of the area of the whole shape.

This fraction can be written as $\frac{1}{2}$.

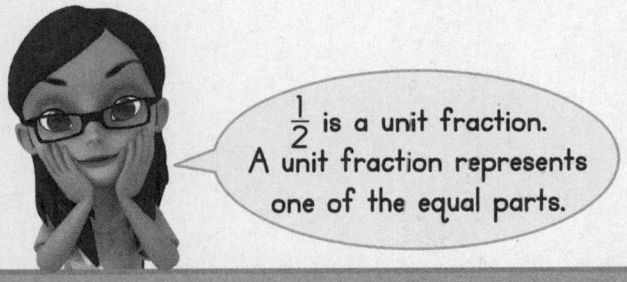

D

The number above the bar in a fraction is called the numerator.

The numerator shows the number of equal parts represented by that fraction.

numerator ⟶ $\frac{1}{2}$
denominator ⟶ $\frac{1}{2}$

The number below the bar in a fraction is called the denominator.

The denominator shows the total number of equal parts in that whole.

Convince Me! Be Precise Divide the grid at the right into thirds. Label each third using a unit fraction. Explain how you knew which fraction to write.

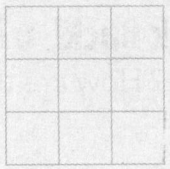

Copyright © Savvas Learning Company LLC. All Rights Reserved.

Name _____

Tools

Guided Practice

Do You Understand?

1. In the examples on page 954, explain how you know the two parts are equal.

In **2** and **3**, tell if each shows equal or unequal parts. If the parts are equal, label one of the parts using a unit fraction.

2. 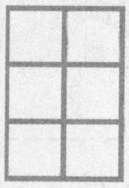

3. 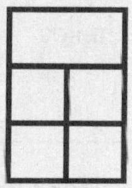

Do You Know How?

4. Draw a rectangle that is divided into fourths. Then, write the fraction that represents one equal part.

Independent Practice

In **5–7**, tell if each shows equal or unequal parts. If the parts are equal, name them.

5. 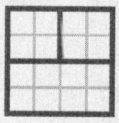

6. 

7. 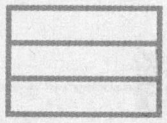

In **8** and **9**, draw lines to divide the shape into the given number of equal parts. Then write the fraction that represents one equal part.

8. 3 equal parts

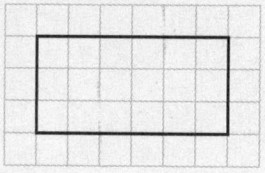

9. 8 equal parts

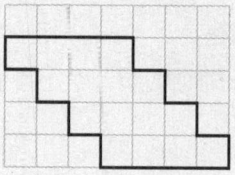

Problem Solving

In **10–13**, use the table of flags.

10. Which nation's flag is $\frac{1}{3}$ white?

11. **Be Precise** What fraction represents the red part of Poland's flag?

12. Which nation's flag does **NOT** have equal parts?

13. Which nation's flag is $\frac{1}{4}$ green?

Flags of Different Nations

Nation	Flag
Mauritius	
Nigeria	
Poland	
Seychelles	

14. **Model with Math** James buys 18 bottles of water. The water comes in packs of 6 bottles. How many packs did he buy? Write an addition equation and a multiplication equation to show your answer.

15. **Higher Order Thinking** Laura's books are shown below. What fraction of her books has a yellow cover?

Assessment

16. On the grid below, draw a rectangle. Divide your rectangle into fourths. Explain how you checked the reasonableness of your work.

Copyright © Savvas Learning Company LLC. All Rights Reserved.

Name _____

Solve

Step Up to Grade 3

Lesson 10
Fractions and Regions

I can ...
show and name part of a region.

SOL 2.4a, 2.4b

Solve & Share

Pat made a garden in the shape of a rectangle and divided it into 4 same-size parts. She planted flowers in one of the parts. Draw a picture of what Pat's garden might look like.

Look Back! Construct Arguments How many parts of Pat's garden do **NOT** have flowers? Explain.

Learn · Glossary

Essential Question

How Can You Show and Name Part of a Region?

A

Mr. Peters served part of a pan of enchilada casserole to a friend. What does each part of the whole pan of casserole represent? What part was served? What part is left?

A fraction is a symbol that names equal parts of a whole. A unit fraction represents one part of a whole that has been divided into equal parts. A unit fraction always has a numerator of 1.

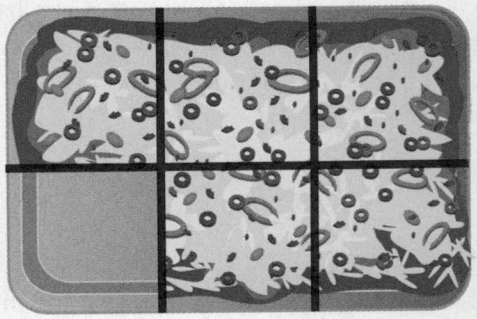

B

What You Think

There are 6 equal pieces in the whole, so each piece is $\frac{1}{6}$.

There is 1 piece missing, so one $\frac{1}{6}$-piece was served.

There are 5 pieces left, so five $\frac{1}{6}$-pieces are left.

The numerator shows how many equal parts are described. The denominator shows the total number of equal parts in a whole.

C

What You Write

$\frac{1}{6}$ ← numerator
$\frac{1}{6}$ ← denominator

$\frac{1}{6}$ of the pan of enchilada casserole was served.

$\frac{5}{6}$ of the pan of enchilada casserole is left.

Do You Understand?

Convince Me! Model with Math Below is a picture of a pie pan. Draw lines and use shading to show that five $\frac{1}{8}$-pieces are still in the pan, and that three $\frac{1}{8}$-pieces were eaten. Remember to draw same-size parts.

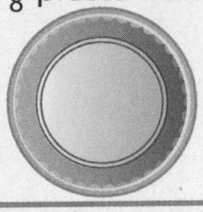

Copyright © Savvas Learning Company LLC. All Rights Reserved.

Name _____

Tools

Guided Practice

Do You Understand?

1. In the problem at the top of page 958, what fraction names all of the pieces in the casserole?

2. **Model with Math** Mrs. Rao made a cake. What fraction of the whole cake does each piece represent?

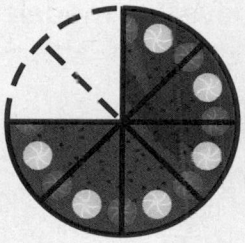

3. In the picture in Item 2, how many $\frac{1}{8}$-pieces were eaten? What fraction of the whole cake was eaten?

Do You Know How?

In **4** through **7**, use the figure below.

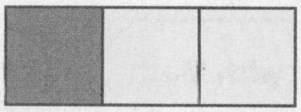

4. Write the unit fraction that represents each part of the whole.

5. How many $\frac{1}{3}$-parts are yellow?

6. What fraction of the whole is yellow?

7. What fraction names *all* of the parts in the whole?

Independent Practice

In **8** through **11**, write the unit fraction that represents each part of the whole. Then write the number of blue parts and the fraction of the whole that is blue.

8. 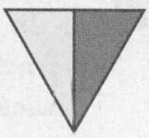

9. 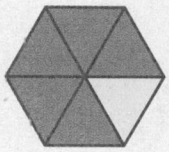

10. 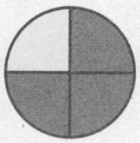

11. 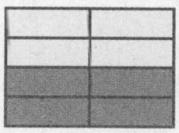

12. Draw a rectangle that shows 6 equal parts. Then shade $\frac{3}{6}$ of the rectangle. Explain how you know you shaded $\frac{3}{6}$ of the rectangle.

Problem Solving

13. Reasoning What is the distance around the baseball card? Write an equation to show and solve the problem.

14. Model with Math Janice has 2 scarves. Carla has 3 times as many scarves as Janice. How many scarves does Carla have? Use the bar diagram to write and solve an equation.

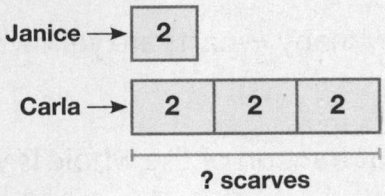

15. Higher Order Thinking Draw a circle that shows 6 equal parts. Shade more than $\frac{3}{6}$ of the circle, but less than $\frac{5}{6}$ of the circle. What fraction have you modeled?

Assessment

In **16** and **17**, use the chart to the right.

16. Kiko and some friends bought a medium party tray. They ate 5 sections of the tray. Which of the following shows the unit fraction, and the fraction of the tray that was **NOT** eaten?

Ⓐ $\frac{1}{8}, \frac{3}{8}$

Ⓑ $\frac{1}{6}, \frac{4}{6}$

Ⓒ $\frac{8}{8}, \frac{2}{8}$

Ⓓ $\frac{1}{6}, \frac{1}{6}$

Size of Tray	Price
Small	$8
Medium	$10
Large	$12

17. Jesse and his friends ordered a large party tray. Which unit fraction does each section of the tray represent?

Ⓐ $\frac{1}{4}$

Ⓑ $\frac{1}{6}$

Ⓒ $\frac{1}{8}$

Ⓓ $\frac{1}{10}$

Copyright © Savvas Learning Company LLC. All Rights Reserved.

Glossary

A

add

When you add, you join groups together.

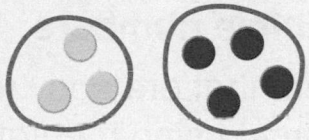

$3 + 4 = 7$

addend

numbers that are added

$2 + 5 = 7$

addends

after

424 comes after 423.

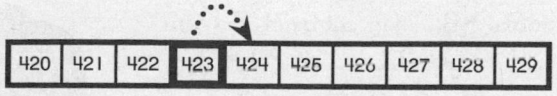

a.m.

clock time from midnight until noon

angle

the corner shape formed by two sides that meet

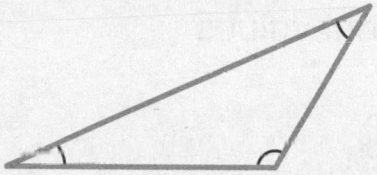

array

a group of objects set in equal rows and columns that forms a rectangle

B

bar diagram

a model for addition and subtraction that shows the parts and the whole

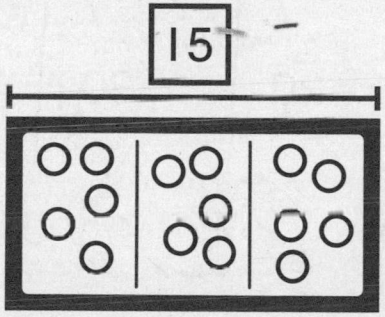

bar graph

A bar graph uses bars to show data.

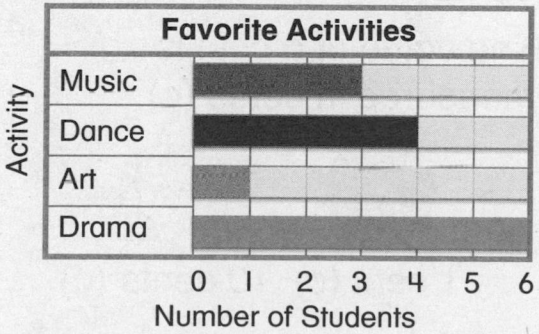

before

420	421	422	423	424	425	426	427	428	429

421 comes before 422.

break apart

You can break apart a number into its place value parts.

27 + 35 = ?

Tens: 20 30

Ones: 7 5

C

cents

The value of a coin is measured in cents (¢).

1 cent (¢)

10 cents (¢)

centimeter (cm)

a metric unit of length that is part of 1 meter

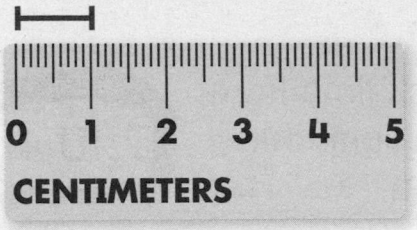

coins

money that is made out of metal and that can have different values

1¢ 5¢ 10¢ 25¢ 50¢

column

objects in an array or data in a table that are shown up and down

column

1	2	3	4	5
11	12	13	14	15
21	22	23	24	25
31	32	33	34	35

compare

When you compare numbers, you find out if a number is greater than, less than, or equal to another number.

147 > 143

147 is greater than 143.

compatible numbers

numbers that are easy to add or subtract using mental math

8 + 2
20 + 7
53 + 10

compensation

a mental math strategy you can use to add or subtract

38 + 24 = ?
+ 2 − 2

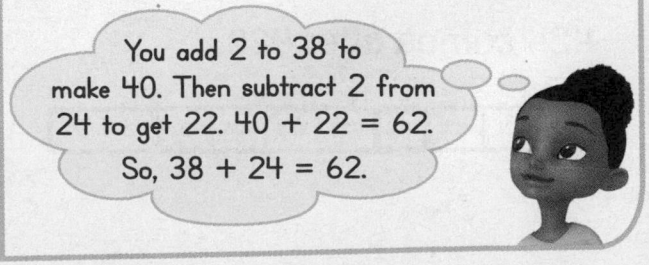

Copyright © Savvas Learning Company LLC. All Rights Reserved.

cone

a solid figure with a circle shaped base and a curved surface that meets at a point

cube

a solid figure with six faces that are matching squares

cylinder

a solid figure with two matching circle shaped bases

D

data

information you collect and can be shown in a table or graph

Favorite Fruit	
Apple	7
Peach	4
Orange	5

decrease

to become lesser in value

600 ⟶ 550

600 decreased by 50 is 550.

denominator

the number below the fraction bar in a fraction, which shows the total number of equal parts

$\frac{3}{4}$ ⟵ denominator

difference

the answer in a subtraction equation or problem

$14 - 6 = 8$

↑ difference

digits

Numbers are made up of 1 or more digits. 43 has 2 digits.

dime

10 cents or 10¢

division

an operation that tells how many equal groups there are or how many are in each group

$12 \div 3 = 4$

divided by

what you say to read a division symbol

$18 \div 3 = 6$

divided by

dollar

One dollar equals 100¢.

dollar bills

paper money that can have different dollar values, such as $1, $5, $10, or $20

dollar sign

a symbol used to show that a number represents money

$37

dollar sign

doubles

addition facts that have two addends that are the same

$4 + 4 = 8$

addend addend

E

edge

a line formed where two faces of a solid figure meet

eighths

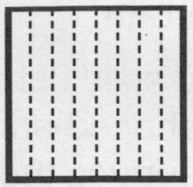

When a whole is separated into 8 equal shares, the parts are called eighths.

equal groups

groups that have the same number of items or objects

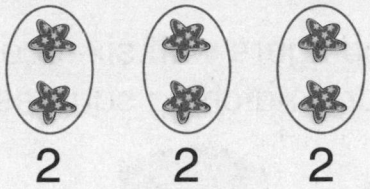

equal shares

parts of a whole that are the same size

All 4 shares are equal.

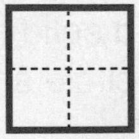

equals (=)

has the same value

$36 = 36$

36 is equal to 36.

Copyright © Savvas Learning Company LLC. All Rights Reserved.

equation

a math sentence that uses an equal sign (=) to show that the value on the left is equal to the value on the right

$$3 + ? = 7$$

$$14 - 6 = 8$$

estimate

When you estimate, you make a good guess.

This table is about 3 feet long.

even

a number that can be shown as a pair of cubes.

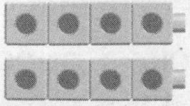

8 is even.

expanded form

a way of writing a number that shows the place value of each digit

$$400 + 60 + 3 = 463$$

F

face

a flat surface of a solid figure that does not roll

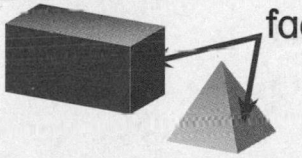

fact family

a group of related addition and subtraction facts

$$2 + 4 = 6$$

$$4 + 2 = 6$$

$$6 - 2 = 4$$

$$6 - 4 = 2$$

factors

numbers that are multiplied together to give a product

$$7 \times 3 = 21$$

factors

flat surface

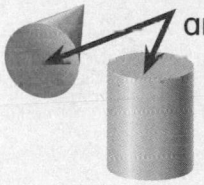

foot (ft)

a standard unit of length equal to 12 inches

fourths

When a whole is divided into 4 equal shares, the shares are called fourths.

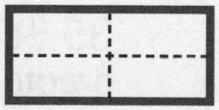

fraction

a number, such as $\frac{1}{2}$ or $\frac{3}{4}$, that names part of a whole or part of a set

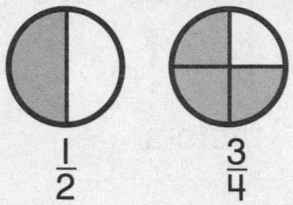

G

greater than (>)

has greater value

$5 > 1$

5 is greater than 1.

greatest

the number in a group with the largest value

35 47 58 61

greatest

greatest value

The coin that has the greatest value is the coin that is worth the most.

The quarter has the greatest value.

H

half-dollar

50 cents or 50¢

half past

30 minutes past the hour

It is half past 9.

halves (half)

When a whole is divided into 2 equal shares, the shares are called halves.

height

how tall an object is from bottom to top

heptagon

a polygon that has 7 sides

hexagon

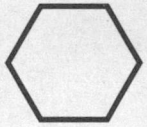

a polygon that has 6 sides

hour

An hour is 60 minutes.

hundred

10 tens make 1 hundred.

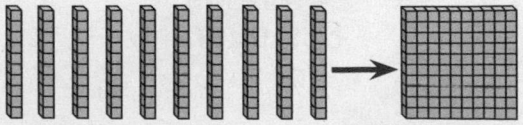

Copyright © Savvas Learning Company LLC. All Rights Reserved.

I

inch (in.)

a standard unit of length that is part of 1 foot

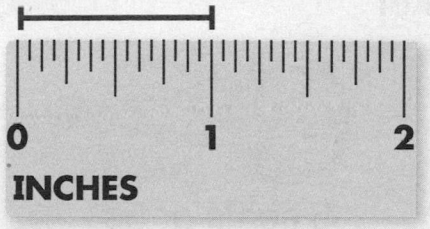

increase

to become greater in value

550 ⟶ 600

550 increased by 50 is 600.

L

least

the number in a group with the smallest value

35 47 58 61

least

least value

The coin that has the least value is the coin that is worth the least.

The dime has the least value.

length

the distance from one end to the other end of an object

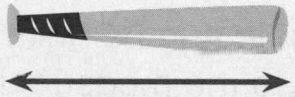

less than (<)

has less value

$2 < 6$

2 is less than 6.

line plot

A line plot uses dots above a number line to show data.

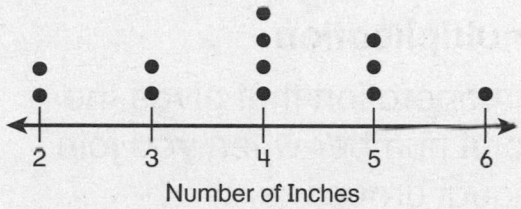

M

mental math

math you do in your head

$23 + 20 = 43$

meter (m)

a metric unit of length equal to 100 centimeters

A long step is about a meter.

minute

a standard length of time

There are 60 minutes in 1 hour.

---

multiplication

an operation that gives the total number when you join equal groups

$$3 \times 2 = 6$$

To multiply 3×2 means to add 2 three times.

$$2 + 2 + 2 = 6$$

N

near doubles

addition facts that have two addends that are close

$$4 + 5 = 9$$

addend addend

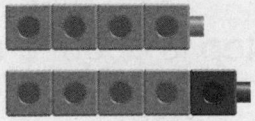

nearest centimeter

The whole number centimeter mark closest to the measure is the nearest centimeter.

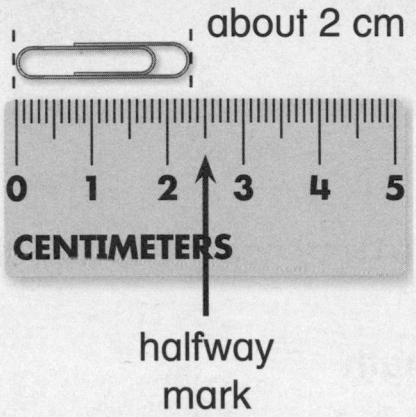

---

nearest inch

The whole number inch mark closest to the measure is the nearest inch.

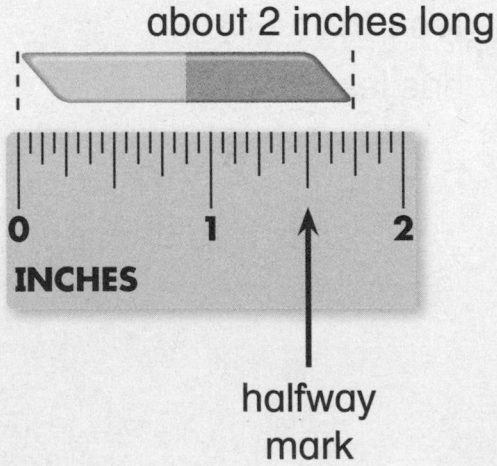

next ten

the first ten greater than a number

30 is the next ten after 27.

---

nickel

5 cents or 5¢

---

nonagon

a polygon that has 9 sides

---

number line

a line that shows numbers in order from left to right

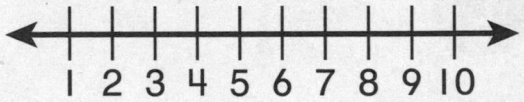

Copyright © Savvas Learning Company LLC. All Rights Reserved.

numerator

the number above the fraction bar in a fraction, which shows how many equal parts are described

$\frac{3}{4}$ ← numerator

O

octagon

a polygon that has 8 sides

odd

a number that can **NOT** be shown as pairs of cubes

9 is odd.

ones

digits that shows how many ones are in a number

54 + 14 = 68

↑ ↑ ↑

open number line

An open number line is a tool that can help you add or subtract. It can begin at any number.

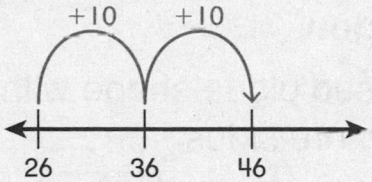

26 + 20 = 46

order

to place numbers from least to greatest or from greatest to least

27 72 107 117 171

least greatest

P

parallelogram

a quadrilateral that has 4 sides and opposite sides parallel

part

a piece of a whole or of a number

2 and 3 are parts of 5.

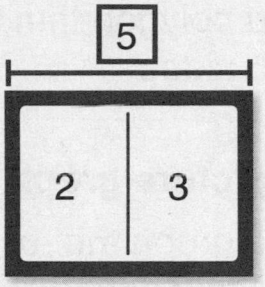

partial sum

When you add numbers, the sum of one of the place values is called a partial sum.

	Tens	Ones	
	5	7	
+	2	8	
	7	0	← partial sum
+	1	5	← partial sum
	8	5	← sum

penny

1 cent or 1¢

pentagon

a polygon that has 5 sides

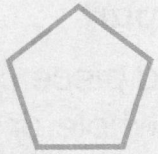

picture graph

a graph that uses pictures to show data

Favorite Ball Games	
Baseball	🧍🧍
Soccer	🧍🧍🧍🧍🧍🧍🧍🧍
Tennis	🧍🧍🧍🧍

Each 🧍 = 1 student

place-value chart

a chart matches each digit of a number with its place

Hundreds	Tens	Ones
3	4	8

plane shape

a flat shape

circle rectangle square triangle

p.m.

clock time from noon until midnight

polygon

a closed plane shape with 3 or more sides

product

the answer to a multiplication problem

$$4 \times 2 = 8$$

↑ product

pyramid

a solid figure with a base that is a polygon and faces that are triangles that meet in a point

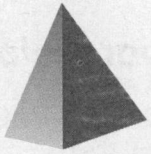

Q

quadrilateral

a polygon that has 4 sides

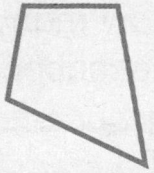

quarter

25 cents or 25¢

quarter past

15 minutes after the hour

It is quarter past 4.

quarter to

15 minutes before the hour

It is quarter to 4.

Copyright © Savvas Learning Company LLC. All Rights Reserved.

R

rectangular prism

a solid figure with bases and faces that are rectangles

regroup

to name a number or part in a different way

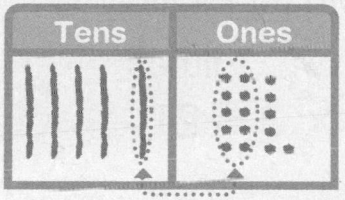

10 ones can be regrouped as 1 ten. 1 ten can be regrouped as 10 ones.

related

Addition facts and subtraction facts are related if they have the same numbers.

$$2 + 3 = 5$$
$$5 - 2 = 3$$

repeated addition

adding the same number repeatedly

$$3 + 3 + 3 + 3 = 12$$

right angle

an angle that forms a square corner

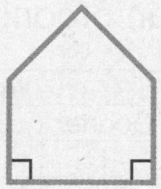

row

objects in an array or data in a table that are shown across

1	2	3	4	5
11	12	13	14	15
21	22	23	24	25
31	32	33	34	35

← row

S

separate

to subtract or to take apart into two or more parts

$$5 - 2 = 3$$

side

a line segment that makes one part of a plane shape

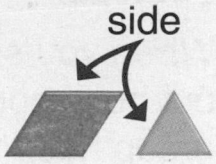

solid figure

a shape that has length, width, and height

These are all solid figures.

sphere

a solid figure that looks like a ball

standard form

a way to write a number using only digits

436

subtract

When you subtract, you find out how many are left or which group has more.

$$5 - 3 = 2$$

sum

the answer to an addition equation or problem

$$3 + 4 = 7$$

$$\begin{array}{r} 4 \\ +\ 3 \\ \hline 7 \end{array}$$

sum → 7

symbol

a picture or character that stands for something

T

tally mark

a symbol used to keep track of each piece of information in an organized list

Ways to Show 30¢			
Quarter	Dime	Nickel	Total
I		I	30¢
	III		30¢
	II	II	30¢
	I	IIII	30¢
		~~IIII~~ I	30¢

tens

the digit that shows how many groups of ten are in a number

238

thirds

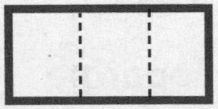

When a whole is divided into 3 equal shares, the shares are called thirds.

thousand

10 hundreds make 1 thousand.

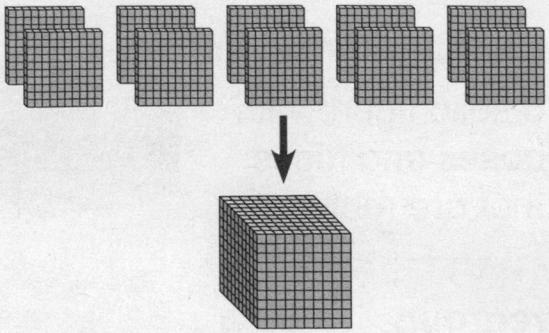

times

another word for multiply

times

$$7 \times 3 = 21$$

trapezoid

a polygon with 4 sides and one pair of sides are parallel

triangular prism

a solid figure that has two triangle shaped bases and three faces that have rectangle shapes.

Copyright © Savvas Learning Company LLC. All Rights Reserved.

U

unequal

Unequal parts are parts that are not equal.

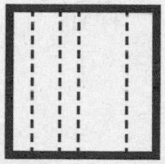

5 unequal parts

unit

You can use different units to measure.

about 12 inches
about 1 foot

unit fraction

a fraction that reperesents one equal part of a whole or a set

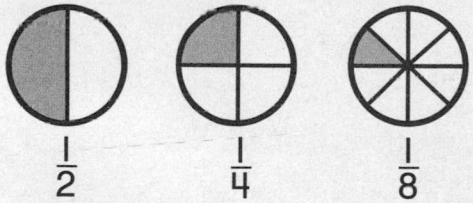

unknown

a symbol that stands for a number in an equation

$$34 + ? = 67$$

unknown

V

vertices (vertex)

corner points where 2 sides of a polygon meet or where edges of a solid figure meet

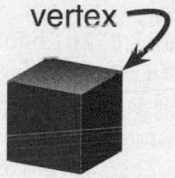

W

whole

a single unit that can be divided into parts

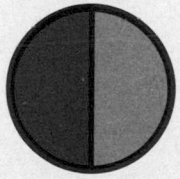

The two halves make one whole circle.

width

the distance across an object

word form

a way to write a number using only words

The word form for 23 is twenty-three.

Y

yard (yd)

a standard unit of length equal to 3 feet

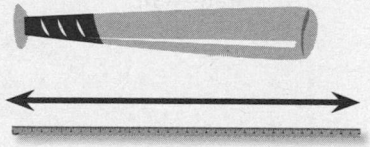

A baseball bat is about a yard long.

enVisionmath 2.0

Photographs

Photo locators denoted as follows: Top (T), Center (C), Bottom (B), Left (L), Right (R), Background (Bkgd)

001BL Lori Martin/Shutterstock;**001BR** An Nguyen/Shutterstock;**001C** Africa Studio/Fotolia;**001L** Africa Studio/Fotolia;**001R** karandaev/Fotolia;**077BL** michaklootwijk/Fotolia;**077BR** Jitka Volfova/Shutterstock;**077L** Charles Brutlag/Shutterstock;**077R** Erni/Fotolia;**119L** FiCo74/Fotolia;**119R** Antonio Scarpi/Fotolia;**189** Beboy/Shutterstock;**253** Deborah Benbrook/Fotolia;**321** GlebStock/Shutterstock;**389** Paylessimages/Fotolia;**435** Ambient Ideas/Shutterstock;**503** Es0lex/Fotolia;**583** kalafoto/Fotolia;**635** Klagyivik Viktor/Shutterstock;**675** Nagel Photography/Shutterstock;**678** Optionm/Shutterstock;**687** Ant Clausen/Fotolia;**759** Bonita R. Cheshier/Shutterstock;**788** Lledó/Fotolia;**790** Ivan Kruk/Fotolia;**799L** Karichs/Fotolia;**799R** Ivonne Wierink/Fotolia;**851** Yurakr/Shutterstock;**868** StudioSmart/Shutterstock;**G10R** United State Mint.

Grade 2 Lessons Exclusively for Virginia

Volume 1

VA 1 **Round Whole Numbers** VA3
(Use after Lesson 4-4.)

VA 2 **Estimate Sums** VA7
(Use after Lesson 4-4.)

Topic 4 Assessment Items for Virginia Lessons 1 and 2 ..... VA9

VA 3 **Estimate Differences** VA11
(Use after Lesson 6-5.)

Topic 6 Assessment Items for Virginia Lesson 3 ..... VA13

VA 4 **Use a Calendar** VA15
(Use after Lesson 8-8.)

Topic 8 Assessment Items for Virginia Lesson 4 ..... VA19

Volume 2

VA 5 **Ordinal Numbers** VA23
(Use before Lesson 9-1.)

Topic 9 Assessment Items for Virginia Lesson 5 ..... VA25

VA 6 **Estimate and Measure Weight** VA27
(Use after Lesson 12-9.)

VA 7 **Temperature** VA31
(Use after Lesson 12-9.)

Topic 12 Assessment Items for Virginia Lessons 6 and 7 ..... VA35

VA 8 **Predict Outcomes** VA37
(Use after Lesson 14-6.)

Topic 14 Assessment Items for Virginia Lesson 8 ..... VA41

VA 9 **Compare 2-Dimensional with 3-Dimensional Shapes** VA43
(Use after Lesson 15-4.)

VA 10 **Symmetry** VA47
(Use after Lesson 15-5.)

VA 11 **Fraction Names** VA51
(Use after Lesson 15-7.)

VA 12 **Fractions of a Set** VA55
(Use after Lesson 15-7.)

VA 13 **Equal Shares, Length** VA59
(Use after Lesson 15-7.)

VA 14 **Compare Unit Fractions** VA63
(Use after Lesson 15-7.)

Topic 15 Assessment Items for Virginia Lessons 9, 10, 11, 12, 13, and 14 ..... VA67

Name _____

Learn Glossary

Virginia Lesson 5 Ordinal Numbers

I can ... use ordinal numbers to 30.

SOL 2.3a, 2.3b

This is an ordered set of 30 peaches. Put an X on the nineteenth peach. Circle the twenty-third peach.

Count in order from the first to the nineteenth peach. Then count on to find the twenty-third peach.

An ordinal number tells the order of something in a list.

Guided Practice

Use the picture of the stars. Solve each problem.

1. Color the third star red.
2. Color the 6th star blue.
3. Color the eleventh star yellow.
4. Color the fifteenth star green.
5. Color the 9th star purple.
6. Color the 13th star orange.

Independent Practice and Problem Solving

Use the picture of the fishes. Solve each problem.

1st

7. Color the 2nd fish blue.

8. Color the seventeenth fish yellow.

9. Color the ninth fish purple.

10. Color the 20th fish green.

11. Color the sixth fish red.

12. Label the fish 2nd through 20th above the fish.

13. **Higher Order Thinking** Jalen put his toy vehicles in a line as shown. He started from the right and ended at the left. Starting from the right, what ordinal number would he use for the school bus?

14. **Be Precise** Katie is ninth in line. Jasmine is right behind her. What position is Jasmine in line?

_____

15. **Be Precise** Jack is twenty-fifth in line to buy a movie ticket. How many people are in front of him?

_____ people

Copyright © Savvas Learning Company LLC. All Rights Reserved.

Name _____

TOPIC 9

Assessment (Additional)

19. Put an **X** on the fifth apple and circle the twentieth apple.

1st

20. What position is the basketball with an **X** drawn over it? Choose all that apply.

1st

- ☐ 17th
- ☐ 18th
- ☐ eighth
- ☐ eighteenth
- ☐ seventeenth

Name _____

Learn Glossary

Virginia Lesson 6 Estimate and Measure Weight

I can ... estimate and measure weight to the nearest pound.

SOL 2.8b

You can measure the **weight** of an object in **pounds (lb)** using a **pan balance**.

Estimate the weight of an object first.

Measure to check your estimate.

Estimate: about 6 pounds
Measure: 5 pounds

Other **scales** can be used to measure weight, too.

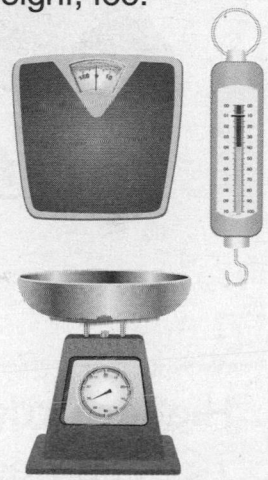

Do You Understand?

Show Me! Is the weight of your desk closer to 1 pound or 10 pounds? Explain.

Guided Practice

Circle the better estimate for the weight of each.

1. 

   1 pound
   10 pounds

2. 

   10 pounds
   4 pounds

3. 

   7 pounds
   75 pounds

4. 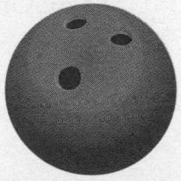

   10 pounds
   1 pound

Independent Practice

Read each scale. Measure the weight of each object in pounds.

Tools Assessment

5.

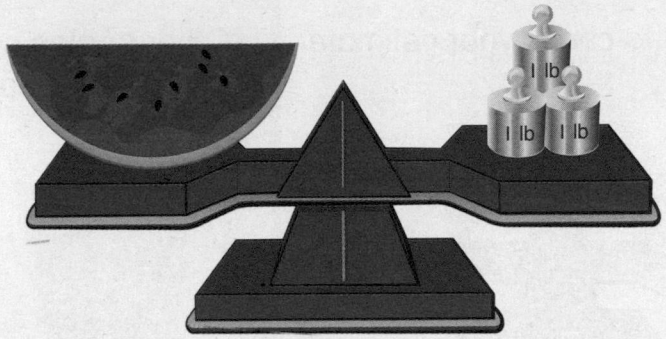

_____

6.

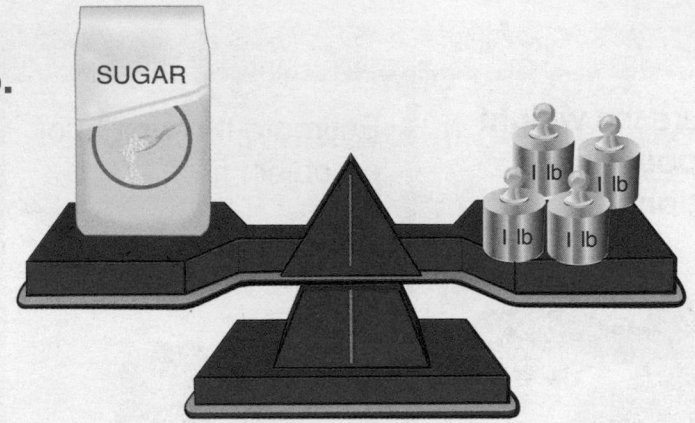

_____

7. **Higher Order Thinking** Hold a 1-pound weight. Find an object in the classroom you think weighs more than 1 pound, but less than 3 pounds. Name the object. Estimate the weight of the object. Then, weigh it to the nearest pound. Record your work.

_____

_____

_____

_____

8. Why do you think this kind of scale is used to weigh vegetables at the grocery store?

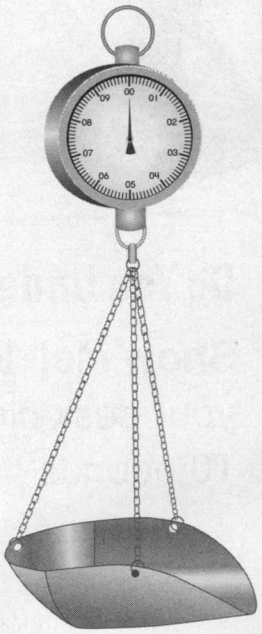

_____

_____

_____

_____

_____

_____

_____

Copyright © Savvas Learning Company LLC. All Rights Reserved.

Name _____

Problem Solving Solve each problem.

9. **Reasoning** One liter of water weighs about 2 pounds. About how much does a 3-liter bottle of water weigh? Write an equation to show how to solve the problem. Then solve.

_____

_____

_____

10. A box can hold 50 pounds. Liam puts an object that weighs 19 pounds and another object that weighs 18 pounds into the box. Can the box hold the weight of both objects? Explain.

_____

_____

_____

11. **Higher Order Thinking** To the nearest pound, Maria's case weighs 37 pounds. Ian's case weighs 45 pounds. Emma does not have the heaviest case. Emma's case is heavier than Maria's. How heavy could Emma's case be?

_____ pounds

12. **Assessment** Look at each object and think about its weight. Draw a line from each weight estimate to a matching object.

about 1 pound	about 10 pounds	about 50 pounds

Homework & Practice

Estimate and Measure Weight

HOME ACTIVITY Help your child find objects at home that weigh about 1 pound. Use a pan balance or scale to measure and record the weight of each object.

Tools Games

Circle the better estimate for the weight of each.

1. 

   1 pound
   8 pounds

2. 

   8 pounds
   80 pounds

3. 

   2 pounds
   15 pounds

4. 

   1 pound
   10 pounds

Find 3 objects that weigh at least 1 pound. Estimate the weight of each object. Then weigh each to the nearest pound using a scale. Record your results.

	Name of Object	Estimate	Measure
5.		about _____ pound(s)	_____ pound(s)
6.		about _____ pound(s)	_____ pound(s)
7.		about _____ pound(s)	_____ pound(s)

Copyright © Savvas Learning Company LLC. All Rights Reserved.

Name _____

Learn Glossary

Virginia Lesson 7 Temperature

I can ... read temperature in degrees Fahrenheit to the nearest 10 degrees.

SOL 2.11, 2.6c

You can use a **thermometer** to measure **temperature** in degrees **Fahrenheit (°F)**.

What temperature is showing? Measure to the nearest 10 degrees.

This is an outdoor thermometer. What is the temperature to the nearest 10 degrees?

about 90 °F

Different thermometers can be used for other activities.

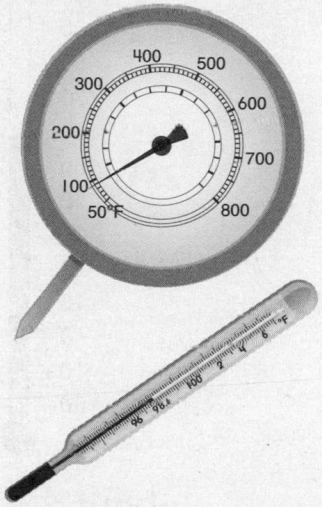

Do You Understand?

Show Me! Why do we use thermometers?

Guided Practice

Write each temperature to the nearest 10 degrees.

1.

about 70 °F

2.

about ____ °F

Independent Practice

Write each temperature to the nearest 10 degrees.

Tools Assessment

3.

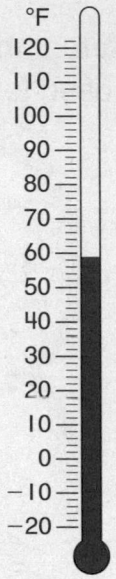

about _____ °F

4.

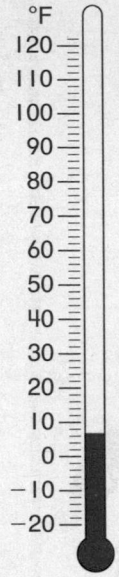

about _____ °F

5.

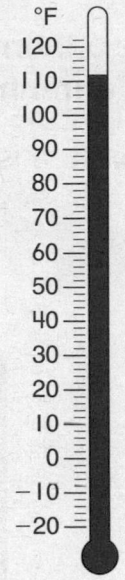

about _____ °F

6.

about _____ °F

7.

about _____ °F

8.

about _____ °F

Copyright © Savvas Learning Company LLC. All Rights Reserved.

Name _____

Problem Solving Solve each problem.

9. **Make Sense** Jon says the difference between 78°F and 29°F is 49°F. How can he estimate to check that his answer is reasonable?

10. Leo and Sam are at the beach. Do you think the temperature is closer to 80°F or 30°F? What kind of thermometer do you think would show this temperature? Explain.

11. **Higher Order Thinking** Write a two-step math story that uses temperatures. Then solve the problem. Write equations to show each step.

12. **Assessment** To the nearest 10 degrees, which temperature does this thermometer show?

Ⓐ about 30°F

Ⓑ about 40°F

Ⓒ about 50°F

Ⓓ about 60°F

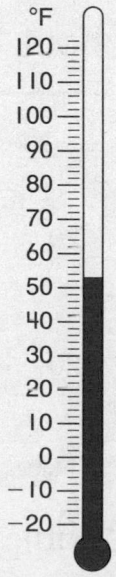

Homework & Practice

Temperature

HOME ACTIVITY Help your child find the daily temperature to the nearest 10 degrees by reading a thermometer. Discuss whether the temperature is hot or cold.

Tools Games

Write each temperature to the nearest 10 degrees.

1.

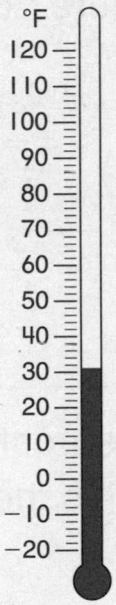

about _____ °F

2.

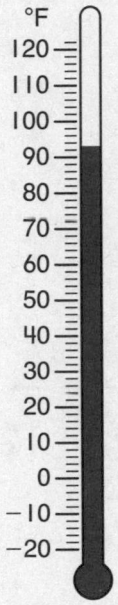

about _____ °F

3.

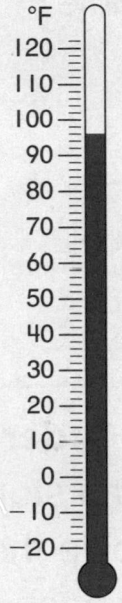

about _____ °F

4.

about _____ °F

5.

about _____ °F

6.

about _____ °F

Copyright © Savvas Learning Company LLC. All Rights Reserved.

Name _____

TOPIC 12 Assessment (Additional)

17. Draw a line from each estimate to a matching object.

about 1 pound	about 8 pounds	about 15 pounds

18. Read the scale. Measure the weight of the shoe in pounds.

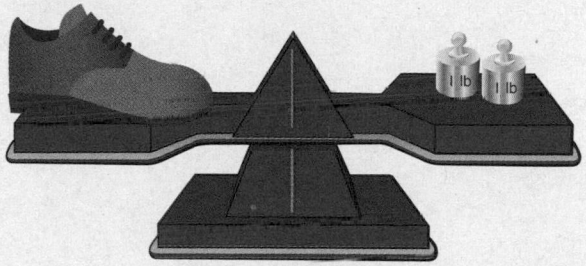

_____ pounds

19. To the nearest 10 degrees, what temperature does this thermometer show?

Ⓐ about 30°F

Ⓑ about 40°F

Ⓒ about 50°F

Ⓓ about 60°F

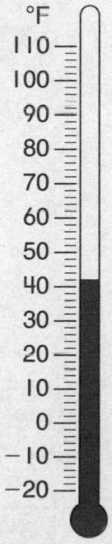

20. Complete the sentences.

The temperature is between _____ and _____. It is closer to _____. The temperature to the nearest 10 degrees is about _____.

Name _____

Learn Glossary

Virginia Lesson 8 Predict Outcomes

I can ... use data to predict outcomes.
SOL 2.14

A bag has some red cubes and some blue cubes.

1 cube is chosen 10 times and put back each time.

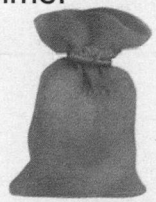

The results are recorded in the chart.

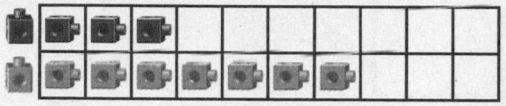

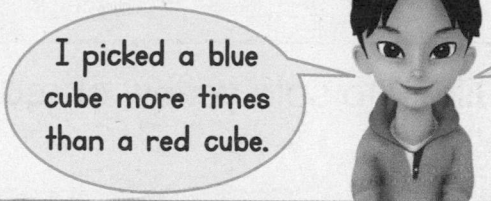

You can predict what will happen if you repeat the activity.

Use the data to predict.

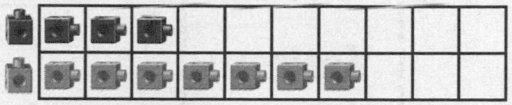

Do You Understand?

Show Me! Is a prediction always true? Explain.

Guided Practice

For this activity, put 10 orange cubes and 5 blue cubes in a bag.

1. Pick 10 cubes, 1 at a time. Put the cube back each time. Record the results.

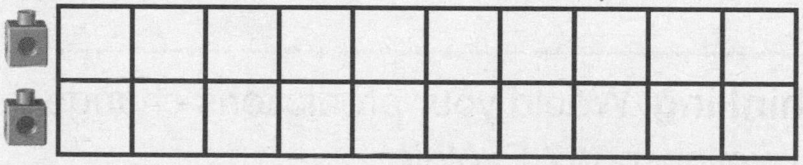

2. Look at the data. If you repeat this activity, are you less likely to pick an orange cube or a blue cube? Explain.

_____

_____

Independent Practice

For this activity, spin the spinner 20 times. Record the results in the tally chart. Then use your data to make two predictions.

Tools Assessment

3.

Red	
Yellow	

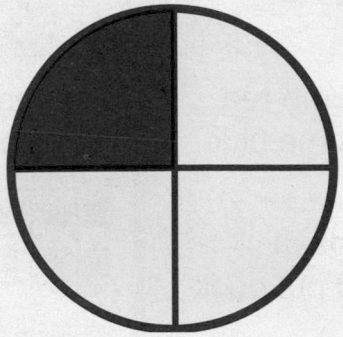

4. If you repeat this activity, are you more likely to spin yellow or red? Explain.

5. If you repeat this activity, are you less likely to spin yellow or red? Explain.

6. **Higher Order Thinking** Would your predictions change if the spinner had 3 red parts and 1 yellow part? Explain.

Copyright © Savvas Learning Company LLC. All Rights Reserved.

Name _____

Problem Solving

Solve each problem.

7. **Reasoning** Evie is picking spotted marbles and striped marbles from a box. She picks 1 marble and puts it back each time. List two things you can tell from Evie's data.

	𝍸 𝍸 𝍸 ||||
	𝍸 𝍸 |

_____

_____

_____

_____

8. **Higher Order Thinking** Micah has a spinner that is equally likely to land on green or yellow if it is spun once. Color to show what Micah's spinner could look like.

9. **Assessment** Look at the data in Item 7. If Evie repeats the activity, is she more likely to pick a striped marble or a spotted marble? Make a prediction. Explain.

_____

_____

_____

_____

_____

_____

Homework & Practice

Predict Outcomes

HOME ACTIVITY Put two different objects, such as two colors of straws, in a bag. Ask your child to pick an object 10 times, putting it back in the bag each time, and record the results. Ask your child to look at the data and predict the results if the activity is repeated.

Tools Games

For this activity, spin the spinner 20 times. Record the results in the tally chart. Then describe your data and make two predictions.

1.

Red	
Purple	

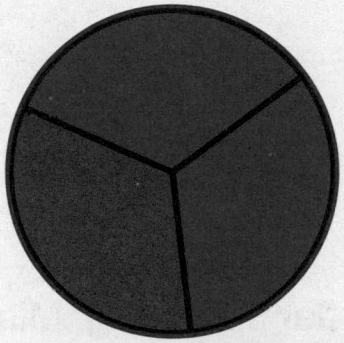

2. Describe something you notice about the data.

3. If you repeat this activity, are you less likely to spin purple or red? Explain.

4. If you repeat this activity, are you more likely to spin purple or red? Explain.

Copyright © Savvas Learning Company LLC. All Rights Reserved.

Name _____

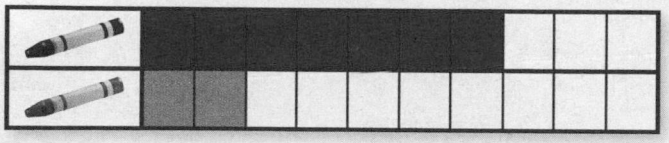

10. Tim is making a prediction from the data above. If this activity is repeated, which prediction makes sense?

Ⓐ Tim is equally likely to pick a blue marker or a red marker.

Ⓑ Tim is more likely to pick a green marker than a blue marker.

Ⓒ Tim is more likely to pick a red marker than a blue marker.

Ⓓ Tim is more likely to pick a blue marker than a red marker.

---

11. Beth spun this spinner 30 times. She recorded the results in the tally chart.

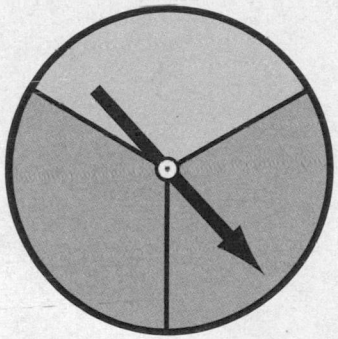

Yellow	𝍸 ||||
Green	𝍸 𝍸 𝍸 𝍸 |

Use the data to make a prediction. If Beth repeats this activity, is she more likely to spin yellow or green? Explain.

_____

_____

Name _____

Learn Glossary

Virginia Lesson 9 Compare 2-Dimensional with 3-Dimensional Shapes

I can ... compare 2-dimensional with 3-dimensional shapes.

SOL 2.13

A **rectangular prism** is a solid figure with 6 faces, 12 edges, and 8 vertices.

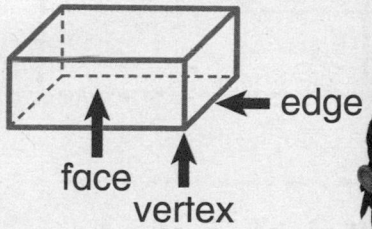

You can trace the faces of a rectangular prism.

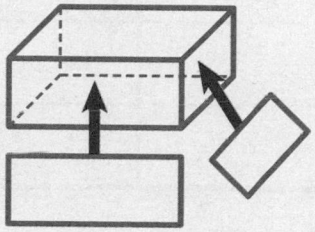

A **sphere** is a solid figure with 0 faces, 0 edges, and 0 vertices.

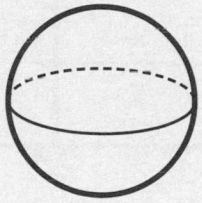

Solids	Related Plane Shapes

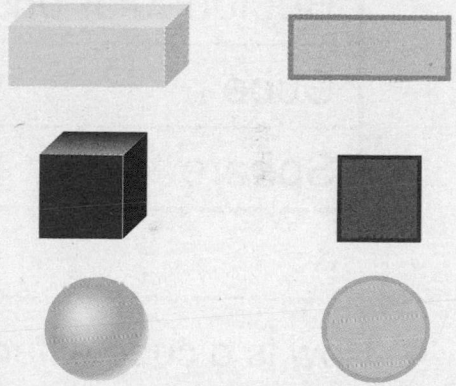

Do You Understand?

Show Me! How is a sphere different from a circle?

Guided Practice

Underline the spheres in the first group of shapes.
Underline the rectangular prisms in the second group.

1.

2.

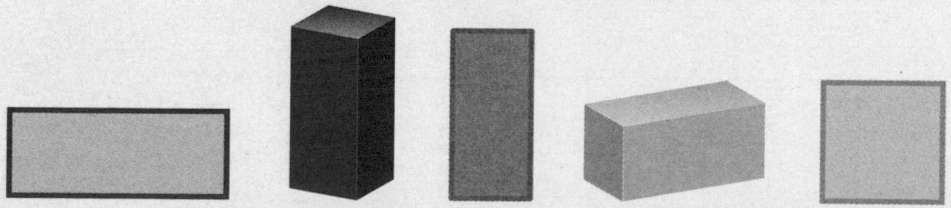

Independent Practice

Complete the table for the three solid figures.

3.

Solid Figure	Number of Faces	Shape of Faces	Number of Edges	Number of Vertices
Rectangular prism				
Cube				
Sphere				

4. How is a cube different from a square?

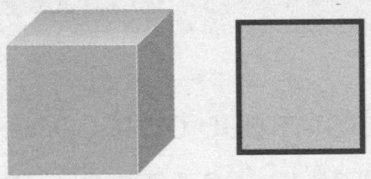

5. How is a rectangular prism different from a rectangle? How are these shapes similar?

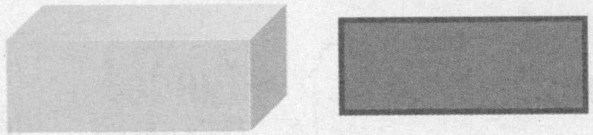

Copyright © Savvas Learning Company LLC. All Rights Reserved.

Name _____

Problem Solving Solve each problem.

6. **Explain** Marie says her soccer ball is a circle. Is she correct?

Explain how you know.

_____

_____

_____

_____

7. Trace the faces of a tissue box on to paper. What shapes have you traced?

_____

8. **Higher Order Thinking** Jon traces the faces of 4 of these boxes. How many rectangles does Jon draw?

_____ rectangles

9. **Assessment** Which shape has 6 faces?

Ⓐ 

Ⓒ 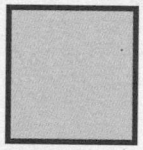

Ⓑ 

Ⓓ 

Homework & Practice

Compare 2-Dimensional with 3-Dimensional Shapes

HOME ACTIVITY Draw a rectangle and ask your child to name the shape. Then help your child identify shapes at home or outside that are rectangular prisms. Ask your child to compare a shape they found with the shape you drew. Repeat for a circle and a sphere.

Tools Games

Underline the rectangular prisms in the first group of shapes. Underline the spheres in the second group. Then explain how you know for each group.

1.

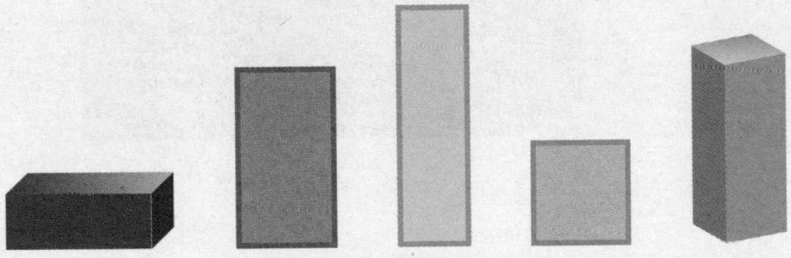

_____

_____

_____

_____

2.

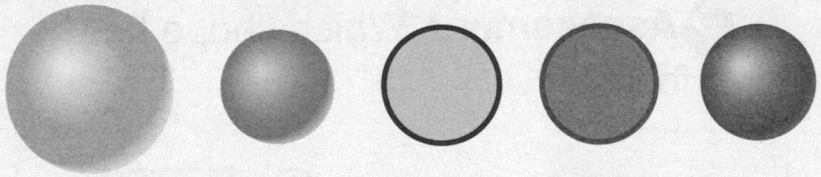

_____

_____

_____

_____

3. Trace all of the faces of a small cube. What shape have you traced?

_____

Copyright © Savvas Learning Company LLC. All Rights Reserved.

Name _____

Learn Glossary

Virginia Lesson 10 Symmetry

I can ... see and draw lines of symmetry.
SOL 2.12a, 2.12b

A shape has **symmetry** if it can be folded into two matching parts.

This shows a line of symmetry.

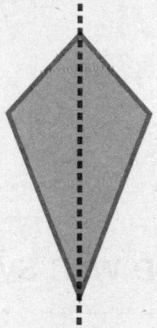

If you fold the shape on the line, there will be two matching parts.

This is not a line of symmetry.

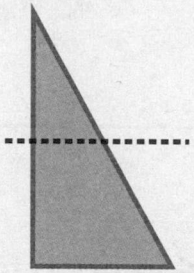

If you fold the shape on the line, the two parts will NOT match.

You can draw the matching part to make a shape that has symmetry.

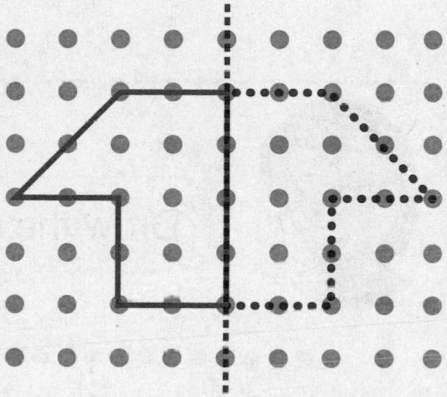

Do You Understand?

Show Me! Does every shape have a line of symmetry? Explain how you know.

Guided Practice

Does the shape have a line of symmetry? Circle yes or no. If yes, draw a line of symmetry.

1.

Yes No

2.

Yes No

Independent Practice

Does the shape have a line of symmetry? Circle yes or no. If yes, draw a line of symmetry.

3. Yes No

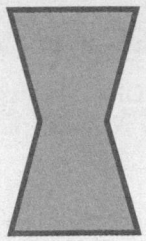

4. Yes No

Draw the matching part in each to make a shape with symmetry.

5.

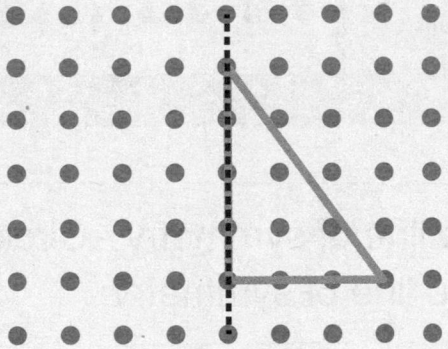

6.

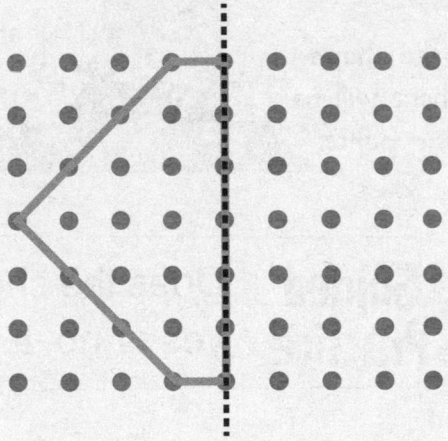

7.

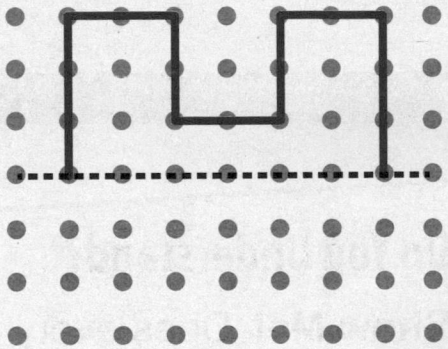

8. **Higher Order Thinking** Draw a shape that has a line of symmetry. Draw a line of symmetry for the shape.

Copyright © Savvas Learning Company LLC. All Rights Reserved.

Name _____

Problem Solving Solve each problem.

9. Beth gave Sara a gift. Draw the matching parts to make letters with symmetry. Use the letters to spell Sara's gift.

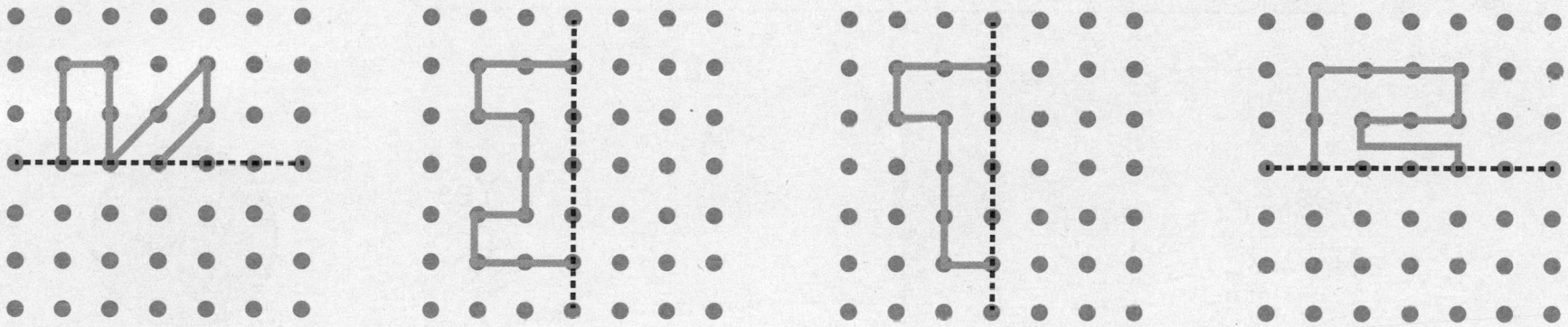

What is Sara's gift? _____

10. **Higher Order Thinking** Draw as many lines of symmetry for this shape as you can. How many lines of symmetry did you draw?

_____

11. **Assessment** Which shapes have a line of symmetry? Choose all that apply.

☐ ☐ ☐ ☐

Homework & Practice

Symmetry

HOME ACTIVITY Help your child identify shapes at home or outside that have at least one line of symmetry. Ask your child to explain how he or she knows the shapes have one or more lines of symmetry.

Tools Games

Does the shape have a line of symmetry? Circle yes or no. If yes, draw a line of symmetry.

1.

Yes

No

2.

Yes

No

Draw the matching part in each to make a shape with symmetry.

3.

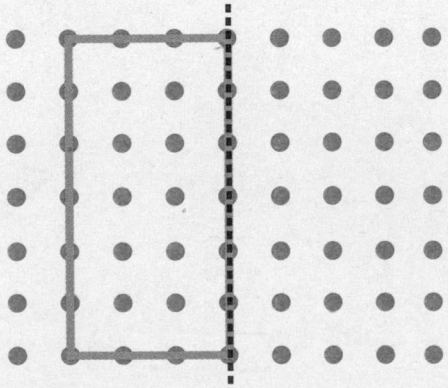

4.

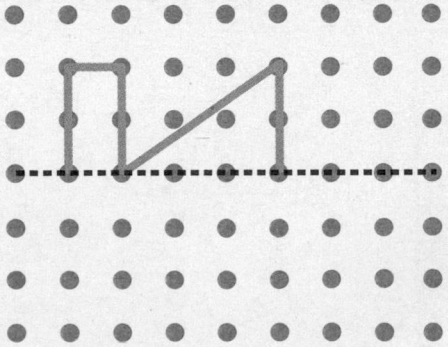

Copyright © Savvas Learning Company LLC. All Rights Reserved.

Name _____

Learn Glossary

Virginia Lesson 11 Fraction Names

I can ... name and represent fractions of regions.

SOL 2.4a, 2.4b

Mr. Peters served part of a pan of enchilada casserole to a friend.

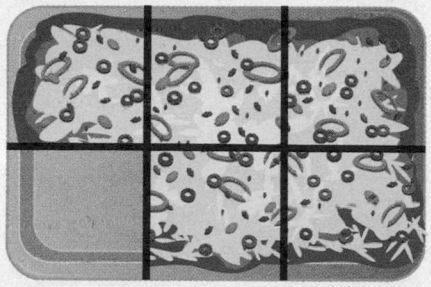

What does each part represent?
What part was served?
What part is left?

A **fraction** names equal parts of a whole. A **unit fraction** represents one part of a whole that is divided into equal parts.

Each piece is $\frac{1}{6}$, so the unit fraction is $\frac{1}{6}$.

$\frac{1}{6}$ ← **numerator**
$\frac{1}{6}$ ← **denominator**

$\frac{1}{6}$ of the pan of enchilada casserole was served.

$\frac{5}{6}$ of the pan of enchilada casserole is left.

The numerator shows how many equal parts are described. The denominator shows the total number of equal parts in a whole.

Do You Understand?

Show Me! What fraction represents the whole pan of casserole before $\frac{1}{6}$ was served? If Mr. Peters served 3 pieces, what fraction of the casserole would be left?

Guided Practice

Use the figure below to solve the problems.

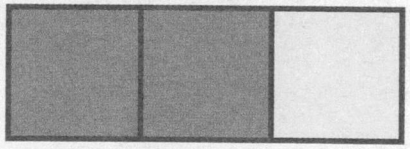

1. What unit fraction represents each part of the whole? _____
2. What fraction of the whole is blue? _____
3. What fraction names *all* the parts of the whole? _____

Independent Practice

Write the unit fraction that represents each part of the whole. Then write the fraction of the whole that is shaded green.

4. 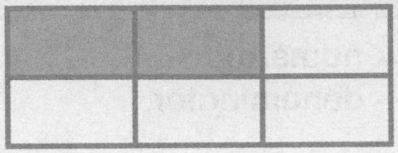

___ ___

5. 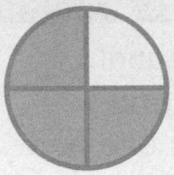

___ ___

6. 

___ ___

7. 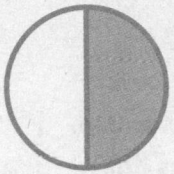

___ ___

8. 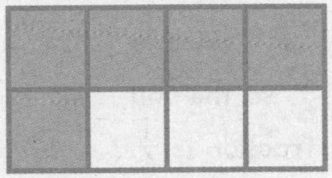

___ ___

9. 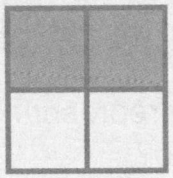

___ ___

10. Draw a rectangle with 8 equal parts with 4 of the parts shaded. Name the fraction for your model.

___

11. **Higher Order Thinking** Draw a circle with 6 equal parts. Shade more than $\frac{4}{6}$ but less than $\frac{6}{6}$ of the circle. What fraction of the circle did you shade?

___

Copyright © Savvas Learning Company LLC. All Rights Reserved.

Name _____

Problem Solving Solve each problem.

12. Mr. Williams divided his garden into six equal parts. Explain what the unit fraction of the garden is.

_____

_____

_____

_____

_____

13. Jacob wants to cut this picture into pieces to make a puzzle. He wants each piece to be $\frac{1}{8}$ of the picture. How many equal pieces should he cut the picture into? Explain.

_____

_____

_____

14. Higher Order Thinking Dale says that $\frac{1}{2}$ of this figure is red. What error is he making? Explain. What fraction of the figure is red?

_____

_____

_____

_____

15. Assessment Write the unit fraction that represents one purple square. What fraction represents the whole? Explain.

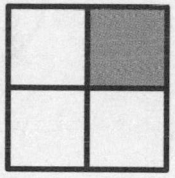

Homework & Practice

Fraction Names

HOME ACTIVITY Have your child draw and label separate models that show the unit fractions for halves, thirds, fourths, sixths, and eighths. Then have your child draw a model that represents $\frac{2}{6}$.

Tools Games

Write the unit fraction that represents each part of the whole. Then write the fraction of the whole that is shaded blue.

1. 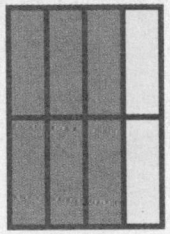

___ ___

2. 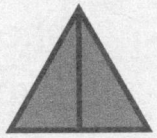

___ ___

3. 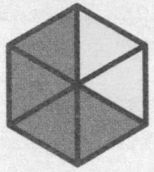

___ ___

4. 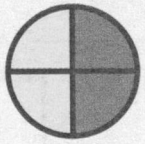

___ ___

5. 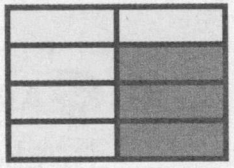

___ ___

6. 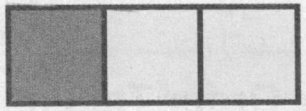

___ ___

7. Draw a rectangle with 6 equal parts with 6 of the parts shaded. Name the fraction for your model.

___

8. Draw a circle with 8 equal parts with 7 parts shaded. Name the fraction for your model.

___

Copyright © Savvas Learning Company LLC. All Rights Reserved.

Name _____

Learn Glossary

Virginia Lesson 12 Fractions of a Set

I can ... name and represent fractions of a set.

SOL 2.4a, 2.4b

Fractions can name part of a **set**. A set is a group of things.

What fraction of the set is red?

2 red fish
3 fish in all

$\frac{2}{3}$ of the fish are red.

Color this set so that $\frac{3}{4}$ of the fish are red.

$\frac{3}{4}$ means 3 out of the 4 fish.

$\frac{3}{4}$ ← red fish
$\frac{3}{4}$ ← fish in all

$\frac{3}{4}$ of the fish are red.

Do You Understand?

Show Me! In the group of three fish, what fraction of the fish is yellow?

In the group of 4 fish, what fraction of the fish is green?

Guided Practice

Write the fraction of each set that is red.

1.

5 red fish

6 fish in all

$\frac{5}{6}$ of the fish are red.

2.

_____ red fish

_____ fish in all

_____ of the fish are red.

Independent Practice

Color to show the fraction of each set.

3.

$\frac{1}{3}$ of the fish are blue.

4.

$\frac{2}{4}$ of the fish are blue.

5.

$\frac{4}{8}$ of the fish are blue.

6. **Higher Order Thinking** Color $\frac{1}{2}$ of the fish blue.

Copyright © Savvas Learning Company LLC. All Rights Reserved.

Name _____

Problem Solving Solve each problem.

7. **Model** Draw a picture to solve the problem.

There are 6 shapes.
3 of the shapes are red.
Show the set of shapes.
What fraction of the shapes are red?

_____

8. **Higher Order Thinking** What fraction of the crayons are NOT blue?

_____

Write the unit fraction for this set of crayons.

_____

9. **Assessment** Which fraction of the fish are yellow?

Ⓐ $\frac{1}{3}$ Ⓑ $\frac{2}{3}$ Ⓒ $\frac{1}{4}$ Ⓓ $\frac{2}{4}$

Homework & Practice

Fractions of a Set

HOME ACTIVITY Show your child a group of 6 or 8 objects, such as buttons or cups, that have different colors. Ask your child to name and write the fraction for a certain part of the buttons or cups. For example, ask: *What fraction of the buttons are brown?* You child might respond, "three eighths," and write the fraction $\frac{3}{8}$.

Color to show the fraction of each set.

1.

$\frac{1}{6}$ of the leaves are green.

2.

$\frac{7}{8}$ of the leaves are green.

3.

$\frac{3}{3}$ of the leaves are green.

4.

$\frac{3}{4}$ of the leaves are green.

5. On the right, draw 3 brown leaves. Draw 5 orange leaves. What fraction of the set is brown? What fraction is orange?

Copyright © Savvas Learning Company LLC. All Rights Reserved.

Name _____

Virginia Lesson 13 Equal Shares, Length

Learn Glossary

I can ... name and represent fractions of lengths.

SOL 2.4a, 2.4b

This fraction strip is divided into two equal shares. Each part is **one half** of the strip.

This fraction strip is divided into three equal shares. Each part is **one third** of the strip.

This fraction strip is divided into four equal shares. Each part is **one fourth** of the strip.

This fraction strip is divided into six equal shares. Each part is **one sixth** of the strip.

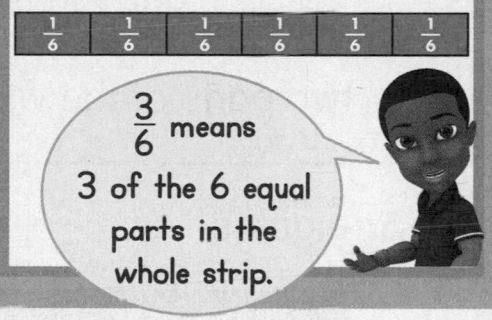

Do You Understand?

Show Me! How many eighths are in the whole strip? Write a fraction for one part of the whole.

Guided Practice

Tell how many equal parts are in the whole fraction strip. Then, write a fraction for the number of parts that are named.

1. fourths

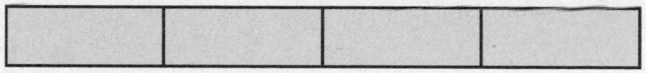

4 parts in the whole

two parts of the whole $\frac{2}{4}$

2. sixths

_____ parts in the whole

four parts of the whole _____

Independent Practice

Divide each fraction strip into the given equal parts. Tell how many parts are in the whole. Then, write a fraction for the number of parts that are named.

Tools Assessment

3. thirds

_____ parts in the whole

two parts of the whole _____

4. halves

_____ parts in the whole

one part of the whole _____

5. eighths

_____ parts in the whole

five parts of the whole _____

6. sixths

_____ parts in the whole

two parts of the whole _____

7. fourths

_____ parts in the whole

three parts of the whole _____

8. Higher Order Thinking Show eighths in the fraction strip below. Color more than $\frac{2}{8}$ but less than $\frac{4}{8}$ of the strip blue. What fraction of the strip have you colored?

_____

Copyright © Savvas Learning Company LLC. All Rights Reserved.

Name _____

Problem Solving Solve each problem.

9. Model Mia wants to cut this ribbon into fourths. Draw lines to show how she should cut it.

10. Reasoning What fraction of the cube train is each color?

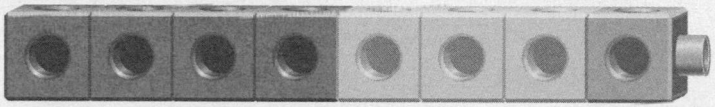

Blue: _____

Yellow: _____

Green: _____

11. Higher Order Thinking Joann cut this loaf of bread into equal parts to share with her friends. The cuts are shown.

How many equal parts are in the loaf? _____

Use words to write a fraction for two of the parts. _____

Use numbers to write a fraction for two of the parts. _____

12. Assessment Which fraction of the strip is shaded orange?

Ⓐ $\frac{5}{8}$

Ⓑ $\frac{5}{6}$

Ⓒ $\frac{4}{6}$

Ⓓ $\frac{4}{5}$

Homework & Practice
Equal Shares, Length

HOME ACTIVITY Give your child three pieces of string or yarn that are the same length. Ask him or her to cut one piece into halves and then write a fraction for one part. Repeat the process with the other pieces for thirds and fourths.

Tools Games

Shade the number of cubes named for each cube train. Then write a fraction for the part that is shaded.

1. one cube

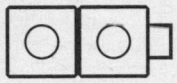

_____

2. two cubes

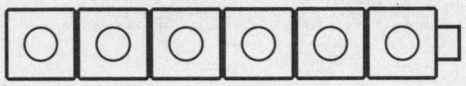

_____

3. three cubes

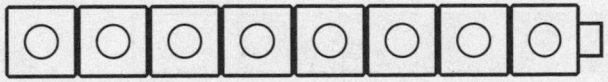

_____

4. seven cubes

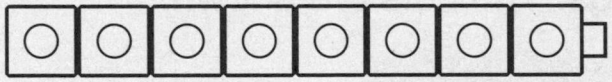

_____

5. three cubes

_____

6. 1 cube

_____

Copyright © Savvas Learning Company LLC. All Rights Reserved.

Name _____

Learn Glossary

Virginia Lesson 14 Compare Unit Fractions

I can ... compare unit fractions.
SOL 2.4c

How do you compare fractions?

Which is greater: $\frac{1}{2}$ or $\frac{1}{4}$?

To model $\frac{1}{2}$, divide a whole strip into two halves. Shade one of them.

To model $\frac{1}{4}$, divide the same-sized whole strip into fourths. Shade one of them.

Which fraction is greater?

Using symbols to compare, you can write $\frac{1}{2} > \frac{1}{4}$.

Do You Understand?

Show Me! In the second box above, $\frac{1}{2}$ of the strip is shaded. What fraction of the strip is NOT shaded?

How can you compare these two fractions?

Guided Practice

Compare. Write > or < in the ◯.

1.

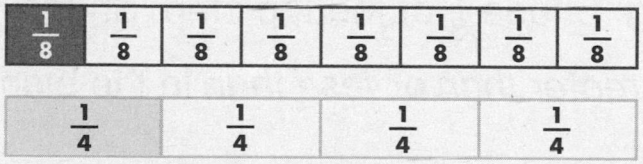

$\frac{1}{8}$ ◯ $\frac{1}{4}$

2.

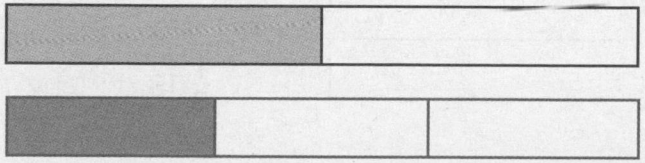

$\frac{1}{2}$ ◯ $\frac{1}{3}$

Independent Practice

Compare. Write > or < in the ◯.

3.

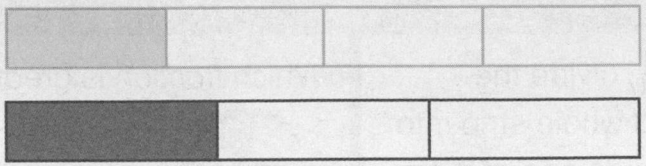

$\frac{1}{4}$ ◯ $\frac{1}{3}$

4.

$\frac{1}{2}$ ◯ $\frac{1}{6}$

Write the fraction for each whole that is shaded. Then compare.

5.

_____ ◯ _____

6.

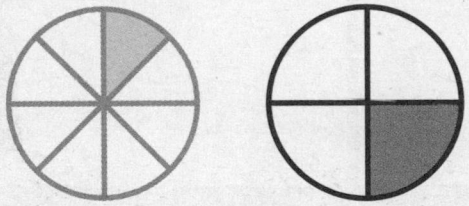

_____ ◯ _____

7. **Higher Order Thinking** Shade $\frac{1}{8}$ of the top strip. Shade $\frac{1}{6}$ of the bottom strip. Then compare. Write *greater than* or *less than* in the blank.

$\frac{1}{8}$ is _____ $\frac{1}{6}$.

Copyright © Savvas Learning Company LLC. All Rights Reserved.

Name _____

Problem Solving Solve each problem.

8. **Reasoning** David and Max shared 8 bottles of water. David drank $\frac{1}{2}$ of them. Max drank $\frac{1}{4}$ of them. Who drank more? Draw a picture to explain your answer.

9. **Higher Order Thinking** This pizza is cut into sixths. Which part of the pizza is larger, $\frac{1}{6}$ or $\frac{1}{3}$? Explain.

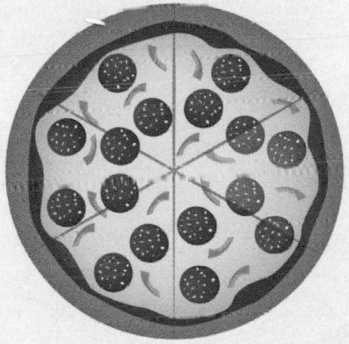

_____

_____

_____

_____

_____

10. **Assessment** Which comparison describes the models below?

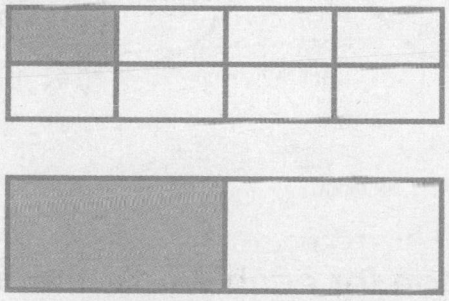

Ⓐ $\frac{1}{2} < \frac{1}{8}$

Ⓑ $\frac{1}{3} > \frac{1}{8}$

Ⓒ $\frac{1}{2} > \frac{1}{4}$

Ⓓ $\frac{1}{2} > \frac{1}{8}$

Homework & Practice
Compare Unit Fractions

HOME ACTIVITY Give your child a sheet of paper. Ask your child to draw a rectangle and model $\frac{1}{2}$ of a pan of brownies and then another same-size rectangle to model $\frac{1}{4}$ of a pan of brownies. Ask your child which fraction is greater and to explain why. Repeat to compare $\frac{1}{4}$ of a pan of brownies to $\frac{1}{8}$ of a pan of brownies.

Tools Games

Compare. Write > or < in the ◯.

1.

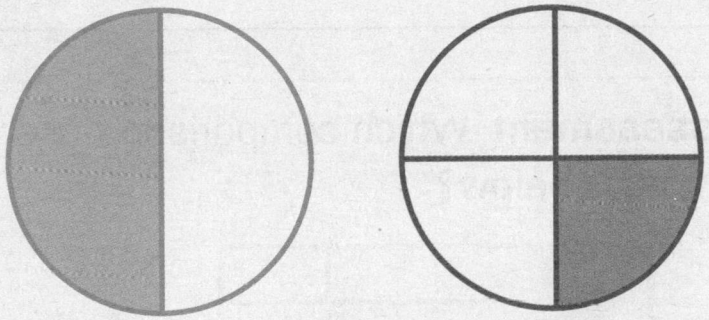

$\frac{1}{2}$ ◯ $\frac{1}{4}$

2.

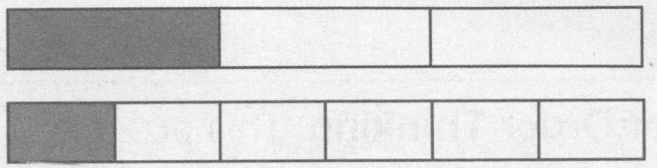

$\frac{1}{3}$ ◯ $\frac{1}{6}$

Write the fraction for each whole that is shaded. Then compare.

3.

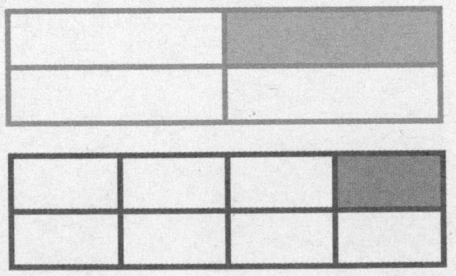

____ ◯ ____

4.

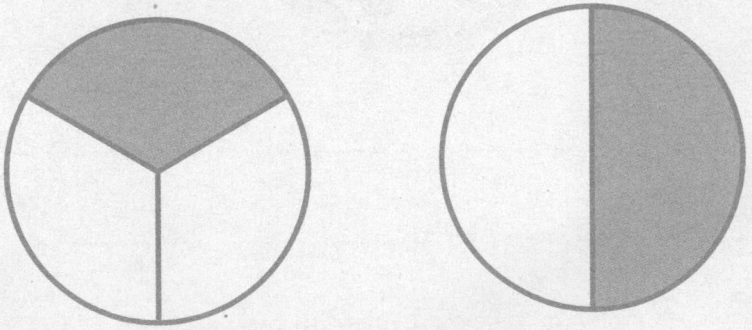

____ ◯ ____

Copyright © Savvas Learning Company LLC. All Rights Reserved.

Name _____

TOPIC 15 Assessment (Additional)

17. Draw a cube train that shows $\frac{1}{2}$ of the train shaded.

18. Which cube train shows $\frac{3}{4}$ of the train red?

Ⓐ 

Ⓑ 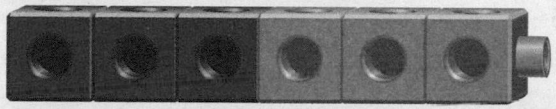

Ⓒ 

Ⓓ 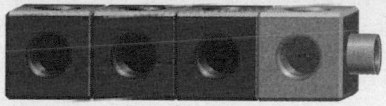

19. Which sentences describe this model? Choose all that apply.

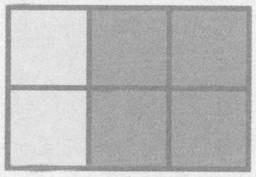

- ☐ $\frac{6}{6}$ of the model is yellow.
- ☐ $\frac{6}{6}$ represents the whole.
- ☐ $\frac{2}{6}$ of the model is yellow.
- ☐ $\frac{1}{6}$ is the unit fraction for the model.
- ☐ $\frac{4}{6}$ of the model is green.

20. Which fraction of the jackets are blue?

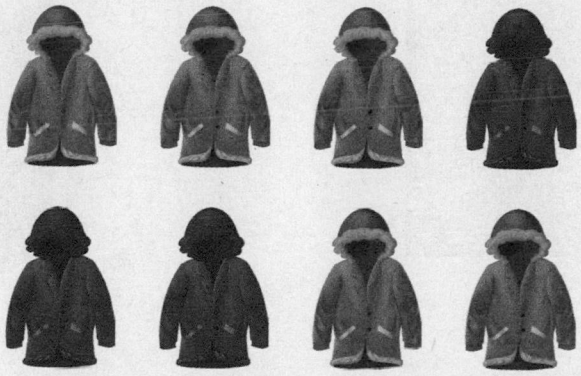

Ⓐ $\frac{3}{8}$

Ⓑ $\frac{5}{8}$

Ⓒ $\frac{5}{6}$

Ⓓ $\frac{3}{4}$

21. Compare. Write > or < in the ◯.

$\frac{1}{6}$ ◯ $\frac{1}{3}$

22. Draw a line of symmetry for this shape. Explain why it is a line of symmetry.

23. Which shapes have 8 vertices? Choose all that apply.

☐ 

☐ 

☐ 

☐ 

Copyright © Savvas Learning Company LLC. All Rights Reserved.